# CONTEMPORARY MUSIC THEORY
## LEVEL TWO
### BY MARK HARRISON

ISBN 0-7935-9882-6

HARRISON
MUSIC
EDUCATION
SYSTEMS

HAL•LEONARD®
CORPORATION
7777 W. BLUEMOUND RD. P.O. BOX 13819 MILWAUKEE, WI 53213

Visit Hal Leonard Online at
**www.halleonard.com**

**W**elcome to *Contemporary Music Theory Level 2*. I have personally taught these concepts to **hundreds of students** in Harmony classes held at the former **Grove School of Music**, and this book is the second in a series used in many schools across the U.S.A. and around the world. As such this book represents a proven and 'battle-tested' approach to the subject matter! During the years I was teaching Harmony and Theory at the Grove School to students from all over the world, I had the best possible opportunity to determine what the theory needs of the contemporary musician were, and what the best method was to communicate these concepts! This process has led to the creation of our *Contemporary Music Theory* book series - *the most thorough music theory courses available for the pop and jazz musician!*

If you really want to understand how harmony and chord progressions work in today's pop and jazz styles, this *Level Two* course is the best method available! Following on from our *Level One* course, in here we completely derive and explain five-part chords, 'definitive' **II-V-I**-style progressions (widely used in jazz and standard styles), chord substitutions, harmonic analysis of tunes, voiceleading, triad and four-part 'upper structures' (widely used in pop, rock and R&B styles), and pentatonic & blues scales and their applications. Everything is presented *from the viewpoint of the contemporary musician* and is information you can then *use right away* in your playing or composing/arranging! To get the best out of the material in this *Level Two* book, you need to have some familiarity with music notation, major scales, intervals, triads and four-part chords, as presented in detail in our *Contemporary Music Theory Level One* book (this information is also reviewed and summarized in Chapter One of this book).

Today's pop and jazz styles are very 'ear-oriented' - in other words they tend to follow a set of rules and expectations that an 'educated ear' will understand. You may have already seen or used our *Contemporary Eartraining* courses (see pages *vi – vii*), which were a fundamental component of the musicianship program at the Grove School. For music theory instruction to be of value to the contemporary musician, the concepts *must be presented in a way that is consistent with how the ear works* - this is the whole philosophy behind our *Contemporary Music Theory* courses. For students wishing to strengthen their overall musicianship, the combination of our *Eartraining* and *Music Theory* methods represents the most efficient and 'targeted' contemporary music program now available!

Each chapter in this book (except for the Chapter One review) is divided into three sections:-

- **Textbook**, containing a complete explanation for each subject area addressed, with various examples of how to apply the theory concepts
- **Workbook Questions**, containing written exercises for each subject area
- **Workbook Answers**, containing answers for all of the written exercises.

This book is ideally suited for self-study, one-on-one music tutoring, and group classes. At the **Grove School of Music** we would typically cover this material in a ten-week class 'quarter', although the material can of course be adapted for use within different course lengths (i.e. a different number of weeks), at the discretion of the teacher or educational institution. There are hundreds of written exercises throughout the book, all with answers provided - a perfect way to consolidate your understanding of how today's music really works!

At the back of the book, I have provided appendices listing 'II-V-I' definitive chords and substitutes in all major and minor keys, voiceleading of 3- & 4-part chords around the circle-of-5ths/4ths, 'upper structure' chords in major and minor keys, and all pentatonic & blues scales. These are followed by a complete glossary of terms used in the book, for your reference and convenience.

Good luck with your study of **Contemporary Music Theory** - and I hope it opens many doors for you as a musician!

*Mark Harrison*
*Harrison Music Education Systems*
*Los Angeles, California*

**M**ARK HARRISON is a keyboardist, composer and educator with over twenty years experience in the industry. Before moving to Los Angeles in 1987, Mark's musical career in his native London included appearances on British national (**BBC**) television as well as extensive club and studio experience. As an active composer for television in both England and the United States, his work is heard internationally in commercials for clients like **American Express** and **CNN**, as well as in numerous dramas and documentaries including **A & E**'s popular **American Justice** series.

Mark was commissioned by the music equipment manufacturers **Roland** and **Gibson** to compose and arrange music for their trade shows, and in 1996 Boston's renowned **Berklee College of Music** invited Mark to showcase his composition **First Light** with Berklee's faculty orchestra. Active in the Los Angeles music scene, Mark has performed with top professional musicians such as **Bruce Hornsby**'s drummer John Molo and **Yanni**'s bassist Rick Fierabracci. He leads and composes for the **Mark Harrison Quintet**, which performs regularly on the L.A. jazz circuit. After a recent show, **Music Connection** magazine noted that the Quintet "excelled at contemporary jazz" and that Mark "played with a high level of skill and passion that gave every song a soul".

After teaching at the internationally-acclaimed **Grove School of Music** for six years, Mark founded the **Harrison School of Music** (a successor institution to the Grove school) in Los Angeles. The Harrison School has since helped hundreds of students achieve their musical goals. Mark's groundbreaking keyboard method **The Pop Piano Book** is endorsed by Grammy-winners **Russell Ferrante** and **Mark James**, as well as other top professional musicians and educators. **Keyboard Magazine** calls his presentation style "warm, humorous and clear", and names The Pop Piano Book "the most accessible and valuable keyboard method available for those interested in popular styles".

Mark has also authored a complete series of instruction books for contemporary music theory and eartraining, which are "first class teaching texts" and "an excellent, plainspoken introduction to understanding music" according to **Jazz Times** magazine. The **Harrison Music Education Systems** product line is published internationally by **Hal Leonard Publications**. Mark's methods are also used and recommended at many educational institutions (including the internationally-famous **Berklee College of Music**) and his materials have been purchased by thousands of students in over twenty-five countries worldwide. Mark has written several 'master class' articles on contemporary rock, R&B and gospel piano styles for **Keyboard Magazine**, and he continues to be in demand as a uniquely effective contemporary music educator. He currently runs a busy private teaching studio in the Los Angeles area.

Here are some more products available from

# *HARRISON MUSIC EDUCATION SYSTEMS:*

## *Contemporary Music Theory Level One Book*

This introductory pop & jazz theory course covers music notation, major and minor scales, key signatures, intervals, triads, four-part chords, modes, diatonic chords, suspensions, and alterations of 3- and 4-part chords. Includes hundreds of written theory exercises, all with answers provided!

## *Contemporary Music Theory Level Three Book* *(available with CDs)*

This more advanced pop & jazz theory course presents the chord tones, extensions, alterations, and scale sources, for all major, minor, dominant and diminished chords. This information is then used to create voicings, polychords, and to harmonize melodies, using our 'contemporary shape concept'. This book is available with CDs of all music examples, and includes hundreds of written theory exercises with answers!

## *The Pop Piano Book* *(available with CDs, cassettes & Midi files)*

A complete method for playing contemporary styles spontaneously on the keyboard. This **500-page** book includes application of harmony to the keyboard in all keys, and then specific instruction for playing in pop, rock, funk, country, ballad, new age and gospel styles. Endorsed by **Grammy**-winners and top educators, this book is available with CDs, cassette tapes and MIDI files of all 800 music examples!

*"This is the most accessible and valuable keyboard method available for those interested in popular styles. Going through the method is just plain fun!"*

**ERNIE RIDEOUT**
Associate Editor, **KEYBOARD MAGAZINE**

## *Contemporary Eartraining Level One Book* *(available with CDs & cassettes)*

A modern eartraining approach to help you hear and transcribe melodies, rhythms, intervals, bass lines and basic chords (available with CDs or cassette tapes of vocal drills and exercises). Developed at the **Grove School of Music** in Los Angeles.

*(more products available contd)*

## Contemporary Eartraining Level Two Book *(available with CDs & cassettes)*

A modern eartraining approach to help you hear and transcribe chord progressions, modes and key changes used in pop and jazz styles (available with CDs or cassette tapes of exercises). Developed at the **Grove School of Music** in Los Angeles.

*If you would like to **order** or **inquire about our products**, or if you are interested in **private instruction with Mark Harrison** in the Los Angeles area, please call toll-free (in the U.S.):*

*(4   6   3   7)*
# 1-800-799-HMES

(**H**arrison **M**usic **E**ducation **S**ystems)

*or visit our website at:*

# www.harrisonmusic.com

*or write to us at:*

## HARRISON MUSIC EDUCATION SYSTEMS
## P.O. BOX 56505
## SHERMAN OAKS
## CA 91413 U.S.A.

## *DICK GROVE*

During the period from 1988 until 1992 I had the pleasure and privilege of teaching a wide range of courses at the **Grove School of Music**, in Los Angeles, California. From the time that **Dick Grove** founded this school in 1973 until the school's closure in 1992, his unique perspective on contemporary music influenced literally thousands of musicians and students from all around the world, as well as those of us on the faculty who were fortunate enough to work in this exceptional institution.

My experience on the Grove School faculty provided an ideal environment for me to develop and fine-tune my own concepts of how contemporary music should be taught, which in turn has helped me create my own series of instruction books and methods. Dick Grove's overall philosophy and concepts of contemporary music were very influential in this process, and I am proud to have been an integral part of the Grove School educational environment.

We were very saddened to hear of Dick's untimely death in December of 1998. I had the honor of speaking at a memorial service held for Dick in Los Angeles, which was attended by several hundred members of the 'Grove community'. Dick was a major influence and inspiration for my own educational career, and I know his legacy and spirit will continue to impact the many lives he has touched.

*Mark Harrison*

# TABLE OF CONTENTS

## Contemporary Music Theory Level 2 by Mark Harrison

*x*

# *Review of Contemporary Music Theory Level One*

## *Introduction*

This chapter reviews the main subject areas covered in **Contemporary Music Theory Level One**. The information is presented here in summary form - for a more detailed analysis and derivation of these concepts, please refer to the **Level One** book as required.

## *Major scales*

The major scale is derived by linking together two '**major tetrachords**', each of which consists of **whole-step**, **whole-step** and **half-step** intervals, as in the following example of a **C major** scale:-

### *Figure 1.1. C major scale showing tetrachords and intervals*

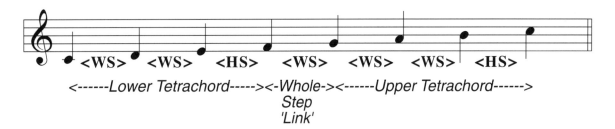

The two major tetrachords are separated by a '**link**' of a **whole-step** interval in between. It is strongly recommended that you always derive and conceptualize major scales this way (i.e. use consecutive ascending note letternames, and then qualify as necessary using sharps or flats to obtain the intervals shown above).

## *Circle-of-fifths and circle-of-fourths*

We can now use the above information to create a 'circle', which is defined as **a series of interlocking major scales with tetrachords in common**. For example, the upper tetrachord of the above **C major** scale is also the lower tetrachord of a **G major** scale, and the lower tetrachord of the above **C major** scale is also the upper tetrachord of an **F major** scale. Therefore the **C major** scale has **F major** and **G major** as its immediate neighbours on the 'circle', as shown in the diagram on the following page:-

## Circle-of-fifths and circle-of-fourths (contd)

### Figure 1.2. Circle diagram showing all major scale/tetrachord relationships

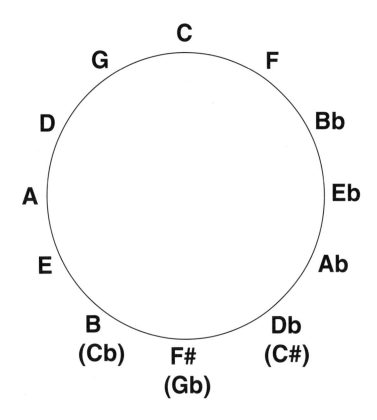

Each note name around the circle **represents a major scale**, and each of these major scales **shares a tetrachord in common with its two most immediate neighbours**.

Now we will arrive at the definition of the terms **'circle-of-fifths'** and **'circle-of-fourths'**, which represent **different movement directions** around the 'circle' shown above.

Each **clockwise** movement around the circle represents a **five-to-one** relationship. For example, **C to F** is a **five-to-one** relationship in **F major** (i.e. the **5th** to the **1st** degree of an **F major** scale), **F to Bb** is a **five-to-one** relationship in **Bb major**, etc. For this reason the clockwise movement direction around the above circle is referred to as **'circle-of-fifths'**.

Each **counter-clockwise** movement around the circle represents a **four-to-one** relationship. For example, **C to G** is a **four-to-one** relationship in **G major** (i.e. the **4th** to the **1st** degree of a **G major** scale), **G to D** is a **four-to-one** relationship in **D major**, etc. For this reason the counter-clockwise movement direction around the above circle is referred to as **'circle-of-fourths'**.

## *Circle-of-fifths and circle-of-fourths (contd)*

The logic and justification behind this approach to 'labelling the circles' (which may be new for you!) is explained in great detail in Chapter One of the **Level One** book. We can briefly summarize the reasons here:-

*1)* It is consistent with our original concept of defining the circle as an **interlocking series of major scales**, with tetrachords in common.

*2)* It neatly **sidesteps any problems** with defining the circles on an 'interval basis'. For example, many people are tempted to label the '**C to F**' direction as 'circle-of-fourths', as **C to F** looks like a 4th interval. Well of course it is if we **ascend** from C to F, but if we **descend** it is a 5th interval! So this method is rather unreliable due to these different interval interpretations (and in any case is a rather superficial approach in my opinion)!

*3)* Perhaps most importantly, it **most accurately reflects how the ear works** to hear progressions and key changes around the circle (i.e. on a **5-to-1** or **4-to-1** basis) - as discussed in detail in my **Contemporary Eartraining Level Two** course.

## *Major key signatures*

Building our major scales using the interval/tetrachord method, we find that as we move clockwise from **C** on the circle diagram, the key of **F** requires **one flat**, the key of **Bb** requires **two flats**, etc. Each time we move clockwise to a new 'flat key', we add a new flat (equivalent to the **4th degree** of the new major scale) to the previously derived key signature. The 'flat key' signatures can therefore be summarized as follows:-

### *Figure 1.3. Summary of all 'flat key' signatures*

(**C** *Major*      **F** *Major*      **Bb** *Major*      **Eb** *Major*
*- no flats)*      *- one flat*      *- two flats*      *- three flats*

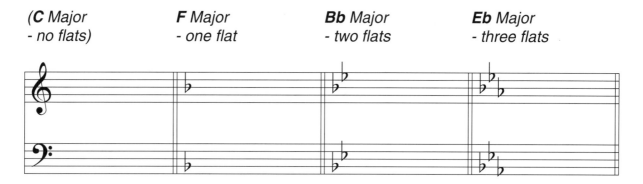

*(continued on next page----->)*

## *Major key signatures (contd)*

### *Figure 1.3. Summary of all 'flat key' signatures (contd)*

**Ab** *Major*          **Db** *Major*          **Gb** *Major*          **Cb** *Major*
*- four flats*          *- five flats*          *- six flats*           *- seven flats*

Again building our major scales using the interval/tetrachord method, we find that as we move counter-clockwise from **C** on the previous circle diagram, the key of **G** requires **one sharp**, the key of **D** requires **two sharps**, etc. Each time we move counter-clockwise to a new 'sharp key', we add a new sharp (equivalent to the **7th degree** of the new major scale) to the previously derived key signature. The 'sharp key' signatures can therefore be summarized as follows:-

### *Figure 1.4. Summary of all 'sharp key' signatures*

*(**C** Major*          **G** *Major*          **D** *Major*          **A** *Major*
*- no sharps)*          *- one sharp*          *- two sharps*          *- three sharps*

*E Major*          *B Major*          *F# Major*          *C# Major*
*- four sharps*    *- five sharps*    *- six sharps*      *- seven sharps*

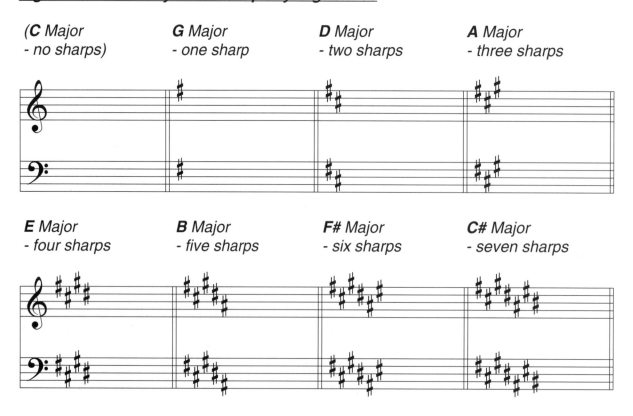

## *Intervals*

An interval in music is defined as the **measurement of distance between any two notes**. Each **interval name** will always have **two components**:-

- a **description** (either major, perfect, minor, augmented or diminished).
- a **number** i.e. 2nd, 3rd, 4th etc.

All intervals will belong to one of two overall categories - **diatonic** or **chromatic**:-

- A **diatonic** interval is created when the **upper** note of an interval **is contained within** the major scale built from the **lower** note.

- A **chromatic** interval is created when the **upper** note of an interval **is not contained within** the major scale built from the **lower** note.

All **diatonic** intervals are either **major** or **perfect**, as shown in the following example:-

### *Figure 1.5. Diatonic intervals within a C major scale*

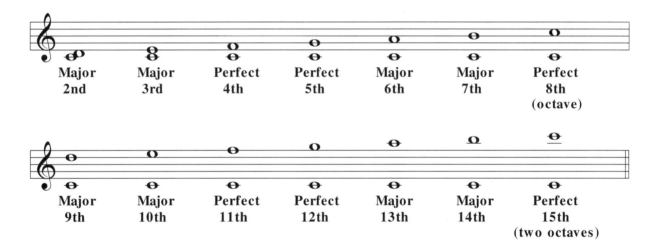

| Major 2nd | Major 3rd | Perfect 4th | Perfect 5th | Major 6th | Major 7th | Perfect 8th (octave) |

| Major 9th | Major 10th | Perfect 11th | Perfect 12th | Major 13th | Major 14th | Perfect 15th (two octaves) |

All **chromatic** intervals are either **minor**, **diminished** or **augmented**, and can be considered as modified versions of the above diatonic intervals:-

- A **major** interval reduced by a half-step becomes a **minor** interval.
- A **minor** interval reduced by a (further) half-step becomes a **diminished** interval.
- A **major** interval increased by a half-step becomes an **augmented** interval.
- A **perfect** interval reduced by a half-step becomes a **diminished** interval.
- A **perfect** interval increased by a half-step becomes an **augmented** interval.

## Triads

The **major** triad is derived by placing **major 3rd** and **perfect 5th** intervals above the root, as follows:-

### Figure 1.6. C major triad - interval construction

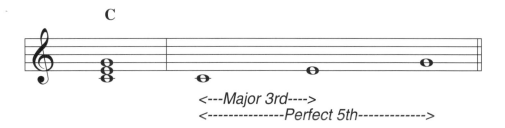

<---Major 3rd---->
<---------------Perfect 5th------------>

The **minor** triad is derived by placing **minor 3rd** and **perfect 5th** intervals above the root, as follows:-

### Figure 1.7. C minor triad - interval construction

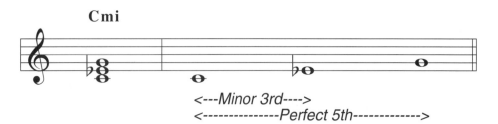

<---Minor 3rd---->
<---------------Perfect 5th------------>

The **augmented** triad is derived by placing **major 3rd** and **augmented 5th** intervals above the root, as follows:-

### Figure 1.8. C augmented triad - interval construction

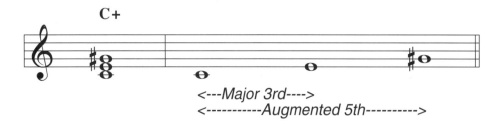

<---Major 3rd---->
<-----------Augmented 5th---------->

The **diminished** triad is derived by placing **minor 3rd** and **diminished 5th** intervals above the root, as shown on the following page:-

### *Triads (contd)*

#### *Figure 1.9. C diminished triad - interval construction*

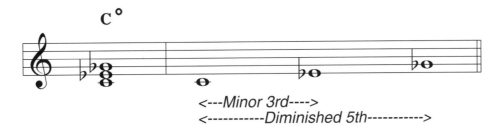

&lt;---Minor 3rd----&gt;
&lt;-----------Diminished 5th-----------&gt;

All of these triads may be **inverted**, as in the following example of a **C major** triad:-

#### *Figure 1.10. C major triad and inversions*

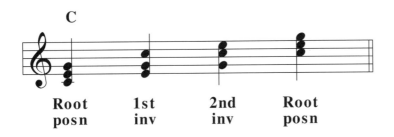

Root        1st        2nd        Root
posn        inv        inv        posn

### *Diatonic triads*

Diatonic triads are **wholly contained within a major scale**. Here are the diatonic triads in the key of **C major**:-

#### *Figure 1.11. Diatonic triads within a C major scale*

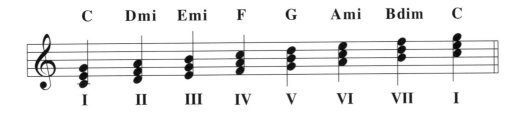

The same triad 'qualities' will also occur within all major scales/keys, as in the summary on the following page:-

## *Diatonic triads (contd)*

- The triad built from the *1st* degree of a major scale is always *major.*
- The triad built from the *2nd* degree of a major scale is always *minor.*
- The triad built from the *3rd* degree of a major scale is always *minor.*
- The triad built from the *4th* degree of a major scale is always *major.*
- The triad built from the *5th* degree of a major scale is always *major.*
- The triad built from the *6th* degree of a major scale is always *minor.*
- The triad built from the *7th* degree of a major scale is always *diminished.*

## *Four-part chords*

The **major 7th** chord is derived by placing **major 3rd**, **perfect 5th** and **major 7th** intervals above the root, as follows:-

### *Figure 1.12. C major seventh chord - interval construction*

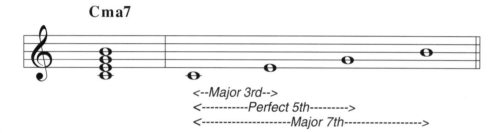

The **major 6th** chord is derived by placing **major 3rd**, **perfect 5th** and **major 6th** intervals above the root, as follows:-

### *Figure 1.13. C major sixth chord - interval construction*

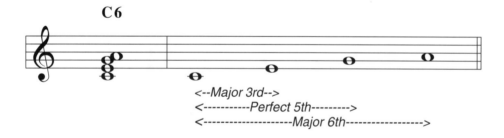

The **minor 7th** chord is derived by placing **minor 3rd**, **perfect 5th** and **minor 7th** intervals above the root, as shown on the following page:-

### *Four-part chords (contd)*

#### *Figure 1.14. C minor seventh chord - interval construction*

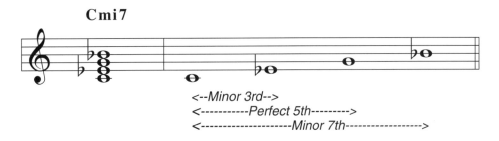

```
<--Minor 3rd-->
<-----------Perfect 5th--------->
<--------------------Minor 7th------------------>
```

The **dominant 7th** chord is derived by placing **major 3rd**, **perfect 5th** and **minor 7th** intervals above the root, as follows:-

#### *Figure 1.15. C dominant seventh chord - interval construction*

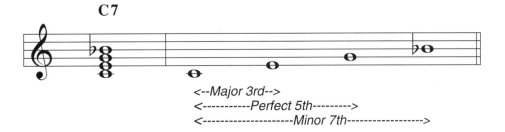

```
<--Major 3rd-->
<-----------Perfect 5th--------->
<--------------------Minor 7th------------------>
```

All of these four-part chords may be **inverted**, as in the following example of a **C major seventh** chord:-

#### *Figure 1.16. C major seventh chord and inversions*

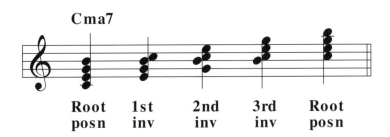

Root    1st    2nd    3rd    Root
posn    inv    inv    inv    posn

(Note that the **major 6th** and **minor 7th** chords can be considered as **inversions** of one another).

## *Diatonic four-part chords*

Diatonic four-part chords are **wholly contained within a major scale**. Here are the diatonic four-part chords in the key of **C major**:-

**Figure 1.17. Diatonic four-part chords within a C major scale**

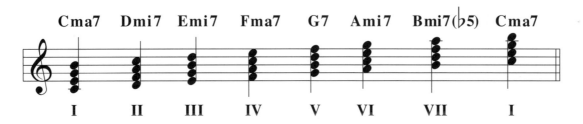

The same four-part chord 'qualities' will also occur within all major scales/keys, as in the following summary:-

-    The four-part chord built from the **1st** degree of a major scale is always a **major 7th** or **major 6th**.
-    The four-part chord built from the **2nd** degree of a major scale is always a **minor 7th**.
-    The four-part chord built from the **3rd** degree of a major scale is always a **minor 7th**.
-    The four-part chord built from the **4th** degree of a major scale is always a **major 7th** or **major 6th**.
-    The four-part chord built from the **5th** degree of a major scale is always a **dominant 7th**.
-    The four-part chord built from the **6th** degree of a major scale is always a **minor 7th**.
-    The four-part chord built from the **7th** degree of a major scale is always a **minor 7th with flatted 5th**.

## *Modal scales*

Modal scales or modes are **displaced versions of major scales**, i.e. they are major scales starting on a note **other than the normal tonic** or 1st degree, as follows:-

-    A **Dorian** mode is a major scale starting from its **2nd** degree.
-    A **Phrygian** mode is a major scale starting from its **3rd** degree.
-    A **Lydian** mode is a major scale starting from its **4th** degree.
-    A **Mixolydian** mode is a major scale starting from its **5th** degree.
-    An **Aeolian** mode is a major scale starting from its **6th** degree.
-    A **Locrian** mode is a major scale starting from its **7th** degree.
-    (An **Ionian** mode is a major scale starting from its **1st** degree i.e. **not** displaced).

## Modal scales (contd)

For example, we can take a **Bb major** scale and displace it to start on its **2nd** degree, creating a **C Dorian** mode:-

### Figure 1.18. C Dorian mode (Bb major scale starting on its 2nd degree)

The **relative major** of a modal scale, is the major scale which has been displaced to create the mode in question - for example, the relative major of the above **C Dorian** mode is **Bb major**. The above mode could therefore be notated using the **relative major key signature** (i.e. two flats) as follows:-

### Figure 1.19. C Dorian mode (notated using Bb major key signature)

## Minor scales, keys and key signatures

There are three minor scales in common usage - **melodic**, **harmonic** and **natural**. In contemporary applications (as opposed to classical music) we do not need different ascending and descending forms of these scales. There are three ways to construct the minor scales - using intervals/tetrachords, altering a major scale, and using a minor key signature (with any necessary accidentals).

Each major key signature as reviewed in **Figs. 1.3. - 1.4.** is also used for a corresponding **relative minor key**. This relative minor is built from the **6th degree** of the corrresponding major key. For example, the key signature of **Eb major** uses **three flats** (see **Fig. 1.3.**), and the **6th** degree of an **Eb major** scale is the note **C** - so the key of **C minor** also uses the same key signature (i.e. three flats).

First we will build the minor scales using intervals and tetrachords, as in the **C minor** scale examples beginning on the following page:-

## *Minor scales, keys and key signatures (contd)*

### *Figure 1.20. C melodic minor scale* *(showing tetrachords and intervals)*

<------- *lower tetrachord* ------>          <------ *upper tetrachord* ------>

### *Figure 1.21. C harmonic minor scale* *(showing tetrachords and intervals)*

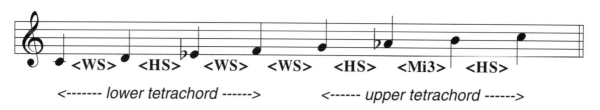

<------- *lower tetrachord* ------>          <------ *upper tetrachord* ------>

### *Figure 1.22. C natural minor scale* *(showing tetrachords and intervals)*

<------- *lower tetrachord* ------>          <------ *upper tetrachord* ------>

Note that the **natural minor** scale is intervallically equivalent to an **Aeolian** mode, and that **all** of the minor scales contain the **same lower tetrachord** (whole-step, half-step, and whole-step). Now we will build the minor scales by altering a major scale (in this case **C major**):-

### *Figure 1.23. C melodic minor scale*
*(built by flatting the 3rd degree of a C major scale)*

### *Figure 1.24. C harmonic minor scale*
*(built by flatting the 3rd and 6th degrees of a C major scale)*

### Minor scales, keys and key signatures (contd)

#### Figure 1.25. C natural minor scale
*(built by flatting the 3rd, 6th and 7th degrees of a C major scale)*

Finally we will build the minor scales using minor key signatures. If a minor key signature is used **with no additional accidentals**, a **natural minor scale** will result as follows:-

#### Figure 1.26. C natural minor scale
*(using the C minor key signature **with no additional accidentals**)*

To obtain a **harmonic minor** scale when a minor key signature is 'in force' we need to **sharp the 7th** degree as follows:-

#### Figure 1.27. C harmonic minor scale
*- using the C minor key signature with the **7th** degree sharped (**Bb --> B**)*

Finally, to obtain a **melodic minor** scale when a minor key signature is 'in force' we need to **sharp the 6th and 7th** degrees as follows:-

#### Figure 1.28. C melodic minor scale
*- using the C minor key signature with the **6th** and **7th** degrees sharped (**Ab --> A, Bb --> B**)*

## *More four-part chords*

The **minor major 7th** chord is built from the **1st** degree of the **melodic minor scale** (see **Fig. 1.20.**), and can be derived by placing **minor 3rd**, **perfect 5th** and **major 7th** intervals above the root, as follows:-

### *Figure 1.29. C minor major seventh chord - interval construction*

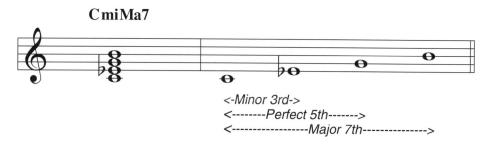

```
<-Minor 3rd->
<--------Perfect 5th------->
<-----------------Major 7th--------------->
```

The **minor 6th** chord is also built from the **1st** degree of the **melodic minor scale**, and can be derived by placing **minor 3rd**, **perfect 5th** and **major 6th** intervals above the root, as follows:-

### *Figure 1.30. C minor sixth chord - interval construction*

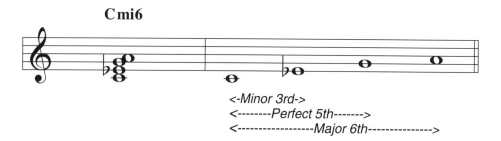

```
<-Minor 3rd->
<--------Perfect 5th------->
<-----------------Major 6th--------------->
```

In all four-part (or larger) chord forms, it is the **3rd** and **7th** (or **6th**) of the chord which defines the basic **chord quality**. Here is a summary of these intervals within the four-part chords:-

| *Type of chord* | *Third interval contained in chord* | *Seventh (or sixth) interval contained in chord* |
| --- | --- | --- |
| *Major 7th* | *Major 3rd* | *Major 7th* |
| *Minor major 7th* | *Minor 3rd* | *Major 7th* |
| *Major 6th* | *Major 3rd* | *Major 6th* |
| *Minor 6th* | *Minor 3rd* | *Major 6th* |
| *Minor 7th* | *Minor 3rd* | *Minor 7th* |
| *Dominant 7th* | *Major 3rd* | *Minor 7th* |

## *Suspended chords*

A 'suspended' chord is one in which the **3rd** has been **replaced** by the note which is a **perfect 4th interval from the root of the chord**. If this occurs within a **C major** triad, the following **Csus** (or **Csus4**) chord is obtained:-

***Figure 1.31. C suspended triad - interval construction***

```
<--Perfect 4th--->
<--------------Perfect 5th------------->
```

If the replacement of the **3rd** (with the **4th**) occurs within a **C minor** triad, the resulting **Cmisus** or **Cmisus4** chord has the same interval structure as the above **Csus** chord.

If the replacement of the **3rd** (with the **4th**) occurs within a **C dominant seventh** four-part chord, the following **C7sus** (suspended dominant 7th) chord is obtained:-

***Figure 1.32. C suspended dominant seventh chord - interval construction***

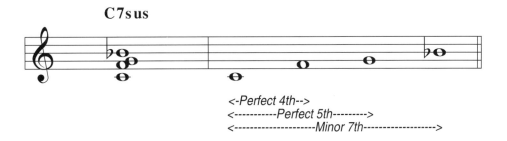

```
<-Perfect 4th-->
<-----------Perfect 5th--------->
<---------------------Minor 7th------------------->
```

## *Altered chords*

An '**altered**' version of a triad or four-part chord is one in which the **5th** of the chord has been flatted or sharped by half-step. (If the **3rd** or **7th/6th** is changed within a chord, the result is a **new chord type**, as shown in the table on the previous page - **not an 'altered' version of the original chord**).

First we will **flat** the **5th** of a **major triad**, as shown on the following page:-

**15**

## *Altered chords (contd)*

### *Figure 1.33. C major triad with flatted 5th - interval construction*

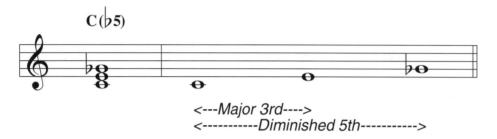

<---Major 3rd---->
<-----------Diminished 5th----------->

We can also **sharp** the **5th** of a **minor triad**, as follows:-

### *Figure 1.34. C minor triad with sharped 5th - interval construction*

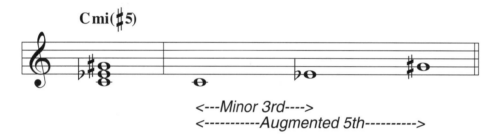

<---Minor 3rd---->
<-----------Augmented 5th---------->

We can also **flat** the **5th** of a **major sixth** chord, as follows:-

### *Figure 1.35. C major 6th with flatted 5th - interval construction*

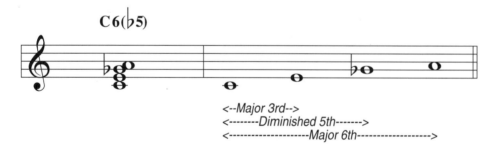

<--Major 3rd-->
<--------Diminished 5th------->
<--------------------Major 6th------------------->

Finally we can both **flat** and **sharp** the **5th** of **major 7th**, **minor 7th** and **dominant 7th** four-part chords, as shown in the examples on the following page:-

16

## Altered chords (contd)

### Figure 1.36. Deriving a 'C major 7th with flatted/sharped 5th' from a C major 7th chord

### Figure 1.37. Deriving a 'C minor 7th with flatted/sharped 5th' from a C minor 7th chord

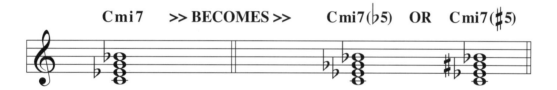

### Figure 1.38. Deriving a 'C dominant 7th with flatted/sharped 5th' from a C dominant 7th chord

# *Five-part chords and the II-V-I progression in major keys*

## *Introduction*

In this chapter we will deal with the following subject areas:-

**1)** We will review the **solfeg** system for labelling the scale degrees of a major scale (i.e. using the syllables **DO**, **RE**, **MI**, **FA**, **SO**, **LA** and **TI**), and in particular the **active** or **resting** qualities of each scale degree with respect to the tonic of the key (or **DO**). You will already have encountered these **solfeg** syllables if you have worked through my *Contemporary Eartraining* courses! This concept will then enable us to understand how a **II - V - I** (two-five-one) progression works, and why the **II - V - I** is so frequently used in jazz and 'standard' tunes.

**2)** We will discuss the function and importance of the **dominant chord** in today's music. We will see the various ways in which this chord 'leads back' to a **I** or **tonic** chord, using the **active** and **resting** scale degree concepts mentioned above. We will also see how the dominant chord can be **suspended**, which happens very frequently in pop styles.

**3)** We will then add the **IImi7** chord to the front of the 'dominant to tonic' sequence above, to create the **II - V - I** progression in a major key. By focusing on the definitive **3rds** and **7ths** of each chord, we will see how the active and resting scale degree concepts work within the progression.

**4)** We will then add **ninths** to all of the chords used in the **II - V - I** progression in major, to create the following **five-part** chords:- *minor 9th, dominant 9th, dominant 9th suspended, major 9th,* and *major 69*. We will also discuss the major and minor **add9** chords.

**5)** Finally we will begin a discussion of **harmonic analysis** as applied to musical styles, and we will then analyze the function of various **II**, **V** and **I** chords used in pairs.

## *Diatonic solfeg review*

We will now review the diatonic solfeg syllables used to label the scale degrees of a major scale (the term 'diatonic' here meaning that we are entirely within a major scale/key restriction). These solfeg syllables can be assigned to a **C major** scale as follows:-

### *Figure 2.1. Diatonic solfeg syllables assigned to a C major scale*

## *Diatonic solfeg review (contd)*

The central point to grasp when using this system is that **each scale degree will have a unique 'active' or 'resting' property with respect to the tonic of the key (or DO)**. As you may know, this concept is the main foundation of our *Contemporary Eartraining* courses (see page **v**). This principle now also becomes an issue in our study of theory and harmony, as it will give us a clear insight into how certain progressions (such as the widely-used **II - V - I** sequence) really work.

Don't forget that **the solfeg system works in all keys** - **DO** can be assigned to any tonic, and the active & resting properties will work in exactly the same manner - the example on the previous page is shown in the key of **C** for convenience. We can review the active and resting properties of each of these major scale degrees as follows:-

**DO** - Being the tonic or 'home base' of the major key we are using, this scale degree is by definition the most **resting** or 'resolved' within the major scale.

**RE** - This is an **active** tone which generally wants to resolve down to **DO** (or up to **MI**). As these resolutions would be via **whole-step** intervals (review **Fig. 1.1.** as necessary), **RE** is only considered to be 'mildly' active (or semi-active) - the resulting **whole-step** movements (i.e. from **RE** down to **DO**, or from **RE** up to **MI**) are not particularly strong or 'leading'.

**MI** - This is another **resting** tone within the major scale, and is considered very 'definitive' as its use clearly signifies a major key quality.

**FA** - This is another active tone which generally wants to resolve down to **MI**. As this resolution would be via a **half-step** interval, **FA** is considered to be very active - the resulting **half-step** movement (i.e. from **FA** down to **MI**) is a strong and 'leading' interval. For reasons more fully explained later, the **FA** to **MI** movement can be considered as the most important and definitive resolution within a major key.

**SO** - This is another resting tone within the major scale - **SO** is considered to have a particularly 'stable' quality.

**LA** - This is an **active** tone which generally wants to resolve down to **SO** (or up to **DO** via **TI**). In a similar manner to **RE** above, **LA** is only considered to be 'mildly' active (or semi-active) as the resulting **whole-step** movement (i.e. from **LA** down to **SO**) is not particularly strong or 'leading'.

**TI** - This is another active tone which generally wants to resolve up to **DO**. As this resolution would be via a **half-step** interval, **TI** is considered to be very active - the resulting **half-step** movement (i.e. from **TI** up to **DO**) is a strong and 'leading' interval.

The above active and resting scale degree properties can be summarized as shown on the following page:-

### *Diatonic solfeg review (contd)*

- **DO**, **MI** and **SO** are considered the **resting** or 'resolved' tones of the major scale.
- **RE** and **LA** are cosidered **mildly active** as they resolve by **whole-step**.
- **FA** and **TI** are considered **very active** as they resolve by **half-step**.

The main active-to-resting resolutions occurring within the major scale are:-

- **RE** down to **DO** (by **whole-step**).
- **FA** down to **MI** (by **half-step**).
- **LA** down to **SO** (by **whole-step**).
- **TI** up to **DO** (by **half-step**).

*(For numerous vocal drills and exercises using these principles, please refer to **Chapter 1** of our **Contemporary Eartraining Level One** course).*

Of the above resolutions, **FA-MI** and **TI-DO** are arguably the most important as **FA** and **TI** are the most active scale degrees within the major scale, and these resolutions are via the strong and leading **half-step** interval. It would not be an exaggeration to say that the '**FA-to-MI**' and '**TI-to-DO**' resolutions are pretty much the basis of Western tonal music as we know it!

Don't forget that using the solfeg syllables is simply a convenient way to label the major scale degrees **in any key**. Some of you may be more accustomed to using scale degree numbers (i.e. **FA-to-MI** is equivalent to **4-to-3**, and **TI-to-DO** is equivalent to **7-to-1**). This is no problem for now, as obviously the same major scale resolution and active-to-resting concepts will apply - however, using numbers can often be inconvenient when doing vocal drills and/or eartraining, particularly when chromatic tones are involved (as presented in **Chapter 4** in this book, and in our **Contemporary Eartraining Level Two** course). For these reasons, I would strongly advise that you familiarize yourself with these solfeg syllables if you have not done so already!

### *The function and importance of the dominant chord*

Back in **Contemporary Music Theory Level One** we derived the four-part **dominant 7th** chord from the 5th degree of a major scale, as follows:-

### *Figure 2.2. Diatonic four-part chords within a C major scale (including the G7 chord)*

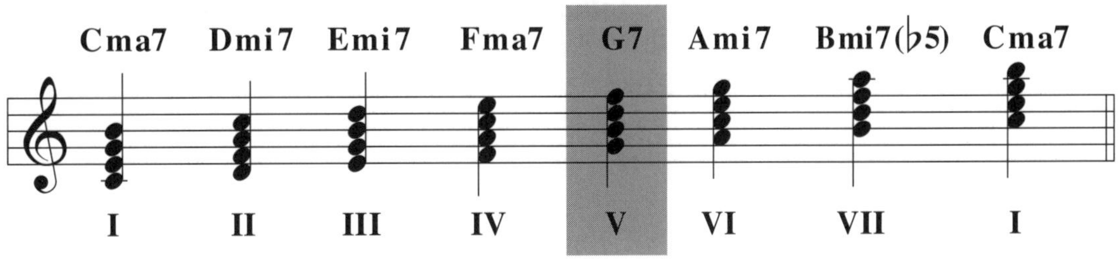

### *The function and importance of the dominant chord (contd)*

We have already seen that it is the **3rd** and **7th** (or **6th**) **intervals** present within four-part chords, which define the basic **vertical quality** of the chord (review the table on **p14** as necessary). In this context we note that a **dominant 7th** chord contains **major 3rd** and **minor 7th** intervals. Having reviewed the active and resting scale degrees in the major scale, we are now in a position to see exactly why the **dominant** chord leads back to the **tonic** or **I** chord - the **3rd** and **7th** of the dominant chord (which give the chord its vertical quality) are also **TI** and **FA** of the major scale, which as we have recently seen are the most active scale degrees in a major key and typically require resolution to the adjacent resting tones. This principle is shown in the following dominant-to-tonic progression (in the key of **C**):-

### *Figure 2.3. G7 to C progression (showing movement between FA-MI and TI-DO)*

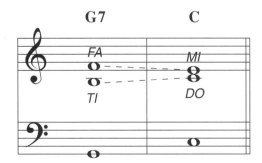

Note that the **G7** chord in the first measure, is shown with a basic **'7-3' voicing** - i.e. we have the **root** of the chord (**G**) in the bass clef, and the **7th** (**F**) and **3rd** (**B**) in the treble clef. This type of voicing has an 'open' sound and yet completely defines the chord quality (for this reason I typically use it as a 'starting' jazz voicing approach for keyboard students).

Let's review again what this example shows us - the definitive **3rd** and **7th** of the dominant chord are also **TI** and **FA** of the key, which resolve to the resting tones **DO** and **MI** respectively within this simple **G7** to **C** progression. This resolution energy or momentum (combined with the bass movement of **G** to **C** which is a strong **circle-of-5ths** motion - review **Fig. 1.2.** as necessary) is the reason why the **dominant** chord leads back to the **tonic** or **I** chord in most conventional Western music styles.

Now we'll look at the effect of using a **suspended dominant 7th chord** on these active-to-resting resolutions. We recall from **Fig. 1.30.** that the '4th has replaced the 3rd' in this chord - in other words, the **3rd** has been replaced by the note which is a **perfect 4th** interval above the root of the chord. Using this principle, we will first of all review how a **G suspended dominant 7th** chord is spelled, as shown on the following page:-

## *The function and importance of the dominant chord (contd)*

### *Figure 2.4. G suspended dominant 7th chord*

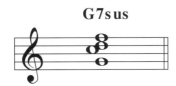

In comparing this **G7sus** chord to the **G7** chord in **Fig. 2.2.**, we note that that the **3rd** of the **G7** (i.e. the note **B**) has been replaced by the note which is a **perfect 4th** interval above the root of the **G7sus** chord (i.e. the note **C**).

What effect does this have on the dominant-to-tonic progression i.e. when the **suspended dominant 7th** chord is used? In a similar manner to the 'G7 to C' progression shown in **Fig. 2.3.**, we can now demonstrate the interior resolutions occurring within a 'G7sus to C' progression, as follows:-

### *Figure 2.5. G7sus to C progression (showing movement between FA-MI)*

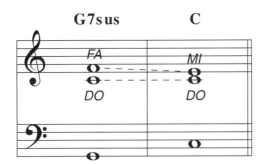

Note that instead of the definitive '**7-3**' voicing shown in the first measure of **Fig. 2.3.** for the **G7** chord, we now effectively have a '**7-4**' voicing in the first measure above, on the **G7sus** chord. From an active/resting (solfeg) standpoint, now instead of the very active combination of **TI** and **FA** present on the **G7** chord, we now have **eliminated TI altogether** from the **G7sus** chord. This has the following implications for the above **G7sus** - **C** chord progression:-

- The resting tone of **DO** is now a commontone across both chords.
- The '**TI to DO**' resolution has been eliminated.
- The dissonant interval between **TI** and **FA** on the dominant chord has been eliminated.
- The resolution of **FA** to **MI** across the dominant-to-tonic progression has been retained.

The sum total of all this is that the resolution of the **suspended dominant** to the **tonic** chord (as shown in **Fig. 2.5.** above) is far 'gentler' and less leading than the resolution of the **regular** (i.e. unsuspended) **dominant** to the **tonic** chord (as shown in **Fig. 2.3.**).

## *The function and importance of the dominant chord (contd)*

At this point it might be helpful to make a stylistic observation - subject to numerous variations and exceptions, we can say that the **regular** (i.e. unsuspended) **dominant** chord shown in **Fig 2.3.** is widely used in jazz, standards and older pop music styles, whereas the **suspended dominant** shown in **Fig. 2.5.** is widely used in modern pop styles.

Now let's return to the use of the **regular** (i.e. unsuspended) dominant in **Fig. 2.3.** In that example, the use of a simple **C** triad as the **I** or **tonic** chord allowed both the active tones (**TI** and **FA**) to resolve to their respective resting tones (i.e. **DO** and **MI**). However we recall from **Fig. 2.2.** that a **C major 7th** four-part chord can be built from the **1st** degree of a **C major** scale - and it is extremely common to use a **major 7th** as a **tonic** chord in jazz and more sophisticated styles. So now we will look at the resolution implications of moving from a **G dominant 7th** chord to a **C major 7th** chord, by again isolating the definitive '7-3' voices as follows:-

### *Figure 2.6. G7 to Cma7 progression (showing movement between FA-MI)*

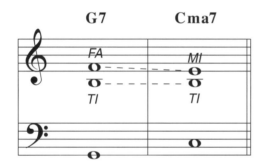

Both of these chords are now shown with a definitive '7-3' voicing:-
- the **G7** chord has the root (G) in the bass clef, and the 7th (F) & 3rd (B) in the treble clef (as in **Fig. 2.3.**)
- the **Cma7** chord has the root (C) in the bass clef, and the 7th (B) & 3rd (E) in the treble clef.

Note that whereas the **G7** chord is no less active than it was in **Fig. 2.3.**, now the **active tone TI is retained** on the **Cma7** chord - in other words the active tone is not resolved (to **DO**) on the tonic chord. This more sophisticated sound (i.e. active tones retained on a tonic chord) is routinely used in jazz styles.

Note also that the consistent factor in all of the dominant-to-tonic variations in **Figs. 2.3.**, **2.5.** and **2.6.** (apart from the root movement) is the **FA-to-MI** resolution (the movement of the **7th** of the dominant chord down to the **3rd** of the tonic chord). We might draw the following conclusions from this observation:-

- The **FA-to-MI** resolution is an essential component of any dominant-to-tonic chord relationship in a major key.
- The **FA-to-MI** resolution is the most important and 'definitive' active-to-resting resolution within the major scale (see **p20** comments).

# Five-part chords and the II-V-I progression in major keys

## ***The II - V - I (two-five-one) progression in major***

Now we will expand on the dominant-to-tonic progression already derived, by putting a **IImi7** chord (i.e. a minor 7th chord built from the 2nd degree of the major scale) in front of it to create a **II - V - I** progression. Again an analysis of the active/resting qualities and resolutions (together with the root movement) will enable us to understand why this progression is so widely used in jazz and 'standard' styles.

First we will review where the **II - V - I** occurs within the overall four-part chord options available from a **C major scale**, as follows:-

***Figure 2.7. Diatonic four-part chords within a C major scale (including the II, V and I)***

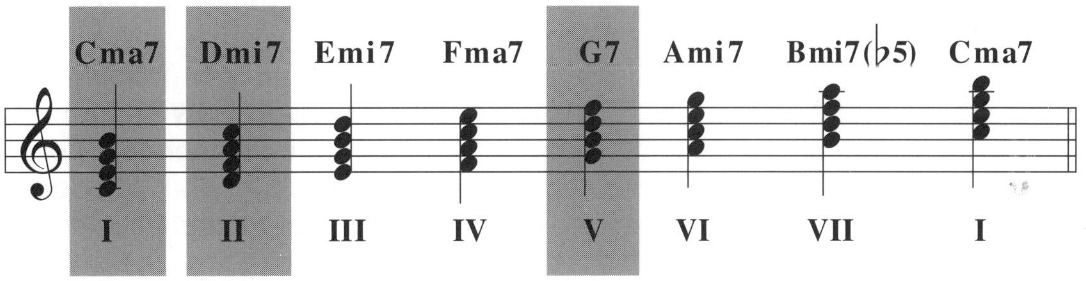

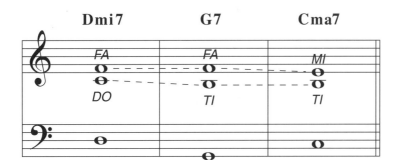

In a similar manner to the previous progression examples, we will now isolate the definitive '**7-3**' voices within the four-part **II - V - I** progression in **C major**, as follows:-

***Figure 2.8. Dmi7 - G7 - Cma7 progression (showing movement between FA-MI and TI-DO)***

*All of these chords are now shown with a definitive '7-3' voicing:-*
- *the **Dmi7** chord has the root (D) in the bass clef, and the 7th (C) & 3rd (F) in the treble clef*
- *the **G7** chord has the root (G) in the bass clef, and the 7th (F) & 3rd (B) in the treble clef (as in **Fig. 2.6.**)*
- *the **Cma7** chord has the root (C) in the bass clef, and the 7th (B) & 3rd (E) in the treble clef (as in **Fig. 2.6.**).*

Here we have effectively added a '**7-3**' voicing for a **Dmi7** chord on to the front of the **G7 - Cma7** progression shown in **Fig. 2.6**. At this time we should note the 'voiceleading' used - in the above example, the **3rd** is the top treble clef note of the **Dmi7** voicing, which then becomes the **7th** on top of the **G7**, finally moving to the **3rd** on top of the **Cma7**. This can therefore be referred to as a **3 - 7 - 3** line, and from a solfeg standpoint this line contains the scale degrees **FA - FA - MI**.

## *The II - V - I (two-five-one) progression in major (contd)*

Now looking at the other 'horizontal line' in the treble clef of the previous example, the **7th** is the bottom treble clef note of the **Dmi7** voicing, which then moves to the **3rd** on the **G7**, finally becoming the **7th** on the **Cma7**. This can therefore be referred to as a **7 - 3 - 7** line, and from a solfeg standpoint this line contains the scale degrees **DO - TI - TI**.

*(For more on 'horizontal lines' within II - V - I progressions from an Eartraining perspective, please refer to **Chapters 7 & 8** of our **Contemporary Eartraining Level Two** course).*

We can now make the following observations about the **II - V - I** sequence shown in **Fig. 2.8.**:-

- The '**7-3**' voicings used, completely define the **minor 7th**, **dominant 7th** and **major 7th** chord qualities respectively - review the table on **p14** as necessary.
- This progression enables us to move between **DO** and **TI** of the key (from the **IImi7** chord to the **V7** chord) and between **FA** and **MI** of the key (from the **V7** chord to the **Ima7** chord). Both of the leading half-steps in the major scale are therefore used, which is the most efficient way to 'let the ear know' which key we are in. **This provides vital 'definition' in jazz and standard styles**, which routinely use 'momentary key changes' in the harmony (as we will shortly discuss).
- The root movement of the **II - V - I** progression uses a strong and leading **circle-of-5ths** motion - review the circle in **Fig. 1.2.** as necessary.
  (Note that the upper voices of the **G7sus** chord as shown in the first measure of **Fig. 2.5.**, are the same as the upper voices on the **Dmi7** chord as shown in the first measure of **Fig. 2.8.** This enables us to see why the **IImi7** chord is sometimes referred to as a 'suspension' or 'delayed resolution' into the **V7** chord).

For these reasons, the **II - V - I** progression is very commonly used in more sophisticated musical styles such as jazz and standards, which typically use four-part (or greater) chord forms. The two 'horizontal lines' shown in the treble clef of **Fig. 2.8.** could also be 'reversed' - i.e. the **7 - 3 - 7** (**DO - TI - TI**) line could be placed on top, as in the following example:-

### *Figure 2.9. Dmi7 - G7 - Cma7 progression (showing movement between FA-MI and TI-DO)*

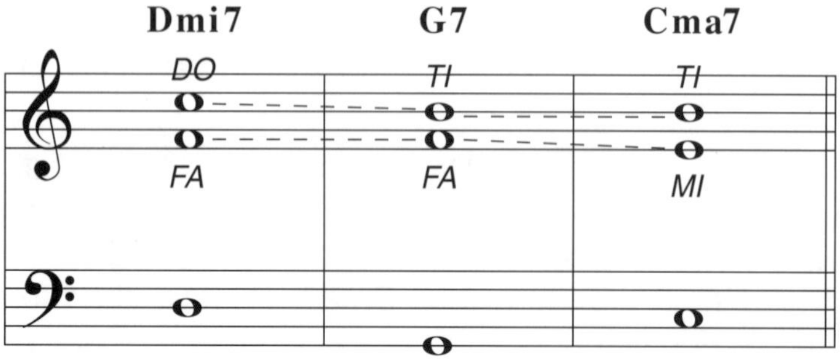

This **II - V - I** progression is now shown with the 7 - 3 - 7 (DO - TI - TI) line on top of the treble clef. (Compare this example to **Fig. 2.8.** as necessary).

## *Using five-part chords within the II - V - I progression in major*

Now that we have analyzed the **II - V - I** progression in major using **four-part** chords, we are now in a position to 'upgrade' these definitve chords to **five-part** versions (sometimes also referred to as 'ninth' chords as these larger chord forms will now include 'ninths'). Note that the addition of a ninth to these chords **does not fundamentally alter the active/resting qualities occurring across the II - V - I progression**, as demonstrated by isolating the definitive '7-3' voices in the previous examples. Rather, the use of these five-part chords can add a more 'lush' or saturated quality to the harmony, **in addition to the definitive qualities already present in the II - V - I progression** as previously described.

First of all we will review the chord 'stacks' for the **four-part II - V - I** chords in major, as in the following example in the key of **C major**:-

### *Figure 2.10. Four-part II - V - I chord 'stacks' in the key of C major*

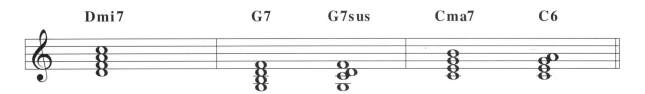

Again note that we have two forms of dominant seventh chord built from the 5th degree of the key - the '**regular**' dominant chord with the **3rd** & **7th** (**TI/FA**) present, and the **suspended** dominant in which the **3rd** has been replaced by the note which is a perfect **4th** interval above the root - review earlier text accompanying **Fig. 2.5.** as necessary. We also recall from our work in *Contemporary Music Theory Level One* (and the review on **p10**) that the four-part chord quality built from the first degree of the major scale, can also be a **major 6th** chord as well as a **major 7th** chord.

Another angle on the use of these alternate chord forms (i.e. the **G7sus** in place of the **G7**, and the **C6** in place of the **Cma7**) is to consider the **melody note** being 'harmonized' by the chords. If the tonic of the key or **DO** (**C** in this case) was in the melody over the dominant chord, we would have a problem if the '**regular**' dominant 7th chord was used, as this chord contains **TI** (**B** in this case) which would create an undesirable dissonance below **DO** in the melody. This problem could be solved by the use of the **suspended dominant 7th** chord (**G7sus** in this case). Similarly, if **DO** was in the melody over the tonic or **I** chord, we would have a problem if the **major 7th** chord was used, as this chord also contains **TI** which again would create an undesirable dissonance below **DO** in the melody. This problem could be solved by the use of the **major 6th** chord (**C6** in this case).

## *Using five-part chords within the II - V - I progression in major (contd)*

We will now go through the process of upgrading each of the chords shown in **Fig. 2.10.** to a **five-part** chord. In each case this will be done by **adding the note which is a major ninth interval above the root of the chord**. With the exception of certain 'altered dominant' chords to be discussed later, the major 9th interval is the **only type of ninth** you will be adding to chords in conventional Western music styles.

First of all we will take the **D minor 7th** chord shown in **Fig. 2.10.**, and upgrade it to a **D minor 9th** chord as follows:-

### *Figure 2.11. D minor 9th chord 'stack' and interval construction*

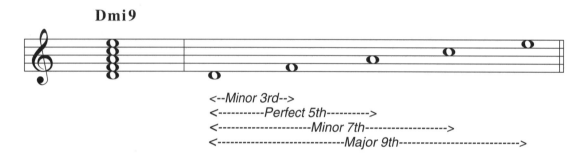

```
<--Minor 3rd-->
<----------Perfect 5th---------->
<---------------------Minor 7th------------------->
<------------------------------Major 9th---------------------------->
```

Again note that this chord can be derived by taking the **Dmi7** chord (as in **Fig. 2.10.**) and adding the note which creates a **major 9th** interval from the root of the chord (i.e. the note **E** above). In total, the intervals created are a **minor 3rd**, **perfect 5th**, **minor 7th**, and **major 9th** respectively above the root of the chord. As discussed in *Contemporary Music Theory Level One*, it is important that you understand the distinction between a **chord description** and an **interval description** - for example, the above **D minor 9th** chord contains a <u>major</u> <u>9th</u> interval! (The '**minor 9th**' chord description is reflective of the fact that the definitive **minor 3rd** and **minor 7th** intervals are still present within the chord).

Note the chord symbol used in the above example ('**Dmi9**'). The suffix '**mi9**' indicates a **minor ninth chord** built from the root i.e. in this case a **D minor ninth chord**. Although using the suffix '**mi9**' is the preferred way to write this chord symbol, you will sometimes encounter other suffixes for the minor ninth chord, as follows:-

-       '**min9**' i.e. as in the chord symbol **Dmin9**. Unnecessary as the suffix '**mi9**' already explicitly defines a minor 9th chord.
-       '**mi7(9)**', '**mi7(add9)**' i.e. as in the chord symbols **Dmi7(9)**, **Dmi7(add9)** etc. Similar comments to above - it is not necessary to indicate that we are 'adding a 9th' to a minor 7th chord - the '**mi9**' chord symbol explicitly includes all the notes that we need.

*(contd on following page>>>)*

### *Using five-part chords within the II - V - I progression in major (contd)*

*(other possible suffixes for the minor 9th chord - contd)*

- **'m9'** i.e. as in the chord symbol **Dm9**. As discussed in *Contemporary Music Theory Level One*, if just a single (lower-case) **'m'** is used within a chord symbol, this can be confused with an upper-case **'M'** which is sometimes used to indicate a major quality. Use **'mi9'** to be explicit.

- **'-9'** i.e. as in the chord symbol **D-9**. Again as discussed in *Contemporary Music Theory Level One*, the **'-'** suffix is often used in older charts and 'illegal' fake books to signify a minor quality, and therefore you will sometimes encounter the **'-9'** suffix for a **minor ninth** chord. However, I personally find the **'mi9'** suffix to be clearer and less error-prone - a view echoed by some of the better 'legal' fake books coming on to the market in recent years.

So - when writing your minor ninth chord symbols, use the **'mi9'** suffix - but **be prepared to recognize** the alternatives listed above! Now we will review how the **D minor 9th** chord can be derived from the **2nd**, **4th**, **6th**, **1st** and **3rd** degrees of a **C major** scale, as follows:-

### *Figure 2.12. Deriving the D minor ninth chord from a C major scale*

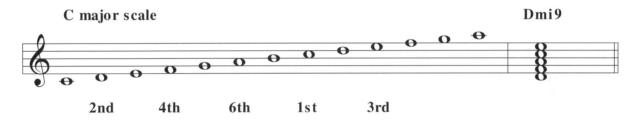

Next we will take the **G dominant 7th** chord shown in **Fig. 2.10.**, and upgrade it to a **G dominant 9th** chord as follows:-

### *Figure 2.13. G dominant 9th chord 'stack' and interval construction*

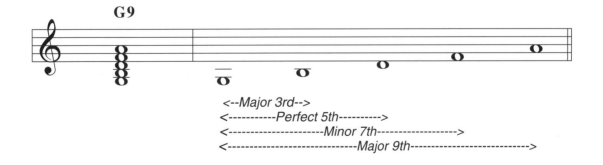

### *Using five-part chords within the II - V - I progression in major (contd)*

Again note that the **G9** chord at the bottom of the previous page can be derived by taking the **G7** chord (as in **Fig. 2.10.**) and adding the note which creates a **major 9th** interval from the root of the chord (i.e. the note **A**). In total, the intervals created are a **major 3rd**, **perfect 5th**, **minor 7th**, and **major 9th** respectively above the root of the chord. (The '**dominant 9th**' chord description is reflective of the fact that the definitive **major 3rd** and **minor 7th** intervals which create the dominant quality, are still present within the chord).

Note the chord symbol used for the **G dominant 9th** chord ('**G9**'). The suffix '**9**' indicates a **dominant ninth chord** built from the root i.e. in this case a **G dominant ninth chord**. We should briefly review the following rules from *Contemporary Music Theory Level One* with regard to chord symbols which consist solely of a root note name followed by a number (i.e. with no other suffix or qualification):-

- If the number in the chord symbol is **less than 7** (i.e. as in the chord symbol **C6**) the chord has a **major** quality or implication.
- If the number in the chord symbol is **7 or greater** (i.e. as in the chord symbols **G7** and **G9**) the chord has a **dominant** quality or implication.

Although using the chord symbol '**G9**' is pretty much the only correct way to write this chord, you may sometimes encounter symbols such as **G7(9)**, **G7(add9)** etc. These symbols are unnecessary and/or incorrect - it is not necessary to indicate that we are 'adding a 9th' to a dominant 7th chord - the '**G9**' chord symbol explicitly includes all the notes that we need.

Now we will review how the **G dominant 9th** chord can be derived from the **5th**, **7th**, **2nd**, **4th** and **6th** degrees of a **C major** scale, as follows:-

### *Figure 2.14. Deriving the G dominant ninth chord from a C major scale*

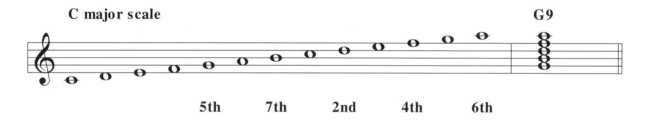

Next we will take the **G suspended dominant 7th** chord shown in **Fig. 2.10.**, and upgrade it to a **G suspended dominant 9th** chord (see example on following page):-

## Using five-part chords within the II - V - I progression in major (contd)

### Figure 2.15. G suspended dominant 9th chord 'stack' and interval construction

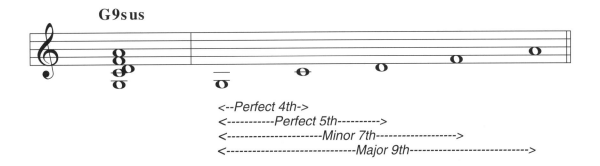

<--Perfect 4th->
<-----------Perfect 5th---------->
<----------------------Minor 7th------------------>
<-----------------------------Major 9th-------------------------->

Again note that this chord can be derived by taking the **G7sus** chord (as in **Fig. 2.10.**) and adding the note which creates a **major 9th** interval from the root of the chord (i.e. the note **A** above). In total, the intervals created are a **perfect 4th**, **perfect 5th**, **minor 7th**, and **major 9th** respectively above the root of the chord. (The '**suspended dominant 9th**' chord description is reflective of the fact that the definitive **perfect 4th** and **minor 7th** intervals which create the suspended dominant quality, are still present within the chord).

Note the chord symbol in the above example ('**G9sus**'). The suffix '**9sus**' indicates a **suspended dominant ninth chord** built from the root (in this case a **G suspended dominant ninth chord**). Although this is the correct way to write this chord symbol, you may sometimes see this chord suffix 'switched around' i.e. written as '**Gsus9**'. As discussed in *Contemporary Music Theory Level One*, when a number is written **after** the '**sus**' in the chord symbol, it is indicating the scale degree which is **replacing the 3rd** of the chord (which most correctly should be the **4th**). So although it is possible that 'replacing the 3rd with the 9th' is intended by this symbol (see '**add9(omit3)**' chord and comments on **p37**), you should most likely assume that a **suspended dominant 9th** chord is intended if you see a chord symbol such as '**Gsus9**'.

Another common and perfectly correct way to write this chord is to use the suffix '**11**' i.e. as in the chord symbol **G11** ('**G eleven**'). Remember that we can replace the **3rd** of the **G9** chord (i.e. the note **B**) with the note which is a perfect **4th** interval above the root (i.e. the note **C**) to create the **G9sus** chord. The note **C** can also be considered as the perfect **11th** interval above the root of the chord, and this interval can be derived by continuing to build the dominant chord 'stack' beyond the **9th** (i.e. by going up a further 3rd interval above the **9th** of the chord, while still staying within the overall **C major** scale restriction - as shown in **Fig. 7.5.**). The use of the chord symbol **G11** therefore implies that we need the note which is a perfect **11th** interval above the root (i.e. the note **C** in this case) - this creates a **suspension** which in turn requires us to eliminate the **3rd** of the chord (i.e. the note **B** in this case). The resulting **G11** chord is therefore identical in spelling and function to the previously derived **G9sus** (suspended dominant 9th) chord.

## *Using five-part chords within the II - V - I progression in major (contd)*

Now we will review how the **G suspended dominant 9th** chord can be derived from the **5th**, **1st**, **2nd**, **4th** and **6th** degrees of a **C major** scale, as follows:-

### *Figure 2.16. Deriving the G suspended dominant ninth chord from a C major scale*

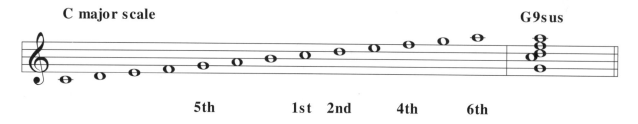

Next we will take the **C major 7th** chord shown in **Fig. 2.10.**, and upgrade it to a **C major 9th** chord as follows:-

### *Figure 2.17. C major 9th chord 'stack' and interval construction*

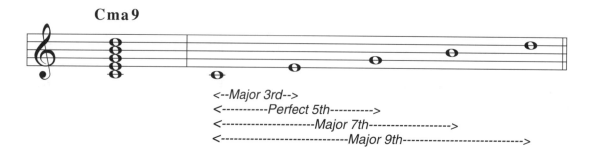

Again note that this chord can be derived by taking the **Cma7** chord (as in **Fig. 2.10.**) and adding the note which creates a **major 9th** interval from the root of the chord (i.e. the note **D** above). In total, the intervals created are a **major 3rd**, **perfect 5th**, **major 7th**, and **major 9th** respectively above the root of the chord.

Note the chord symbol in the above example ('**Cma9**'). The suffix '**ma9**' indicates a **major ninth chord** built from the root i.e. in this case a **C major ninth chord**. Although using the suffix '**ma9**' is the preferred way to write this chord symbol, you will sometimes encounter other suffixes for the major ninth chord, as follows:-

- '**Maj9**', '**maj9**', i.e. as in the chord symbols **CMaj9**, **Cmaj9**. Unnecessary as the suffix '**ma9**' already explicitly defines a major ninth chord.

    *(contd on following page>>>)*

## Using five-part chords within the II - V - I progression in major (contd)

*(other possible suffixes for the major 9th chord - contd)*

- **'Ma7(9)'**, **'ma7(9)'**, **'Ma7(add9)'**, **'ma7(add9)'** i.e. as in the chord symbols **CMa7(9)**, **Cma7(9)**, **CMa7(add9)**, **Cma7(add9)** etc. Again these suffixes are redundant - it is unnecessary to indicate that we are 'adding a 9th' to a major 7th chord. (We will soon see that the **'add9'** suffix should only be used if the chord has no **6th** or **7th**).

- **'M9'** i.e. as in the chord symbol **CM9**. As already discussed, the single upper-case **'M'** can be confused with **'m'** (lower-case) which is sometimes used to signify a **minor** quality.

- **'Δ9'** i.e. as in the chord symbol **CΔ9**. As discussed in ***Contemporary Music Theory Level One***, the 'triangle symbol' is sometimes used in older charts and fake books to indicate a major quality. However, I personally find the **'ma9'** suffix to be clearer and less error-prone - again a view echoed by some of the better 'legal' fake books now on the market.

So - when writing your **major ninth** chord symbols, use the **'ma9'** suffix - but **be prepared to recognize** the alternative chord suffixes listed above. Now we will review how the **C major 9th** chord can be derived from the **1st**, **3rd**, **5th**, **7th** and **2nd** degrees of a **C major** scale, as follows:-

### Figure 2.18. Deriving the C major ninth chord from a C major scale

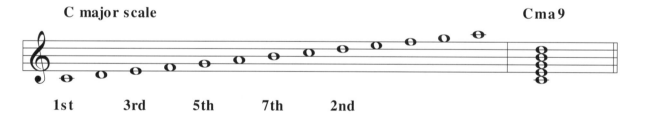

Finally we will take the **C major 6th** chord shown in **Fig. 2.10.**, and upgrade it to a **C major six nine** chord as follows:-

### Figure 2.19. C major six nine chord 'stack' and interval construction

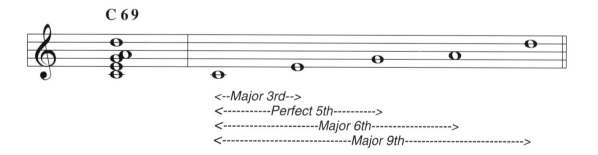

<--Major 3rd-->
<----------Perfect 5th---------->
<---------------------Major 6th------------------->
<----------------------------Major 9th---------------------------->

### *Using five-part chords within the II - V - I progression in major (contd)*

Again note that the **C major six nine** chord shown on the bottom of the previous page, can be derived by taking the **C6** chord (as in **Fig. 2.10.**) and adding the note which creates a **major 9th** interval from the root of the chord (i.e. the note **D**). In total, the intervals created are a **major 3rd**, **perfect 5th**, **major 6th**, and **major 9th** respectively above the root of the chord.

Note the chord symbol used for the **C major six nine chord** ('C69'). The suffix '**69**' indicates a **major six nine chord** built from the root i.e. in this case a **C major six nine chord**. Although using the suffix '**69**' is the preferred way to write this chord symbol, you will sometimes encounter other suffixes for the major six nine chord, as follows:-

- '**Ma69**', '**ma69**', '**Maj69**', '**maj69**', **ma6(9)** etc. as in the chord symbols **CMa69**, **Cma69**, **CMaj69**, **Cmaj69**, **Cma6(9)** etc. These are acceptable alternatives, however strictly speaking the 'major' qualification is redundant.
- **6(add9)**, **ma6(add9)** etc. as in the chord symbols **C6(add9)**, **Cma6(add9)** etc. As we will shortly see, the '**add9**' suffix should only be used on chords with **no 6th or 7th** present - so strictly speaking these are incorrect chord symbols.
- '**M69**' i.e. as in the chord symbol **CM69**. As already discussed, the single upper-case '**M**' can be confused with '**m**' (lower-case) which is sometimes used to signify a **minor** quality.
- '**Δ69**' i.e. as in the chord symbol **CΔ69**. Review comments on the previous page concerning my reservations about using the 'triangle' symbol for major chords!

A common factor in the above suffixes (apart from the '**6(add9)**' suffix) is that they are trying to convey a major quality - which is not necessary as the suffix '**69**' explicitly defines the chord. So - when writing your **major six nine** chord symbols, use the '**69**' suffix - but as usual **be prepared to recognize** the alternative chord suffixes listed above. Now we will review how the **C major six nine** chord can be derived from the **1st**, **3rd**, **5th**, **6th** and **2nd** degrees of a **C major** scale, as follows:-

### *Figure 2.20. Deriving the C major six nine chord from a C major scale*

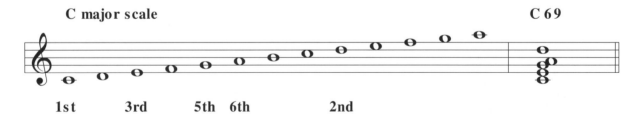

Now that we have upgraded all of the four-part **II - V - I** chords (as originally shown in **Fig. 2.10.**) to five-part chords, we can now summarize all of the new chord 'stacks' (including the 'ninths' in each case) as shown in the example on the following page:-

## *Using five-part chords within the II - V - I progression in major (contd)*

### *Figure 2.21. Five-part II - V - I chord 'stacks' in the key of C major*

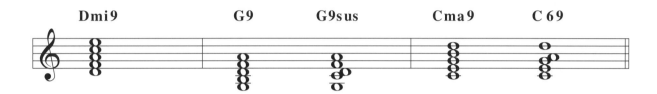

*(compare to the four-part **II - V - I** chords shown in **Fig. 2.10.** as necessary).*

## *Major and minor 'add9' chords*

You will recall that, while 'upgrading' the four-part **II - V - I** sequence to five-part chords, we added a **major 9th** interval to the **major 7th** and **minor 7th** chords, to create **major 9th** and **minor 9th** chords respectively. However, there will be times (particularly in contemporary applications) where we need the ninth on a major or minor chord, **but without including the seventh** (or the **sixth**) **of the chord**. This is equivalent to taking a major or minor triad and adding a ninth, as we can see in the following examples:-

### *Figure 2.22. Creating a C major 'add nine' chord by adding a ninth to a C triad*

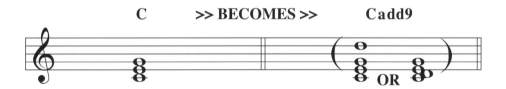

### *Figure 2.23. Creating a C minor 'add nine' chord by adding a ninth to a C minor triad*

Note the chord symbols used for the **C major 'add nine'** and **C minor 'add nine'** chords ('**Cadd9**' and '**Cmiadd9**' respectively). The suffixes '**add9**' and '**miadd9**' indicate a **major 'add nine' chord** and a **minor 'add nine' chord** built from the root, respectively.

## *Major and minor 'add9' chords (contd)*

Sometimes you will see these chord symbols written with parentheses i.e. as **C(add9)** and **Cmi(add9)**, and this is perfectly correct and acceptable. However, there are some other ways that the **add9** chord is indicated on pop charts and sheet music, which are dubious to say the least! These other 'suffixes' are listed below, and discussed in the context of the **major 'add nine'** chord (as we will see later, they are also sometimes used on the **minor 'add nine'** chord):-

-   **'(9)'**   i.e. as in the chord symbol **C(9)**. This incorrect chord symbol still shows up on a lot of printed music! We are used to seeing chord symbols simply consisting of a note name followed by a number, which (if the number is **7** or greater) indicates a dominant chord - see review on **p30**. However, if you were to interpret this chord (on a typical pop chart) as a **dominant 9th**, it would most probably sound very wrong indeed! So if you see this on a chart, assume that a **major 'add nine'** quality is intended.

-   **'9'**   i.e. as in the chord symbol **C9**. A rather worse version of the above problem! The symbol '**C9**' is the correct symbol for a **C dominant 9th** chord (see **Fig. 2.13.** and accompanying text), and is of course a **completely incorrect** symbol for a **C major 'add nine'** chord. So how do you know **not** to interpret this chord as a **dominant 9th** on the chart that you're looking at? Basically you have to make a stylistic and contextual judgement. On a typical contemporary **pop** tune (and in particular if the chord is a **I** or tonic chord of the key, for example) the use of the **major 'add nine'** quality is much more likely to be correct than the use of the **dominant 9th** quality. However, in a more **blues-** or **jazz**-oriented style, the **dominant 9th** quality is more likely to be correct....it's a judgement call!

-   **'2'**, **'add2'**, **'(2)'**, **'(add2)'**, i.e. as in the chord symbols **C2**, **Cadd2**, **C(2)**, **C(add2)**. At least there's one good thing about these chord symbols - you're less likely to mistake them for dominant chords! As discussed in *Contemporary Music Theory Level One*, the implication of the chord suffix containing '**2**' is that we are adding the **2nd** degree (i.e. the note which is a whole-step above the root) to the major triad, which of course is then equivalent to the **major 'add nine'** chord. From a harmony standpoint, I believe that this is an incorrect usage of the number '**2**' - for example, while technically the note **D** is a whole-step above the note **C**, there is no such thing as the '**2nd**' of a **C major chord** - the note **D** is correctly termed a **ninth** on a **C** major chord (as seen in **Fig. 2.17.**) as it really is an **upper extension** of the chord, regardless of where it is actually 'voiced' in the chord or which other chord tones may be present. Another problem with the usage of the '**2**' suffix which I sometimes see on pop charts, is that it is not always clear whether or not the **3rd** of the chord should also be included - more about this shortly.

Less frequently, you may also see the above suffixes used for the **minor 'add nine'** chord i.e. **Cmi(9)**, **Cmi2**, **Cmi(add2)** etc. Again assume that a **minor 'add nine'** chord is intended!

### *Major and minor 'add9' chords (contd)*

So - when writing your **major 'add nine'** chord symbols, use the **'add9'** or **'(add9)'** suffix, and when writing your **minor 'add nine'** chord symbols, use the **'miadd9'** or **'mi(add9)'** suffix - but be prepared to recognize (and in some cases make a judgement on) the various possibilities discussed on the previous page!

We will now look at one more variation on the **'add nine'** chord. Sometimes it will be necessary to **omit the 3rd** from a **major 'add nine'** chord, resulting in a **major 'add nine omit three'** chord. This is shown in the following example:-

#### *Figure 2.24. Creating a C major 'add nine omit three' chord*
*(by adding a **ninth** to, and omitting the **third** from, a **C triad**)*

Depending upon the context, the implication of this chord will most often be major, even though of course the **3rd** is not present. The resulting **major 'add nine omit three'** chord consists of the **root**, **5th** and **9th** only - another way of arriving at this would be to take the **Cma9** chord 'stack' (as shown in **Fig. 2.17.**) and remove the **3rd** and **7th** of the chord. This helps to explain why this **'add nine omit three'** chord sounds so 'transparent' and non-definitive - we have already seen that the 3rd and 7th of these 4- and 5-part chords are responsible for defining the quality of the chord, and the chord shown above contains **no 3rd or 7th**. This more 'open' sound is often used in more evolved pop music styles. (Note that if you were to take a **C minor** triad, and then add the **9th** and remove the **3rd**, you would arrive at the same result as shown in the right-hand measure above).

Note the chord symbol used in the above example which is **'Cadd9(omit3)'**. The alternative symbol **'Cadd9(no3)'** is also perfectly correct. However, as with the **major 'add nine'** chord, there are some other ways in which this chord may be indicated, as follows:-

- **'sus2'** i.e. as in the chord symbol **'Csus2'**. You may recall that we encountered this chord symbol in **Contemporary Music Theory Level One** when discussing suspended chords. The intention behind this chord symbol is that the **'2nd'** (which as mentioned on the previous page, is more correctly termed the **9th**) has replaced the **3rd** of the chord. Although strictly speaking the use of a **suspended** symbol implies that the **3rd** of a chord has been replaced by the note which is a **perfect 4th** above the root of the chord, sometimes suffixes such as **sus2** are used to replace the **3rd** of the chord with another scale degree (i.e. the '2nd' in this case).

**37**

## *Major and minor 'add9' chords (contd)*

*(other possible suffixes for the major 'add nine omit three' chord - contd)*

- '**2**', '**(2)**', i.e. as in the chord symbols '**C2**', '**C(2)**'. We have already discussed this suffix back on **p36** - but now we need to be additionally aware that this suffix is some-times used for the '**add nine omit three**' chord as well as the '**add nine**' chord! So if you're faced with this symbol, you'll need to make a judgement call (based on the style and musical context) whether or not to include the **3rd** of the chord.

So - when writing your **major 'add nine omit three'** chord symbols, use the '**add9(omit3)**' or '**add9(no3)**' suffix - but again be prepared to recognize (and in some cases make a judgement on) the possibilities discussed above and on the previous page!

## *Five-part or 'ninth' chord recognition method and examples*

We will now establish some rules for recognizing the five-part or 'ninth' chords studied in this chapter, when written on the staff. This section of the chapter can be viewed as a follow-up to the four-part chord recognition techniques covered in ***Contemporary Music Theory Level One***. Now we will see how to recognize the following new five-part or 'ninth' chords (in root position) introduced in this chapter:-

- **Minor 9th** chords, as in **Figs. 2.11. - 2.12.**
- **Dominant 9th** chords, as in **Figs. 2.13. - 2.14.**
- **Suspended dominant 9th** chords, as in **Figs. 2.15. - 2.16.**
- **Major 9th** chords, as in **Figs. 2.17. - 2.18.**
- **Major '69'** chords, as in **Figs. 2.19. - 2.20.**
- **Major** and **minor 'add9'** chords, as in **Figs. 2.22. - 2.23.**

Note that all of the above chords will include **major 9th** and **perfect 5th intervals** with respect to the root - so while we should observe that these intervals are present (and that we are dealing with 'ninth' chords), this will not help us to distinguish between the chord types listed above. What we additionally need to do is to recognize the other chord tones as follows:-

- If the chord contains a **3rd** and a **7th**, then (within the current possibilities) it will be either a **minor 9th**, **dominant 9th** or **major 9th** chord. At this point we are back to the same range of **3rd/7th** options as analyzed in ***Contemporary Music Theory Level One*** for diatonic four-part chords (and included in the table on **p14**). To briefly review:-
  - If the chord contains **minor 3rd** and **minor 7th** intervals, we have a **minor 9th** chord.
  - If the chord contains **major 3rd** and **minor 7th** intervals, we have a **dominant 9th** chord.
  - If the chord contains **major 3rd** and **major 7th** intervals, we have a **major 9th** chord.
  *(contd on next page>>>)*

### Five-part or 'ninth' chord recognition method and examples (contd)

- If the chord contains a **3rd** and a **6th**, then (within the current possibilities) it will be a **major '69'** chord. We should verify that the chord contains the necessary **major 3rd** and **major 6th** intervals, as shown in **Fig. 2.19.** for the **major '69'** chord (and summarized in the table on **p14** for the **major 6th** chord).
- If the chord contains a '**4th**' (i.e. the note which is a **4th** interval above the root) and a **7th**, then (within the current possibilities) it will be a **suspended dominant 9th** chord. We should verify that the chord contains the necessary **perfect 4th** and **minor 7th** intervals, as shown in **Fig. 2.15.** for the **suspended dominant 9th** chord (and as reviewed in **Fig. 1.32.** for the **suspended dominant 7th** chord).
- If the chord contains a **3rd** but no **6th** or **7th**, then (within the current possibilities) it will be either a **major 'add9'** or **minor 'add9'** chord. If the chord contains a **major 3rd**, then we have a **major 'add9'** chord as shown in **Fig. 2.22.** If the chord contains a **minor 3rd**, then we have a **minor 'add9'** chord as shown in **Fig. 2.23.**

All the following chord recognition examples will be presented in root position. You need to be familiar with basic interval recognition techniques as covered in *Contemporary Music Theory Level One* (for example, in order to find out what type of **3rd** or **7th** is present in a chord) - review interval concepts as necessary on **p5**.

### Figure 2.25. Five-part or 'ninth' chord recognition example #1

First of all we note that the chord has **3rd** and **7th intervals** present, which (within the current possibilities) means that we are looking at either a **minor 9th**, **dominant 9th** or **major 9th** chord. We then analyze the **3rd** and **7th** intervals as follows:-

- the **3rd** interval (**F#** up to **A**) is a **minor 3rd**, and
- the **7th** interval (**F#** up to **E**) is a **minor 7th**.

Reviewing the directions at the bottom of the previous page, we note that the five-part chord containing **minor 3rd** and **minor 7th intervals** is a **minor 9th chord**. (We recall from **Fig. 2.11.** that this chord also contains **perfect 5th** and **major 9th** intervals - the above **5th** interval of **F#** up to **C#** is a **perfect 5th**, and the above **9th** interval of **F#** up to **G#** is a **major 9th**). The chord in example #1 is therefore an **F# minor 9th** chord, for which the correct chord symbol would be **F#mi9**.

## *Five-part or 'ninth' chord recognition method and examples (contd)*

### *Figure 2.26. Five-part or 'ninth' chord recognition example #2*

First of all we note that the chord has **3rd** and **7th intervals** present, which again means that we are looking at either a **minor 9th**, **dominant 9th** or **major 9th** chord. We then analyze the **3rd** and **7th** intervals as follows:-

- the **3rd** interval (**A** up to **C#**) is a **major 3rd**, and
- the **7th** interval (**A** up to **G**) is a **minor 7th**.

Reviewing the directions at the bottom of **p38**, we note that the five-part chord containing **major 3rd** and **minor 7th intervals** is a **dominant 9th chord**. (We recall from **Fig. 2.13.** that this chord also contains **perfect 5th** and **major 9th** intervals - the above **5th** interval of **A** up to **E** is a **perfect 5th**, and the above **9th** interval of **A** up to **B** is a **major 9th**). The chord in example **#2** is therefore an **A dominant 9th** chord, for which the correct chord symbol would be **A9**.

### *Figure 2.27. Five-part or 'ninth' chord recognition example #3*

First of all we note that the chord has **3rd** and **6th intervals** present, which (within the current possibilities) means that we are looking at a **major '69'** chord. We can further verify the definitive **3rd** and **6th** intervals as follows:-

- the **3rd** interval (**Eb** up to **G**) is a **major 3rd**, and
- the **6th** interval (**Eb** up to **C**) is a **major 6th**.

We recall from **Fig. 2.19.** that the **major '69'** chord also contains **perfect 5th** and **major 9th** intervals - the above **5th** interval of **Eb** up to **Bb** is a **perfect 5th**, and the above **9th** interval of **Eb** up to **F** is a **major 9th**. We have confirmed that the chord in example **#3** is therefore an **Eb major '69'** chord, for which the correct chord symbol would be **Eb69**.

### Five-part or 'ninth' chord recognition method and examples (contd)

#### Figure 2.28. Five-part or 'ninth' chord recognition example #4

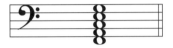

First of all we note that the chord has **3rd** and **7th intervals** present, which again means that we are looking at either a **minor 9th**, **dominant 9th** or **major 9th** chord. We then analyze the **3rd** and **7th** intervals as follows:-

- the **3rd** interval (**F** up to **A**) is a **major 3rd**, and
- the **7th** interval (**F** up to **E**) is a **major 7th**.

Reviewing the directions at the bottom of **p38**, we note that the five-part chord containing **major 3rd** and **major 7th intervals** is a **major 9th chord**. (We recall from **Fig. 2.17.** that this chord also contains **perfect 5th** and **major 9th** intervals - the above **5th** interval of **F** up to **C** is a **perfect 5th**, and the above **9th** interval of **F** up to **G** is a **major 9th**). The chord in example #4 is therefore an **F major 9th** chord, for which the correct chord symbol would be **Fma9**.

#### Figure 2.29. Five-part or 'ninth' chord recognition example #5

First of all we note that the chord has **4th** and **7th intervals** present, which (within the current possibilities) means that we are looking at a **suspended dominant 9th** chord. We can further verify the definitive **4th** and **7th** intervals as follows:-

- the **4th** interval (**D** up to **G**) is a **perfect 4th**, and
- the **7th** interval (**D** up to **C**) is a **minor 7th**.

We recall from **Fig. 2.15.** that the **suspended dominant 9th** chord also contains **perfect 5th** and **major 9th** intervals - the above **5th** interval of **D** up to **A** is a **perfect 5th**, and the above **9th** interval of **D** up to **E** is a **major 9th**. We have confirmed that the chord in example #5 is therefore a **D suspended dominant 9th** chord, for which the correct chord symbol would be **D9sus**.

### Five-part or 'ninth' chord recognition method and examples (contd)

### Figure 2.30. Five-part or 'ninth' chord recognition example #6

First of all we note that the chord has a **3rd interval** but no **6th** or **7th intervals** present. This means that (within the current possibilities) we are looking at either a **major 'add nine'** or **minor 'add nine'** chord. We then analyze the **3rd** interval as follows:-

-        the **3rd** interval (**B** up to **D#**) is a **major 3rd**.

Reviewing the directions at the top of **p39**, we note that the '**add nine**' chord containing a **major 3rd interval** is a **major 'add nine'** chord. (We recall from **Fig. 2.22.** that this chord also contains **perfect 5th** and **major 9th** intervals - the above **5th** interval of **B** up to **F#** is a **perfect 5th**, and the above **9th** interval of **B** up to **C#** is a **major 9th**). The chord in example #6 is therefore a **B major 'add nine'** chord, for which the correct chord symbol would be **Badd9** or **B(add9)**.

### Introduction to harmonic analysis

Over the next several chapters, we will developing an approach to 'harmonic analysis' of tunes (i.e. analyzing the chord progression which is used). This type of analysis will depend upon the musical style of the tune. In this book we will be looking at the following styles:-

-        ***Jazz and standards***                These tunes use a lot of **II - V - I** progressions, with some substitutions (as in **Chapters 2 through 5**). Chords are almost always four-part (i.e. 'seventh' chords) or larger. Harmony is frequently chromatic to the key signature (i.e. moves to other keys).

-        ***'Classic' pop & rock***              These tunes also use **II - V - I** progressions, but with more
        *(i.e. Beatles)*                substitutions in major keys (see **Chapter 3**). Triads and four-part chords are used. Harmony is generally diatonic to the key signature.

*(contd. on next page>>>)*

### Introduction to harmonic analysis (contd)

| | | |
|---|---|---|
| - | **Contemporary pop, rock, and R&B** | These tunes are generally not **II - V - I** -oriented. They use a lot of '**upper structure**' chords (i.e. triad-over-root as in **Chapter 7**, and 4-part-over-root as in **Chapter 8**), as well as basic triad symbols and suspensions. Harmony is most often built from the major and natural minor scales, and is frequently non-definitive (i.e. the chords can belong to different keys) and non-leading (i.e. dominant chords are less common). |
| - | **Blues and blues/rock** | These tunes start from a basis of building dominant chords from the **I**, **IV** and/or **V** of a key (as opposed to other styles which use the **V** dominant as an 'active' chord to lead back to the **I** or tonic chord) - more about blues applications in **Chapter 9**. |

When looking at a chord progression for a tune, we will therefore use the above information to assess the general style of the tune, which in turn will suggest the type of 'harmonic analysis' which is feasible. For the **jazz** and **standard** tunes which use key changes in the harmony, it is helpful to determine **which** keys are being used throughout the tune (we will refer to these as **momentary keys**), as well as the **function** of each chord (i.e. **II**, **V**, etc) within these keys. For the more **contemporary** tunes which generally do not use key changes in the harmony, we can still assess the **function** of each chord, relative to the key signature used by the tune. (More on the chord structures and harmonic analysis for contemporary styles in **Chapters 7** through **9**).

Here in **Chapters 2** through **5** we will develop a harmonic analysis approach for the first two musical styles listed i.e. **jazz/standards** and '**classic' pop**, which as discussed are generally oriented around **II - V - I** progressions with substitutes. For these styles, we will now analyze:-

- the **function** of each chord i.e. is it a **II**, **V** or **I** chord (or some other function)?
- the **relationship** that a chord may have to other chords either side of it.
- the **momentary key** that each chord is a part of.

Now we shall discuss further the term **momentary key** which was introduced above. If you are familiar with **jazz standard** tunes at all, you may have noticed that, while these tunes will be notated in a certain key and while the melody will for the most part be diatonic to the key signature, the harmony (chord symbols) seems at times to have very little to do with the key signature! What is happening here is that the **harmony has moved to some other momentary key** which is different to the key indicated by the key signature. We will now develop a method for **determining the momentary key** 'in force' for **each chord** in a given (**II - V - I**-oriented) progression. This will then be a major asset in terms of better understanding the tune in general, as well as enabling players & writers to construct more meaningful lines, voiceleading and/or solos etc. over the chord changes of the tune in question!

### *Introduction to harmonic analysis (contd)*

When analyzing a chord progression using this '**momentary key**' method, we will first look for the **dominant chords**. We have already discussed the uniquely 'definitive' nature of the dominant chord (see **Figs. 2.2. - 2.6.** and accompanying text). The fact that each dominant chord can only be 'built from' the **5th** degree of a particular major scale, and that the dominant chord uses the identifying active scale degrees **TI** and **FA**, means that at this stage we can assume that each **dominant** chord is functioning as a **V (five)** chord in a **momentary major key**. (Later in *Chapter 4* we will discuss dominant chords in momentary minor keys).

Once we have identified a dominant chord as being a **V chord** in a **momentary major key**, we will then look 'either side' of it to see if we can connect these neighboring chords to the same key. We have already seen that the **II - V - I** progression is very commonly used, and so we will look to see if the **V** dominant chord (at this stage either a **V7** or **V9**) is preceded by a **II** chord (at this stage either a **IImi7** or **IImi9**) and/or if it is followed by a **I** or tonic chord (at this stage either a **Ima7**, **I6**, **Ima9** or **I69**). We will begin this process by looking at 'pairs' of chords which include a dominant chord. After determining which momentary major key the dominant chord is the **V** of, we will then establish the function of the other chord in the progression, beginning with the following example:-

### *Figure 2.31. Harmonic analysis progression example #1*

First we look at the dominant chord (**E7**) - we know this is a **V** chord in a momentary major key. As **E** is the **5th** degree of an **A major** scale, this is therefore a **V in A major**. We then look at the preceding chord (**Bmi7**) to see if it also is found within the key of **A major**, and we see that this chord is built from the **2nd** degree of an **A major** scale. Therefore overall the above progression is a **II - V** in **A major**. *(If you're not sure why **Bmi7** is the **II** chord in **A major**, review **Chapter 7** and **Appendix 3** of **Contemporary Music Theory Level One**, and/or the diatonic four-part chord review in **Chapter 1** of this book, as necessary).*

### *Figure 2.32. Harmonic analysis progression example #2*

## Introduction to harmonic analysis (contd)

### (analysis of Fig. 2.32. contd)

Again we first look at the dominant chord (**Db9**) - we know this is a **V** chord in a momentary major key. As **Db** is the **5th** degree of a **Gb major** scale, this is therefore a **V in Gb major**. We then look at the preceding chord (**Abmi9**) to see if it also is found within the key of **Gb major**, and we see that this chord is built from the **2nd** degree of a **Gb major** scale. Therefore overall the above progression is a **II - V in Gb major**.

### Figure 2.33. Harmonic analysis progression example #3

Again we first look at the dominant chord (**A7**) - we know this is a **V** chord in a momentary major key. As **A** is the **5th** degree of a **D major** scale, this is therefore a **V in D major**. We then look at the following chord (**Dma7**) to see if it also is found within the key of **D major**, and of course this chord is built from the **1st** degree of a **D major** scale. Therefore overall the above progression is a **V - I in D major**.

### Figure 2.34. Harmonic analysis progression example #4

Again we first look at the dominant chord (**Bb9**) - we know this is a **V** chord in a momentary major key. As **Bb** is the **5th** degree of an **Eb major** scale, this is therefore a **V in Eb major**. We then look at the following chord (**Ebma9**) to see if it also is found within the key of **Eb major**, and of course this chord is built from the **1st** degree of an **Eb major** scale. Therefore overall the above progression is a **V - I in Eb major**.

In **Chapter 3** we will expand our harmonic analysis to include substitutes for the **II - V - I** chords in major, and we will begin working on progressions typically used for jazz standards and 'classic' pop tunes.

## Chapter Two Workbook Questions

### 1.   *Five-part chord spelling*

Write the notes on the staff (in root position) corresponding to the following major 9th and major '69' chord symbols:-

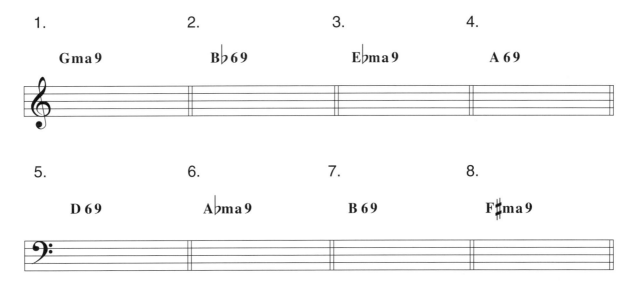

|  1. | 2. | 3. | 4. |
| --- | --- | --- | --- |
| Gma9 | Bb69 | Ebma9 | A69 |

|  5. | 6. | 7. | 8. |
| --- | --- | --- | --- |
| D69 | Abma9 | B69 | F#ma9 |

Write the notes on the staff (in root position) corresponding to the following minor 9th chord symbols:-

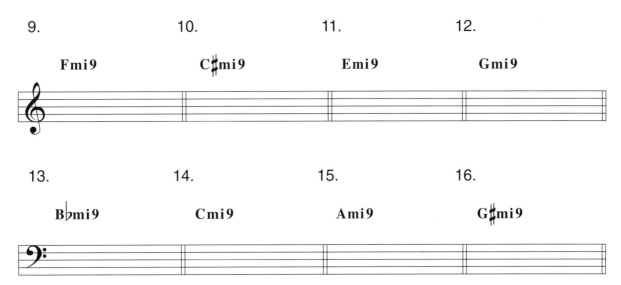

|  9. | 10. | 11. | 12. |
| --- | --- | --- | --- |
| Fmi9 | C#mi9 | Emi9 | Gmi9 |

|  13. | 14. | 15. | 16. |
| --- | --- | --- | --- |
| Bbmi9 | Cmi9 | Ami9 | G#mi9 |

### 1. *Five-part chord spelling (contd)*

Write the notes on the staff (in root position) corresponding to the following dominant 9th chord symbols:-

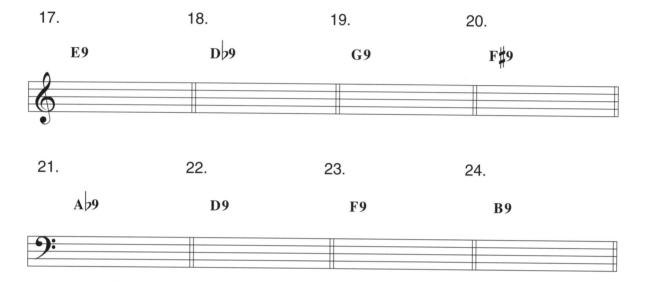

Write the notes on the staff (in root position) corresponding to the following suspended dominant 9th chord symbols:-

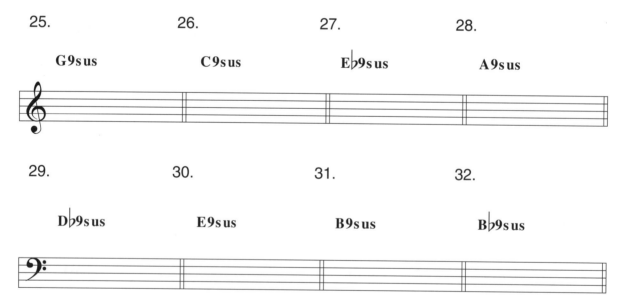

### 1. *Five-part chord spelling (contd)*

Write the notes on the staff (in root position) corresponding to the following major 'add 9' and minor 'add 9' chord symbols:-

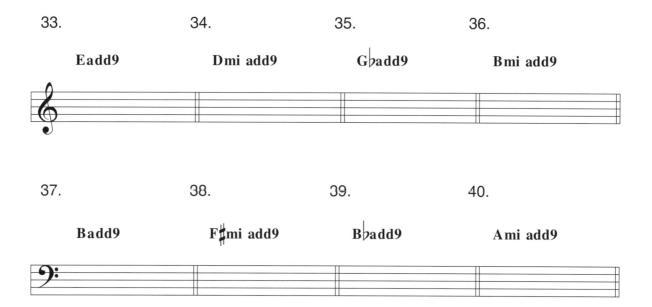

33.
Eadd9

34.
Dmi add9

35.
G♭add9

36.
Bmi add9

37.
Badd9

38.
F♯mi add9

39.
B♭add9

40.
Ami add9

## 2. *Five-part chord recognition*

This section contains a mixture of (root-position) major 9th, major '69', major 'add 9', minor 9th, minor 'add 9', dominant 9th, and suspended dominant 9th chords. Write the chord symbol above the staff for each question:-

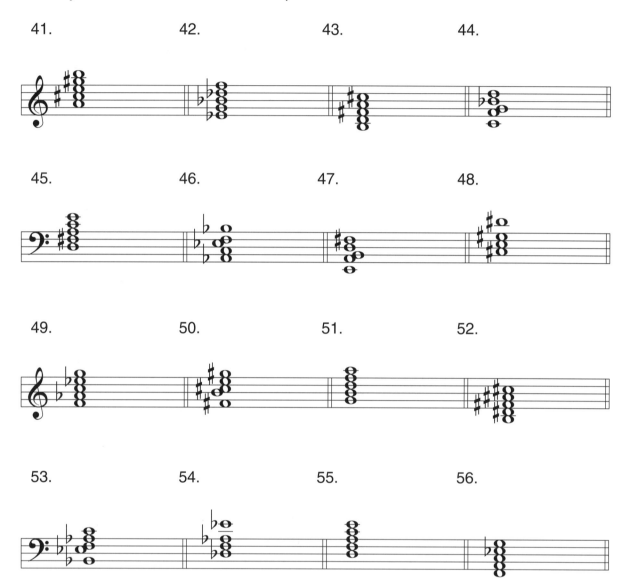

41.          42.          43.          44.

45.          46.          47.          48.

49.          50.          51.          52.

53.          54.          55.          56.

## 2.    _Five-part chord recognition (contd)_

57.    58.    59.    60.

61.    62.    63.    64.

65.    66.    67.    68.

69.    70.    71.    72.

### 3. Writing the II-V-I progression in major keys

You are to write the '**7-3**' (seven-three) voicings on the treble clef staff and the root on the bass clef staff, for the **II-V-I** progressions in the following major keys. You are to 'voicelead' the '7-3' voices across each progression. Be sure to include all necessary accidentals. (Review **Figs. 2.8.** and **2.9.** in the text as necessary).

For questions 73 and 75, you are to begin with the **7th** of the IImi7 chord as the top voice on the treble clef staff (i.e. as in **Fig. 2.9.** in the text).

For questions 74 and 76, you are to begin with the **3rd** of the IImi7 chord as the top voice on the treble clef staff (i.e. as in **Fig. 2.8.** in the text).

73. *Key of **Bb** major*          74. *Key of **G** major*

| Cmi7 | F7 | Bbma7 | Ami7 | D7 | Gma7 |

75. *Key of **Db** major*          76. *Key of **D** major*

| Ebmi7 | Ab7 | Dbma7 | Emi7 | A7 | Dma7 |

### 3. _Writing the II-V-I progression in major keys (contd)_

You are to write the five-part chord 'stack' on the staff (with all necessary accidentals), and chord symbols above the staff, for the **II-V-I** progressions in the following major keys.

For questions 77 - 80, you are to use the regular (i.e. <u>un</u>suspended) dominant chord form on the **V** chord, and the major 9th chord form on the **I** chord.

77. _Key of **Eb** major_           78. _Key of **A** major_

79. _Key of **B** major_           80. _Key of **F** major_

For questions 81 - 84, you are to use the suspended dominant chord form on the **V** chord, and the major '69' chord form on the **I** chord.

81. _Key of **Bb** major_           82. _Key of **D** major_

83. _Key of **Ab** major_           84. _Key of **E** major_

**4.** **_Chord progression analysis_**

The following examples consist of 'pairs' of chords within a major key. You are to write the key for each question, and the function (i.e. **II**, **V** or **I**) of each chord:-

85. *Key of* _____          86. *Key of* _____

    *Function* _____     *Function* _____     *Function* _____     *Function* _____

    **Emi7**             **A7**            **B♭mi7**          **E♭7**

87. *Key of* _____          88. *Key of* _____

    *Function* _____     *Function* _____     *Function* _____     *Function* _____

    **C♯mi9**         **F♯9**          **Gmi9**          **C9**

89. *Key of* _____          90. *Key of* _____

    *Function* _____     *Function* _____     *Function* _____     *Function* _____

    **B7**            **Ema7**         **A♭7**         **D♭ma7**

91. *Key of* _____          92. *Key of* _____

    *Function* _____     *Function* _____     *Function* _____     *Function* _____

    **F9**            **B♭ma9**        **A9**          **D 69**

## *Chapter Two Workbook Answers*

**_1._**   **_Five-part chord spelling - answers_**

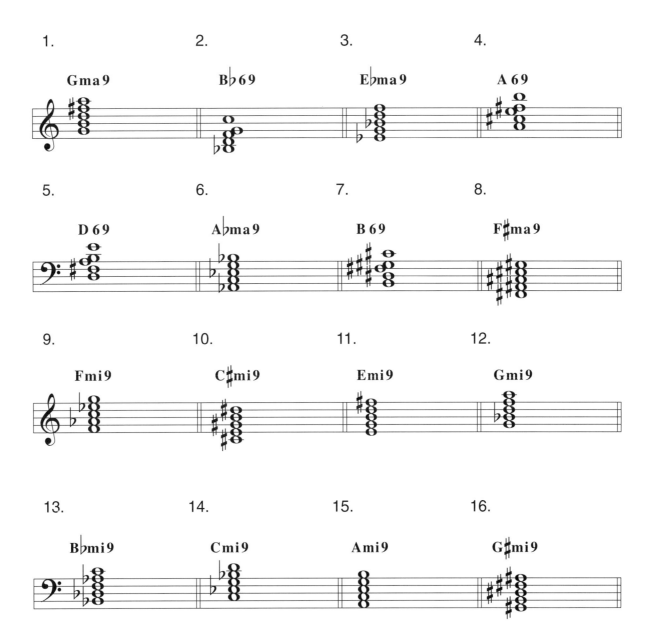

## 1. _Five-part chord spelling - answers (contd)_

**1.** *Five-part chord spelling - answers (contd)*

33.       34.       35.       36.

Eadd9     Dmi add9     G♭add9     Bmi add9

37.       38.       39.       40.

Badd9     F♯mi add9     B♭add9     Ami add9

**2.** **_Five-part chord recognition - answers_**

**2.** *Five-part chord recognition - answers (contd)*

### 3. *Writing the II-V-I progression in major keys - answers*

*('7-3' voices)*

73. *Key of **Bb** major*          74. *Key of **G** major*

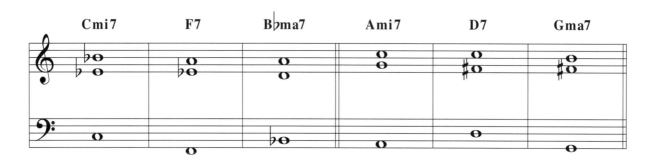

75. *Key of **Db** major*          76. *Key of **D** major*

**_3._**  **_Writing the II-V-I progression in major keys - answers (contd)_**

*(five-part chord 'stacks')*

77. *Key of **Eb** major*

78. *Key of **A** major*

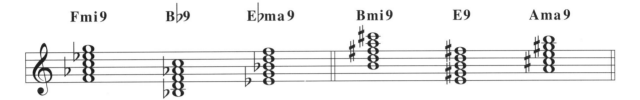

79. *Key of **B** major*

80. *Key of **F** major*

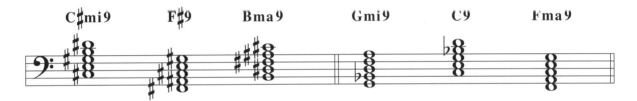

81. *Key of **Bb** major*

82. *Key of **D** major*

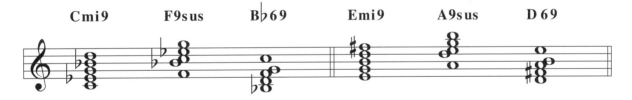

83. *Key of **Ab** major*

84. *Key of **E** major*

## 4. Chord progression analysis - answers

85. Key of **D**
86. Key of **Ab**

Function:- **II**    Function:- **V**    Function:- **II**    Function:- **V**

Emi7    A7    B♭mi7    E♭7

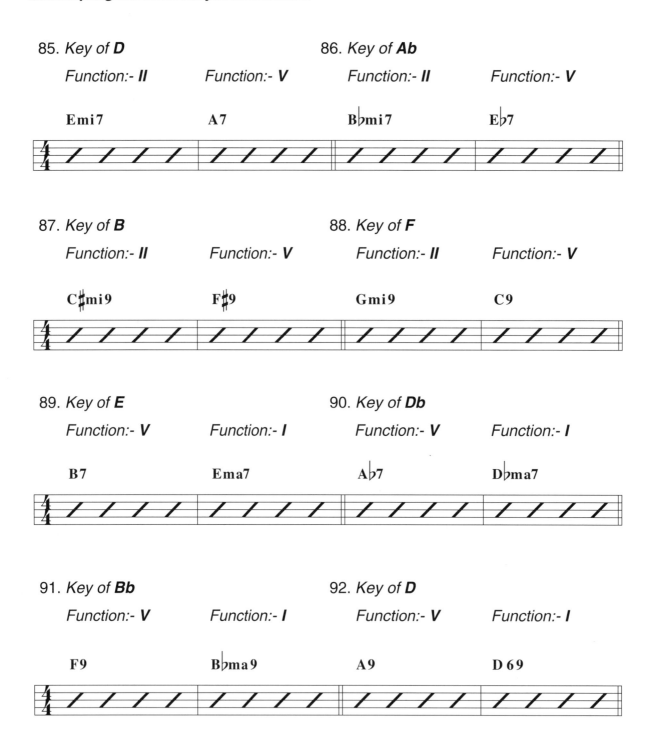

87. Key of **B**
88. Key of **F**

Function:- **II**    Function:- **V**    Function:- **II**    Function:- **V**

C♯mi9    F♯9    Gmi9    C9

89. Key of **E**
90. Key of **Db**

Function:- **V**    Function:- **I**    Function:- **V**    Function:- **I**

B7    Ema7    A♭7    D♭ma7

91. Key of **Bb**
92. Key of **D**

Function:- **V**    Function:- **I**    Function:- **V**    Function:- **I**

F9    B♭ma9    A9    D 69

# Plural substitute chords and harmonic analysis in major keys

## Introduction

In this chapter we will determine the **plural substitute** chords which may be used instead of either the **II**, the **V** or the **I** chord in a major key. At this stage the substitute chords will be '**diatonic**' substitutes - in other words they will still be diatonic to the major key being used. We will then use our knowledge of **II - V - I** and **substitute** chords in major keys, to begin working on the **harmonic analysis** of chord progressions typically used in jazz/standards and older (or 'classic') pop styles.

## Plural substitute chords for the II - V - I in major

We will now establish the criteria for chords which can **substitute** for the **II**, **V** and **I** chords in a major key. (We have already seen in **Chapter 2** that the **II - V - I** progression is the most efficient way to 'define' the key center to our ear). In order to preserve the main 'harmonic sense' or intent of the progression, these **diatonic substitutions** will need to possess the following characteristics:-

- the substitute chord(s) will need to have substantial **plurality** (i.e. notes in common) with the definitive chord being substituted.
- the substitute chord(s) will need similar **active/resting qualities** to the definitive chord being substituted.

We saw in **Chapter 2** that isolating the definitive '7-3' voices across the **II - V - I** progression, resulted in movements between the critical half-steps (**FA-MI** & **TI-DO**) of the major key. This is shown again below for your convenience:-

### Figure 3.1. Dmi7 - G7 - Cma7 progression (showing movement between FA-MI and TI-DO)

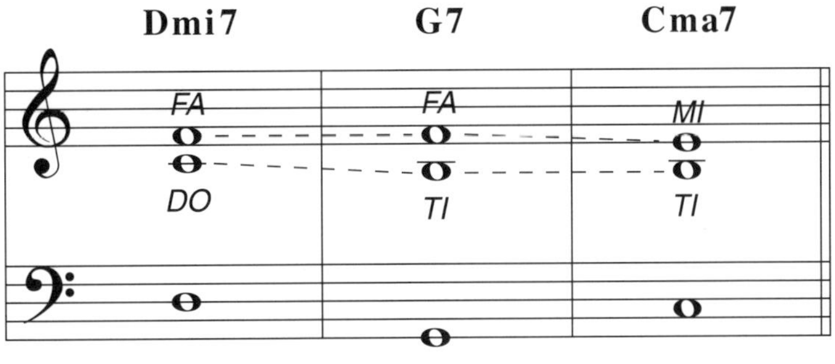

### *Plural substitute chords for the II - V - I in major (contd)*

Reviewing the movements between **FA-MI** and **TI-DO** across the **II - V - I** progression at the bottom of the previous page, we can make the following conclusions regarding the active and/or resting tones required for the substitute chords:-

-   The **II** chord (in this case **Dmi7**) has the critical active tone **FA**, which we know has a tendency to resolve to **MI** (review **Fig. 2.1.** and accompanying text as necessary). Also (as noted in the comments on **p26**) the **II** chord can be thought of as a 'suspension' or 'delayed resolution' into the **V** chord, and this is as a result of the resting tone **DO** on the **II** chord moving to the active tone **TI** on the **V** chord. Therefore in order to preserve the 'harmonic sense' of the progression, **any diatonic substitution for the II chord should contain the active tone FA and the resting tone DO.**
-   The **V** chord (in this case **G7**) also has the critical active tone **FA** (see above comments). The resting tone **DO** on the **II** chord has now moved to the (other) active tone **TI** on the **V** chord. The sound of **TI** and **FA** together create a particularly active and dissonant quality which requires resolution (i.e. into the **I** or **tonic** chord). Therefore in order to preserve the 'harmonic sense' of the progression, **any diatonic substitution for the V chord should contain the active tones TI and FA.**
-   The **I** chord (in this case **Cma7**) has the critical resting tone **MI**, which we know is the most 'definitive' resting tone within the major scale. (The **major 7th** form of the **I** chord also contains the active tone **TI**, although we have seen that other forms of the **I** chord such as the **major 6th** do not contain this active tone). Therefore in order to preserve the 'harmonic sense' of the progression, **any diatonic substitution for the I chord should contain the resting tone MI.**

In **Fig. 2.7.** we reviewed the origin of the definitive **II - V - I** progression within the four-part diatonic chords available from a major scale. What we will now see is that the remaining diatonic chords (i.e. the **III**, **IV**, **VI** and **VII**) will be used as diatonic substitutes for either the **II**, **V** or **I** chord, based on the **plurality** and **active/resting** criteria detailed above.

We will begin by taking the **minor ninth** form of the **II** chord in the key of **C** (i.e. **Dmi9**, as first derived in **Fig. 2.11.**). If we take the top four notes (i.e. the **3rd**, **5th**, **7th** and **9th**) of this chord, an **Fma7** chord is created as shown in the following example:-

### *Figure 3.2. Creating an Fma7 chord by taking the top four notes of a Dmi9 chord*

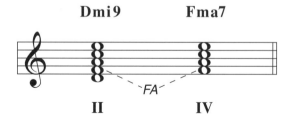

*(The solfeg shown is with respect to the key of C - the note F is 'FA' in this key).*

### *Plural substitute chords for the II - V - I in major (contd)*

In comparing the **Fma7** chord (which as we saw in **Fig. 2.7.** is the four-part **IV** chord in **C major**) to the **Dmi9** chord, we can observe the following:-

- There is significant **plurality** between the two chords (four notes in common).
- The critical active tone **FA** is shared by both chords (as indicated on **Fig. 3.2.**).

As a result of this, we can conclude that **the IV chord can substitute for the II chord in a major key**. For example, we could take the following **II - V - I** progression in the key of **Eb major**:-

### *Figure 3.3. II - V - I progression in the key of Eb major*

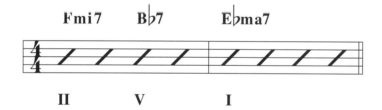

and substitute the **IV** chord for the **II** chord as follows:-

### *Figure 3.4. IV - V - I progression in the key of Eb major (with IV-for-II substitution)*

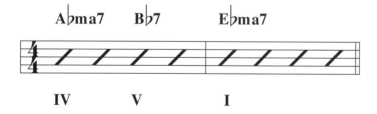

All melody notes which work over the original **II** chord (**Fmi7** in the above example) will also work over the substitute **IV** chord (**Abma7** in the above example). Subject to style considerations, all common forms of the **IV** chord (i.e. **Ab, Ab6, Abma7, Ab69, Abma9** in the above example) will substitute for all common forms of the **II** chord (i.e. **Fmi, Fmi7, Fmi9** etc.).

What is the effect of such a substitution on the original **II - V - I** progression, and why would we use it? Well, this type of substitution **changes the chord quality** (in this case from a **minor 7th** chord to a **major 7th** chord) and **changes the root movement** (in this case from the **circle-of-5ths** motion of **F** to **Bb**, to the the 'scalewise' motion of **Ab** to **Bb**) but **without fundamentally altering the movement between the critical active and resting tones** (i.e. **FA-MI** and **TI-DO**) - so it is a harmonically 'safe' way to vary the **II - V - I** progression!

### *Plural substitute chords for the II - V - I in major (contd)*

Next we will take the **dominant ninth** form of the **V** chord in the key of **C** (i.e. **G9**, as first derived in **Fig. 2.13.**). If we take the top four notes (i.e. the **3rd**, **5th**, **7th** and **9th**) of this chord, a **Bmi7(b5)** chord is created as shown in the following example:-

### *Figure 3.5. Creating a Bmi7(b5) chord by taking the top four notes of a G9 chord*

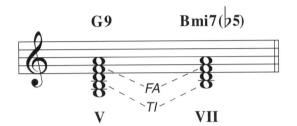

*(Again the solfeg shown is with respect to the key of **C** - the note **F** is '**FA**', and the note **B** is '**TI**', in this key).*

In comparing the **Bmi7(b5)** chord (which as we saw in **Fig. 2.7.** is the four-part **VII** chord in **C major**) to the **G9** chord, we can observe the following:-

- There is significant **plurality** between the two chords (again four notes in common).
- The critical active tones **TI** and **FA** are shared by both chords (as indicated above).

As a result of this, we can conclude that **the VII chord can substitute for the V chord in a major key**. For example, we can take the following **II - V - I** progression in the key of **A major**:-

### *Figure 3.6. II - V - I progression in the key of A major*

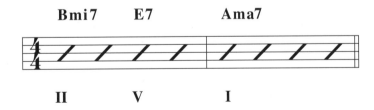

and substitute the **VII** chord for the **V** chord as follows:-

### *Figure 3.7. II - VII - I progression in the key of A major (with VII-for-V substitution)*

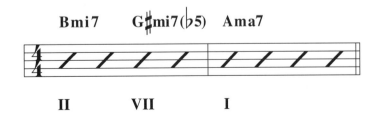

### *Plural substitute chords for the II - V - I in major (contd)*

All melody notes which work over the original **V** chord (**E7** in the example at the bottom of the previous page) will also work over the substitute **VII** chord (**G#mi7(b5)** in this example). The **VII** chord will substitute for the four- and five-part forms of the **V** chord (i.e. **E7** and **E9** in this case).

Next we will take the **major ninth** form of the **I** chord in the key of **C** (i.e. **Cma9**, as first derived in **Fig. 2.17.**). If we take the top four notes (i.e. the **3rd**, **5th**, **7th** and **9th**) of this chord, an **Emi7** chord is created as shown in the following example:-

### *Figure 3.8. Creating an Emi7 chord by taking the top four notes of a Cma9 chord*

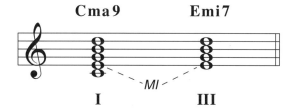

*(Again the solfeg shown is with respect to the key of C - the note E is 'MI' in this key).*

In comparing the **Emi7** chord (which as we saw in **Fig. 2.7.** is the four-part **III** chord in **C major**) to the **Cma9** chord, we can observe the following:-

- There is significant **plurality** between the two chords (again four notes in common).
- The critical resting tone **MI** is shared by both chords (as indicated above).

As a result of this, we can conclude that **the III chord can substitute for the I chord in a major key**. For example, we can take the following **II - V - I** progression in the key of **Bb major**:-

### *Figure 3.9. II - V - I progression in the key of Bb major*

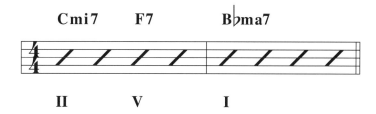

and substitute the **III** chord for the **I** chord as shown on the following page:-

## *Plural substitute chords for the II - V - I in major (contd)*

### *Figure 3.10. II - V - III progression in the key of Bb major (with III-for-I substitution)*

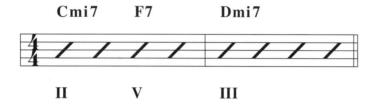

All melody notes which work over the original **I** chord (**Bbma7** in the above example) will also work over the substitute **III** chord (**Dmi7** in the above example), with the exception of **DO** in the melody which clashes with the **TI** in the **IIImi7** chord (in the above key, this would be the melody note **Bb** clashing with the note **A** which is the **5th** of the **Dmi7** chord). Subject to style considerations, the triad and four-part forms of the **III** chord (i.e. **Dmi** and **Dmi7** in the above example) will substitute for all common forms of the **I** chord (i.e. **Bb**, **Bb6**, **Bbma7**, **Bb69**, **Bbma9** etc.). The five-part form of the **III** chord **cannot** arbitrarily be used as a substitute for the **I** chord, as the **9th** of the **III** chord is not diatonic to the major key (in the above example, the **9th** of a **Dmi9** chord is the note **E**, which is not diatonic to **Bb major**).

Finally in this section we will take the **major sixth** form of the **I** chord in the key of **C** (i.e. **C6**, as reviewed in **Fig. 2.10.**). If we rearrange (or invert) the four notes in this chord, an **Ami7** chord is created as shown in the following example:-

### *Figure 3.11. Creating an Ami7 chord by inverting the four notes of a C6 chord*

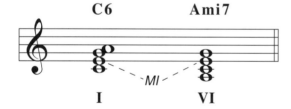

*(Again the solfeg shown is with respect to the key of **C** - the note **E** is 'MI' in this key).*

In comparing the **Ami7** chord (which as we saw in **Fig. 2.7.** is the four-part **VI** chord in **C major**) to the **C6** chord, we can observe the following:-

-    There is of course complete **plurality** between the two chords.
-    The critical resting tone **MI** is shared by both chords (as indicated above).

## *Plural substitute chords for the II - V - I in major (contd)*

As a result of this, we can conclude that **the VI chord can substitute for the I chord in a major key**. For example, we can take the following **II - V - I** progression in the key of **E major**:-

*Figure 3.12. II - V - I progression in the key of E major*

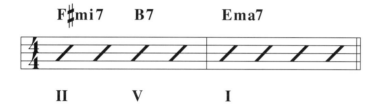

and substitute the **VI** chord for the **I** chord as follows:-

*Figure 3.13. II - V - VI progression in the key of E major (with VI-for-I substitution)*

All melody notes which work over the original **I** chord (**Ema7** in the above example) will also work over the substitute **VI** chord (**C#mi7** in the above example). Subject to style considerations, all common forms of the **VI** chord (i.e. **C#mi, C#mi7, C#mi9** in the above example) will substitute for all common forms of the **I** chord (i.e. **E, E6, Ema7, E69, Ema9** etc.).

We can summarize these plural substitute relationship in major keys, as follows:-

- The **IV** chord can substitute for the **II** chord (as in **Fig. 3.2.**).
- The **VII** chord can substitute for the **V** chord (as in **Fig. 3.5.**).
- The **III** chord and the **VI** chord can substitute for the **I** chord (as in **Figs. 3.8.** and **3.11.**).

These substitute relationships are now shown in the key of **C** (see summary example on following page):-

CHAPTER THREE - Textbook

## *Plural substitute chords for the II - V - I in major (contd)*

### *Figure 3.14. Summary of plural substitute relationships in the key of C major*

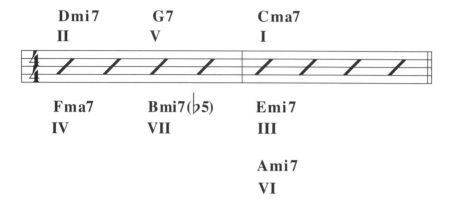

In the above example, the definitive **II - V - I** chords are shown above the staff, and the corresponding substitute chords are shown below the staff.

## *Harmonic analysis in major keys*

Following on from our introductory work in **Chapter 2** on analyzing 'pairs' of **II - V** and **V - I** chord relationships, we will now begin to analyze longer progressions in major keys. Review as necessary our discussion on **p42-43** concerning the overall harmonic analysis approach for different musical styles. We concluded then that jazz/standards and older (or 'classic') pop styles used **II - V - I** progressions and substitutes, with the jazz tunes additionally featuring **momentary key changes** in the harmony. The result of our harmonic analysis on these **II - V - I** -oriented tunes will tell us the **key** in which each chord is functioning (either the key corresponding to the key signature, or some other momentary key), and the **function** (i.e. **I**, **II**, **III** etc.) of the chord in that key. In some cases the same chord may function in **two consecutive** momentary keys within a progression, and these '**linking**' chords will also be analyzed.

We will go through the following stages to analyze progressions in major keys:-

*1)*     **Look for the dominant chords first.** At this stage we can assume that the dominant chord is functioning as a **V** chord in a major key.

*2)*     Look to see if the dominant chord is **preceded by the II chord** from the same key, and/or **followed by the I chord** from the same key (resulting in a **II - V**, **V - I**, or **II - V - I** progression).

*(contd>>>)*

## *Harmonic analysis in major keys (contd)*

*(Harmonic analysis method contd)*

**3)**    Look for chords which are **diatonic to the key signature** (and will therefore function in that key). Here are some examples of situations where this will prove helpful:-
-      It is not uncommon in jazz standard tunes for a chord diatonic to the key signature (often a **I** or tonic chord) to be 'sandwiched' in between other chords in different momentary keys - as in our first progression example (**Fig. 3.15. - 3.16.**).
-      In more 'pop'-oriented tunes we may not have any dominant (7th or 9th) chords to begin with - however we may still be using **II - V - I** chords and substitutes, but in triad forms which are generally diatonic to the key signature - as in our fourth progression example (**Fig. 3.21. - 3.22.**).

**4)**    Any chord still remaining to be analyzed after the above steps, is likely to be one of the following:-

-      **plural substitute** chords, in either:-
    -      the **preceding** momentary key within the progression, or
    -      the **following** momentary key within the progression.

-      isolated '**momentary I**' (one) chords in a new momentary key.

-      'passing' or embellishment chords.

We will now work through a series of progressions to apply these harmonic analysis principles, beginning with the following example:-

### *Figure 3.15. Harmonic analysis progression example #1*
*(this progression is typically used for the first eight measures*
*of the jazz standard tune "I Remember You")*

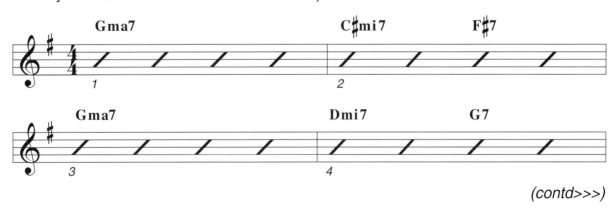

*(contd>>>)*

## *Harmonic analysis in major keys (contd)*

### *Figure 3.15. Harmonic analysis progression example #1 (contd)*

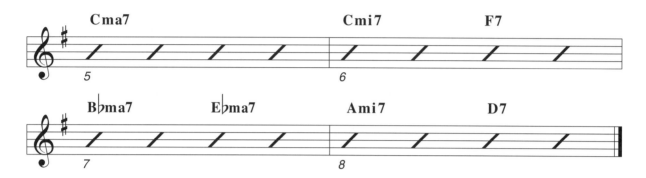

We will now apply the method outlined on **p70-71** to this progression as follows:-

**Stage 1**    We can analyze the dominant chords as follows:-

- The **F#7** in measure **2** will be a **V** chord in the momentary key of **B major**.
- The **G7** in measure **4** will be a **V** chord in the momentary key of **C major**.
- The **F7** in measure **6** will be a **V** chord in the momentary key of **Bb major**.
- The **D7** in measure **8** will be a **V** chord in the key of **G major** (corresponding to the key signature of the tune).

**Stage 2**    We can analyze the chords preceding and following the above dominant chords (i.e. to check for **II** or **I** chords functioning in the same momentary key) as follows:-

- The **C#mi7** preceding the **F#7** in measure **2**  also functions in the momentary key of **B major**, as a **II** chord. We have a **II - V** progression in **B major**.
- (The **Gma7** following the **F#7** in measure **2** does not function in **B major**).
- The **Dmi7** preceding the **G7** in measure **4** also functions in the momentary key of **C major**, as a **II** chord.
- The **Cma7** following the **G7** (in measure **5**) also functions in the momentary key of **C major**, as a **I** chord. In total we have a **II - V - I** progression in **C major**.
- The **Cmi7** preceding the **F7** in measure **6** also functions in the momentary key of **Bb major**, as a **II** chord.
- The **Bbma7** following the **F7** (in measure **7**) also functions in the momentary key of **Bb major**, as a **I** chord. In total we have a **II - V - I** progression in **Bb major**.
- The **Ami7** preceding the **D7** in measure **8** also functions in the key of **G major** (corresponding to the key signature of the tune), as a **II** chord. We have a **II - V** progression in **G major**.

## Harmonic analysis in major keys (contd)

### (Harmonic analysis of progression example #1 contd)

(So far we have taken care of all the chords except for the **Gma7** in measures **1** and **3**, and the **Ebma7** in measure **7**).

**Stage 3**    We can analyze any remaining chords which are diatonic to the key signature as follows:-

- The **Gma7** in measure **1** will be a **I** chord in the key of **G**. (It is not uncommon for jazz standards to begin with the **I** or tonic chord of the key signature).
- The **Gma7** in measure **3** will also be a **I** chord in the key of **G**. (This is the situation referred to at the top of **p71**, with the **I** chord of the key signature being 'sandwiched' in between other momentary keys).
- (The **Ebma7** in measure **7** is not diatonic to the key of **G major**).

**Stage 4**    We can analyze any remaining chords to see if they could function as plural substitutes within either the preceding or following momentary keys, as follows:-

- The **Ebma7** in measure **7** is found within the preceding momentary key of **Bb major** (defined by the **Cmi7 - F7 - Bbma7** progression in measures **6 - 7**), as a **IV** chord. It could therefore be considered as a **IV-for-II** substitution in the momentary key of **Bb major**.

We can now summarize the analysis of this progression as follows:-

### Figure 3.16. Harmonic analysis completed for progression example #1

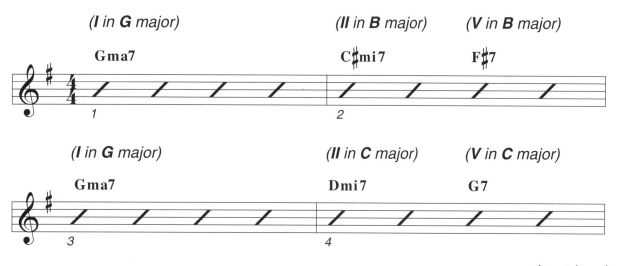

(contd>>>)

### *Harmonic analysis in major keys (contd)*

**(Figure 3.16. contd)**

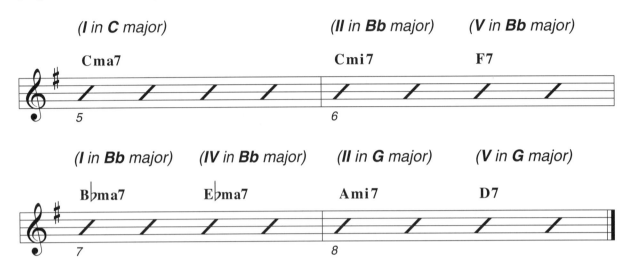

Note that, even though technically the **Cma7** in measure **5** is a **IV** chord with respect to the key signature (i.e. in the key of **G major**), it is primarily heard as a '**momentary I**' or tonic chord as a result of the preceding **Dmi7 - G7** progression in measure **4**. This illustrates why we look for the definitive progressions in other momentary keys (in **Stages 1-2**) before we look for chords diatonic to the key signature (in **Stage 3**), as of course **we need our harmonic analysis to reflect how the ear hears and understands the progression.**

Now we will analyze the next harmonic progression example as follows:-

### *Figure 3.17. Harmonic analysis progression example #2*
*(this progression is typically used for the first eight measures
of the jazz standard tune "Misty")*

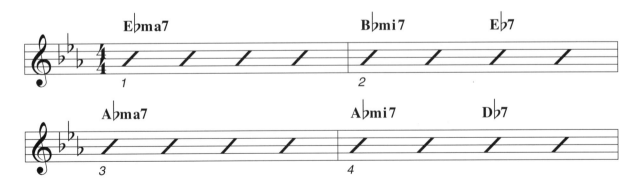

(contd>>>)

## *Harmonic analysis in major keys (contd)*

### *Figure 3.17. Harmonic analysis progression example #2 (contd)*

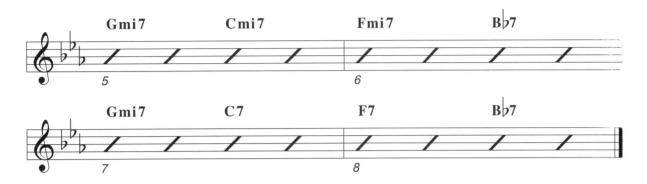

Again we will apply the same analysis method to this progression as follows:-

**Stage 1**    We can analyze the dominant chords as follows:-

- The **Eb7** in measure **2** will be a **V** chord in the momentary key of **Ab major**.
- The **Db7** in measure **4** will be a **V** chord in the momentary key of **Gb major**.
- The **Bb7** in measure **6** will be a **V** chord in the key of **Eb major** (corresponding to the key signature of the tune).
- The **C7** in measure **7** will be a **V** chord in the momentary key of **F major**.
- The **F7** in measure **7** will be a **V** chord in the momentary key of **Bb major**.
- The **Bb7** in measure **8** will again be a **V** chord in the key of **Eb major** (corresponding to the key signature of the tune).

**Stage 2**    We can analyze the chords preceding and following the above dominant chords (i.e. to check for **II** or **I** chords functioning in the same momentary key) as follows:-

- The **Bbmi7** preceding the **Eb7** in measure **2** also functions in the momentary key of **Ab major**, as a **II** chord.
- The **Abma7** following the **Eb7** (in measure **3**) also functions in the momentary key of **Ab major**, as a **I** chord. In total we have a **II - V - I** progression in **Ab major**.
- The **Abmi7** preceding the **Db7** in measure **4** also functions in the momentary key of **Gb major**, as a **II** chord. We have a **II - V** progression in **Gb major**.
- (The **Gmi7** following the **Db7** in measure **5** does not function in **Gb major**).
- The **Fmi7** preceding the **Bb7** in measure **6** also functions in the momentary key of **Eb major**, as a **II** chord. We have a **II - V** progression in **Eb major**.

*(contd>>>)*

## *Harmonic analysis in major keys (contd)*

**(Harmonic analysis of progression example #2 contd)**

**Stage 2 (contd)**

- The **Gmi7** preceding the **C7** in measure **7** also functions in the momentary key of **F major**, as a **II** chord. We have a **II - V** progression in **F major**.
- **HOWEVER,**
    - note that this **Gmi7** chord is also found in the preceding momentary key of **Eb major** (as defined by the **Fmi7 - Bb7** progression in measure **6**), as a **III** chord. It could therefore be considered as a **III-for-I** substitution in the momentary key of **Eb major** (which is of course also the key signature of the tune).
    - we will therefore refer to this **Gmi7** chord as a 'linking' chord, as **it is found within the preceding and following momentary keys** (i.e. the keys of **Eb** and **F** in this case).

(So far we have taken care of all the chords except for the **Ebma7** in measure **1** and the **Gmi7** and **Cmi7** in measure **5**).

**Stage 3**  We can analyze any remaining chords which are diatonic to the key signature as follows:-

- The **Ebma7** in measure **1** will be a **I** chord in the key of **Eb**. (As previously noted, it is not uncommon for jazz standards to begin with the **I** or tonic chord of the key signature).
- The **Gmi7** in measure **5** is also diatonic to the key signature - it is a **III** chord in the key of **Eb** (and therefore could be considered as a **III-for-I** substitution).
- The **Cmi7** in measure **5** is also diatonic to the key signature - it is a **VI** chord in the key of **Eb** (and therefore could be considered as a **VI-for-I** substitution).

No further analysis stages are required, as we now have dealt with all of the chords within the progression. We can now summarize the analysis of this progression as follows:-

### *Figure 3.18. Harmonic analysis completed for progression example #2*

(contd>>>)

### Harmonic analysis in major keys (contd)

#### (Figure 3.18. contd)

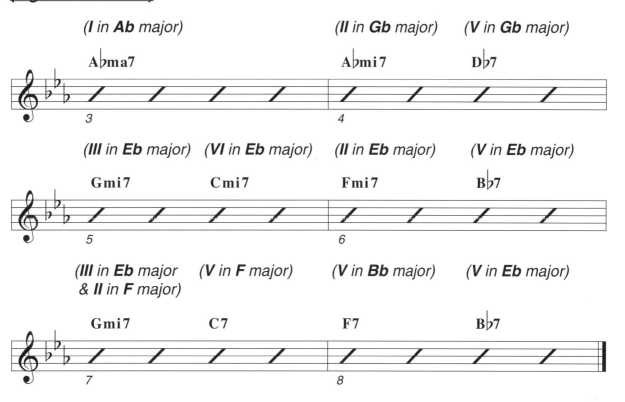

Note that (similar to the analysis of the **Cma7** chord in measure **5** of progression example **#1**), even though technically the **Abma7** in measure **3** above is a **IV** chord with respect to the key signature (i.e. in the key of **Eb major**), it is primarily heard as a '**momentary I**' or tonic chord as a result of the preceding **Bbmi7 - Eb7** progression in measure **2**. Now we will analyze the next harmonic progression example as follows:-

#### Figure 3.19. Harmonic analysis progression example #3
(this progression is typically used for the first eight measures
of the early-70s pop ballad "Killing Me Softly With His Song")

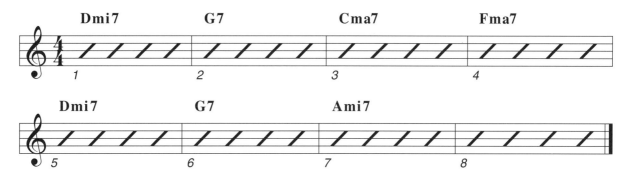

## Harmonic analysis in major keys (contd)

Again we will apply the same analysis method to the progression at the bottom of the previous page, as follows:-

**Stage 1**      We can analyze the dominant chords as follows:-

-      The **G7** in measure **2** will be a **V** chord in the key of **C major** (corresponding to the key signature of the tune).
-      The **G7** in measure **6** will also be a **V** chord in the key of **C major** (again corresponding to the key signature of the tune).

**Stage 2**      We can analyze the chords preceding and following the above dominant chords (i.e. to check for **II** or **I** chords functioning in the same momentary key) as follows:-

-      The **Dmi7** preceding the **G7** (in measure **1**) also functions in the key of **C major**, as a **II** chord.
-      The **Cma7** following the **G7** (in measure **3**) also functions in the key of **C major**, as a **I** chord. In measures **1 - 3** we have a **II - V - I** progression in **C major**.
-      The **Dmi7** preceding the **G7** (in measure **6**) also functions in the key of **C major**, as a **II** chord. In measures **5 - 6** we have a **II - V** progression in **C major**.
-      (The **Ami7** following the **G7** in measures **7 & 8** is not a **I** or tonic chord, however it still functions in the key of **C major** - see **stage 3**).

**Stage 3**      We can analyze any remaining chords which are diatonic to the key signature as follows:-

-      The **Fma7** in measure **4** is also diatonic to the key signature - it is a **IV** chord in the key of **C** (and therefore could be considered as a **IV-for-II** substitution).
-      The **Ami7** in measures **7 & 8** is also diatonic to the key signature - it is a **VI** chord in the key of **C** (and therefore could be considered as a **VI-for-I** substitution).

Note that in this case (as with many pop-oriented tunes) there were no momentary key changes i.e. all of the chords were diatonic to the key signature.

No further analysis stages are required, as we now have dealt with all of the chords within the progression. We can now summarize the analysis of this progression on the following page:-

### Harmonic analysis in major keys (contd)

#### Figure 3.20. Harmonic analysis completed for progression example #3

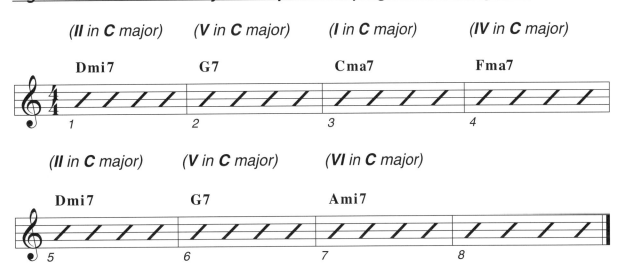

Now we will analyze the final harmonic progression example in this chapter, as follows:-

#### Figure 3.21. Harmonic analysis progression example #4
*(this progression is typically used for the first sixteen measures
of the 70s pop/rock tune "Lyin' Eyes" by the Eagles)*

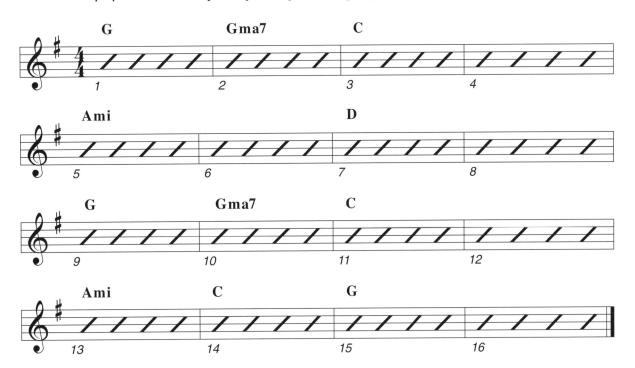

## *Harmonic analysis in major keys (contd)*

Note that the progression at the bottom of the previous page consists mainly of **3-part** chord forms (triads), with occasional **4-part** chords used. When analyzing the progression, we will refer to the **3-part** chords as '**incomplete**' as they are non-definitive (with no **6th** or **7th** present in the chord) and could therefore be plural to a number of different keys. In applying the previous analysis method to this progression, we note that:-

**Stage 1**     is redundant as there are no dominant (7th or 9th) chords present, and so

**Stage 2**     is also redundant as of course we have no **II** or **I** chords 'either side' of dominants.

We continue with the analysis method as follows:-

**Stage 3**     We can analyze chords which are diatonic to the key signature as follows:-

-     The **G** chord in measure **1** is an 'incomplete' **I** or tonic chord in the key of **G**.
-     The **Gma7** chord in measure **2** is a 'complete' (and definitive) **I** or tonic chord in the key of **G**.
-     The **C** chord in measures **3 & 4** is an 'incomplete' **IV** chord in the key of **G** (and therefore could be considered as a **IV-for-II** substitution).
-     The **Ami** chord in measures **5 & 6** is an 'incomplete' **II** chord in the key of **G**.
-     The **D** chord in measures **7 & 8** is an 'incomplete' **V** chord in the key of **G**.
-     (Measures **9 -12** are a repeat of measures **1 - 4**).
-     The **Ami** chord in measure **13** is an 'incomplete' **II** chord in the key of **G**.
-     The **C** chord in measure **14** is an 'incomplete' **IV** chord in the key of **G** (and therefore could again be considered as a **IV-for-II** substitution).
-     The **G** chord in measures **15 & 16** is again an 'incomplete' **I** or tonic chord in the key of **G**.

Note that, as in the previous progression example #3 (**Figs. 3.19. - 3.20.**), there were no momentary key changes in the progression at the bottom of the previous page i.e. all of the chords were diatonic to the key signature.

No further analysis stages are required, as we now have dealt with all of the chords within the progression. We can now summarize the analysis of this progression on the following page:-

### Harmonic analysis in major keys (contd)

**Figure 3.22. Harmonic analysis completed for progression example #4**

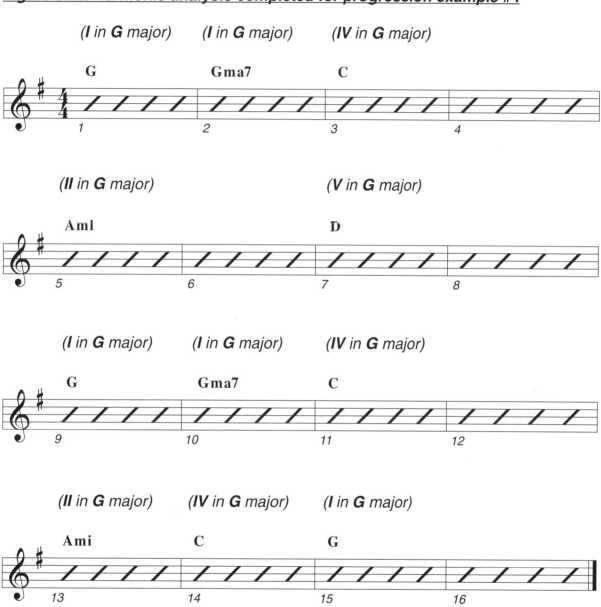

## Chapter Three Workbook Questions

### 1. *Determining plural substitutes in major keys*

Each of the following **II-V-I** progressions has one chord marked with asterisks. You are to determine which chord would substitute for the chord indicated, and then write the notes of the substitute chord on the staff (in root position) together with a chord symbol above the staff, in the blank measure(s) after each question. When the **I** chord is being substituted, you are to write notes and chord symbols for <u>both</u> of the possible substitutes.

**1.** *Determining plural substitutes in major keys (contd)*

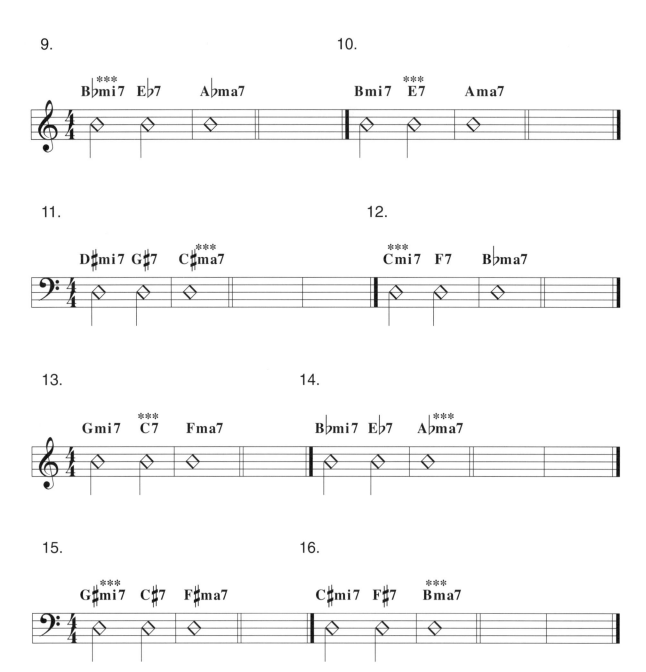

**2.** *Determining (original) definitive chords in major keys*

Each of the following progressions represents a **II-V-I** in which <u>one</u> of the chords has been substituted. You are to determine which chord is the substitute in each progression, and write asterisks over the appropriate chord symbol (in a similar manner as shown in questions 1 - 16). You are then to determine which (original) definitive chord has been substituted, and write the notes of the definitive chord (in root position) together with a chord symbol above the staff, in the blank measure after each question.

## 2. *Determining (original) definitive chords in major keys (contd)*

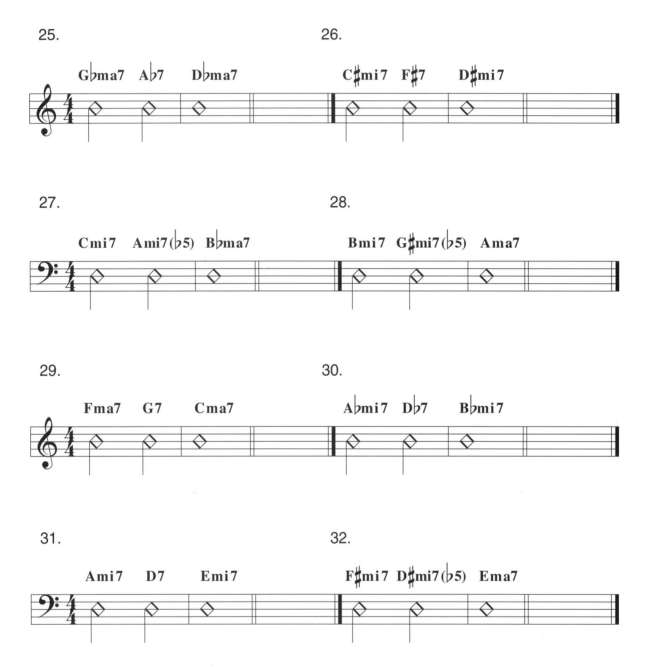

### 3. _Determining functions and keys for given chord symbols_

You are to determine the functions and (major) keys for the following chord symbols.
For example:-

- an _Ami7_ is a **II in G**, a **III in F** and a **VI in C**.
- an _A7_ is a **V in D**.
- an _Ama7_ is a **I in A** and a **IV in D**.

33. **Fmi7**   is a   ___ in ___
                      ___ in ___
                      ___ in ___

34. **Bmi7**   is a   ___ in ___
                      ___ in ___
                      ___ in ___

35. **Ab7**    is a   ___ in ___

36. **D7**     is a   ___ in ___

37. **Ema7**   is a   ___ in ___
                      ___ in ___

38. **Bbma7**  is a   ___ in ___
                      ___ in ___

### 4. _Chord progression analysis_

You are to determine the functions and keys for each chord in the following progressions,
in a similar manner as for section **3** above. Where a 'linking' chord occurs (i.e. belonging
to the preceding and following key centers) you are to indicate all applicable keys and
functions. Write the functions and keys in the spaces provided below each progression:-

_Chord Progression #1_
_(typically used for the first 16 measures of the jazz standard "All The Things You Are")_

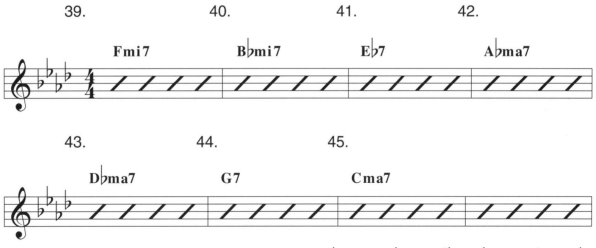

39.    40.    41.    42.

Fmi7    Bbmi7    Eb7    Abma7

43.    44.    45.

Dbma7    G7    Cma7

_(progression continued on next page)>>_

## 4. *Chord progression analysis (contd)*

*(Chord Progression #1 contd)*

46.         47.         48.         49.

50.         51.         52.

Write your answers here:-

| | | | |
|---|---|---|---|
| 39. _____ | | 40. _____ | |
| 41. _____ | | 42. _____ | |
| 43. _____ | | 44. _____ | |
| 45. _____ | | 46. _____ | |
| 47. _____ | | 48. _____ | |
| 49. _____ | | 50. _____ | |
| 51. _____ | | 52. _____ | |

# Plural substitute chords and harmonic analysis in major keys

**4.** ***Chord progression analysis (contd)***

*Chord Progression **#2***
*(typically used for the first 16 measures of the jazz standard "Just Friends")*

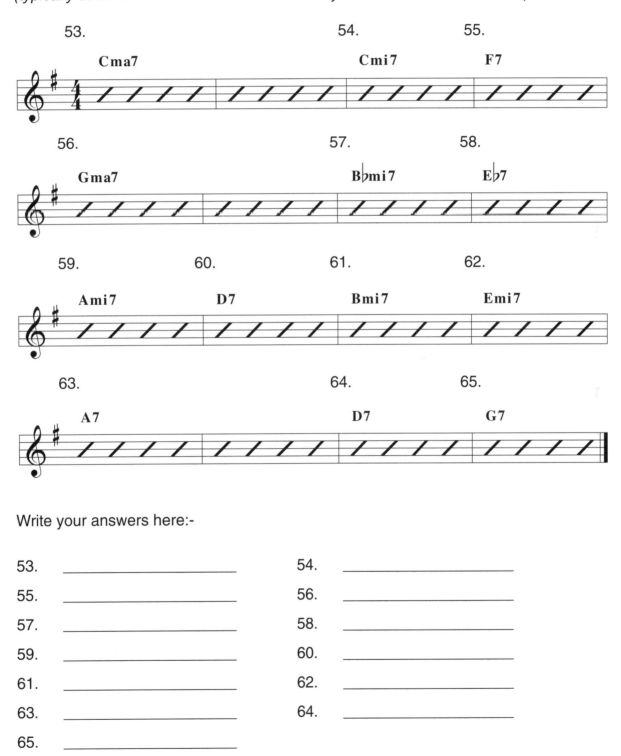

Write your answers here:-

53. _____    54. _____

55. _____    56. _____

57. _____    58. _____

59. _____    60. _____

61. _____    62. _____

63. _____    64. _____

65. _____

### 4. Chord progression analysis (contd)

*Chord Progression #3*
*(typically used for the first 8 measures of the jazz standard "Satin Doll")*

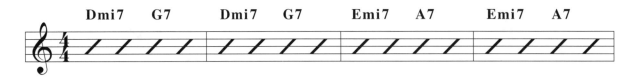

Write your answers here:-

66. _____      67. _____

68. _____      69. _____

70. _____      71. _____

72. _____      73. _____

74. _____      75. _____

76. _____      77. _____

78. _____      79. _____

80. _____

## 4. *Chord progression analysis (contd)*

*Chord Progression #4*
*(typically used for the last 6 measures of the jazz standard "A Foggy Day")*

81.     82.     83.     84.     85.     86.

Fma7     Gmi7     Ami7     B♭6     Ami7     Dmi7

87.     88.     89.          90.     91.

Gmi7     C7     Fma7          Gmi7     C7

Write your answers here:-

81. _____          82. _____

83. _____          84. _____

85. _____          86. _____

87. _____          88. _____

89. _____          90. _____

91. _____

### 4. *Chord progression analysis (contd)*

*Chord Progression #5*
*(typically used for the first 9 measures of the Beatles tune "I Will")*

Write your answers here:-

| | | | |
|---|---|---|---|
| 92. _____ | | 93. _____ | |
| 94. _____ | | 95. _____ | |
| 96. _____ | | 97. _____ | |
| 98. _____ | | 99. _____ | |
| 100. _____ | | 101. _____ | |
| 102. _____ | | 103. _____ | |
| 104. _____ | | 105. _____ | |
| 106. _____ | | 107. _____ | |
| 108. _____ | | 109. _____ | |

## *Chapter Three Workbook Answers*

**1.** *Determining plural substitutes in major keys - answers*

1.  *Determining plural substitutes in major keys - answers (contd)*

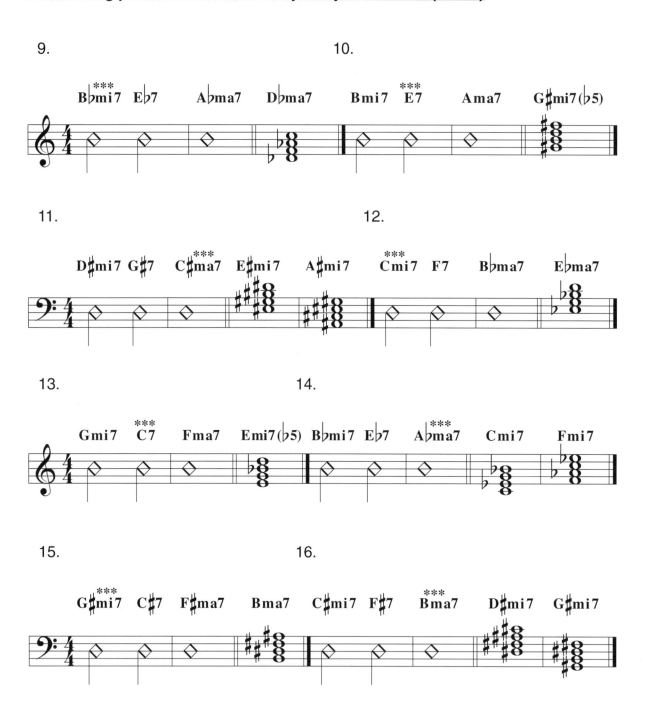

**_2._**   **_Determining (original) definitive chords in major keys - answers_**

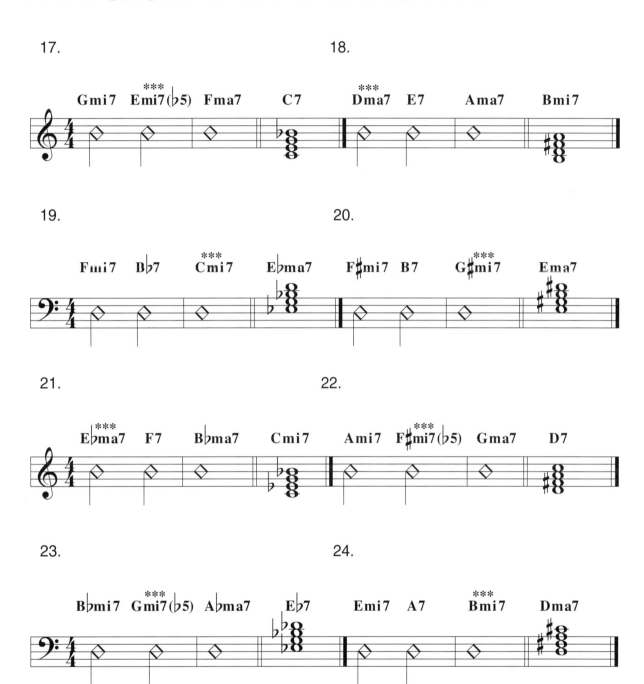

**_2._**     **_Determining (original) definitive chords in major keys - answers (contd)_**

_**3.**_    _**Determining functions and keys for given chord symbols - answers**_

| 33. | **Fmi7** | is a | **II** in Eb<br>**III** in Db<br>**VI** in Ab | 34. | **Bmi7** | is a | **II** in A<br>**III** in G<br>**VI** in D |

| 35. | **Ab7** | is a | **V** in Db | 36. | **D7** | is a | **V** in G |

| 37. | **Ema7** | is a | **I** in E<br>**IV** in B | 38. | **Bbma7** | is a | **I** in Bb<br>**IV** in F |

_**4.**_    _**Chord progression analysis - answers**_

_(Chord Progression #1)_

| 39. | **VI** in Ab | 40. | **II** in Ab |
| 41. | **V** in Ab | 42. | **I** in Ab |
| 43. | **IV** in Ab | 44. | **V** in C |
| 45. | **I** in C | 46. | **VI** in Eb |
| 47. | **II** in Eb | 48. | **V** in Eb |
| 49. | **I** in Eb | 50. | **IV** in Eb |
| 51. | **V** in G | 52. | **I** in G |

_(Chord Progression #2)_

| 53. | **I** in C | 54. | **II** in Bb |
| 55. | **V** in Bb | 56. | **I** in G |
| 57. | **II** in Ab | 58. | **V** in Ab |
| 59. | **II** in G | 60. | **V** in G |
| 61. | **III** in G, **VI** in D | 62. | **VI** in G, **II** in D |
| 63. | **V** in D | 64. | **V** in G |
| 65. | **V** in C | | |

4.    *Chord progression analysis - answers (contd)*


(Chord Progression *#3*)

| | | | | |
|---|---|---|---|---|
| 66. | *II* in C | 67. | *V* in C |
| 68. | *II* in C | 69. | *V* in C |
| 70. | *III* in C, *II* in D | 71. | *V* in D |
| 72. | *II* in D | 73. | *V* in D |
| 74. | *II* in G | 75. | *V* in G |
| 76. | *II* in Gb | 77. | *V* in Gb |
| 78. | *I* in C | 79. | *III* in C, *II* in D |
| 80. | *V* in D | | |


(Chord Progression *#4*)

| | | | | |
|---|---|---|---|---|
| 81. | *I* in F | 82. | *II* in F |
| 83. | *III* in F | 84. | *IV* in F |
| 85. | *III* in F | 86. | *VI* in F |
| 87. | *II* in F | 88. | *V* in F |
| 89. | *I* in F | 90. | *II* in F |
| 91. | *V* in F | | |


(Chord Progression *#5*)

| | | | | |
|---|---|---|---|---|
| 92. | *I* in F | 93. | *VI* in F |
| 94. | *II* in F | 95. | *V* in F |
| 96. | *I* in F | 97. | *VI* in F |
| 98. | *III* in F | 99. | *V* in Bb |
| 100. | *I* in Bb , *IV* in F | 101. | *V* in F |
| 102. | *VI* in F | 103. | *I* in F |
| 104. | *IV* in F | 105. | *V* in F |
| 106. | *I* in F | 107. | *VI* in F |
| 108. | *II* in F | 109. | *V* in F |

# Five-part chords and the II-V-I progression in minor keys

## Introduction

In this chapter we will deal with the following subject areas:-

**1)** Following on from our work in *Chapters 2 & 3* on 'diatonic solfeg', we will now review the **chromatic solfeg** syllables. These syllables will be used for labelling tones which are **not** contained within the major scale of the key signature 'in force'. (You may have already been exposed to 'chromatic solfeg' via our *Contemporary Eartraining Level Two* course). This expansion of the 'solfeg' system will then enable us to understand how resolutions (and therefore definitive progressions such as the **II - V - I**) work in minor key areas.

**2)** In reviewing the three minor scales (**melodic**, **harmonic** and **natural**) available within a minor key, we will now assign chromatic solfeg syllables throughout these scales. We will then use this to help define the critical **active-to-resting resolutions** present within a minor key area.

**3)** From the choices available within the different minor scales, we will then derive the 'definitive' **II**, **V** and **I** chords in a minor key, according to the following selection criteria:-
- the **II - V - I** chords in minor must be different from their 'major counterparts'.
- the **II - V - I** chords in minor must allow the critical **active-to-resting resolutions** to occur (as mentioned above).

**4)** Where appropriate, we will then add **ninths** to the chords used in the **II - V - I** progression in minor, to create **five-part** chords.

**5)** Finally we will expand our work on **harmonic analysis** of tunes, by including the **II - V - I** progression in minor, and by **mixing together** the **II - V - I** progressions from major and minor keys.

## Chromatic solfeg review

We have already been introduced to the diatonic solfeg syllables used to label the scale degrees of a major scale, in *Chapter 2*. These are repeated below for your convenience:-

### Figure 4.1. Diatonic solfeg syllables assigned to a C major scale

DO    RE    MI    FA    SO    LA    TI    DO

## *Chromatic solfeg review (contd)*

We now need to move beyond this diatonic restriction, to label the **chromatic tones** i.e. those which are **not** within the major scale of the key signature. You will recall our discussion towards the end of *Chapter 2* concerning how our harmonic analysis techniques are influenced by the **style** of the music in question. We noted then for example that a lot of **jazz standards** have melodies which are generally diatonic to the key signature, and yet use chord progressions from other momentary keys. In these situations it is best to keep **DO** assigned to the key of the key signature, and to cater for chromatic tones (i.e. in the harmony) using **chromatic solfeg** syllables. This is the most consistent approach, as the key signature is wielding considerable influence over the tune as a whole (most obviously in the melody), despite any momentary key changes used in the harmony. This method is sometimes referred to as the 'Fixed DO' approach (see *Chapter 3* in our *Contemporary Eartraining Level Two* course).

Chromatic solfeg syllables have enharmonic equivalents in a similar fashion to the enharmonics existing between sharp and flat note names. For example, the notes **C#** and **Db** are the same pitch, but we would use one name or the other depending on the context i.e. whether we were actually sharping the note **C** or flatting the note **D**. Similarly, we will use a different chromatic solfeg syllable if we are sharping **DO** than if we are flatting **RE** - this concept will then of course work in all keys! The following examples show all of the chromatic solfeg syllables, using the key of **C** (i.e. assigning **DO** to **C**) for the purposes of illustration:-

### *Figure 4.2. Ascending chromatic solfeg syllables (with DO assigned to the note C)*

DO   **DI**   RE   **RI**   MI   FA   **FI**   SO   **SI**   LA   **LI**   TI   DO

### *Figure 4.3. Descending chromatic solfeg syllables (with DO assigned to the note C)*

DO   TI   **TE**   LA   **LE**   SO   **SE**   FA   MI   **ME**   RE   **RA**   DO

The new chromatic syllables are shown in bold underlined type in each case. Note that the syllables for the sharped pitches (shown in **Fig. 4.2.**) all end with the vowel "**I**" ( pronounced "**ee**" as in "dee", "ree" etc.), and that the syllables for the flatted pitches (shown in **Fig. 4.3.**) end with the vowel "**E**" (pronounced "**ay**" as in "tay", "lay" etc.), with the exception of the flatted **RE** which becomes **RA** (pronounced "**rah**"). Don't forget that this works in all keys (not just **C**)!

### Minor scales and active-to-resting resolutions in minor keys

We saw in *Contemporary Music Theory Level 1* (and reviewed in **Figs. 1.20. - 1.28.** of this book) that there were three minor scales in common usage - **melodic**, **harmonic** and **natural**. In minor key applications we now have all of these scales available to us! As you can imagine, this potentially complicates the process of deriving definitive chords (such as the **II - V - I** progression) in minor keys. However, using the recently reviewed **chromatic solfeg** as a tool, we will determine the **active-to-resting resolutions** available within the minor scales, which will in turn then help us to derive the definitive **II - V - I** progression in minor.

First we will look at these three scales again, this time adding the solfeg (including any necessary chromatic syllables), again assigning **DO** to **C** as follows:-

*Figure 4.4. C melodic minor scale showing solfeg syllables (with DO assigned to C)*

*Figure 4.5. C harmonic minor scale showing solfeg syllables (with DO assigned to C)*

*Figure 4.6. C natural minor scale showing solfeg syllables (with DO assigned to C)*

Note that in doing a solfeg comparison between the above **C minor** scales and the **C major** scale (shown in **Fig. 4.1.**):-

- in the **melodic** minor scale, **ME** has replaced **MI**.
- in the **harmonic** minor scale, **ME** has replaced **MI** and **LE** has replaced **LA**.
- in the **natural** minor scale, **ME** has replaced **MI**, **LE** has replaced **LA** and **TE** has replaced **TI**.

## *Minor scales and active-to-resting resolutions in minor keys (contd)*

Back in *Chapter 2* when reviewing diatonic solfeg, we concluded that the **FA to MI** and **TI to DO** resolutions were the most important within a major key. As discussed, this is largely because **these active-to-resting resolutions were via the strong and leading half-step interval**. We can summarize these resolutions in major, as follows:-

### *Figure 4.7. Active-to-resting resolutions in major (with DO assigned to C)*

(DO)        FA------>MI        TI------>DO

Now we can analyze how this **active-to-resting** situation will change in a minor key (in the light of the tones available within the three minor scales in **Figs. 4.4. - 4.6.**) as follows:-

- **the FA to MI resolution is no longer available**. (Note that **ME** has replaced **MI** in all three minor scales). **ME** (the **3rd** degree of all the minor scales) is very 'definitive' of minor in that it immediately lets our ear know we are in minor instead of major. The **FA to ME** resolution (found in all the minor scales) is now available in a minor key. However, because this resolution is via a **whole-step** interval, it is **not** as strong or leading as the **FA to MI** resolution is in major.
- **the TI to DO resolution is still available** (within the melodic and harmonic minor scales). The use of **TI** allows a **dominant** chord quality to be built from the **5th** degree of the key (as first seen in **Fig. 2.3.**) - this will be needed in minor (as well as major) keys.
- **the LE to SO resolution is now available** (within the harmonic and natural minor scales). Now in minor we are able to resolve into the resting tone **SO** via the **leading half-step** interval (i.e. from **LE**) - this of course was not possible in a major key. **The LE to SO resolution now becomes an important and definitive relationship in a minor key**.

We can now summarize these resolutions available in minor, as follows:-

### *Figure 4.8. Active-to-resting resolutions in minor (with DO assigned to C)*

(DO)        FA------>ME        LE------>SO        TI-------->DO

## *Deriving the II - V - I (two-five-one) progression in minor*

We will now take the three minor scales (**melodic**, **harmonic** and **natural**) presented in **Figs. 4.4. - 4.6.**, and evaluate the nature of the **II**, **V** and **I** chords that can be built from each of these scales. As mentioned in the introduction at the beginning of this chapter, we will then assess the usefulness of the resulting chords from the following standpoints:-

- are the **II**, **V** and/or **I** chords in minor different from their 'major counterparts'? For example, if a **II** chord in minor was the same as a **II** chord in major, it would not create a recognizably different sound to the major key, and would therefore not be 'definitive' of minor.

- do the **II**, **V** and/or **I** chords in minor contain the appropriate active/resting qualities? From our analysis of resolutions in minor keys (and how this compared to major keys) on the previous page, we can establish the following criteria:-

    - the **active** chords in any **II - V - I** progression are the **II** and the **V** chords. In major keys we saw that **FA** was an important component of these active chords, and this will still be the case in minor keys. On the previous page we also noted the importance of the new **LE to SO** resolution in minor. We can conclude therefore that the presence of **LE** within the **II** and the **V** chord in minor, is very desirable as it gives an additional **active quality to these chords which is definitive of a minor key**.

    - as first discussed in **Chapter 2**, the 'heart' of any **II - V - I** progression is the dominant chord. As mentioned on the previous page, the **V** chord in a minor key will still need to have a dominant quality. We can conclude therefore that the presence of **TI** within the **V** chord in minor, is very desirable as it will (together with **FA** as mentioned above) **impart the necessary 'dominant quality'** to this chord.

    - the **resting** chord in any **II - V - I** progression is the **I** chord. In major keys we saw that **MI** was an important component of the resting chord. In minor keys however we have seen that **ME** has replaced **MI**, and that **ME** is very 'definitive' of minor. We can conclude therefore that the presence of **ME** within the **I** chord in minor is very desirable as it has a **resting quality which is definitive of minor**.

The good news (!) is that, once we apply the above criteria to the various **II**, **V** and **I** chords available from the different minor scales, we will see that many of these chords fail one or other of these tests, and we are left with a small number of definitive choices to use within minor keys. During this process, we will attempt to construct **five-part** as well as **four-part** **II**, **V** and **I** chords from the different scales, although as we shall see this will lead to some vertical contradictions (i.e. incorrect chords) in some cases. We will begin by examining the **four-** and **five-part** chords built from the **second degree** of the **C melodic**, **C harmonic**, and **C natural minor** scales (as shown on the following page):-

### Deriving the II - V - I (two-five-one) progression in minor (contd)

### Figure 4.9. Four- and five-part 'II' chords built from the C melodic minor scale

### Figure 4.10. Four- and five-part 'II' chords built from the C harmonic minor scale

### Figure 4.11. Four- and five-part 'II' chords built from the C natural minor scale

Note that the **five-part** chord produced in each case (in the shaded areas) is described as an 'incorrect chord'. This is because of the dissonant **minor 9th** interval occurring between the root of **D** and the top note of **Eb** in each case. In conventional Western music styles, minor 9th intervals (referred to as 'flatted 9ths') are tonally acceptable **only on dominant chords**. As you can see, these chords are not dominant - the bottom four notes (of the five-part chords) are either **minor 7th** or **minor 7th with flatted 5th** chords. None of the above five-part chords are therefore suitable for our purposes.

Now we will evaluate the remaining **four-part** chords derived above. The **Dmi7** built from the **2nd** degree of the **C melodic** minor scale, fails our selection criteria as it is the same chord as its 'major key counterpart' (review **Fig. 2.10.** as necessary). However the **Dmi7(b5)** built from the **2nd** degree of the **C harmonic** and **C natural** minor scales, looks promising for these reasons (see following page):-

**104**

### Deriving the II - V - I (two-five-one) progression in minor (contd)

- The chord is recognizably different from its 'major key counterpart' i.e. the **Dmi7(b5)** chord quality is not the same as a **Dmi7** chord.
- The chord has the important active tone **LE** (the note **Ab** in the key of **C**) which as discussed is the active component of the critical **LE to SO** resolution in minor.

For these reasons, **we will choose the IImi7(b5) as the definitive II chord within a minor key.**

*[As we saw on the previous page, there are no useful five-part options available within the various minor scales - however we should mention that it is possible to add a **major 9th** interval to a **minor 7th with flatted 5th** chord, creating a **minor 9th with flatted 5th** five-part chord - in this case a **Dmi9(b5)**. Analyzing the solfeg however, we see that the **9th** of this chord is **MI** (E in this case), which can cause problems in simpler minor key applications - we recall that a central difference between minor and major keys is the overall use of **ME** instead of **MI**. This five-part form of the **II** chord is a colorful option in more advanced jazz styles, but would certainly **not** be used on a routine basis].*

Next we will examine the four- and five-part chords built from the **fifth degree** of the **C melodic**, **C harmonic**, and **C natural minor** scales, as follows:-

### Figure 4.12. Four- and five-part 'V' chords built from the C melodic minor scale

### Figure 4.13. Four- and five-part 'V' chords built from the C harmonic minor scale

*(contd---->)*

### *Deriving the II - V - I (two-five-one) progression in minor (contd)*

#### *Figure 4.14. Four- and five-part 'V' chords built from the C natural minor scale*

Note that the five-part chord produced in **Fig. 4.14.** above is described as an 'incorrect chord', again because of the **minor 9th** interval added to the **minor 7th** chord (see **p104** comments). In evaluating the remaining **V** (five) chords shown in the preceding examples, we note that the **G7** built from the **5th** degree of the **C melodic** and **C harmonic** minor scales, and the **G9** built from the **5th** degree of the **C melodic** minor scale, all fail our selection criteria as these chords are the same as would be available in a major key. Also we see that the **Gmi7** built from the **5th** degree of the **C natural** minor scale above, also fails our selection criteria as it does not have a **dominant quality** (being a minor chord, containing a **minor 3rd** interval) and therefore will not provide the necessary dominant-to-tonic chord movement within the **II - V - I** progression *[although it will be a useful option in more 'modal' and less II - V - I -oriented applications]*.

However, the **G7(b9)** built from the **5th** degree of the **C harmonic** minor scale, looks promising for the following reasons:-

-   The chord is recognizably different from its 'major key counterpart' **provided we select the five-part chord available within the scale** - the **G7(b9)** chord quality is not the same as the corresponding **G9** chord found within the major scale.
-   The chord again has the important active tone **LE** (the note **Ab** in the key of **C**) which as discussed is the active component of the critical **LE to SO** resolution in minor.

For these reasons, **we will choose the V7(b9) as the definitive V chord within a minor key.** *[In future harmony studies we shall see that the dominant chord actually has four potential 'alterations' available - the b5 (also referred to as the #11), #5 (also referred to as the b13), b9 (as shown in Fig. 4.13.) and #9. The presence of any or all of these alterations on the dominant chord, is consistent with the chord functioning as a V in a minor key].*

This **dominant 7th with flatted 9th** chord available within the harmonic minor scale, is a new chord which we should look at in more detail. As discussed on **p104**, the dominant is the only type of chord (in conventional Western music) which will support a minor or 'flatted' **9th**. This is because (in the context of a **dominant-to-tonic** progression in minor) the horizontal energy of **LE** resolving to **SO** (as in **Fig. 4.8.**) combined with the **circle-of-5ths** root movement of **SO** to **DO**, is sufficiently strong to counteract the vertical dissonance of the **minor 9th** interval.

### *Deriving the II - V - I (two-five-one) progression in minor (contd)*

The chord 'stack' and interval construction of the **dominant 7th with flatted 9th** chord can be shown as follows:-

***Figure 4.15. G dominant 7th with flatted 9th chord 'stack' and interval construction***

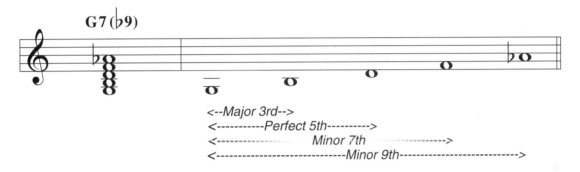

```
<--Major 3rd-->
<-----------Perfect 5th---------->
<---------------- Minor 7th ---------------->
<-----------------------------Minor 9th----------------------------->
```

We note that this **G7(b9)** can be derived by taking a **G7** chord (as in **Fig. 2.10.**) and adding the note which creates a **minor 9th** interval from the root of the chord (i.e. the note **Ab**). In total, the intervals created are a **major 3rd**, **perfect 5th**, **minor 7th**, and **minor 9th** respectively above the root of the chord.

Note the chord symbol used for the **G dominant 7th with flatted 9th** chord i.e. **G7(b9)**. The suffix '**7(b9)**' indicates a **dominant 7th with flatted 9th chord** built from the root i.e. in this case a **G dominant 7th with flatted 9th chord**. Although using the suffix '**7(b9)**' is the preferred way to write this chord symbol, you will sometimes encounter other suffixes for the dominant 7th with flatted 9th chord, as follows:-

-     '**7b9**'   i.e. as in the chord symbol **G7b9**. This is generally correct and acceptable (i.e. with the parentheses omitted) as it is still clear that the '**b**' (flat sign) is referring to the **9th** of the chord.

-     '**7(-9)**', '**7-9**' i.e. as in the chord symbols **G7(-9)**, **G7-9**. As previously noted (i.e. in the text accompanying **Fig. 2.11.**), you will sometimes encounter the use of the '**-**' suffix to signify minor (in this case a minor 9th interval on the chord). Again I think that the use of the '**b**' (flat sign) in the chord suffix is clearer and more explicit.

So - when writing your **dominant 7th with flatted 9th** chord symbols, use the '**7(b9)**' or '**7b9**' suffix - but again **be prepared to recognize** the alternative chord suffixes listed above.

Finally in this section of the chapter we will examine the four- and five-part chords built from the **first degree** of the **C melodic**, **C harmonic**, and **C natural minor** scales, as shown on the following page:-

## *Deriving the II - V - I (two-five-one) progression in minor (contd)*

### *Figure 4.16. Four- and five-part 'I' chords built from the C melodic minor scale*

### *Figure 4.17. Four- and five-part 'I' chords built from the C harmonic minor scale*

### *Figure 4.18. Four- and five-part 'I' chords built from the C natural minor scale*

In evaluating the **I** or **tonic** chords in minor shown above, we note that all of the above chords are different from the **I** chords available in major (i.e. as shown in **Figs. 2.10.** and **2.21.**). However, there is a similarity in the construction of the **I** or **tonic** chords within the **major** scale and within the **melodic minor** scale, in that in both cases we can build '**sixth**' and '**seventh**' **four-part** forms, and in both cases we can add **major 9th** intervals to these chords to create **five-part** forms.

We see also that the choices available from the **harmonic minor** scale above are a **subset** of (i.e. are contained within) the choices available from the **melodic minor** scale. From a solfeg viewpoint, we recall from **Figs. 4.4. - 4.5.** that the only difference between these scales is that the melodic minor scale contains **LA**, while the harmonic minor scale contains **LE**. We recall that **LE** is a particularly active tone in minor, and is therefore unlikely to be very useful on the **I** or **tonic** chord - effectively then we no longer need to concern ourselves with the **harmonic minor** scale as a source for the **I** or **tonic** chord in minor.

### *Deriving the II - V - I (two-five-one) progression in minor (contd)*

The choices for the **I** or **tonic** chord in the key of **C minor** are therefore as follows:-

- the **four-part Cmi6** & **CmiMa7**, and **five-part Cmi69** & **CmiMa9**, available from the **C melodic minor** scale.
- the **four-part Cmi7**, and **five-part Cmi9**, available from the **C natural minor** scale.

With regard to our original selection criteria for definitive chords in minor, these chords are all potentially suitable because:-

- they are all recognizably different from their 'major key counterparts', and
- they all contain **ME** which is the **definitive** resting tone in minor (as well as the resting tone **SO**) - review **Fig. 4.8.** and accompanying text as necessary.

What we see therefore is that, in contrast to the previous derivation of the definitive **IImi7(b5)** and **V7(b9)** chords in minor (where we really no longer need concern ourselves with which minor scale these chords came from), now we have **legitimate alternatives** for the **I** or **tonic** chord from both the **melodic** and **natural** minor scales. From a solfeg standpoint, all of the **melodic-minor based I** or **tonic** chords will contain **LA** or **TI** (which can be viewed as being functionally interchangeable, as they were on the **I** or **tonic** chords in major keys), whereas the **natural-minor based I** or **tonic** chords will contain **TE**.

These two distinct categories of **I** or **tonic** chords in minor (i.e. **melodic-minor based** and **natural-minor based**) have specific stylistic implications. In almost all **contemporary** or **pop** applications using **I** or **tonic** chords in minor which are larger than triads, the **natural-minor based I** or **tonic** chord (i.e. the **mi7** or **mi9** form) will be used. By contrast, in **jazz** styles the **melodic-minor based I** or **tonic** chord in minor (i.e. the **mi6**, **miMa7**, **mi69** or **miMa9** form) is arguably predominant, although **jazz** styles will also make use of the **natural-minor based I** or **tonic** chords.

Now we will look at the interval constructions of these chords a little more closely. So far in this book we have already reviewed and/or derived the following chords:-

- the **Cmi6** chord (from the **C melodic minor** scale in **Fig. 4.16.**) was reviewed in **Fig. 1.30.**
- the **CmiMa7** chord (from the **C melodic minor** scale in **Fig. 4.16.**) was reviewed in **Fig. 1.29.**
- the **Cmi7** chord (from the **C natural minor** scale in **Fig. 4.18.**) was reviewed in **Fig. 1.14.**
- the intervals used in the **Cmi9** chord (from the **C natural minor** scale in **Fig. 4.18.**) were derived in **Fig. 2.11.** (in that case using a **Dmi9** chord as an example).

We will now analyze the chord 'stacks' and interval construction of the remaining **mi69** and **miMa9** chords (from **melodic minor**), beginning on the following page:-

### *Deriving the II - V - I (two-five-one) progression in minor (contd)*

**Figure 4.19. C minor six nine chord 'stack' and interval construction**

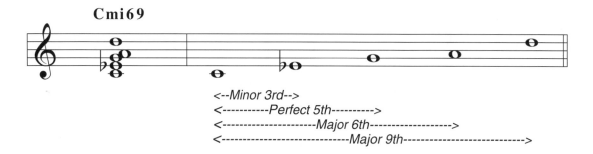

We note that the **C minor six nine** chord shown above, can be derived by taking the **Cmi6** chord (as in **Fig. 1.30.**) and adding the note which creates a **major 9th** interval from the root of the chord (i.e. the note **D**). In total, the intervals created are a **minor 3rd**, **perfect 5th**, **major 6th**, and **major 9th** respectively above the root of the chord.

Note the chord symbol used for the **C minor six nine chord** ('**Cmi69**'). The suffix '**mi69**' indicates a **minor six nine chord** built from the root i.e. in this case a **C minor six nine chord**. Although using the suffix '**mi69**' is the preferred way to write this chord symbol, you will sometimes encounter other suffixes for the minor six nine chord, as follows:-

-    '**min69**', **mi6(9)**, **mi(69)** etc. as in the chord symbols **Cmin69**, **Cmi6(9)**, **Cmi(69)** etc. These are acceptable alternatives, however strictly speaking the '**min**' suffix and the parentheses are redundant.
-    **mi6(add9)** as in the chord symbol **Cmi6(add9)**. As we saw in *Chapter 2*, the '**add9**' suffix should only be used on chords with **no 6th or 7th** present - so strictly speaking this is an incorrect chord symbol.
-    '**m69**' i.e. as in the chord symbol **Cm69**. As already discussed, the single lower-case '**m**' can be confused with '**M**' (upper-case) which is sometimes used to signify a **major** quality.
-    '**-69**' i.e. as in the chord symbol **C-69**. Review earlier comments (i.e. in *Chapter 2*) concerning my reservations about using the '**-**' suffix for minor chords!

So - when writing your **minor six nine** chord symbols, use the '**mi69**' suffix - but again **be prepared to recognize** the alternative chord suffixes listed above.

We will now analyze the chord 'stack' and interval construction of the **miMa9** chord (again from the **melodic minor** scale as shown in **Fig. 4.16.**), as shown on the following page:-

### *Deriving the II - V - I (two-five-one) progression in minor (contd)*

#### *Figure 4.20. C minor major ninth chord 'stack' and interval construction*

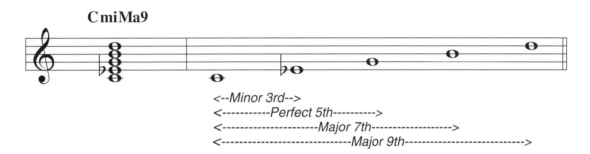

```
                     <--Minor 3rd-->
                   <-----------Perfect 5th---------->
                   <----------------------Major 7th------------------->
                   <-----------------------------Major 9th---------------------------->
```

We note that the **C minor major ninth** chord shown above, can be derived by taking the **CmiMa7** chord (as in **Fig. 1.29.**) and adding the note which creates a **major 9th** interval from the root of the chord (i.e. the note **D**). In total, the intervals created are a **minor 3rd**, **perfect 5th**, **major 7th**, and **major 9th** respectively above the root of the chord.

Note the chord symbol used in the above example ('**CmiMa9**'). The chord suffix '**miMa9**' indicates a **minor major ninth chord** built from the root i.e. in this case a **C minor major ninth chord**. In a sinilar manner to the '**miMa7**' suffix analyzed in ***Contemporary Music Theory Level One***, the '**mi**' in the '**miMa9**' suffix refers to the **minor 3rd** interval present, and the '**Ma**' in the '**miMa9**' suffix refers to the **major 7th** interval present (in other words the '**Ma**' in this chord symbol is **not** referring to the '**9**' which is immediately following).

Although using the suffix '**miMa9**' is the preferred way to write this chord symbol, you will sometimes encounter other suffixes for the minor major ninth chord, as follows:-

-        '**mima9**', '**minmaj9**', '**minMaj9**', i.e. as in the chord symbols **Cmima9, Cminmaj9, CminMaj9** etc. These would be acceptable variations, however I feel that the '**miMa9**' suffix is the clearest and most explicit.
-        '**mi△9**' i.e. as in the chord symbol **Cmi△9**. We have already expressed reservations (in ***Chapter 2***) about using the 'triangle symbol' to indicate a major quality (in this case a major 7th interval within the chord) - again I feel this can be confusing, particularly in the context of the minor major 9th chord.
-        '**-ma9**', '**-maj9**', etc. as in the chord symbols **C-ma9, C-maj9** etc. Again we have already expressed reservations (in ***Chapter 2***) about using the '**-**' suffix to indicate a minor quality (in this case a minor 3rd interval within the chord) - again I feel this can be confusing, particularly in the context of the minor major 9th chord.
-        '**-△9**' i.e. as in the chord symbol **C-△9**. A combination of the above problems - there is even more potential for confusion with this chord symbol!

*(contd on following page>>>)*

### Deriving the II - V - I (two-five-one) progression in minor (contd)

*(other possible suffixes for the minor major 9th chord - contd)*

- 'mM9' i.e. as in the chord symbol **CmM9**. We have already seen that the use of the single upper case '**M**' to signify major, and of the single lower-case '**m**' to signify minor, can cause difficulty if the difference between the upper-case and lower-case is unclear. This chord symbol I believe rather compounds that problem!

- **miMa7(9)**, **miMa7(add9)** etc. as in the chord symbols **CmiMa7(9)**, **CmiMa7(add9)** etc. Again these suffixes are redundant - it is unnecessary to indicate that we are 'adding a 9th' to a minor major 7th chord. (Also as we saw in **Chapter 2**, the 'add9' suffix should only be used if the chord has no **6th** or **7th**).

So - when writing your minor major ninth chord symbols, use the '**miMa9**' suffix - but again **be prepared to recognize** the alternatives listed above!

Now we can finally summarize the definitive **II - V - I** chord choices available in minor, using the key of **C minor** for illustration as follows:-

### Figure 4.21. Summary of definitive II - V - I chord choices in the key of C minor

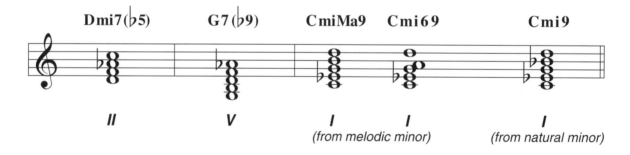

Note that where possible or appropriate, we have used **five-part** chord forms in the above examples. The previously analyzed **four-part** and/or **five-part** chord availability within the **II**, **V** and **I** in minor can be summarized as follows:-

- on the **II** chord (as shown in **Figs. 4.9. - 4.11.** and accompanying text) there are no useful **five-part** forms available from the minor scales - so we use the **four-part mi7(b5)** form.
- on the **V** chord (as shown in **Figs. 4.12. - 4.14.** and accompanying text) we need to go to the **five-part** form (i.e. **beyond** the **four-part** form) to derive the definitive **V** dominant chord in minor - so we use the **five-part 7(b9)** form.
- on the **I** chord (as shown in **Figs. 4.16. - 4.18.** and accompanying text) we have legitimate **four-part** and **five-part** alternatives from both the **melodic** and **natural** minor scales. The **five-part** forms (i.e. **miMa9**, **mi69** and **mi9**) are shown above.

### *Mixing the II - V - I progressions between major and minor keys*

We have now derived the definitive **II - V - I** progression in **major** keys (in *Chapter 2*) and in **minor** keys (in this chapter). What we will now see is that **II - V - I** progressions in major and minor keys are routinely **mixed together** in jazz applications. In other words, any of the **II**, **V** or **I** chords could come from either the **major** key or the **minor** key (built from the same tonic). The overall possibilities for this '**mixed II - V - I**' concept are shown in the following diagram, which summarizes all of the definitive **II**, **V** and **I** chords available within the keys of **C major** and **C minor**:-

#### *Figure 4.22. Overall summary of II - V - I chord choices in C major and C minor*

| MAJOR:- | Dmi7 | G7 | C6 | |
|---|---|---|---|---|
| | Dmi9 | G9 | Cma7 | |
| | | | C 69 | |
| | | | Cma9 | |
| | | | | |
| MINOR:- | Dmi7(♭5) | G7(♭9) | Cmi6 | Cmi7 |
| | | | CmiMa7 | Cmi9 |
| | | | Cmi69 | |
| | | | CmiMa9 | |

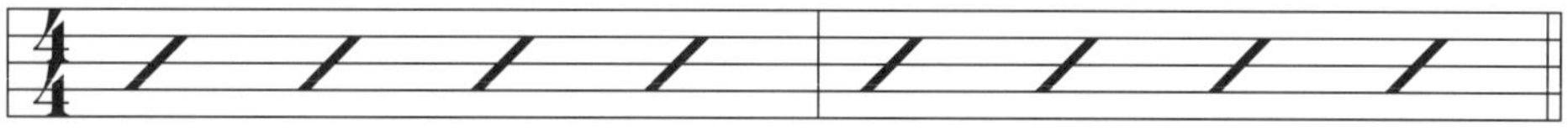

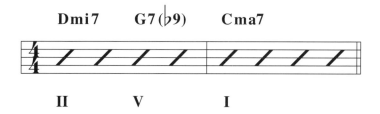

We will now look at some examples of this '**mixed II - V - I**' concept within progressions, beginning with the following example:-

#### *Figure 4.23. 'Mixed II - V - I' progression example #1*

Dmi7    G7(♭9)    Cma7

II    V    I

Following our normal 'harmonic analysis' method of looking at the **dominant** chord first, we note that it is a **dominant 7th with flatted 9th** chord. This tells us the chord is a **V in minor** (in this case **C minor**). To summarize - if the dominant chord has an **alteration** (which at this stage will be a '**flatted 9th**'), it will be a **V in minor**, otherwise it will be a **V in major**.

### *Mixing the II - V - I progressions between major and minor keys (contd)*

*(analysis of Fig. 4.23. contd)*

As we have a **V chord** in **C minor** in the progression at the bottom of the previous page, we might perhaps also expect the **II** and the **I** chord (either side of the **V** chord) to come from the key of **C minor**. However, we see that the **II** chord used is actually **Dmi7** from the key of **C major** - **not** the altered form **Dmi7(b5)** from the key of **C minor** (review the overall chord options in **Fig. 4.22.** as necessary). Similarly, the **I** chord used is **Cma7** which is a four-part **I** chord within the key of **C major**. We can therefore summarize this progression in **Fig. 4.23.** as follows:-

- the **Dmi7** used is a **II** chord in **C major**.
- the **G7(b9)** used is a **V** chord in **C minor**.
- the **Cma7** used is a **I** chord in **C major**.

Note that we have moved between **major** and **minor** keys during this progression - however the tonic (i.e. the note **C**) remains the same throughout. Now we will look at a second 'mixed **II - V - I**' example as follows:-

### *Figure 4.24. 'Mixed II - V - I' progression example #2*

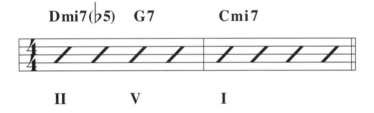

As with the previous example in **Fig. 4.23.**, we have again looked at the **dominant** chord first, we note that it is a regular **dominant 7th** (i.e. unaltered) which tells us the chord is a **V in major** (in this case **C major**). However, we see that the **II** chord used is actually **Dmi7(b5)** from the key of **C minor** - **not** the unaltered form **Dmi7** from the key of **C major** (again review the options in **Fig. 4.22.** as necessary). Similarly, the **I** chord used is **Cmi7** which is one of the four-part **I** chord options within the key of **C minor**. We can therefore summarize the above progression as follows:-

- the **Dmi7(b5)** used is a **II** chord in **C minor**.
- the **G7** used is a **V** chord in **C major**.
- the **Cmi7** used is a **I** chord in **C minor**.

As with the previous example in **Fig. 4.23.**, we have again moved between **major** and **minor** keys during this progression, with the overall tonic remaining the same throughout.

## *Mixing the II - V - I progressions between major and minor keys (contd)*

It is worth making the further point here that the availability of the **II - V - I** progression in minor (and in particular the use of the **minor 7th** and **minor 9th** forms as **I** or **tonic** chords in minor) will significantly increase the occurrence of **linking chords** i.e. 'plural' chords which belong to both the **preceding** and **following** momentary keys within a progression. (Review **p76** comments as necessary, concerning the use of **linking chords** within the progression shown in **Fig. 2.17.**). For example, in the progression shown in **Fig. 4.24.** on the previous page, the **Cmi7** chord (analyzed as a **I** in **C minor**) could be subsequently used as a **II** chord in **Bb major**, for example if the **Cmi7** was immediately followed by an **F7** (or **F9**) chord. This type of **linking chord** situation (i.e. where a **I** chord in the previous minor key is also a **II** chord in the following major key) is commonly used, as we will see in subsequent progression analysis examples.

## *More harmonic analysis - now using minor keys*

Following on from our work in *Chapter 3* on analyzing progressions in major keys, we will now incorporate the **II - V - I** progression in minor within the range of possibilities. At this point in our harmonic analysis, we therefore have the following chord options available:-

- The **II - V - I** progression in **major** keys (as derived in *Chapter 2*).
- **Plural substitutes** for the **II - V - I** progression in **major** keys (as derived in *Chapter 3*).
- The **II - V - I** progression in **minor** keys (as derived in this chapter).

The analysis method outlined for **major keys** in *Chapter 3* (**p70-71**) now needs to be amended to take **minor keys** into account, as follows:-

*1)*     **Look for the dominant chords first.** Now however the dominant chord can function as a **V** chord in either a **major** or **minor** key. As previously discussed, if the dominant chord contains an **alteration** (which will be a '**flatted 9th**' at this stage) then it will function as a **V in minor**, otherwise it will function as a **V in major**.

*2)*     Look to see if the dominant chord is **preceded by the II chord** from the same **major** or **minor** key, and/or **followed by the I chord** from the same **major** or **minor** key (resulting in a **II - V**, **V - I**, or **II - V - I** progression in the same **major** or **minor** key).

*3)*     If the dominant chord is a **V in major**, look to see if it is **preceded by the II chord** from the **minor** key built from the same tonic, and/or **followed by the I chord** from the **minor** key built from the same tonic (as in **Fig. 4.24.** on the previous page). If the dominant chord is a **V in minor**, look to see if it is **preceded by the II chord** from the **major** key built from the same tonic, and/or **followed by the I chord** from the **major** key built from the same tonic (as in **Fig. 4.23.**). These are examples of '**mixed II - V - I**' progressions.

### More harmonic analysis - now using minor keys (contd)

*(Harmonic analysis method contd)*

Subsequent stages in the analysis are for the moment similar to those used in **Chapter 3** when analyzing major key progressions:-

**4)** Again look for chords which are **diatonic to the key signature** (and will therefore function in that major key) - as previously discussed, this is helpful in detecting **momentary I** chords as well as non-definitive (i.e. triad) chord forms within the key.

**5)** Again any chord still remaining to be analyzed after the above steps, is likely to be one of the following:-

- **plural substitute** chords, in either:-
  - the **preceding** momentary (major) key within the progression, or
  - the **following** momentary (major) key within the progression.
- isolated **'momentary I'** (one) chords in a new momentary (major) key.
- 'passing' or embellishment chords.

We will now work through a series of progressions to apply these harmonic analysis principles, beginning with the following example:-

### Figure 4.25. Harmonic analysis progression example #1
*(this progression is typically used for the first eight measures of the jazz standard tune "My Romance")*

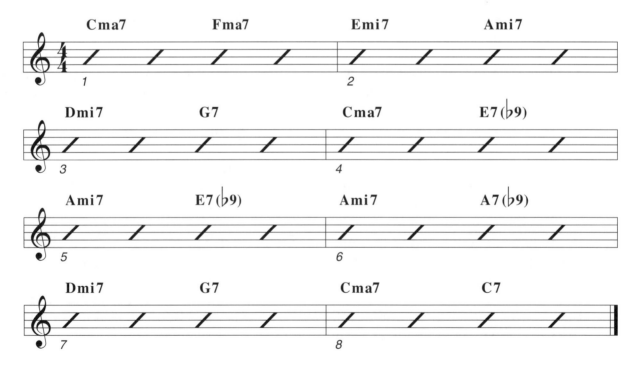

### *More harmonic analysis - now using minor keys (contd)*

We will now apply the method outlined on **p115-116** to the progression in example **#1** (**Fig. 4.25.**) as follows:-

**Stage 1**    We can analyze the dominant chords as follows:-

- The **G7** in measure **3** will be a **V** chord in the key of **C major** (corresponding to the key signature of the tune).
- The **E7(b9)** in measure **4** will be a **V** chord in the momentary key of **A minor**.
- The **E7(b9)** in measure **5** will again be a **V** chord in the momentary key of **A minor.**
- The **A7(b9)** in measure **6** will be a **V** chord in the momentary key of **D minor**.
- The **G7** in measure **7** will again be a **V** chord in the key of **C major** (corresponding to the key signature of the tune).
- The **C7** in measure **8** will be a **V** chord in the momentary key of **F major**.

**Stage 2**    We can analyze the chords preceding and following the above dominant chords to check for **II** or **I** chords functioning in the **same major or minor key**, as follows:-

- The **Dmi7** preceding the **G7** in measure **3** also functions in the key of **C major** (corresponding to the key signature of the tune), as a **II** chord.
- The **Cma7** following the **G7** (in measure **4**) also functions in the key of **C major** (corresponding to the key signature of the tune), as a **I** chord. In total we have a **II - V - I** progression in **C major**.
- The **Ami7** following the **E7(b9)** (in measure **5**) also functions in the momentary key of **A minor**, as a **I** chord. We have a **V - I** progression in **A minor**.
- Similarly, the **Ami7** following the **E7(b9)** (in measure **6**) also functions as a **I** chord in the momentary key of **A minor** - so again we have a **V - I** progression in **A minor**.
- The **Dmi7** following the **A7(b9)** (in measure **7**) also functions in the momentary key of **D minor**, as a **I** chord. We have a **V - I** progression in **D minor**. **However,** this **Dmi7** is also preceding the **G7** in measure **7** and therefore functions in the key of **C major** (corresponding to the key signature of the tune) as a **II** chord. This is another example of a '**linking**' chord i.e. the **Dmi7** functions in both the preceding and following keys (in this case as a **I** in **D minor** and as a **II** in **C major**).
- The **Cma7** following the **G7** (in measure **8**) also functions in the key of **C major** (corresponding to the key signature of the tune), as a **I** chord. Again we have a **II - V - I** progression in **C major**.

**Stage 3**    This is the stage where we see if any **V** chords in major are preceded or followed by **II** or **I** chords from the minor key built from the same tonic, and vice-versa (see comments at the bottom of **p115**). This situation does not occur in progression example **#1** on the previous page.

## *More harmonic analysis - now using minor keys (contd)*

**(Harmonic analysis of progression example #1 contd)**

**Stage 4**    We can analyze any remaining chords which are diatonic to the key signature as follows:-

- The **Cma7** in measure **1** will be a **I** chord in the key of **C** (corresponding to the key signature of the tune).
- The **Fma7** in measure **1** is also diatonic to the key signature - it is a **IV** chord in the key of **C** (and therefore could be considered as a **IV-for-II** substitution).
- The **Emi7** in measure **2** is also diatonic to the key signature - it is a **III** chord in the key of **C** (and therefore could be considered as a **III-for-I** substitution).
- The **Ami7** in measure **2** is also diatonic to the key signature - it is a **VI** chord in the key of **C** (and therefore could be considered as a **VI-for-I** substitution).

No further analysis stages are required, as we now have dealt with all of the chords within the progression. We can now summarize the analysis of this progression as follows:-

**Figure 4.26. Harmonic analysis completed for progression example #1**

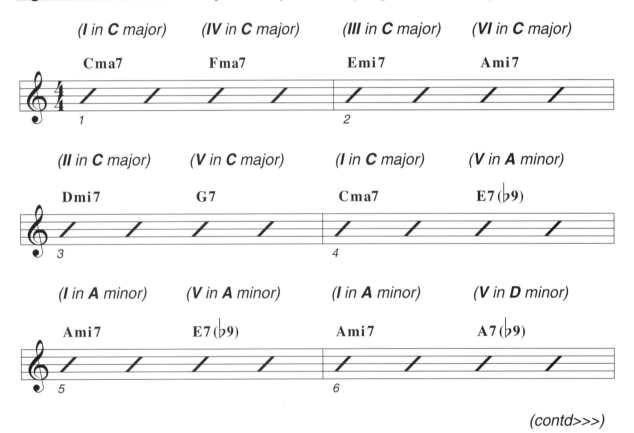

*(contd>>>)*

### More harmonic analysis - now using minor keys (contd)

**(*Figure 4.26. contd*)**

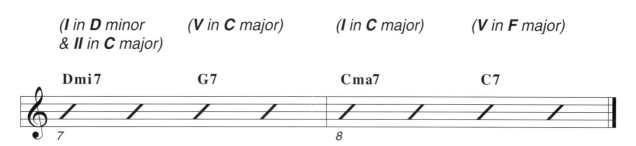

(*I* in *D* minor
& *II* in *C* major)     (*V* in *C* major)     (*I* in *C* major)     (*V* in *F* major)

Dmi7          G7          Cma7          C7

Note that even though technically the **Ami7** chords in measures **5** & **6** are **VI** chords with respect to the key signature (i.e. in the key of **C major**), they are primarily heard here as '**momentary I**' or tonic chords as a result of the preceding **E7(b9)** dominant chords used.

Now we will analyze the next harmonic progression example as follows:-

### Figure 4.27. Harmonic analysis progression example #2
*(this progression is typically used for the first sixteen measures
of the jazz standard tune "Fly Me To The Moon")*

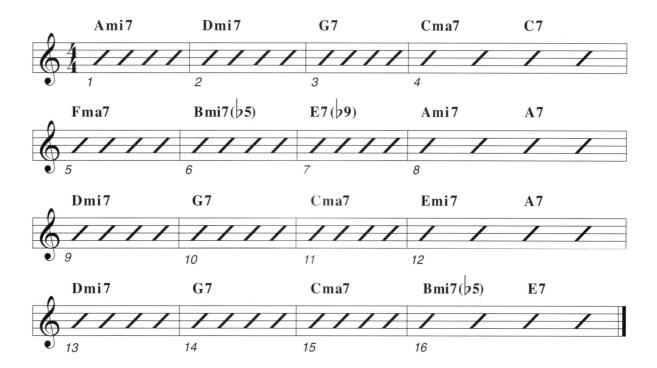

## *More harmonic analysis - now using minor keys (contd)*

Again we will apply the same analysis method to progression **#2** (shown on the previous page) as follows:-

**Stage 1**     We can analyze the dominant chords as follows:-

- The **G7** in measure **3** will be a **V** chord in the key of **C major** (corresponding to the key signature of the tune).
- The **C7** in measure **4** will be a **V** chord in the momentary key of **F major**.
- The **E7(b9)** in measure **7** will be a **V** chord in the momentary key of **A minor**.
- The **A7** in measure **8** will be a **V** chord in the momentary key of **D major**.
- The **G7** in measure **10** will again be a **V** chord in the key of **C major** (corresponding to the key signature of the tune).
- The **A7** in measure **12** will again be a **V** chord in the momentary key of **D major**.
- The **G7** in measure **14** will again be a **V** chord in the key of **C major** (corresponding to the key signature of the tune).
- The **E7** in measure **16** will be a **V** chord in the momentary key of **A major**.

**Stage 2**     We can analyze the chords preceding and following the above dominant chords to check for **II** or **I** chords functioning in the **same major or minor key**, as follows:-

- The **Dmi7** preceding the **G7** (in measure **2**) also functions in the key of **C major** (corresponding to the key signature of the tune), as a **II** chord.
- The **Cma7** following the **G7** (in measure **4**) also functions in the key of **C major** (corresponding to the key signature of the tune), as a **I** chord. In total we have a **II - V - I** progression in **C major**.
- The **Fma7** following the **C7** (in measure **5**) also functions in the momentary key of **F major**, as a **I** chord. We have a **V - I** progression in **F major**.
- The **Bmi7(b5)** preceding the **E7(b9)** (in measure **6**) also functions in the momentary key of **A minor**, as a **II** chord.
- The **Ami7** following the **E7(b9)** (in measure **8**) also functions in the momentary key of **A minor**, as a **I** chord. In total we have a **II - V - I** progression in **A minor**.
- The **Dmi7** preceding the **G7** (in measure **9**) also functions in the key of **C major** as a **II** chord. This chord will also function in a **'linking'** capacity, as we shall see in **Stage 3**.
- The **Cma7** following the **G7** (in measure **11**) also functions in the key of **C major** as a **I** chord. Again we have a **II - V - I** progression in **C major**.

*(contd>>>)*

## More harmonic analysis - now using minor keys (contd)

### (Harmonic analysis of progression example #2 contd)

**Stage 2** (contd)

- The **Emi7** preceding the **A7** in measure **12** also functions in the momentary key of **D major**, as a **II** chord. We have a **II - V** progression in **D major**. However, we note that this **Emi7** chord is also found in the preceding key of **C major** (as defined by the **II - V - I** progression in measures **9 - 11**), as a **III** chord. It could therefore be considered as a **III-for-I** substitution in the key of **C major**. This is therefore another example of a '**linking**' chord i.e. the **Emi7** functions in both the preceding and following keys (in this case as a **III** in **C major** and as a **II** in **D major**).
- The **Dmi7** preceding the **G7** (in measure **13**) also functions in the key of **C major** as a **II** chord. Again this chord will also function in a '**linking**' capacity, as we shall see in **Stage 3**.
- The **Cma7** following the **G7** (in measure **15**) also functions in the key of **C major** as a **I** chord. Again we have a **II - V - I** progression in **C major**.

**Stage 3**  We can now analyze the chords preceding and following the dominant chords to see if any **mixed** (i.e. between major and minor) **II - V**, **V - I**, or **II - V - I** progressions are being used, as follows:-

- We have established that the **A7** in measure **8** is functioning as a **V** in **D major**. The following **Dmi7** in measure **9**, although not functioning as a **I** in **D major**, does function as a **I** in **D minor**. We therefore have a **mixed V - I** progression here (i.e. using a **V** in **D major** and a **I** in **D minor**). The **Dmi7** in measure **9** could also therefore be considered as a '**linking**' chord, as we have already established that it is functioning as a **II** chord in the following key of **C major**.
- Similarly, we have established that the **Emi7 - A7** in measure **12** is functioning as a **II - V** in **D major**. Again the following **Dmi7** in measure **13** can function as a **I** in **D minor**, giving us a **mixed II - V - I** progression (i.e. using a **II - V** in **D major** and a **I** in **D minor**), and again the **Dmi7** is a '**linking**' chord to the following key of **C major**.
- We have established that the **E7** in measure **16** is functioning as a **V** in **A major**. The preceding **Bmi7(b5)** in measure **16**, although not functioning as a **II** in **A major**, does function as a **II** in **A minor**. We therefore have a **mixed II - V** progression here (i.e. using a **II** in **A minor** and a **V** in **A major**). The **Bmi7(b5)** could also be considered as a '**linking**' chord, as it is found in the preceding key of **C major** as a **VII** chord (and could therefore be considered as a **VII-for-V** substitution).

### More harmonic analysis - now using minor keys (contd)

**(Harmonic analysis of progression example #2 contd)**

**Stage 4**    We can analyze any remaining chords which are diatonic to the key signature as follows:-

-    The **Ami7** in measure **1** will be a **VI** chord in the key of **C** (and therefore could be considered as a **VI-for-I** substitution). An alternative interpretation for the first chord of this tune is to hear it as a momentary **I** chord in **A minor** (which of course is the relative minor of **C major**) - particularly if we repeat back from measure **16**, resulting in a mixed **V - I** progression.

No further analysis stages are required, as we now have dealt with all of the chords within the progression. We can now summarize the analysis of this progression as follows:-

*Figure 4.28. Harmonic analysis completed for progression example #2*

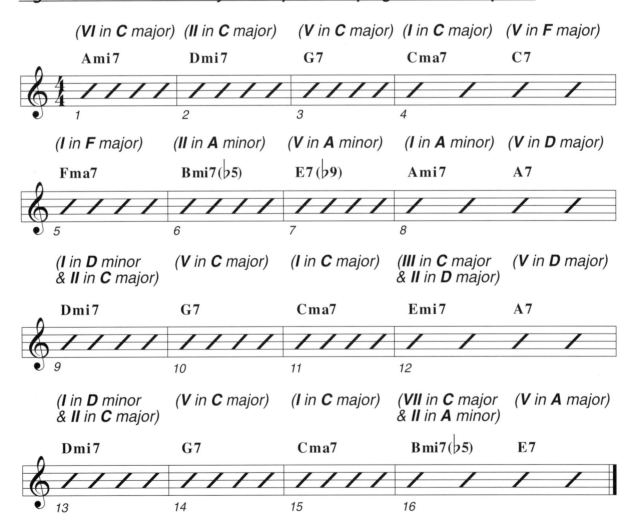

### More harmonic analysis - now using minor keys (contd)

Now we will analyze the final harmonic progression example in this chapter, as follows:-

**Figure 4.29. Harmonic analysis progression example #3**
*(this progression is typically used for the first seven measures
of the Beatles tune "Yesterday")*

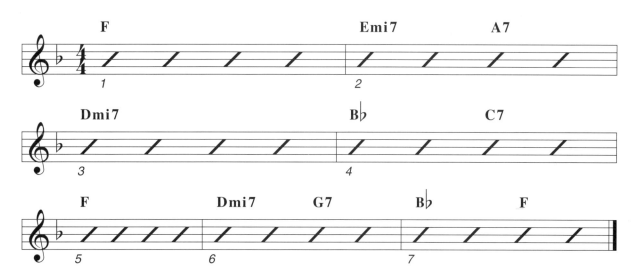

Note that this more **pop-oriented** progression mixes together **3-part** (triad) and **4-part** chord forms. Again we will apply the same analysis method to this progression as follows:-

**Stage 1**      We can analyze the dominant chords as follows:-

- The **A7** in measure **2** will be a **V** chord in the momentary key of **D major**.
- The **C7** in measure **4** will be a **V** chord in the key of **F major** (corresponding to the key signature of the tune).
- The **G7** in measure **6** will be a **V** chord in the momentary key of **C major**.

**Stage 2**      We can analyze the chords preceding and following the above dominant chords to check for **II** or **I** chords functioning in the **same major or minor key**, as follows:-

- The **Emi7** preceding the **A7** in measure **2** also functions in the momentary key of **D major**, as a **II** chord. We have a **II - V** progression in **D major**.
- The **F** chord following the **C7** (in measure **5**) also functions in the key of **F major** (corresponding to the key signature of the tune), as a triad form of the **I** chord. We have a **V - I** progression in **F major**.

*(contd>>>)*

**123**

## *More harmonic analysis - now using minor keys (contd)*

*(Harmonic analysis of progression example #3 contd)*

**Stage 2 (contd)**

- The **Dmi7** preceding the **G7** in measure **6** also functions in the momentary key of **C major**, as a **II** chord. We have a **II - V** progression in **C major**. However, we note that this **Dmi7** chord is also found in the preceding key of **F major**, as a **VI** chord. It could therefore be considered as a **VI-for-I** substitution in the key of **F major**. The **Dmi7** is therefore a '**linking**' chord (functioning as a **VI** in **F major** and as a **II** in **C major**).

**Stage 3**    We can now analyze the chords preceding and following the dominant chords to see if any **mixed (**i.e. between major and minor) **II - V**, **V - I**, or **II - V - I** progressions are being used, as follows:-

- We have established that the **A7** in measure **2** is functioning as a **V** in **D major**. The following **Dmi7** in measure **3**, although not functioning as a **I** in **D major**, does function as a **I** in **D minor**. We therefore have a **mixed V - I** progression here (i.e. using a **V** in **D major** and a **I** in **D minor**).

**Stage 4**    We can analyze any remaining chords which are diatonic to the key signature as follows:-

- The **F** chord in measure **1** is an 'incomplete' (i.e. triad form) **I** or tonic chord in the key of **F major**.
- The **Bb** chord in measure **4** is an 'incomplete' **IV** chord in the key of **F major** (and therefore could be considered as a **IV-for-II** substitution).
  *[It could consequently be argued that the preceding **Dmi7** in measure 3 is a '**linking**' chord, as in addition to functioning as a **I** in **D minor** it is also a **VI** chord (and potentially a **VI-for-I** substitution) in the following key of **F major**].*
- The **Bb** chord in measure **7** is again an 'incomplete' **IV** chord in the key of **F major** which could be considered as a **IV-for-II** substitution.
- The **F** chord in measure **7** is again an 'incomplete' **I** chord in the key of **F major**.

No further analysis stages are required, as we now have dealt with all of the chords within the progression. We can now summarize the analysis of this progression on the following page:-

### More harmonic analysis - now using minor keys (contd)

#### Figure 4.30. Harmonic analysis completed for progression example #3

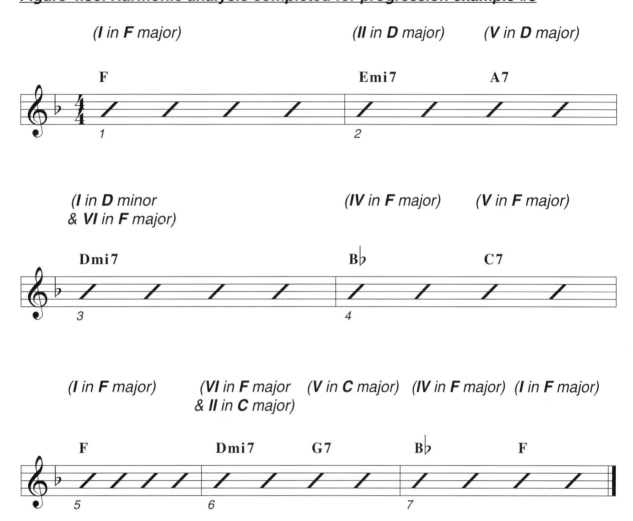

## Chapter Four Workbook Questions

**1.** **_Writing the IImi7(b5) chord in minor keys_**

You are to write the notes on the staff, and chord symbols above the staff, for the **_IImi7(b5)_** chord in the following minor keys:-

1. *Key of G minor*   2. *Key of Eb minor*   3. *Key of C minor*   4. *Key of Ab minor*

5. *Key of F# minor*   6. *Key of D minor*   7. *Key of Bb minor*   8. *Key of B minor*

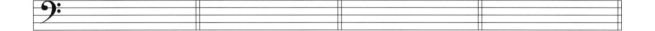

**2.** **_Writing the V7(b9) chord in minor keys_**

You are to write the notes on the staff, and chord symbols above the staff, for the **_V7(b9)_** chord in the following minor keys:-

9. *Key of A minor*   10. *Key of C minor*   11. *Key of F# minor*   12. *Key of Db minor*

13. *Key of Bb minor* 14. *Key of Eb minor* 15. *Key of G minor* 16. *Key of E minor*

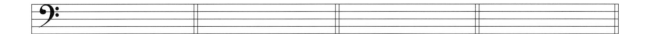

### 3. *Writing the Imi9 chord in minor keys*

You are to write the notes on the staff, and chord symbols above the staff, for the **Imi9** chord in the following minor keys:-

17. *Key of A minor*   18. *Key of Eb minor*   19. *Key of B minor*   20. *Key of G minor*

21. *Key of D minor*   22. *Key of Bb minor*   23. *Key of C minor*   24. *Key of F minor*

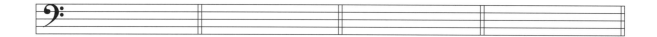

### 4. *Writing the Imi69 and ImiMa9 chord in minor keys*

You are to write the notes on the staff, and chord symbols above the staff, for the **Imi69** and **ImiMa9** chords in the following minor keys:-

25. *Key of E minor*   26. *Key of F# minor*   27. *Key of A minor*   28. *Key of Db minor*

29. *Key of C# minor*  30. *Key of D minor*   31. *Key of B minor*   32. *Key of G# minor*

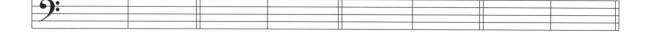

## 5. *Writing the II-V-I progression in minor keys*

You are to write the five-part chord voicings on the staff (with all necessary accidentals), and chord symbols above the staff, for the **II-V-I** progressions in the following minor keys.

For questions 33 - 36, you are to derive the **I** chord from the *natural minor scale* (i.e. use the *Imi9* form).

33.   *Key of **D** minor*          34.   *Key of **Bb** minor*

35.   *Key of **G** minor*          36.   *Key of **Ab** minor*

For questions 37 - 40, you are to write both forms of the **I** chord derived from the *melodic minor scale* (i.e. both the *Imi69* and *ImiMa9* forms).

37.   *Key of **C** minor*          38.   *Key of **F** minor*

39.   *Key of **Eb** minor*          40.   *Key of **B** minor*

### 6. Chord progression analysis

The following examples consist of 'pairs' of chords within a minor key. You are to write the key for each question, and the function (i.e. **II**, **V** or **I**) of each chord:-

41. Key of _____

Function _____      Function _____

Ebmi7(b5)        Ab7(b9)

42. Key of _____

Function _____      Function _____

Bmi7(b5)        E7(b9)

43. Key of _____

Function _____      Function _____

Ami7(b5)        D7(b9)

44. Key of _____

Function _____      Function _____

F#mi7(b5)        B7(b9)

45. Key of _____

Function _____      Function _____

C7(b9)        Fmi9

46. Key of _____

Function _____      Function _____

A7(b9)        Dmi7

47. Key of _____

Function _____      Function _____

Bb7(b9)        Ebmi69

48. Key of _____

Function _____      Function _____

G7(b9)        CmiMa9

## 6.    *Chord progression analysis (contd)*

The following examples consist of 'mixed' **II-V-I** progressions, in which any or all of the
**II**, **V** and **I** chords can come from either a major key or corresponding minor key. Note
that within each question, the 'tonic' note of the key remains the same - the only variable
is whether the key is *major* or *minor*. You are to write the key and function for each chord:-

49. *Key* _____   *Key* _____   *Key* _____       50. *Key* _____   *Key* _____   *Key* _____
    *Func* ___   *Func* ___   *Func* ___              *Func* ___   *Func* ___   *Func* ___

    Dmi7        G7(♭9)       Cma9                     Emi7(♭5)   A9          Dma9

51. *Key* _____   *Key* _____   *Key* _____       52. *Key* _____   *Key* _____   *Key* _____
    *Func* ___   *Func* ___   *Func* ___              *Func* ___   *Func* ___   *Func* ___

    B♭mi7       E♭7(♭9)      A♭69                     F♯mi7(♭5)   B7(♭9)      Ema7

53. *Key* _____   *Key* _____   *Key* _____       54. *Key* _____   *Key* _____   *Key* _____
    *Func* ___   *Func* ___   *Func* ___              *Func* ___   *Func* ___   *Func* ___

    Gmi7(♭5)   C9          Fmi69                      Ami7        D7(♭9)       Gma9

55. *Key* _____   *Key* _____   *Key* _____       56. *Key* _____   *Key* _____   *Key* _____
    *Func* ___   *Func* ___   *Func* ___              *Func* ___   *Func* ___   *Func* ___

    Bmi7        E7          Ami9                       Fmi7        B♭7(♭9)     E♭miMa9

### 6. *Chord progression analysis (contd)*

You are to determine the functions and keys for each chord in the following progressions, in a similar manner as for the previous sections. Where a 'linking' chord occurs (i.e. belonging to the preceding and following key centers) you are to indicate all applicable keys and functions. Write the functions and keys in the spaces provided below each progression:-

*Chord Progression #1*
*(typically used for the first 16 measures of the jazz standard "Stella By Starlight")*

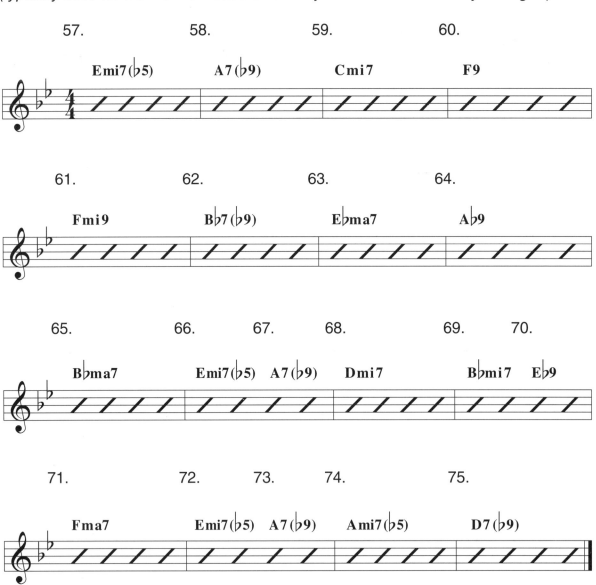

**6.**     ***Chord progression analysis (contd)***

*(Chord Progression #1 contd)*

Write your answers here:-

57. _____          58. _____

59. _____          60. _____

61. _____          62. _____

63. _____          64. _____

65. _____          66. _____

67. _____          68. _____

69. _____          70. _____

71. _____          72. _____

73. _____          74. _____

75. _____


*Chord Progression #2*
*(typically used for the first 16 measures of the jazz standard*
*"There Will Never Be Another You")*

76.                              77.              78.

79.                              80.              81.

*(progression continued on next page)>>*

**6.** *__Chord progression analysis (contd)__*

*(Chord Progression #2 contd)*

82.              83.      84.      85.           86.

87.              88.     89.     90.           91.

Write your answers here:-

76. _____       77. _____

78. _____       79. _____

80. _____       81. _____

82. _____       83. _____

84. _____       85. _____

86. _____       87. _____

88. _____       89. _____

90. _____       91. _____

*134*

**6.** *Chord progression analysis (contd)*

*Chord Progression #3*
*(typically used for the first 8 measures of the Beatles tune*
*"You Never Give Me Your Money")*

Write your answers here:-

92. _____        93. _____

94. _____        95. _____

96. _____        97. _____

98. _____        99. _____

**135**

--- NOTES ---

136

## Chapter Four Workbook Answers

### 1. Writing the IImi7(b5) chord in minor keys - answers

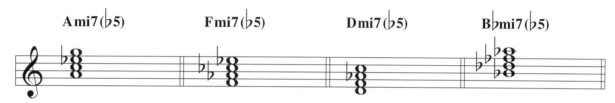

### 2. Writing the V7(b9) chord in minor keys - answers

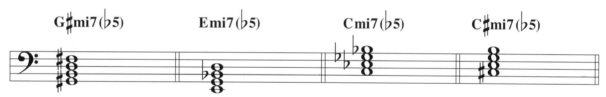

### 3. *Writing the Imi9 chord in minor keys - answers*

17. *Key of A minor*    18. *Key of Eb minor*   19. *Key of B minor*   20. *Key of G minor*

21. *Key of D minor*   22. *Key of Bb minor*   23. *Key of C minor*   24. *Key of F minor*

### 4. *Writing the Imi69 and ImiMa9 chord in minor keys - answers*

25. *Key of E minor*    26. *Key of F# minor*   27. *Key of A minor*   28. *Key of Db minor*

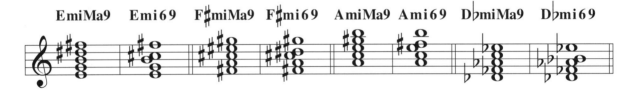

29. *Key of C# minor* 30. *Key of D minor* 31. *Key of B minor* 32. *Key of G# minor*

**5.** *Writing the II-V-I progression in minor keys - answers*

33. *Key of **D** minor*

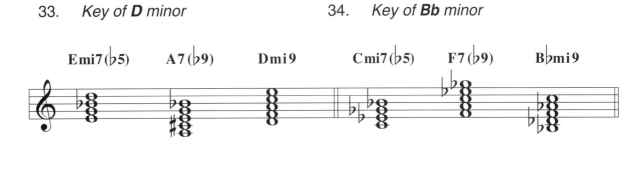

34. *Key of **Bb** minor*

35. *Key of **G** minor*

36. *Key of **Ab** minor*

37. *Key of **C** minor*

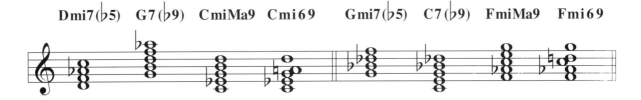

38. *Key of **F** minor*

39. *Key of **Eb** minor*

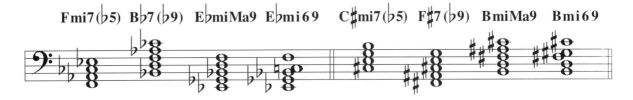

40. *Key of **B** minor*

**139**

## 6. *Chord progression analysis - answers*

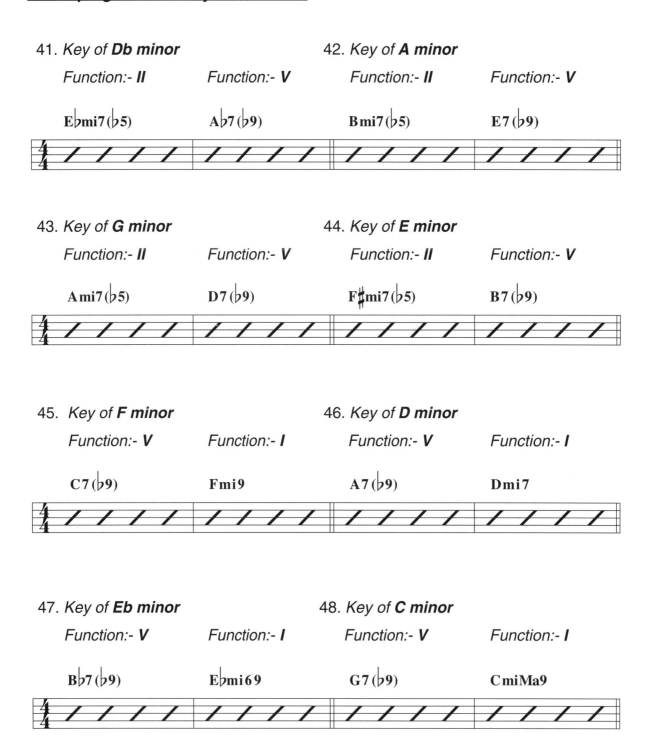

41. *Key of **Db minor***

Function:- *II*   Function:- *V*

E♭mi7(♭5)   A♭7(♭9)

42. *Key of **A minor***

Function:- *II*   Function:- *V*

Bmi7(♭5)   E7(♭9)

43. *Key of **G minor***

Function:- *II*   Function:- *V*

Ami7(♭5)   D7(♭9)

44. *Key of **E minor***

Function:- *II*   Function:- *V*

F♯mi7(♭5)   B7(♭9)

45. *Key of **F minor***

Function:- *V*   Function:- *I*

C7(♭9)   Fmi9

46. *Key of **D minor***

Function:- *V*   Function:- *I*

A7(♭9)   Dmi7

47. *Key of **Eb minor***

Function:- *V*   Function:- *I*

B♭7(♭9)   E♭mi6 9

48. *Key of **C minor***

Function:- *V*   Function:- *I*

G7(♭9)   CmiMa9

**6.** **_Chord progression analysis - answers (contd)_**

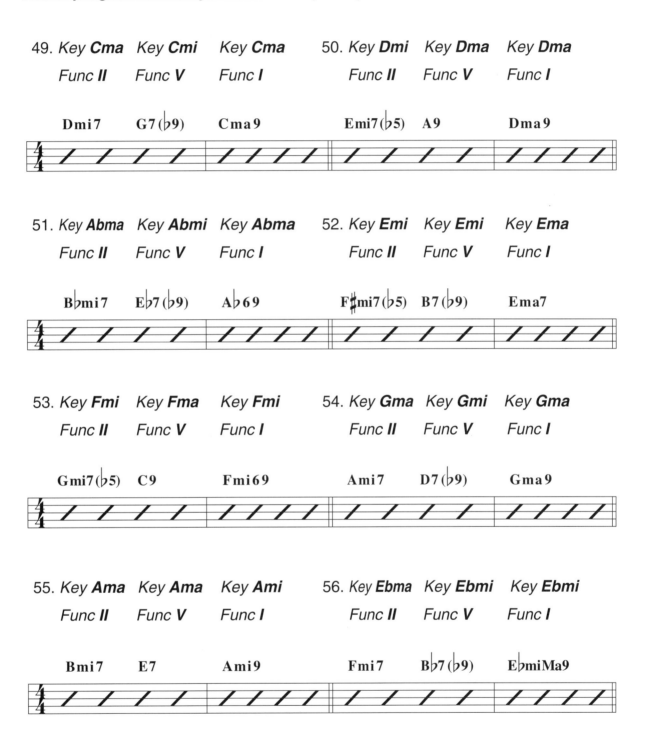

49. *Key **Cma***    *Key **Cmi***    *Key **Cma***
   *Func **II***    *Func **V***    *Func **I***

Dmi7    G7(♭9)    Cma9

50. *Key **Dmi***    *Key **Dma***    *Key **Dma***
   *Func **II***    *Func **V***    *Func **I***

Emi7(♭5)    A9    Dma9

51. *Key **Abma***    *Key **Abmi***    *Key **Abma***
   *Func **II***    *Func **V***    *Func **I***

B♭mi7    E♭7(♭9)    A♭69

52. *Key **Emi***    *Key **Emi***    *Key **Ema***
   *Func **II***    *Func **V***    *Func **I***

F♯mi7(♭5)    B7(♭9)    Ema7

53. *Key **Fmi***    *Key **Fma***    *Key **Fmi***
   *Func **II***    *Func **V***    *Func **I***

Gmi7(♭5)    C9    Fmi69

54. *Key **Gma***    *Key **Gmi***    *Key **Gma***
   *Func **II***    *Func **V***    *Func **I***

Ami7    D7(♭9)    Gma9

55. *Key **Ama***    *Key **Ama***    *Key **Ami***
   *Func **II***    *Func **V***    *Func **I***

Bmi7    E7    Ami9

56. *Key **Ebma***    *Key **Ebmi***    *Key **Ebmi***
   *Func **II***    *Func **V***    *Func **I***

Fmi7    B♭7(♭9)    E♭miMa9

*141*

### 6.    *Chord progression analysis (contd)*

*(Chord Progression #1)*

| | | | |
|---|---|---|---|
| 57. | *II in D minor* | 58. | *V in D minor* |
| 59. | *II in Bb major* | 60. | *V in Bb major* |
| 61. | *II in Eb major* | 62. | *V in Eb minor* |
| 63. | *I in Eb major* | 64. | *V in Db major* |
| 65. | *I in Bb major* | 66. | *II in D minor* |
| 67. | *V in D minor* | 68. | *I in D minor* |
| 69. | *II in Ab major* | 70. | *V in Ab major* |
| 71. | *I in F major* | 72. | *VII in F major, II in D minor* |
| 73. | *V in D minor* | 74. | *II in G minor* |
| 75. | *V in G minor* | | |

*(Chord Progression #2)*

| | | | |
|---|---|---|---|
| 76. | *I in Eb major* | 77. | *II in C minor* |
| 78. | *V in C minor* | 79. | *I in C minor, III in Ab major* |
| 80. | *II in Ab major* | 81. | *V in Ab major* |
| 82. | *I in Ab major* | 83. | *II in Eb minor* |
| 84. | *V in Eb minor* | 85. | *I in Eb major* |
| 86. | *VI in Eb major, II in Bb major* | 87. | *V in Bb major* |
| 88. | *II in Bb major* | 89. | *V in Bb major* |
| 90. | *II in Eb major* | 91. | *V in Eb major* |

*(Chord Progression #3)*

| | | | |
|---|---|---|---|
| 92. | *VI in Bb major* | 93. | *II in Bb major* |
| 94. | *V in Bb major* | 95. | *I in Bb major* |
| 96. | *IV in Bb major* | 97. | *II in G minor* |
| 98. | *V in G major* | 99. | *I in G minor* |

# Plural substitute chords and harmonic analysis in minor keys

## Introduction

In this chapter we will determine the **plural substitute** chords which may be used instead of either the **II**, the **V** or the **I** chord in a **minor** key. This can be considered a parallel process to the derivation of plural substitutes in major keys, which was presented in **Chapter 3**. However, we recall that when deriving the **II - V - I** progression in **minor** keys (in **Chapter 4**), there were important differences between this and the corresponding **II - V - I** in **major** keys (as seen in **Chapter 2**). Significant among these differences (from the perspective of deriving substitute chords in minor keys) are:-

- while we were able to reduce the various options for the **II** and **V** chords in minor down to one basic definitive choice - i.e. the **IImi7(b5)** and the **V7(b9)**, we still have different choices for the **I** chord in minor depending on the desired scale source - i.e. the **Imi6**, **ImiMa7**, **Imi69** & **ImiMa9** from **melodic** minor, and the **Imi7** & **Imi9** from **natural** minor.
- the addition of the important **LE to SO** resolution within minor keys, which we would expect to be available between active (i.e. the **II** and/or the **V**) and resting (i.e. the **I** or tonic) chords in minor.

Once we have derived the **substitute** chords in minor keys, we will then incorporate these new relationships into our **harmonic analysis** of chord progressions. We will also see how both **definitive** and **substitute** chords from **major** and **minor** keys can all be mixed together to create many more variations of the **II - V - I** progression. This will then complete our work in this book concerning the types of progressions most typically found in **jazz** and **standard** tunes.

## Plural substitute chords for the II - V - I in minor

We will now establish the criteria for chords which can **substitute** for the **II**, **V** and **I** chords in a minor key. In order to preserve the main 'harmonic sense' or intent of the progression, these substitutions will need to possess the following characteristics:-

- the substitute chord(s) will need to have substantial **plurality** (i.e. notes in common) with the definitive chord being substituted.
- the substitute chord(s) will need similar **active/resting qualities** to the definitive chord being substituted.

(These criteria correspond to the characteristics for substitutes in major keys - review **Chapter 3** as required).

*143*

### Plural substitute chords for the II - V - I in minor (contd)

First of all we will review the **active-to-resting** resolutions occurring in minor keys (first derived in *Chapter 4*) as follows:-

### Figure 5.1. Active-to-resting resolutions in minor (with DO assigned to C)

(DO)          FA------>ME          LE------>SO          TI------->DO

We will also review the definitive **II - V - I** chords in minor (again derived in *Chapter 4*) as follows:-

### Figure 5.2. Summary of definitive II - V - I chord choices in the key of C minor

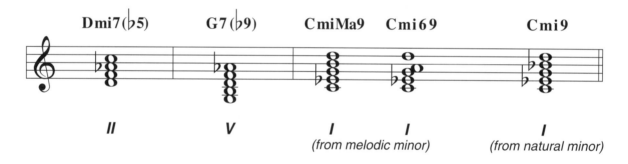

In reviewing the above active-to-resting resolutions and **II - V - I** chords in minor, we can now make the following conclusions regarding the active and/or resting qualities required for the substitute chords in minor keys:-

- The **II** chord (in this case **Dmi7(b5)**) has the critical active tones **FA** and **LE**, which will ultimately resolve to **ME** and **SO** respectively. (Also the resting tone **DO** on the **II** chord will generally move to the active tone **TI** on the **V** chord, in a similar manner as for major keys). Therefore in order to preserve the 'harmonic sense' of the progression, **any diatonic substitution for the II chord in minor should contain the active tones FA and LE** (and the resting tone **DO**).
- The **V** chord (in this case **G7(b9)**) also has the active tones **FA** and **LE**, as well as the active tone **TI** which as we have seen is essential for the 'dominant quality' of the chord. Therefore **any diatonic substitution for the V chord in minor should contain the active tones FA, LE and TI.**

*(contd>>>)*

### Plural substitute chords for the II - V - I in minor (contd)

- The various **I** or tonic chords in minor, all contain the critical definitive tone **ME**, which our ear needs to distinguish the tonic chord in minor from the corresponding chord in major. Therefore **any diatonic substitution for the I chord in minor should contain the definitive** (resting) **tone ME**. We recall that different choices exist for the **I** chord in minor (i.e. from either the melodic or natural minor scales), and we will additionally see that substitutes for these **I** or tonic chords will use the same scale source as the chord being substituted.

We will begin by looking at the **II** chord in the key of **C minor** - i.e. **Dmi7(b5)**, as first derived in **Figs. 4.9. - 4.11.** and accompanying text. If we rearrange (or invert) the four notes in this chord, an **Fmi6** chord is created as shown in the following example:-

### Figure 5.3. Creating an Fmi6 chord by inverting the four notes of a Dmi7(b5) chord

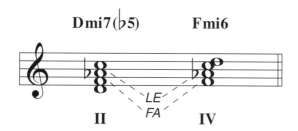

*(The solfeg shown is with respect to the key of C - the note F is 'FA', and the note Ab is 'LE', in this key).*

(Review as necessary the structure of the **minor 6th** chord in **Fig. 1.28.**) In comparing the **Fmi6** chord to the **Dmi7(b5)** chord, we can observe the following:-

- There is of course complete **plurality** between the two chords.
- The critical active tones **FA** and **LE** are shared by both chords (as indicated above).

As a result of this, we can conclude that **the IVmi6 chord can substitute for the IImi7(b5) chord in a minor key**. For example, we could take the following **II - V - I** progression in the key of **D minor**:-

### Figure 5.4. II - V - I progression in the key of D minor

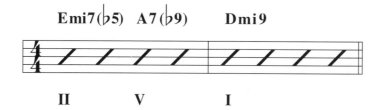

and substitute the **IVmi6** chord for the **IImi7(b5)** chord as shown on the following page:-

## *Plural substitute chords for the II - V - I in minor (contd)*

### *Figure 5.5. IV - V - I progression in the key of D minor (with IV-for-II substitution)*

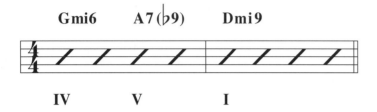

All melody notes which work over the original **IImi7(b5)** chord - **Emi7(b5)** in the example at the bottom of the previous page - will also work over the substitute **IVmi6** chord (**Gmi6** in the above example).

Next we will look at the **V** chord in the key of **C minor** - i.e. **G7(b9)**, as first derived in **Figs. 4.12. - 4.14.** and accompanying text. If we take the top four notes of this chord (i.e. the **3rd**, **5th**, **7th** and **9th**), we create a new chord known as a **diminished seventh** chord (in this case a **B diminished 7th**):-

### *Figure 5.6. Creating a Bdim7 chord by taking the top four notes of a G7(b9) chord*

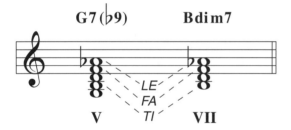

*(Again the solfeg shown is with respect to the key of **C** - the note **B** is 'TI', the note **F** is '**FA**', and the note **Ab** is '**LE**', in this key).*

The chord 'stack' and interval construction of this new **diminished 7th** chord can be shown as follows:-

### *Figure 5.7. B diminished 7th chord 'stack' and interval construction*

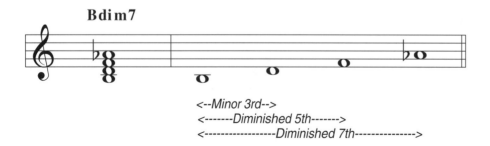

### *Plural substitute chords for the II - V - I in minor (contd)*

Note the chord symbol used for the **B diminished 7th** chord i.e. **Bdim7**. The suffix 'dim7' indicates a **diminished 7th** chord built from the root i.e. in this case a **B diminished 7th** chord. The suffix '**°7**' (i.e. as in the chord symbol **B°7**) is also a commonly-used and correct alternative for this chord.

In comparing the **Bdim7** chord to the original **G7(b9)** chord (as shown in **Fig. 5.6.** on the previous page), we can observe the following:-

- There is significant **plurality** between the two chords (again four notes in common).
- The critical active tones **TI**, **FA** and **LE** are shared by both chords.

As a result of this, we can conclude that **the VIIdim7 chord can substitute for the V7(b9) chord in a minor key**. For example, we can take the following **II - V - I** progression in the key of **E minor**:-

### *Figure 5.8. II - V - I progression in the key of E minor*

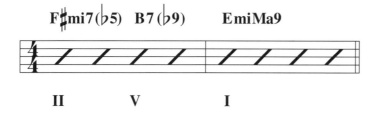

and substitute the **VIIdim7** chord for the **V7(b9)** chord as follows:-

### *Figure 5.9. II - VII - I progression in the key of E minor (with VII-for-V substitution)*

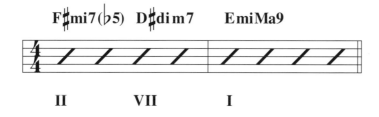

All melody notes which work over the original **V7(b9)** chord - **B7(b9)** in this example - will also work over the substitute **VIIdim7** chord (**D#dim7** in this example).

### Plural substitute chords for the II - V - I in minor (contd)

Next we will take the **minor ninth** form of the **I** chord in the key of **C minor** (i.e. **Cmi9**, as first derived in **Fig. 4.18.** from the **natural minor** scale). If we take the top four notes (i.e. the **3rd**, **5th**, **7th** and **9th**) of this chord, an **Ebma7** chord is created as follows:-

### Figure 5.10. Creating an Ebma7 chord by taking the top four notes of a Cmi9 chord

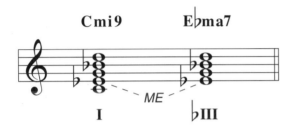

*(Again the solfeg shown is with respect to the key of C - the note Eb is 'ME' in this key).*

In comparing this **Ebma7** chord to the **Cmi9** chord, we can observe the following:-

- There is significant **plurality** between the two chords (again four notes in common).
- The critical definitive (resting) tone **ME** is shared by both chords (as indicated above).

As a result of this, we can conclude that **the bIIIma7 chord can substitute for the Imi9 chord** (derived from the natural minor scale), **in a minor key**. As noted on **p109**, the natural minor-based **I** chord in minor contains '**TE**' (**Bb** in this key), which distinguishes it from the melodic minor-based **I** chords - we see that the above **Ebma7** chord also contains '**TE**'.

As an example of this substitution, we can take the following **II - V - I** progression in the key of **Ab minor**:-

### Figure 5.11. II - V - I progression in the key of Ab minor

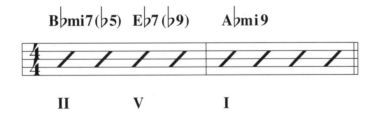

and substitute the **bIIIma7** chord for the **Imi9** chord as shown on the following page:-

### *Plural substitute chords for the II - V - I in minor (contd)*

#### *Figure 5.12. II - V - bIII progression in the key of Ab minor (with bIII-for-I substitution)*

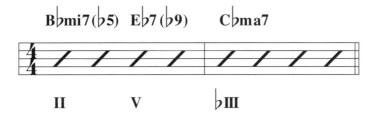

All melody notes which work over the original **I** chord in minor (**Abmi9** in the example at the bottom of the previous page) will also work over the substitute **bIII** chord (**Cbma7** in the above example). Subject to style considerations, all common forms of the **bIII** major chord (i.c. **Cb**, **Cb6**, **Cbma7**, **Cb69**, **Cbma9** in this case) will substitute for the **natural minor**-based **I** or tonic chords in minor (i.e. **Abmi7** and **Abmi9** in this case).

Next we will take the **minor sixth** form of the **I** chord in the key of **C minor** (i.e. **Cmi6**, as first derived in **Fig. 4.16.** from the **melodic minor** scale). If we rearrange (or invert) the four notes in this chord, an **Ami7(b5)** chord is created as shown in the following example:-

#### *Figure 5.13. Creating an Ami7(b5) chord by inverting the four notes of a Cmi6 chord*

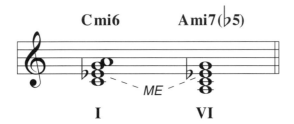

*(Again the solfeg shown is with respect to the key of **C** - the note **Eb** is 'ME' in this key).*

In comparing the **Ami7(b5)** chord to the **Cmi6** chord, we can observe the following:-

- There is of course complete **plurality** between the two chords.
- The critical definitive (resting) tone **ME** is shared by both chords (as indicated above).

As a result of this, we can conclude that **the VImi7(b5) chord can substitute for the Imi6 chord** (derived from the melodic minor scale)**, in a minor key**. As noted on **p109**, the melodic minor-based **I** chords in minor contain the functionally interchangeable tones 'LA' or 'TI' (**A** or **B** in this key), which distinguishes them from the natural minor-based **I** chords - we see that the above **Cmi6** and **Ami7(b5)** chords contain 'LA'.

## *Plural substitute chords for the II - V - I in minor (contd)*

As an example of this **VI-for-I** substitution in minor, we can take the following **II - V - I** progression in the key of **F minor**:-

### *Figure 5.14. II - V - I progression in the key of F minor*

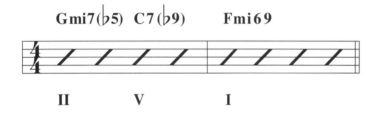

and substitute the **VImi7(b5)** chord for the **Imi69** chord as follows:-

### *Figure 5.15. II - V - VI progression in the key of F minor (with VI-for-I substitution)*

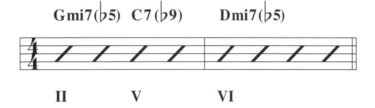

All melody notes which work over the original **I** chord in minor (**Fmi69** in the above example) will also work over the substitute **VI** chord - **Dmi7(b5)** in the above example. This **VI-for-I** substitution will work for all **melodic minor**-based **I** or **tonic** chords in minor (i.e. **Fmi6**, **FmiMa7**, **Fmi69** and **FmiMa9** in the above example).

Now we will take a closer look at the types of **IV** chord available in a minor key. We have already seen in **Fig. 5.3.** that the **IVmi6** chord can substitute for the **IImi7(b5)** chord in minor. However it is also possible to derive the **IVmi7** and **IVmi9** chords in a minor key, for example from the natural minor scale as follows:-

### *Figure 5.16. Fmi7 & Fmi9 chords built from the 4th degree of the C natural minor scale*

### *Plural substitute chords for the II - V - I in minor (contd)*

How then do these new **IVmi7** and **IVmi9** chords fit into our structure of 'definitive' and 'substitute' chords in minor? Well, we might at first be tempted to use these chords as additional substitutes for the **IImi7(b5)** chord - however, I do not feel that this is functionally correct from a solfeg standpoint. The problem here is that '**ME**' (**Eb** in the key of **C minor**) is present in the **IVmi7** and **IVmi9** chords - while we know that **ME** is a critical definitive note within the **I** or tonic chord in minor (see **p103** & **p145** comments), it would **not be available** on the **II** chord in minor (as we saw in **Figs. 4.9. - 4.11.**). Consequently the use of **ME** (on the **IVmi7** and **IVmi9** chords) imparts a harmonic 'sense' or implication which is different from the **IImi7(b5)** chord, and so these chords would **not** be considered as substitutes for the **II** chord in minor.

However, these chords are clearly available within a minor key, and if we do not consider them as substitute chords, we might then (by default) consider them to be **new definitive IV chords in minor**. If we then look at the **minor ninth** form of the **IV** chord in the key of **C minor** (i.e. **Fmi9**, as shown in **Fig. 5.16.** on the previous page) and take the top four notes (i.e. the **3rd**, **5th**, **7th** and **9th**) of this chord, an **Abma7** chord can now be created as follows:-

### *Figure 5.17. Creating an Abma7 chord by taking the top four notes of an Fmi9 chord*

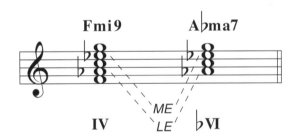

*(Again the solfeg shown is with respect to the key of C - the note Ab is 'LE', and the note Eb is 'ME', in this key).*

Both of these **IVmi9** and **bVIma7** chords share some interesting solfeg (i.e. active/resting) characteristics. The presence of **LE** ensures that both chords have an active quality, however **ME** is also included which as we have seen is very definitive of minor.

In comparing the above **Abma7** chord to the **Fmi9** chord, we observe the following:-

-        There is significant **plurality** between the two chords (again four notes in common).
-        The definitive tones **LE** and **ME** are shared by both chords (as indicated above).

As a result of this (and making the assumption that the **IVmi9** is by default a 'definitive' chord in its own right) we can conclude that **the bVIma7 chord can substitute for the IVmi9 chord in a minor key**. Note that this **bVI-for-IV** substitute relationship in minor (shown in **Fig. 5.17.** above) is structurally similar to the **bIII-for-I** substitute relationship (first seen in **Fig. 5.10.**).

## *Plural substitute chords for the II - V - I in minor (contd)*

As an example of this (**bVI-for-IV**) substitution, we can take the following **IV**(mi9) **- V - I** progression in the key of **C minor**:-

### *Figure 5.18. IV - V - I progression in the key of C minor*

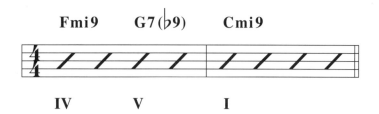

*(Again note that the **IVmi9** chord is **not** a substitute for a **II** chord in minor - we are considering it as a **definitve IV** chord in its own right).*

and substitute the **bVIma7** chord for the **IVmi9** chord as follows:-

### *Figure 5.19. bVI - V - I progression in the key of C minor (with bVI-for-IV substitution)*

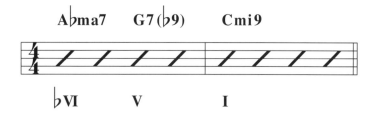

All melody notes which work over the original **IVmi9** chord in minor (**Fmi9** in the example at the top of this page) will also work over the substitute **bVIma7** chord (**Abma7** in the above example). Subject to style considerations, all common forms of the **bVI** major chord (i.e. **Ab, Ab6, Abma7, Ab69, Abma9** in this case) will substitute for the **IVmi7** and **IVmi9** chords in minor (i.e. **Fmi7** and **Fmi9** in this case).

We might also be tempted to think that these new **IV**(mi7 & mi9) and **bVI**(ma7) chords might be used as substitutes for the **I** or tonic chord in minor. The root, 3rd and 5th of all of the **I** chords in minor (**DO, ME** and **SO**, which in the key of **C minor** are the notes **C, Eb** and **G**) are present in the **IV**(mi7 & mi9) and **bVI**(ma7) chords, so clearly there is a lot of 'plurality' between these chords and the various **I** chords in minor. However, we recall that the other main criteria for a chord to be a suitable substitute, was that it should share the same **active** and/or **resting characteristics** as the chord being substituted. In this case, the **IV**(mi7 & mi9) and **bVI**(ma7) chords contain the very active tone **LE** (**Ab** in the key of **C minor**), which prevent these chords from being functionally suitable substitutes for the **I** chord in minor - all of the **I** chords (and their substitutes as derived in this chapter) contain the resting tone **SO**, which is the destination to which the active tone **LE** normally resolves.

## Plural substitute chords for the II - V - I in minor (contd)

We can now summarize these plural substitute relationships in minor keys, as follows:-

- The **IVmi6** chord can substitute for the **IImi7(b5)** chord (as in **Fig. 5.3.**).
- The **VIIdim7** chord can substitute for the **V7(b9)** chord (as in **Fig. 5.6.**).
- The **bIIIma7** chord can substitute for the **natural minor**-based forms of the I chord (for example the **Imi9**, as in **Fig. 5.10.**).
- The **VImi7(b5)** chord can substitute for the **melodic minor**-based forms of the I chord (for example the **Imi6**, as in **Fig. 5.13.**).
- The **bVIma7** chord can substitute for the **IVmi9** (and **IVmi7**) chord (as in **Fig. 5.17.**).

We can now summarize all of the definitive and substitute chords relating to the **II - V - I** progression in the keys of **C major** and **C minor**, as follows:-

*Figure 5.20. Summary of all definitive (II - V - I) and substitute chords in the keys of C major and C minor*

| MAJOR:- | Dmi7 | G7 | C6 | |
|---|---|---|---|---|
| | Dmi9 | G9 | Cma7 | |
| | | | C69 | |
| | | | Cma9 | |
| Subs:- | F6 | Bmi7(b5) | Emi7 | |
| | Fma7 | | Ami7 | |
| | F69 | | Ami9 | |
| | Fma9 | | | |
| MINOR:- | Dmi7(b5) | G7(b9) | Cmi6 | Cmi7 |
| | | | CmiMa7 | Cmi9 |
| | | | Cmi69 | |
| | | | CmiMa9 | |
| Subs:- | Fmi6 | Bdim7 | Ami7(b5) | Eb6 |
| | | | | Ebma7 |
| | | | | Eb69 |
| | | | | Ebma9 |

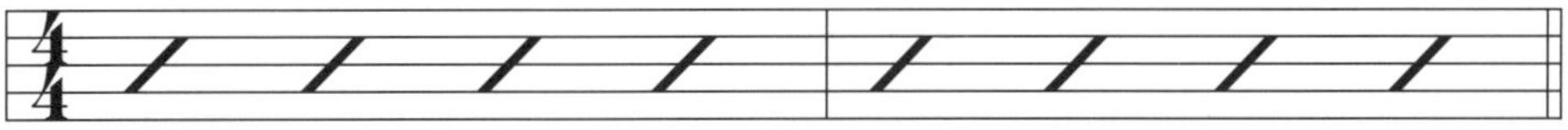

II     V     I

### *Mixing the II - V - I chords and substitutes from major and minor keys*

We have already seen in *Chapter 4* that it is common in jazz and standard tunes for **II - V - I** progressions to be 'mixed' between major and minor keys (review **Figs. 4.23. - 4.24.** as necessary). Now we can add the plural substitutes in both major and minor keys to this overall picture - in other words all of the chords shown in **Fig. 5.20.** on the previous page, could (subject to melodic and stylistic considerations) be mixed together within a given progression.

We will now look at some examples of this '**mixed II - V - I with substitutes**' concept within progressions, beginning with the following example:-

*Figure 5.21. 'Mixed II - V - I with substitutes' progression example #1*

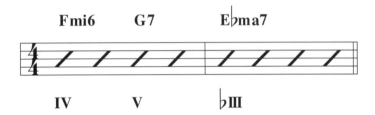

Following our normal 'harmonic analysis' method of looking at the **dominant** chord first, we note that it is a regular **dominant 7th** (i.e. unaltered) which tells us the chord is a **V in major** (in this case **C major**). We might therefore expect to see a **II** chord in either **C major** or **C minor** - i.e. a **Dmi7** or **Dmi7(b5)** - before the **G7** chord. However, instead we see the **IVmi6** chord which we note is a substitution for the **IImi7(b5)** chord in minor (as first seen in **Fig. 5.3.**). Similarly, we might expect to see one of the various forms of **I** or tonic chord in either **C major** or **C minor**, after the **G7** chord. However, instead we see the **bIIIma7** chord which we note is a substitution for the **Imi9** chord in minor (as first seen in **Fig. 5.10.**). We can therefore summarize the above progression as follows:-

- the **Fmi6** used is a substitute **IV-for-II** chord in **C minor**.
- the **G7** used is a definitive **V** chord in **C major**.
- the **Ebma7** used is a substitute **bIII-for-I** chord in **C minor**.

Now we will look at a second '**mixed II - V - I with substitutes**' example as follows:-

*Figure 5.22. 'Mixed II - V - I with substitutes' progression example #2*

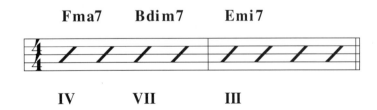

# Plural substitute chords and harmonic analysis in minor keys

## Mixing the II - V - I chords and substitutes from major and minor keys (contd)

Analyzing the progression at the bottom of the previous page, we see that there is no dominant chord present - however, we do have a **VIIdim7** which we note is a substitute for the **V7(b9)** in minor (as first seen in **Fig. 5.6.**). Again we can then look for **either** a **II** chord **or** a suitable substitute (in the keys of **C major** or **C minor**) before the **Bdim7** chord. We see the **IVma7** chord which we note is a substitution for the **IImi7** chord in major (as first seen in **Fig. 3.2.**). Similarly, we can then look for **either** a **I** chord **or** a suitable substitute (in the keys of **C major** or **C minor**) after the **Bdim7** chord. We see the **IIImi7** chord which we note is a substitution for the **Ima9** chord in major (as first seen in **Fig. 3.8.**). We can therefore summarize the above progression as follows:-

-     the **Fma7** used is a substitute **IV-for-II** chord in **C major**.
-     the **Bdim7** used is a substitute **VII-for-V** chord in **C minor**.
-     the **Emi7** used is a substitute **III-for-I** chord in **C major**.

## Chord plurality between major and minor keys

Now with the full range of definitive and substitute chords available in major and minor keys, we have significantly increased the possibilities for '**linking**' chords, which we recall were chords which 'belonged' to both the preceding and following momentary key within a progression. This is a consequence of having an increased number of chords which are found within more than one major or minor key. It would be useful at this point to summarize these '**plural**' chord options, as follows:-

-     the **major 7th** chord has been found to function as:-
    -     a **I** or tonic chord in **major** (as in **Fig. 2.10.**) i.e. **Cma7** is a **I** chord in the key of **C major**.
    -     a **IV-for-II** substitute in major (as in **Fig. 3.2.**) i.e. the same **Cma7** is also a **IV** chord in the key of **G major**.
    -     a **bIII-for-I** substitute in minor (as in **Fig. 5.10.**) i.e. the same **Cma7** is also a **bIII** chord in the key of **A minor**.
    -     a **bVI-for-IV** substitute in minor (as in **Fig. 5.17.**) i.e. the same **Cma7** is also a **bVI** chord in the key of **E minor**.

-     the **minor 7th** chord has been found to function as:-
    -     a **II** chord in **major** (as in **Fig. 2.10.**) i.e. **Dmi7** is a **II** chord in the key of **C major**.
    -     a **III-for-I** substitute in major (as in **Fig. 3.8.**) i.e. the same **Dmi7** is also a **III** chord in the key of **Bb major**.

*(contd on following page>>>)*

## *Chord plurality between major and minor keys (contd)*

*(Analysis of the minor 7th chord contd)*

- a **VI-for-I** substitute in **major** (as in **Fig. 3.11.**) i.e. the same **Dmi7** is also a **VI** chord in the key of **F major**.
- a **I** or tonic chord in **minor** (as in **Fig. 4.18.**) i.e. the same **Dmi7** is also a **I** chord in the key of **D minor**.
- a **IV** chord in **minor** (as in **Fig. 5.16.**) i.e. the same **Dmi7** is also a **IV** chord in the key of **A minor**.

- the **minor 7th with flatted 5th** chord has been found to function as:-
  - a **VII-for-V** substitute in **major** (as in **Fig. 3.5.**) i.e. **Bmi7(b5)** is a **VII** chord in the key of **C major**.
  - a **II** chord in **minor** (as in **Fig. 4.10.**) i.e. the same **Bmi7(b5)** is also a **II** chord in the key of **A minor**.
  - a **VI-for-I** substitute in **minor** (as in **Fig. 5.13.**) i.e. the same **Bmi7(b5)** is also a **VI** chord in the key of **D minor**.

- the **minor 6th** chord has been found to function as:-
  - a **I** or tonic chord in **minor** (as in **Fig. 4.16.**) i.e. **Cmi6** is a **I** chord in the key of **C minor**.
  - a **IV-for-II** substitute in **minor** (as in **Fig. 5.3.**) i.e. the same **Cmi6** is also a **IV** chord in the key of **G minor**.

Other chord types we have encountered so far, have only been found in one place in either a major or minor key, as follows:-

- the **dominant 7th** chord functions as a **V** in **major** i.e. **G7** is a **V** chord in the key of **C major**.

- the **dominant 7th with flatted 9th** chord functions as a **V** in **minor** i.e. **G7(b9)** is a **V** chord in the key of **C minor**.

- the **diminished 7th** chord functions as a **VII-for-V** substitute in **minor** i.e. **Bdim7** is a **VII** chord in the key of **C minor**.

This increased chord plurality between major and minor keys adds considerably to the chord progression possibilities available in jazz and more evolved contemporary styles. However, it also increases the 'detective work' required to analyze progressions using these harmonic options, as we shall now see in the following section which incorporates substitute chords in minor within our harmonic analysis techniques.

## *More harmonic analysis - now using minor keys with substitutes*

Following on from our work in *Chapter 4* on analyzing progressions in major and minor keys, we will now incorporate substitute chords for the **II - V - I** progression in minor, within the range of possibilities. At this point in our harmonic analysis, we therefore have the following chord options available:-

-       The **II - V - I** progression in **major** keys (as derived in *Chapter 2*).
-       **Plural substitutes** for the **II - V - I** progression in **major** keys (as derived in *Chapter 3*).
-       The **II - V - I** progression in **minor** keys (as derived in *Chapter 4*).
-       **Plural substitutes** for the **II - V - I** progression in **minor** keys (as derived in this chapter).

The analysis method previously outlined in *Chapter 4* (**p115-116**) now needs to be amended to take **substitute chords in minor keys** into account, as follows:-

*1)*     As usual, we **look for the dominant chords first.** (As previously noted, if the dominant chord contains an **alteration** it will function as a **V in minor**, otherwise it will function as a **V in major**). **However:-**
-       we now have an increased possibility of a **VII-for-V** substitution for the dominant chord (i.e. in major or minor). We may need to use some **contextual judgement** to determine whether a **VII** chord has substituted for a **V** chord in a minor (or less frequently, in a major) key. For example, if a **diminished 7th** chord (which we know can substitute for a **V dominant** chord in a minor key) is followed by a major or minor chord, and the root interval between the chords is an ascending half-step, this is strong evidence that we have a **VII-to-I** (with the **VII** therefore substituting for the **V**) progression. (See first example progression in **Figs. 5.23. - 5.24.**).

*2)*     We then look to see if the dominant chord (or its substitute as discussed above) is **preceded by a II chord** in **major** or **minor**, and/or **followed by a I chord** in **major** or **minor**. This will include all major, minor and 'mixed' progressions as shown in **Fig. 4.22**.

*3)*     We then look to see if the dominant chord (or its substitute as discussed above) is **preceded by a substitute for the II chord** in **major** or **minor**, and/or **followed by a substitute for the I chord** in **major** or **minor**. This will therefore include all substitute possibilities in major and minor, as shown in **Fig. 5.20.** in this chapter.

*4)*     Chords still remaining to be analyzed, are likely to fall in one of the following categories:-

-       diatonic chords to the key signature (i.e. **I** or tonic chords).
-       a **IV**(mi7, mi9 etc.) or **VI**(ma6,ma7 etc.) in a minor key, as in **Figs. 5.16. - 5.19.**
-       plural substitute chords in either the preceding or following momentary key.
-       isolated '**momentary I**' (one) chords in a new momentary key.
-       'passing' or embellishment chords.

### *More harmonic analysis - now using minor keys with substitutes (contd)*

In general because of the increased chord 'plurality' resulting from combining all of these chords in major and minor keys, there will sometimes be more than one way to analyze a given progression. As previously mentioned, at times some contextual judgement will therefore be required - and at least we will have developed a 'framework' or structure within which we can make these assessments! We will now work through two progressions to apply these expanded harmonic analysis principles, beginning with the following example:-

### *Figure 5.23. Harmonic analysis progression example #1*
*(this progression is typically used for the first four measures*
*of the jazz standard tune "Imagination")*

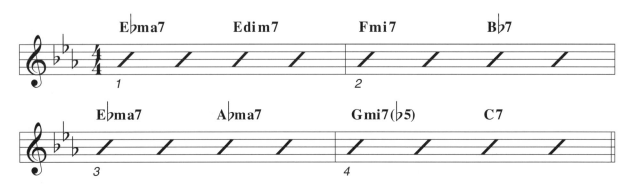

We will now apply the method outlined on the previous page, to the above progression as follows:-

**Stage 1**    We can analyze the dominant chords as follows:-

- The **Bb7** in measure **2** will be a **V** chord in the key of **Eb major** (corresponding to the key signature of the tune).
- The **C7** in measure **4** will be a **V** chord in the momentary key of **F major**.

    We are also looking for any possible **VII-to-I** progressions (evidence that the dominant chord has been substituted, as discussed on the previous page):-

- The root of the **Edim7** in measure **1**, moves up by half-step to the root of the following **Fmi7** in measure **2**. The **Edim7** is therefore a **VII** chord (and could be considered as a **VII-for-V** substitution - review **Figs. 5.6. - 5.9.** as necessary) in the momentary key of **F minor**.

### *More harmonic analysis - now using minor keys with substitutes (contd)*

#### *(Harmonic analysis of progression example #1 contd)*

**Stage 2**    We can analyze the chords preceding and following the dominant chords (or substitutions for dominant chords), to check for **II** or **I** chords in major or minor, as follows:-

- As noted at the bottom of the previous page, the **Fmi7** following the **Edim7** (in measure **2**) functions as a **I** in **F minor**. **However**, this **Fmi7** is also preceding the **Bb7** in measure **7** and therefore functions in the key of **Eb major** (corresponding to the key signature of the tune) as a **II** chord. This is another example of a '**linking**' chord i.e. the **Fmi7** functions in both the preceding and following keys (in this case as a **I** in **F minor** and as a **II** in **Eb major**).
- The **Ebma7** following the **Bb7** (in measure **3**) also functions in the key of **Eb major** (corresponding to the key signature of the tune), as a **I** chord. In total we have a **II - V - I** progression in **Eb major**.
- We have established that the **C7** in measure **4** is functioning as a **V** in **F major**. The preceding **Gmi7(b5)**, although not functioning as a **II** in **F major**, does function as a **II** in **F minor**. We therefore have a **mixed II - V** progression here (i.e. using a **II** in **F minor** and a **V** in **F major**).

As we have now analyzed all of the chords adjacent to dominant chords (or substitutions for dominants), **Stage 3** is therefore redundant in this case. However, the remaining chords to be analyzed fall into the **Stage 4** categories (see bottom of **p157**) as follows:-

- The **Ebma7** in measure **1** will be a **I** chord in the key of **Eb** (corresponding to the key signature of the tune).
- The **Abma7** in measure **3** is potentially a 'linking' chord as it has two possible functions:-
    - with respect to the key of **Eb** (corresponding to the key signature of the tune, and defined by the preceding **II - V - I** progression), this chord will be a **IV** chord (and therefore could be considered as a **IV-for-II** substitution).
    - we have established that the following **Gmi7(b5)** in measure **4**, is functioning as a **II** in **F minor**. The **Abma7** chord also functions in the key of **F minor**, as a **bIII** chord (and therefore could be considered as a **bIII-for-I** substitution) - review **Figs. 5.10. - 5.12.** as necessary.

    (Although both of these conclusions are valid, in general this **Abma7** chord will be heard as a **IV** in **Eb** major).

We can now summarize the analysis of this progression on the following page:-

## *More harmonic analysis - now using minor keys with substitutes (contd)*

### *Figure 5.24. Harmonic analysis completed for progression example #1*

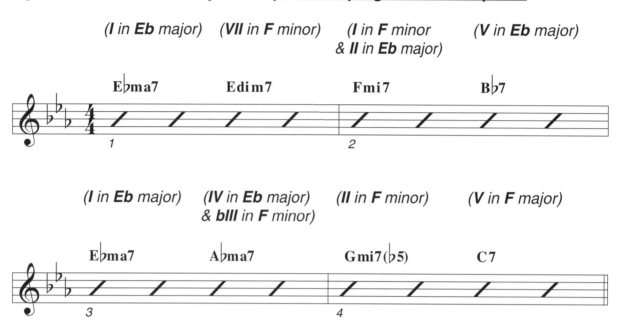

### *Figure 5.25. Harmonic analysis progression example #2*
*(this progression is typically used for the first eight measures*
*of the Beatles tune "Because")*

Now we will analyze the final harmonic progression example in this chapter, as follows:-

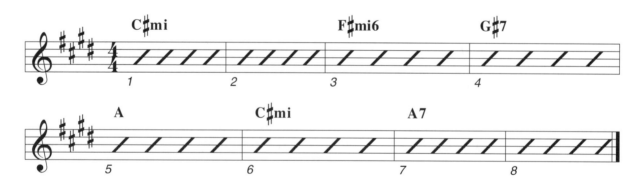

Again we will apply the harmonic analysis method outlined on p**157**, beginning on the following page:-

### *More harmonic analysis - now using minor keys with substitutes (contd)*

#### *(Harmonic analysis of progression example #2)*

**Stage 1**    We can analyze the dominant chords as follows:-

-    The **G#7** in measure **4** will be a **V** chord in the momentary key of **C# major**.
-    The **A7** in measure **7** will be a **V** chord in the momentary key of **D major**.

**Stage 2**    Analyzing the chords preceding and following the dominant chords, we see that they do not function as **II** or **I** chords in major or minor. For example, we have established that the **G#7** in measure **4**, is functioning as a **V** in **C# major**. The **II** chord preceding this, would need to be either a **D#mi7** (in the key of **C# major**) or a **D#mi7(b5)** (in the key of **C# minor**). However what we actually have is an **F#mi6** chord preceding the **G#7** chord (in measure **3**). In general then **Stage 2** (i.e. looking for **II** and/or **I** chords either side of dominants) does not help us to further analyze this particular progression example.

**Stage 3**    However, looking further at the chords preceding and following the **G#7** in measure **4**, we see that while they have no function in the key of **C# major**, they can be considered as **substitutes** within the key of **C# minor**, as follows:-

-    The **F#mi6** in measure **3** can be considered a **IV-for-II** substitution (as first seen in **Fig. 5.3.**) in the key of **C# minor**. In this case the original **II** chord being substituted is a **D#mi7(b5)** chord.
-    The **A** (chord) in measure **5** can be considered a (triad form of the) **bVI-for-IV** substitution (as first seen in **Fig. 5.17.**) again in the key of **C# minor**. In this case the original **IV**(mi7) chord being substituted is an **F#mi7** chord.

**Stage 4**    We can analyze any remaining chords which are diatonic to the key signature as follows:-

-    The **C#mi** chord in measures **1** and **6** could technically be (a triad form of) either a **VI** in **E major** or a **I** or tonic chord in **C# minor** (the **relative minor** of E major). We need to make a contextual judgement as to which of these interpretations is most appropriate. As we have decided that the chords in measures **3** and **5** function in **C# minor** (as a **IV** and **bVI** respectively), and that the **G#7** in measure **4** is a **V** in the major key built from the same tonic (i.e. **C# major**), this evidence would suggest that the **C#mi** triads in measures **1** and **6** be interpreted as **I** or tonic chords in the key of **C# minor**.

As we have now dealt with all the chords in the progression, the analysis can now be summarized as shown on the following page:-

### More harmonic analysis - now using minor keys with substitutes (contd)

#### Figure 5.26. Harmonic analysis completed for progression example #2

## *Chapter Five Workbook Questions*

*1.* *Determining plural substitutes in minor keys*

Each of the following **II-V-I** progressions has one chord marked with asterisks. You are to determine which chord would substitute for the chord indicated, and then write the notes of the substitute chord on the staff (in root position) together with a chord symbol above the staff, in the blank measure after each question.

**1.** *Determining plural substitutes in minor keys (contd)*

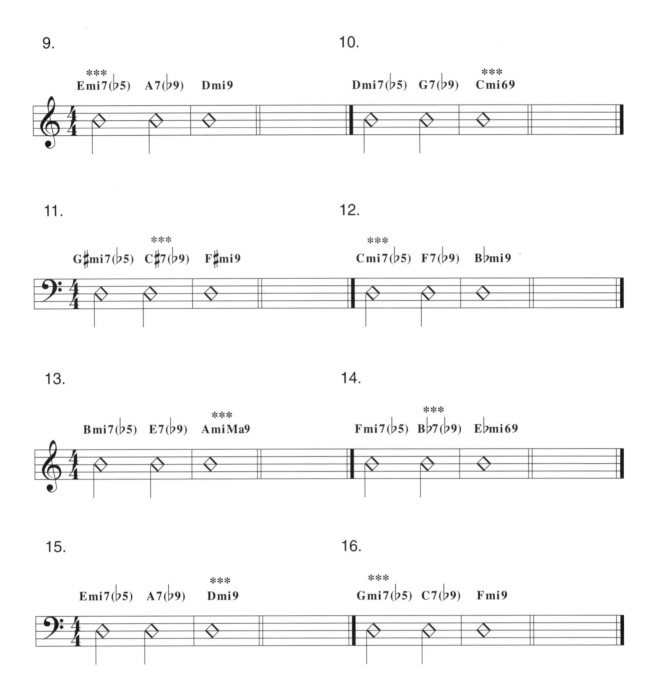

## 2. Determining (original) definitive chords in minor keys

Each of the following progressions represents a **II-V-I** in which <u>one</u> of the chords has been substituted. You are to determine which chord is the substitute in each progression, and write asterisks over the appropriate chord symbol (in a similar manner as shown in questions 1 - 16). You are then to determine which (original) definitive chord has been substituted, and write the notes of the definitive chord (in root position) together with a chord symbol above the staff, in the blank measure after each question. If you decide that a *melodic minor-based* **I** chord is being substituted, you should write the ***Imi69*** chord form.

17.

Bbmi6    C7(b9)    Fmi9

18.

Cmi7(b5)    Adim7    Bbmi69

19.

Bbmi7(b5)    Eb7(b9)    Fmi7(b5)

20.

Ami7(b5)    D7(b9)    Bbma7

21.

Dmi7(b5)    Bdim7    Cmi9

22.

Dmi6    E7(b9)    AmiMa9

23.

C#mi7(b5)    F#7(b9)    Dma7

24.

Gmi7(b5)    Edim7    Fmi9

**2.** *Determining (original) definitive chords in minor keys (contd)*

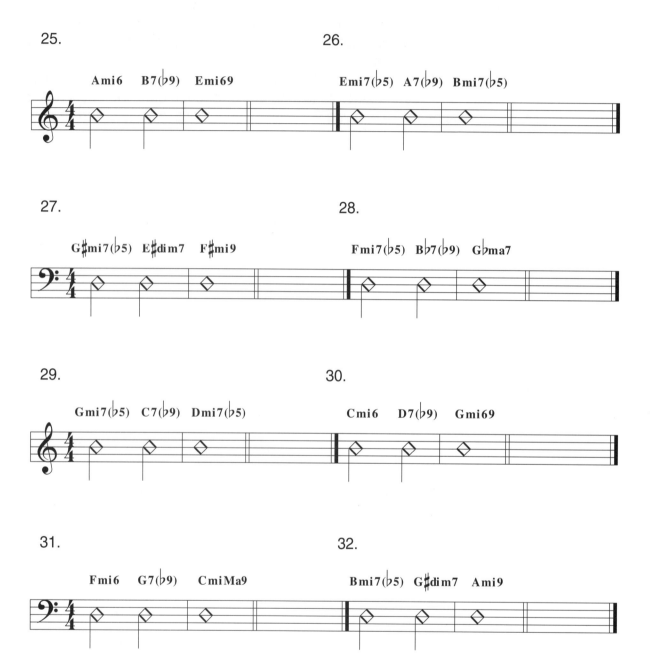

25.    Ami6    B7(♭9)    Emi69

26.    Emi7(♭5)    A7(♭9)    Bmi7(♭5)

27.    G♯mi7(♭5)    E♯dim7    F♯mi9

28.    Fmi7(♭5)    B♭7(♭9)    G♭ma7

29.    Gmi7(♭5)    C7(♭9)    Dmi7(♭5)

30.    Cmi6    D7(♭9)    Gmi69

31.    Fmi6    G7(♭9)    CmiMa9

32.    Bmi7(♭5)    G♯dim7    Ami9

### 3.   *Determining functions and keys for given chord symbols*

You are to determine the functions and keys for the following chord symbols.
*Remember that certain chords will now function in both major and minor keys.*

33.   **Ami7**      is a   ___ in ___
                           ___ in ___
                           ___ in ___
                           ___ in ___
                           ___ in ___

34.   **B7b9**      is a   ___ in ___

35.   **Ebma7**     is a   ___ in ___
                           ___ in ___
                           ___ in ___
                           ___ in ___

36.   **Fmi7(b5)**  is a   ___ in ___
                           ___ in ___
                           ___ in ___

37.   **G9**        is a   ___ in ___

38.   **Cdim7**     is a   ___ in ___

39.   **Fmi7**      is a   ___ in ___
                           ___ in ___
                           ___ in ___
                           ___ in ___
                           ___ in ___

40.   **Dma7**      is a   ___ in ___
                           ___ in ___
                           ___ in ___
                           ___ in ___

**167**

**4.** ***Chord progression analysis***

You are to determine the functions and keys for each chord in the following progressions, in a similar manner as for section 3 above. Where a 'linking' chord occurs (i.e. belonging to the preceding and following key centers) you are to indicate all applicable keys and functions. Write the functions and keys in the spaces provided below each progression:-

*Chord Progression #1*
*(typically used for the first 8 measures of the jazz standard "Autumn Leaves")*

Write your answers here:-

41. _____      42. _____

43. _____      44. _____

45. _____      46. _____

47. _____

### 4.   _Chord progression analysis (contd)_

_Chord Progression #2_
_(typically used for the first 8 measures of the jazz standard "It Could Happen To You")_

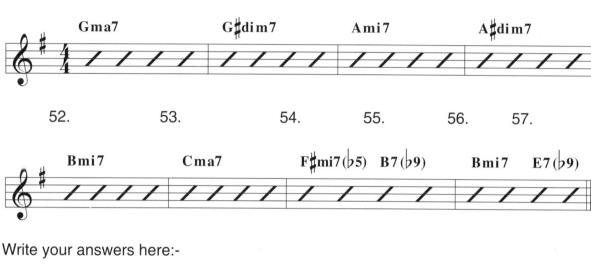

Write your answers here:-

48. _____    49. _____
50. _____    51. _____
52. _____    53. _____
54. _____    55. _____
56. _____    57. _____

_Chord Progression #3_
_(typically used for the first 8 measures of the jazz standard "A Foggy Day")_

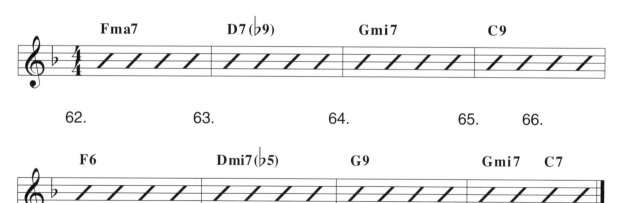

### 4. Chord progression analysis (contd)

*(Chord Progression #3 contd)*

Write your answers here:-

58. _____     59. _____

60. _____     61. _____

62. _____     63. _____

64. _____     65. _____

66. _____

*Chord Progression #4*
*(typically used for the first 8 measures of the jazz standard "I Love You")*

67.          68.          69.          70.

71.          72.          73.

Write your answers here:-

67. _____     68. _____

69. _____     70. _____

71. _____     72. _____

73. _____

## Chapter Five Workbook Answers

### 1. Determining plural substitutes in minor keys - answers

**1.** *Determining plural substitutes in minor keys - answers (contd)*

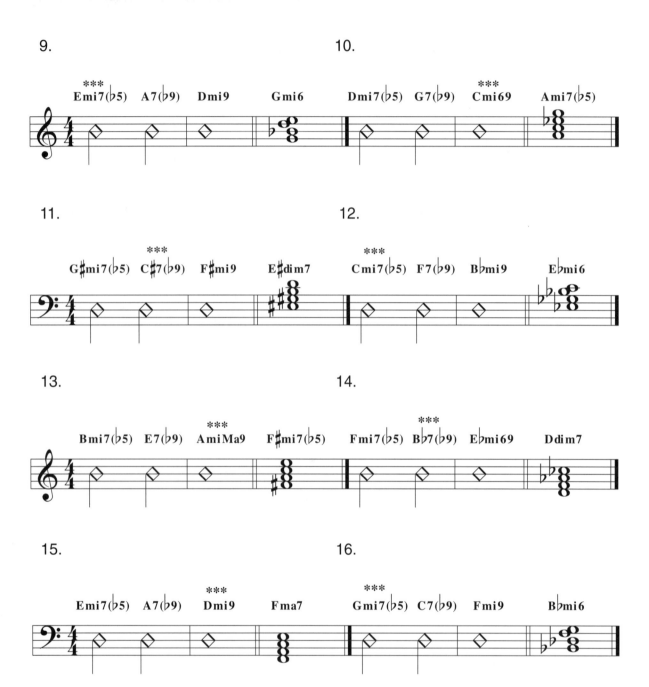

**2.** *Determining (original) definitive chords in minor keys - answers*

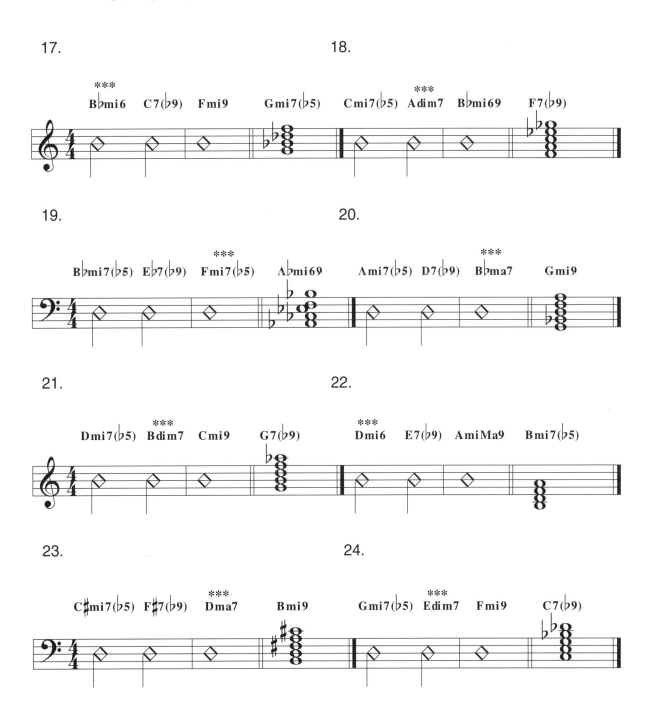

17.

18.

19.

20.

21.

22.

23.

24.

**2.** *Determining (original) definitive chords in minor keys - answers (contd)*

25.                                          26.

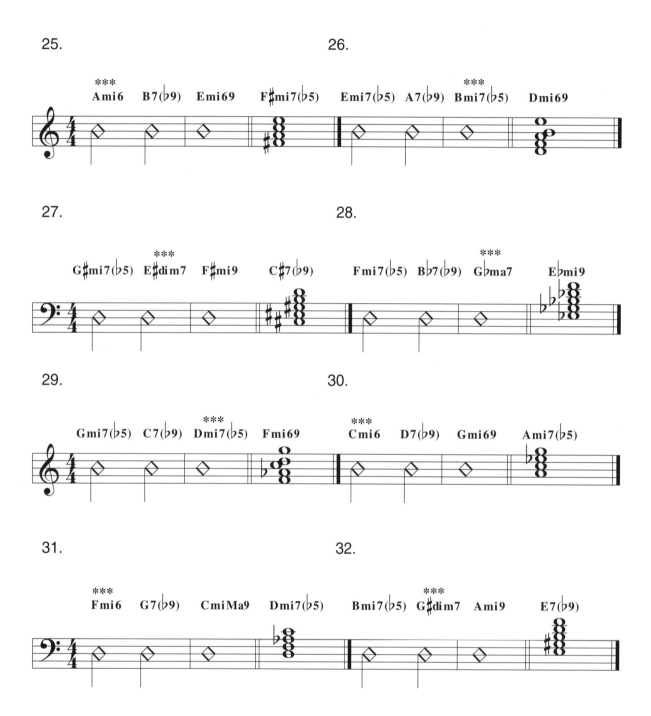

### 3. *Determining functions and keys for given chord symbols - answers*

33. **Ami7**    is a    *II* in G major
                                *III* in F major
                                *VI* in C major
                                *I* in A minor
                                *IV* in E minor

34. **B7b9**    is a    *V* in E minor

35. **Ebma7**    is a    *I* in Eb major
                                *IV* in Bb major
                                *bIII* in C minor
                                *bVI* in G minor

36. **Fmi7(b5)**    is a    *VII* in Gb major
                                    *II* in Eb minor
                                    *VI* in Ab minor

37. **G9**    is a    *V* in C major

38. **Cdim7**    is a    *VII* in Db minor

39. **Fmi7**    is a    *II* in Eb major
                                *III* in Db major
                                *VI* in Ab major
                                *I* in F minor
                                *IV* in C minor

40. **Dma7**    is a    *I* in D major
                                    *IV* in A major
                                    *bIII* in B minor
                                    *bVI* in F# minor

### 4. *Chord progression analysis - answers*

*(Chord Progression #1)*

41.    *II* in G major

42.    *V* in G major

43.    *I* in G major

44.    *IV* in G major

45.    *II* in E minor

46.    *V* in E major

47.    *I* in E minor

*175*

**4.** *Chord progression analysis - answers (contd)*

*(Chord Progression #2)*

| | | | |
|---|---|---|---|
| 48. | *I in G major* | 49. | *VII in A minor* |
| 50. | *I in A minor, II in G major* | 51. | *VII in B minor* |
| 52. | *I in B minor, III in G major* | 53. | *IV in G major* |
| 54. | *II in E minor* | 55. | *V in E minor* |
| 56. | *II in A major* | 57. | *V in A minor* |

*(Chord Progression #3)*

| | | | |
|---|---|---|---|
| 58. | *I in F major* | 59. | *V in G minor* |
| 60. | *I in G minor, II in F major* | 61. | *V in F major* |
| 62. | *I in F major* | 63. | *II in C minor, VI in F minor* |
| 64. | *V in C major* | 65. | *II in F major* |
| 66. | *V in F major* | | |

*(Chord Progression #4)*

| | | | |
|---|---|---|---|
| 67. | *IV in F minor* | 68. | *V in F minor* |
| 69. | *I in F major* | 70. | *VI in F major* |
| 71. | *II in F major* | 72. | *V in F major* |
| 73. | *I in F major* | | |

# Voiceleading of triads and four-part chords

## Introduction

The term '**voiceleading**' is used to describe the smooth horizontal movement (i.e. without unnecessary interval leaps) between consecutive chord 'voicings' in a given piece of music. We have already been introduced to the concept of '**7-3 line voiceleading**' in **Chapter 1** (see **Figs. 2.8. - 2.9.**), where the **7-3** lines were 'voiceled' across the **II - V - I** progression. Now in this chapter we will apply the concept of voiceleading to three-part (triad) and four-part chords. These voiceleading techniques will then not only be used within basic three-part and four-part harmonic contexts (for example, diatonic chord progressions), but also within the various **upper structure** chords which are so widely used in today's pop styles (as we shall see in **Chapters 7** and **8**).

Voiceleading three- and four-part chords requires the use of inversions to achieve the smooth horizontal movement required. (Review 3- and 4-part inversions in *Contemporary Music Theory Level One*, and **Figs. 1.10. & 1.16.** in this book, as necessary). Often a 'static' voiceleading effect is required (i.e. minimal horizontal movement between consecutive chord voicings), although there will be times when an ascending or descending result is preferred. The voiceleading examples for the three-part and the four-part chords in this chapter consist of the following types of progression:-

- **diatonic** chord sequences i.e. where all of the **3-** or **4**-part chords belong to the same key.
- chord sequences around the **circle-of-5ths** and **circle-of-4ths** (review **Fig. 1.2.** and accompanying text as necessary). While consecutive chords within these 'circular' progressions could belong to the same key, these progressions as a whole will typically imply key changes in the harmony. These **circle-of-5ths/4ths** voiceleading concepts will be particularly useful when dealing with **upper structure** chords in **Chapters 7** and **8**.

## Triad voiceleading

Now we will consider how to 'voicelead' various progressions using triads. First we will look at the following example:-

### Figure 6.1. Two-chord major triad progression without voiceleading

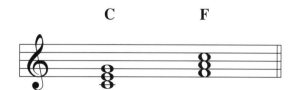

### *Triad voiceleading (contd)*

Note that there are some different interpretations of the **C** to **F** chord progression at the bottom of the previous page, as follows:-

-     it could be a **diatonic triad** progression in the key of **C**.
-     it could be a **diatonic triad** progression in the key of **F**.
-     it could be a **circle-of-5ths triad** progression (we see in **Fig. 1.2.** that movement between the **C** and **F** chords can be considered as '**circle-of-5ths**').

Note also that as a root-position triad voicing was used for each chord in the preceding example, we did not have any voiceleading - in other words we have a (potentially undesirable) interval skip occurring between the two 'top notes' of **G** and **C** respectively. As the ear is often drawn to the '**top note**' used in a chord voicing, looking at this **top note movement** is normally a good way to assess the voiceleading used within a chord progression.

In order to then apply voiceleading to the preceding progression, we would **determine which inversion** of the second chord (i.e. the **F major** triad) would result in a **top note that was closest** to the note **G** (the top note of the first **C major** triad). The **F major** triad could be inverted to place the notes **F** or **A** on top, either of which would be closer to the first top note of **G** (on the **C major** triad) than the top note of **C** currently being used on the **F major** triad. If an 'ascending' top line was preferred (which would depend on the overall musical context) then we would follow the **root position C major** triad with a **second inversion F major** triad, as follows:-

### *Figure 6.2. Two-chord major triad progression with voiceleading*

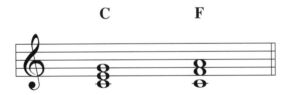

Now we will look at the next triad progression, this time using minor triads as follows:-

### *Figure 6.3. Two-chord minor triad progression without voiceleading*

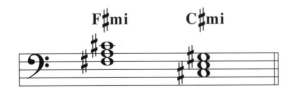

### *Triad voiceleading (contd)*

Again note that there are some different interpretations of the **F#mi** to **C#mi** chord progression at the bottom of the previous page, as follows:-

- it could be a **diatonic triad** progression in the key of **E**.
- it could be a **diatonic triad** progression in the key of **A**.
- it could be a **circle-of-4ths triad** progression (we see in **Fig. 1.2.** that movement between the **F#mi** and **C#mi** chords can be considered as '**circle-of-4ths**').

Now we will apply voiceleading to the preceding progression, and we will assume for the purposes of this example that the (root position) voicing for the **C#mi** chord is to be retained. We would then determine which inversion of the first chord (i.e. the **F# minor** triad) would result in a **top note that was closest** to the note G# (the top note of the second **C# minor** triad). The **F# minor** triad could be inverted to place the notes F# or A on top, either of which would be closer to the second top note of G# (on the **C# minor** triad) than the top note of C# currently being used on the **F# minor** triad. If a 'descending' top line was preferred (which again would depend on the overall musical context) then we would precede the **root position C# minor** triad with a **second inversion F# minor** triad, as follows:-

### *Figure 6.4. Two-chord minor triad progression with voiceleading*

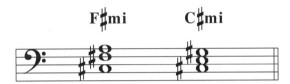

Now we will look at some longer examples of **diatonic triad progressions** (using four chords each) and consider how voiceleading might be applied. When voiceleading these chord progressions, it will often be desirable to use a **commontone** (i.e. the same note belonging to successive chords) as a top note 'across' those chords where possible, as this will provide the smoothest horizontal result. However, when a commontone is **not** available as a top note between successive chords, a decision (based on the musical context) will be needed to determine whether the voiceleading should be **ascending** or **descending**. We will now see these principles at work, beginning with the first four-chord diatonic triad progression as follows:-

### *Figure 6.5. Four-chord diatonic triad progression without voiceleading (key of C)*

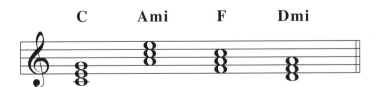

## *Triad voiceleading (contd)*

For the purposes of the preceding example, we will apply an **ascending** voiceleading direction if a commontone is not available as a top note between successive chords. We can analyze the inversions required for the chords following the first **C major** triad in the preceding progression, as follows:-

**Ami** chord  -  This triad does not contain the previous top note of **G** (on the **C** chord), and so a commontone is not available as a top note across this chord (**Ami**) and the preceding **C** chord (assuming that the **C** major triad remains in root position). The nearest available top note (moving in an **ascending** direction) would be the note **A**, which requires the **Ami** triad to be in **first inversion**.

**F** chord  -  Following on from the previous top note of **A** derived above, we see that the note **A** is also contained within the **F** triad - therefore this note is available as a 'commontone top note' across this chord (**F**) and the preceding chord (**Ami**). This requires the **F** triad to be in **second inversion**.

**Dmi** chord  -  Following on from the previous top note of **A** derived above, we see that the note **A** is also contained within the **Dmi** triad (and is already on top as the **Dmi** triad is in root position). Therefore this note is available as a 'commontone top note' across this chord (**Dmi**) and the preceding chord (**F**). This requires the **Dmi** triad to remain in **root position**.

The above voiceleading and inversion choices can now be shown as follows:-

### *Figure 6.6. Four-chord diatonic triad progression with voiceleading (key of C)*

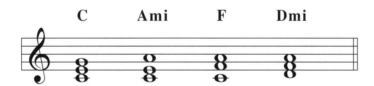

Now we will look at another four-chord diatonic triad progression as follows:-

### *Figure 6.7. Four-chord diatonic triad progression without voiceleading (key of Ab)*

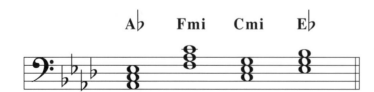

### *Triad voiceleading (contd)*

For the purposes of the preceding example, we will apply a **descending** voiceleading direction if a commontone is not available as a top note between successive chords, and we will (arbitrarily) use the beginning **Ab** major triad in **second inversion** (resulting in a starting top note of **C**). We can then analyze the inversions required for the chords following this **Ab major** triad in the preceding progression, as follows:-

**Fmi** chord - Following on from the previous top note of **C** resulting from the **Ab** triad being in second inversion, we see that the note **C** is also contained within the **Fmi** triad (and is already on top as the **Fmi** triad is in root position) - therefore this note is available as a 'commontone top note' across this chord (**Fmi**) and the preceding chord (**Ab**). This requires the **Fmi** triad to remain in **root position**.

**Cmi** chord - Following on from the previous top note of **C** derived above, we see that the note **C** is also contained within the **Cmi** triad - therefore this note is available as a 'commontone top note' across this chord (**Cmi**) and the preceding chord (**Fmi**). This requires the **Cmi** triad to be in **first inversion**.

**Eb** chord - This triad does not contain the previous top note of **C** (on the **Cmi** chord), and so this note is not available as a 'commontone top note' across this chord (**Eb**) and the preceding **Cmi** chord. The nearest available top note (moving in a **descending** direction) would be the note **Bb**, which requires the **Eb** triad to remain in **root position**.

The above voiceleading and inversion choices can now be shown as follows:-

#### *Figure 6.8. Four-chord diatonic triad progression with voiceleading (key of Ab)*

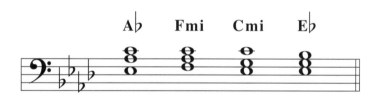

Next we will look at some four-chord examples of triad progressions moving around the **circle-of-5ths** and the **circle-of-4ths**. We have already seen that the progressions shown in **Figs. 6.1. - 6.4.** can be interpreted as '**circular**'-type progressions. As previously mentioned, these types of progressions can imply key changes in the harmony, corresponding to the various stages around the circle (again review **Fig. 1.2.** as required). Our first 'circular' four-chord triad progression contains **major triads** moving around the **circle-of-5ths**, as shown in the example on the following page:-

### Triad voiceleading (contd)

**Figure 6.9. Four-chord major triad progression around the circle-of-5ths, without voiceleading**

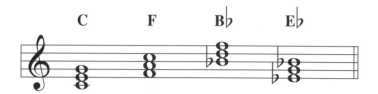

In a circle-of-5ths triad sequence such as the above example, we can see that there will always be **one commontone** between successive chords. The **root** of each triad is always present in the following triad i.e. the root of the first triad (**C**) is contained within the second triad (**F** major), the root of the second triad (**F**) is contained within the third triad (**Bb** major) and so on.

Although different voiceleading directions can be applied to these 'circular' sequences, we will for the moment use what I call a '**commontone voiceleading**' rule which I believe results in the most 'natural' voiceleading for this type of progression. Applying this principle means that the commontone **retains its relative position between successive chords**. For example, the commontone of **C** between the first two chords in the above example, is the **bottom** voice of the first **C** major triad (assuming that this **C** major triad remains in **root position**) and we will therefore **retain it as the bottom voice** of the following **F** major triad (which in turn requires the **F** major triad to be in **second inversion**). Applying this principle throughout the above progression, we find that an **ascending** voiceleading direction results, as follows:-

**Figure 6.10. Four-chord major triad progression around the circle-of-5ths, with voiceleading**

*(Note that the dotted lines are being used to connect the commontones between successive chords).*

We can analyze the voiceleading used for the chords following the first (root position) **C** major triad, as follows:-

F chord       -        As discussed above, the commontone of **C** (between this **F** major triad and the preceding **C** major triad) is the **bottom voice** of the preceding **C** major triad, and we will therefore **retain it as the bottom voice** of this **F** major triad. This requires the **F** major triad to be in **second inversion**, resulting in a top note on this triad of **A**.

## *Triad voiceleading (contd)*

**(Analysis of Fig. 6.10. contd)**

**Bb** chord     -     The commontone of **F** (between this **Bb** major triad and the preceding **F** major triad) is the **middle voice** of the preceding **F** major triad, and we will therefore **retain it as the middle voice** of this **Bb** major triad. This requires the **Bb** major triad to be in **first inversion**, resulting in a top note on this triad of **Bb**.

**Eb** chord     -     The commontone of **Bb** (between this **Eb** major triad and the preceding **Bb** major triad) is the **top voice** of the preceding **Bb** major triad, and we will therefore **retain it as the top voice** of this **Eb** major triad. This requires the **Eb** major triad to remain in **root position**, resulting in a top note on this triad of **Bb**.

     If we were now to continue this voiceleading technique within major triads around the **entire circle-of-5ths**, we can derive the following example:-

### *Figure 6.11. Major triad progression around the (complete) circle-of-5ths, with voiceleading*

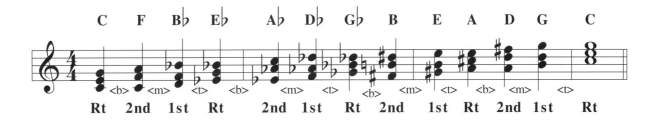

     Note that in the above example, the ending **C** major triad is exactly **one octave higher** that the beginning **C** major triad - so it takes us one octave to voicelead around the complete circle-of-5ths using this method. The following information is provided in the above example:-

- the **commontones between successive chords** are indicated by the **<b>**, **<m>**, and **<t>** symbols, signifying **bottom**, **middle** and **top** notes respectively. (For example, the **bottom** note of **C** is the commontone between the first **C** major triad and the following **F** major triad - hence the symbol **<b>** between these two triads).
- the **inversions used** for each chord are indicated by the symbols **Rt** (root position), **1st** (first inversion) and **2nd** (second inversion). Note that in this case the sequence of **Rt**, **2nd** & **1st** (inversions) repeats throughout the entire progression.

*(These circle-of-5ths/4ths triad voiceleading concepts are presented from a keyboard perspective in **Chapter 4** of our **Pop Piano Book** keyboard method - please see **page vi**).*

## *Triad voiceleading (contd)*

Again note that in the circle-of-5ths voiceleading example on the previous page, we began and ended with a **root position C** major triad. We could similarly have started on either **first** or **second** inversion triads, in which case all the commontones and subsequent inversions would be **correspondingly displaced** throughout. *(Please see **Appendix 3** for a complete summary of all major and minor triad progressions around the circle-of-5ths/4ths, using all possible starting inversions).*

Next we will look at a 'circular' four-chord triad progression with **minor triads** moving around the **circle-of-4ths**, as shown in the following example:-

### *Figure 6.12. Four-chord minor triad progression around the circle-of-4ths, without voiceleading*

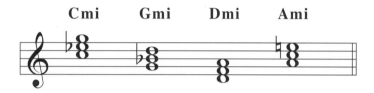

In a circle-of-4ths triad sequence such as the above example, we can again see that there will always be **one commontone** between successive chords. The **fifth** of each triad is always present in the following triad i.e. the fifth of the first triad (**G**) is contained within the second triad (**G minor**), the fifth of the second triad (**D**) is contained within the third triad (**D minor**) and so on.

Again here we will use '**commontone voiceleading**' i.e. the commontone **retains its relative position between successive chords**. For example, the commontone of **G** between the first two chords in the above example, is the **top** voice of the first **C** minor triad (assuming that this **C** minor triad remains in **root position**) and we will therefore **retain it as the top voice** of the following **G** minor triad (which in turn requires the **G** minor triad to be in **first inversion**). Applying this principle throughout the above progression, we find that a **descending** voiceleading direction results, as follows:-

### *Figure 6.13. Four-chord minor triad progression around the circle-of-4ths, with voiceleading*

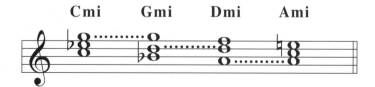

*(Note again that the dotted lines are being used to connect the commontones between successive chords).*

### *Triad voiceleading (contd)*

We can analyze the voiceleading used for the chords following the first (root position) **C** minor triad in the example at the bottom of the previous page, as follows:-

**Gmi** chord    -    As discussed on the previous page, the commontone of **G** (between this **G** minor triad and the preceding **C** minor triad) is the **top voice** of the preceding **C** minor triad, and we will therefore **retain it as the top voice** of this **G** minor triad. This requires the **G** minor triad to be in **first inversion**, resulting in a top note on this triad of **G**.

**Dmi** chord    -    The commontone of **D** (between this **D** minor triad and the preceding **G** minor triad) is the **middle voice** of the preceding **G** minor triad, and we will therefore **retain it as the middle voice** of this **D** minor triad. This requires the **D** minor triad to be in **second inversion**, resulting in a top note on this triad of **F**.

**Ami** chord    -    The commontone of **A** (between this **A** minor triad and the preceding **D** minor triad) is the **bottom voice** of the preceding **D** minor triad, and we will  therefore **retain it as the bottom voice** of this **A** minor triad. This requires the **A** minor triad to remain in **root position**, resulting in a top note on this triad of **E**.

If we were now to continue this voiceleading technique within minor triads around the **entire circle-of-4ths**, we can derive the following example:-

### *Figure 6.14. Minor triad progression around the (complete) circle-of-4ths, with voiceleading*

Note that in the above example, the ending **C** minor triad is exactly **one octave lower** than the beginning **C** minor triad - so it takes us one octave to voicelead around the complete circle-of-4ths using this method. The commontone symbols (i.e. <b>, <m>, <t>) and inversions (i.e. **Rt**, **1st**, **2nd**) in this example are used in the same way as for the previous major triad example around the entire circle-of-5ths (see **Fig. 6.11.** and accompanying text). Again note that we could have started on different inversions of the first **C** minor triad, resulting in the subsequent 'displacement' of the commontones and triad inversions *(please see Appendix 3)*. Although in a 'real-life' context we are unlikely to voicelead a progression around the **entire** circle-of-5ths/4ths (!), in contemporary situations we **very often** need to voicelead between **2**, **3** or **4** stages around the circle, especially when using **upper structure** chords (as in **Chapter 7**).

### *Four-part chord voiceleading*

Now we will consider how to 'voicelead' various progressions using four-part chords. First we will look at the following example, using **major 7th** four-part chords:-

### *Figure 6.15. Two-chord major 7th progression without voiceleading*

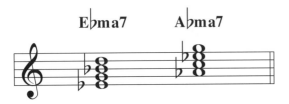

Note that there are some different interpretations of the **Ebma7** to **Abma7** chord progression shown above, as follows:-

-   it could be a **diatonic four-part** chord progression in the key of **Eb**.
-   it could be a **circle-of-5ths four-part** chord progression (review **Fig. 1.2.** as necessary to see that movement between these **Ebma7** and **Abma7** chords can be considered as 'circle-of-5ths').

Again in order to apply voiceleading to the above progression, we would **determine which inversion** of the second chord (i.e. the **Abma7**) would result in a **top note that was closest** to the note **D** (the top note of the **Ebma7** chord). The **Abma7** chord could be inverted to place the notes **C** or **Eb** on top, either of which would be closer to the first top note of **D** (on the **Ebma7** chord) than the top note of **G** currently being used on the **Abma7** chord. If a 'descending' top line was preferred (which would depend on the overall musical context) then we would follow the **root position Ebma7** chord with a **second inversion Abma7** chord, as follows:-

### *Figure 6.16. Two-chord major 7th progression with voiceleading*

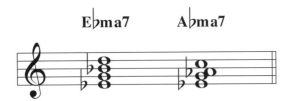

*(Note that in general when voiceleading four-part chords, we will often try to avoid using **first inversions**, as this creates an 'exposed' second interval on top of the chord. This creates a dissonance which is often undesirable, particularly on the first inversion **major 7th** chord - review **Fig. 1.16.** as necessary).*

### *Four-part chord voiceleading (contd)*

Now we will look at the next four-part chord progression, this time using **minor 7th** chords as follows:-

#### *Figure 6.17. Two-chord minor 7th progression without voiceleading*

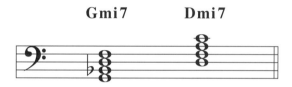

Again note that there are some different interpretations of the **Gmi7** to **Dmi7** chord progression in the above example, as follows:-

-     it could be a **diatonic four-part** chord progression in the key of **F**.
-     it could be a **diatonic four-part** chord progression in the key of **Bb**.
-     it could be a **circle-of-4ths four-part** chord progression (review **Fig. 1.2.** as necessary to see that movement between these **Gmi7** and **Dmi7** chords can be considered as '**circle-of-4ths**').

Now we will apply voiceleading to the above progression, and we will assume for the purposes of this example that the (root position) voicing for the **Dmi7** chord is to be retained. We would then determine which inversion of the first chord (i.e. the **Gmi7**) would result in a **top note that was closest** to the note C (the top note of the second **Dmi7** chord). The **Gmi7** could be inverted to place the notes **Bb** or **D** on top, either of which would be closer to the second top note of C (on the **Dmi7**) than the top note of **F** currently being used on the **Gmi7** chord. If an 'ascending' top line was preferred (which again would depend on the overall musical context) then we would precede the **root position Dmi7** chord with a **second inversion Gmi7** chord, as follows:-

#### *Figure 6.18. Two-chord minor 7th progression with voiceleading*

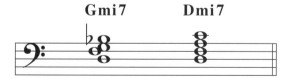

Now we will look at some longer examples of **diatonic four-part** chord progressions (using four chords each) and consider how voiceleading might be applied. Again it will often be desirable to use **commontones** (where possible) as the top voice of successive chords, and where this is not possible we will **ascend** or **descend** depending on the musical context.

### *Four-part chord voiceleading (contd)*

Now we will look at the first four-chord, diatonic four-part progression as follows:-

### *Figure 6.19. Four-chord diatonic four-part progression without voiceleading (key of D)*

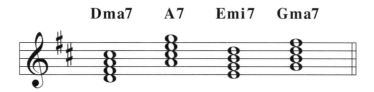

For the purposes of the above example, we will apply an **ascending** voiceleading direction if a commontone is not available as a top note between successive chords. We can analyze the inversions required for the chords following the first **Dma7** chord as follows:-

**A7** chord   -    This chord contains the previous top note of **C#** (on the **Dma7** chord) - therefore this note is available as a 'commontone top note' across this chord (**A7**) and the preceding **Dma7** chord (assuming that the **Dma7** remains in root position). This requires the **A7** chord to be in **second inversion**.

**Emi7** chord   -    This chord does not contain the previous top note of **C#** (on the **A7** chord), and so this note is not available as a 'commontone top note' across this chord (**Emi7**) and the preceding **A7** chord. The nearest available top note (moving in an **ascending** direction) would be the note **D**, which requires the **Emi7** chord to remain in **root position**.

**Gma7** chord   -    Following on from the previous top note of **D** derived above, we see that the note **D** is also contained within the **Gma7** chord - therefore this note is available as a 'commontone top note' across this chord (**Gma7**) and the preceding chord (**Emi7**). This requires the **Gma7** to be in **third inversion**.

The above voiceleading and inversion choices can now be shown as follows:-

### *Figure 6.20. Four-chord diatonic four-part progression with voiceleading (key of D)*

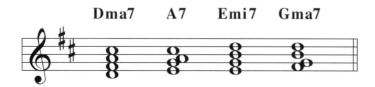

Now we will look at another four-chord, diatonic four-part progression as shown on the following page:-

## *Four-part chord voiceleading (contd)*

### *Figure 6.21. Four-chord diatonic four-part progression without voiceleading (key of Bb)*

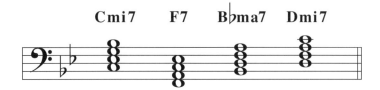

For the purposes of the above example, we will apply a **descending** voiceleading direction if a commontone is not available as a top note between successive chords. We can analyze the inversions required for the chords following the first **Cmi7** chord as follows:-

| | | |
|---|---|---|
| **F7** chord | - | This chord does not contain the previous top note of **Bb** (on the **Cmi7** chord), and so this note is not available as a 'commontone top note' across this chord (**F7**) and the preceding **Cmi7** chord. The nearest available top note (moving in a **descending** direction, and assuming that the **Cmi7** remains in root position) would be the note **A**, which requires the **F7** chord to be in **second inversion**. |
| **Bbma7** chord | - | Following on from the previous top note of **A** derived above, we see that the note **A** is also contained within the **Bbma7** chord - therefore this note is available as a 'commontone top note' across this chord (**Bbma7**) and the preceding chord (**F7**). This requires the **Bbma7** to remain in **root position**. |
| **Dmi7** chord | - | Following on from the previous top note of **A** derived above, we see that the note **A** is also contained within the **Dmi7** chord - therefore this note is available as a 'commontone top note' across this chord (**Dmi7**) and the preceding chord (**Bbma7**). This requires the **Dmi7** to be in **third inversion**. |

The above voiceleading and inversion choices can now be shown as follows:-

### *Figure 6.22. Four-chord diatonic four-part progression with voiceleading (key of Bb)*

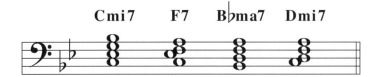

### *Four-part chord voiceleading (contd)*

Next we will look at some four-chord examples of four-part chord progressions moving around the **circle-of-5ths** and the **circle-of-4ths**. (Again we have already seen that the four-part chord progressions shown in **Figs. 6.15. - 6.18.** can be interpreted as '**circular**'-type progressions, which can imply key changes in the harmony). In this section we will focus on **major 7th** and **minor 7th** chords, as later on these will be the most useful four-part chords to use within **upper structure** voicings (as we shall see in **Chapter 8**). Our first 'circular' four-chord, four-part progression contains **major 7th** chords moving around the **circle-of-5ths**, as shown in the following example:-

### *Figure 6.23. Four-chord major 7th progression around the circle-of-5ths, without voiceleading*

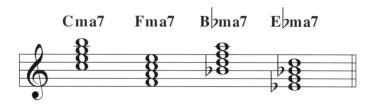

In a circle-of-5ths four-part chord sequence such as the above example, we can see that there will always be **two commontones** between successive chords. The **root** and **third** of each four-part chord is always present in the following chord i.e. the root and third of the first chord (**C** and **E**) are contained within the second chord (**Fma7**), the root and third of the second chord (**F** and **A**) are contained within the third chord (**Bbma7**) and so on.

Although different voiceleading directions can be applied to these four-part 'circular' sequences, we will again for the moment use a '**commontone voiceleading**' approach i.e. the two commontones **retain their relative position between successive chords**. For example, the commontones of **C** and **E** between the first two chords in the above example, are the **bottom** voices of the first **Cma7** chord (assuming that this chord remains in **root position**) and we will therefore **retain these notes as the bottom voices** of the following **Fma7** chord (which in turn requires the **Fma7** chord to be in **second inversion**). Applying this principle throughout the above progression, we find that a **descending** voiceleading direction results, as follows:-

### *Figure 6.24. Four-chord major 7th progression around the circle-of-5ths, with voiceleading*

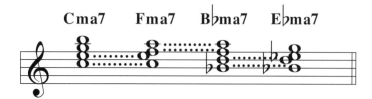

*(Note again that the dotted lines are being used to connect the commontones between successive chords).*

### *Four-part chord voiceleading (contd)*

We can analyze the voiceleading used for the chords following the first (root position) **Cma7** chord in the example on the previous page, as follows:-

**Fma7** chord   -   As discussed on the previous page, the commontones of **C** and **E** (between this **Fma7** chord and the preceding **Cma7** chord) are the **bottom voices** of the preceding **Cma7** chord, and we will therefore **retain them as the bottom voices** of this **Fma7** chord. This requires the **Fma7** chord to be in **second inversion**, resulting in a top note on this chord of **A**.

**Bbma7** chord  -   The commontones of **F** and **A** (between this **Bbma7** chord and the preceding **Fma7** chord) are the **top voices** of the preceding **Fma7** chord, and we will therefore **retain them as the top voices** of this **Bbma7** chord. This requires the **Bbma7** chord to remain in **root position**, resulting in a top note on this chord of **A**.

**Ebma7** chord  -   The commontones of **Bb** and **D** (between this **Bbma7** chord and the preceding **Bbma7** chord) are the **bottom voices** of the preceding **Bbma7** chord, and we will therefore **retain them as the bottom voices** of this **Ebma7** chord. This requires the **Ebma7** chord to be in **second inversion**, resulting in a top note on this chord of **G**.

Note that when we use this 'commontone voiceleading' approach for these **four-part** chords moving around the circle-of-5ths, this resulted in a **descending** voiceleading direction (as opposed to the **triads** which voiceled around the circle-of-5ths in an **ascending** manner, as shown in **Figs. 6.10. - 6.11.**). Also note that this four-part voiceleading effectively results in an alternation between **root position** and **second inversion** chords. It is also possible to achieve a similar alternation between first and third inversion four-part chords around the 'circle', although as previously mentioned the first inversion is often less useful due to the 'exposed' second interval dissonance on top (see **p186** comments).

If we were now to continue this voiceleading technique within **major 7th** chords around the **entire circle-of-5ths**, we can derive the following example:-

### *Figure 6.25. Major 7th progression around the (complete) circle-of-5ths, with voiceleading*

*(contd>>>)*

## *Four-part chord voiceleading (contd)*

### *(Figure 6.25. contd)*

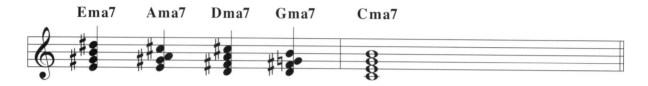

Note again that we have two commontones between each pair of consecutive chords, and that we are alternating between **root position** and **second inversion** chords throughout. In a similar manner to the triad progressions around the 'circle', the ending **Cma7** chord in the above example is exactly **one octave lower** than the beginning **Cma7** chord (at the bottom of the previous page) - so again it takes us one octave to voicelead around the complete circle-of-5ths using this method.

*(These circle-of-5ths/4ths four-part chord voiceleading concepts are presented from a keyboard perspective in **Chapter 6** of our **Pop Piano Book** keyboard method).*

Again note that in the preceding circle-of-5ths four-part voiceleading example, we began and ended with a **root position Cma7** chord. We could similarly have started on a **second inversion** chord, in which case all the commontones and subsequent inversions would be **correspondingly displaced** throughout. *(Please see **Appendix 3** for a complete summary of all major 7th and minor 7th four-part chord progressions around the circle-of-5ths/4ths, starting in root position and second inversion).*

Our next 'circular' four-chord, four-part progression contains **minor 7th** chords moving around the **circle-of-4ths**, as shown in the following example:-

### *Figure 6.26. Four-chord minor 7th progression around the circle-of-4ths, without voiceleading*

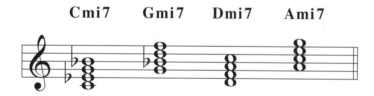

In a circle-of-4ths four-part chord sequence such as the above example, we can again see that there will always be **two commontones** between successive chords. The **fifth** and **seventh** of each chord is always present in the following chord i.e. the fifth & seventh of the first chord (**G** and **Bb**) are contained within the second chord (**Gmi7**), the fifth & seventh of the second chord (**D** and **F**) are contained within the third chord (**Dmi7**) and so on.

### Four-part chord voiceleading (contd)

Again here we will use a '**commontone voiceleading**' approach i.e. the two common-tones **retain their relative position between successive chords**. For example, the common-tones of **G** and **Bb** between the first two chords in the preceding example, are the **top** voices of the first **Cmi7** chord (assuming that this chord remains in **root position**) and we will there-fore **retain these notes as the top voices** of the following **Gmi7** chord (which in turn requires the **Gmi7** chord to be in **second inversion**). Applying this principle throughout this progression, we find that an **ascending** voiceleading direction results, as follows:-

**Figure 6.27. Four-chord minor 7th progression around the circle-of-4ths, with voiceleading**

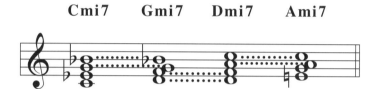

(Note again that the dotted lines are being used to connect the commontones between successive chords).

We can analyze the voiceleading used for the chords following the first (root position) **Cmi7** chord in the above example, as follows:-

**Gmi7** chord    -    As discussed above, the commontones of **G** and **Bb** (between this **Gmi7** chord and the preceding **Cmi7** chord) are the **top voices** of the preceding **Cmi7** chord, and we will therefore **retain them as the top voices** of this **Gmi7** chord. This requires the **Gmi7** chord to be in **second inversion**, resulting in a top note on this chord of **Bb**.

**Dmi7** chord -    The commontones of **D** and **F** (between this **Dmi7** chord and the preceding **Gmi7** chord) are the **bottom voices** of the preceding **Gmi7** chord, and we will therefore **retain them as the bottom voices** of this **Dmi7** chord. This requires the **Dmi7** chord to remain in **root position**, resulting in a top note on this chord of **C**.

**Ami7** chord -    The commontones of **A** and **C** (between this **Ami7** chord and the preceding **Dmi7** chord) are the **top voices** of the preceding **Dmi7** chord, and we will therefore **retain them as the top voices** of this **Ami7** chord. This requires the **Ami7** chord to be in **second inversion**, resulting in a top note on this chord of **C**.

### Four-part chord voiceleading (contd)

Note that when we use this 'commontone voiceleading' approach for these **four-part** chords moving around the circle-of-4ths, this resulted in an **ascending** voiceleading direction (as opposed to the **triads** which voiceled around the circle-of-4ths in a **descending** manner, as shown in **Figs. 6.13. - 6.14.**). Again note that the preceding voiceleading example resulted in an alternation between **root position** and **second inversion** chords.

If we were now to continue this voiceleading technique within **minor 7th** chords around the **entire circle-of-4ths**, we can derive the following example:-

### Figure 6.28. Minor 7th progression around the (complete) circle-of-4ths, with voiceleading

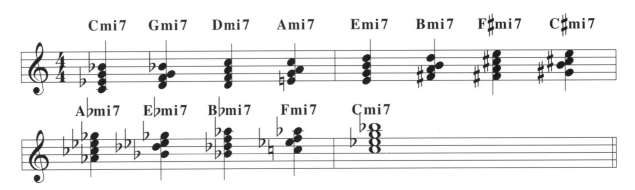

Note again that we have two commontones between each pair of consecutive chords, and that we are alternating between **root position** and **second inversion** chords throughout. The ending **Cmi7** chord in the above example is exactly **one octave higher** than the beginning **Cmi7** chord - so again it takes us one octave to voicelead around the complete circle-of-4ths using this method.

As with the previous circle-of-5ths four-part voiceleading example, we could have started the above progression with a **second inversion** chord, in which case all the commontones and subsequent inversions would be **correspondingly displaced** throughout.

## Chapter Six Workbook Questions

### 1.   *Diatonic triad voiceleading*

You are to voicelead the following diatonic triad progressions. This requires you to decide which inversion is needed for each chord symbol, and then write the chosen inversion on the staff following the first chord provided. You are to maintain 'static' voiceleading where possible i.e. where a commontone is available as the top voice of consecutive chords, you should keep this voice on top.

For questions 1 - 5, in situations where a commontone is not available as the top voice of consecutive chords, you are to voicelead the top voice in an *ascending* manner.

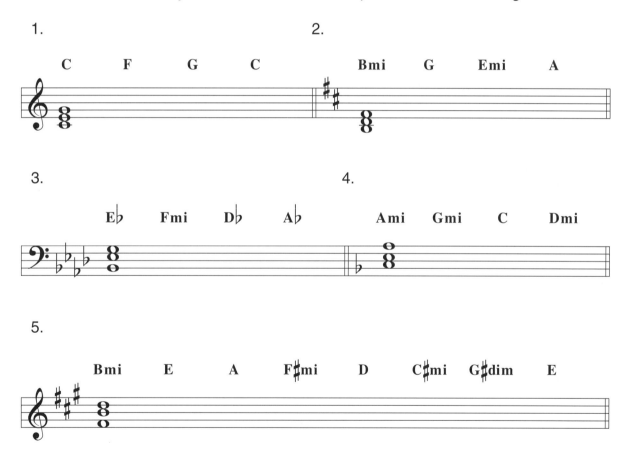

### 1. *Diatonic triad voiceleading (contd)*

For questions 6 - 10, in situations where a commontone is not available as the top voice of consecutive chords, you are to voicelead the top voice in a *descending* manner.

## 2. *Diatonic four-part chord voiceleading*

You are to voicelead the following diatonic four-part chord progressions. Again this requires you to decide which inversion is needed for each chord symbol, and then write the chosen inversion on the staff following the first chord provided. For the purpose of these exercises you should avoid using the first inversion four-part chord shape (with the less desirable 2nd interval on top). As in the previous section, you are to maintain 'static' voiceleading where possible i.e. where a commontone is available as the top voice of consecutive chords, you should keep this voice on top.

For questions 11 - 15, in situations where a commontone is not available as the top voice of consecutive chords, you are to voicelead the top voice in an *ascending* manner.

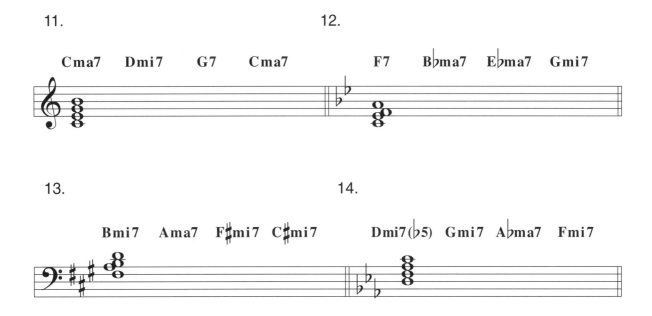

11.

Cma7    Dmi7    G7    Cma7

12.

F7    B♭ma7    E♭ma7    Gmi7

13.

Bmi7    Ama7    F♯mi7    C♯mi7

14.

Dmi7(♭5)    Gmi7    A♭ma7    Fmi7

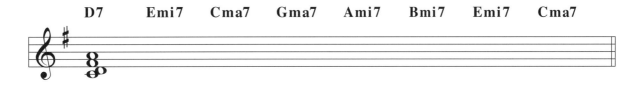

15.

D7    Emi7    Cma7    Gma7    Ami7    Bmi7    Emi7    Cma7

## 2. *Diatonic four-part chord voiceleading (contd)*

For questions 16 - 20, in situations where a commontone is not available as the top voice of consecutive chords, you are to voicelead the top voice in a *descending* manner.

16.

17.

18.

19.

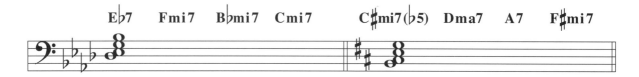

20.

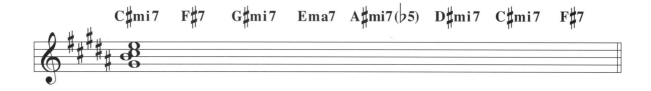

### 3.    *Triad voiceleading around the circle-of-fifths/fourths*

You are to voicelead the following triad progressions by writing the required inversions on the staff below the chord symbols, again following on from the first chord inversion provided. For the purpose of these exercises, you are to voicelead triads moving around the circle-of-5ths in a *static or ascending* manner, and triads moving around the circle-of-fourths in a *static or descending* manner.

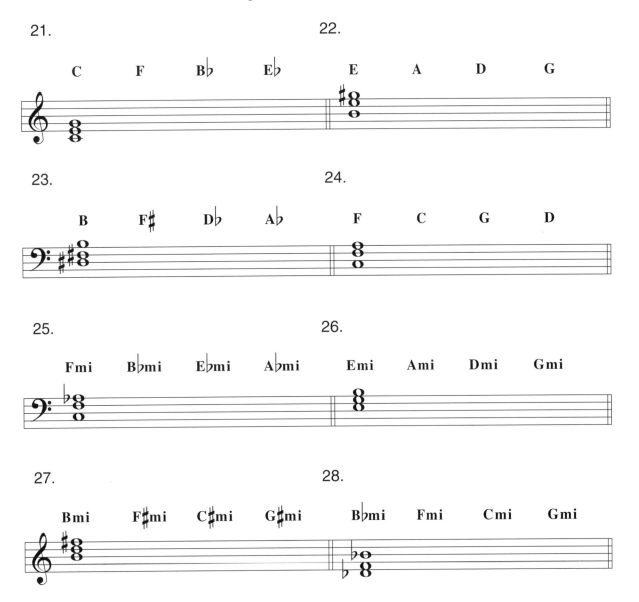

*4.* **_Four-part chord voiceleading around the circle-of-fifths/fourths_**

You are to voicelead the following four-part chord progressions by writing the required inversions on the staff below the chord symbols. For the purpose of these exercises, you are to voicelead four-part chords moving around the circle-of-5ths in a *static or descending* manner, and four-part chords moving around the circle-of-fourths in a *static or ascending manner.*

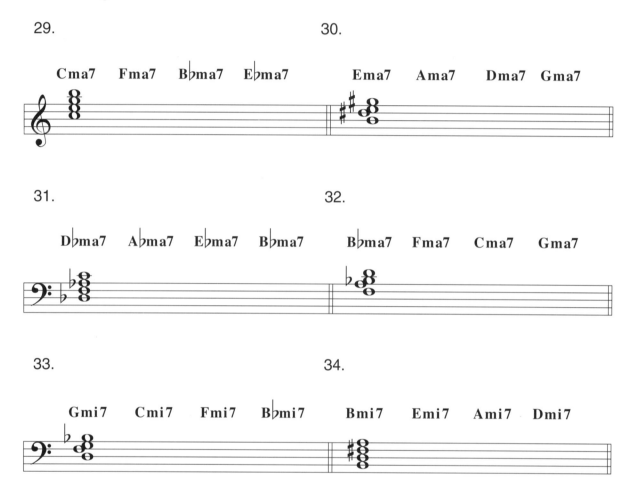

29.

Cma7    Fma7    B♭ma7    E♭ma7

30.

Ema7    Ama7    Dma7    Gma7

31.

D♭ma7    A♭ma7    E♭ma7    B♭ma7

32.

B♭ma7    Fma7    Cma7    Gma7

33.

Gmi7    Cmi7    Fmi7    B♭mi7

34.

Bmi7    Emi7    Ami7    Dmi7

35.

Fmi7    Cmi7    Gmi7    Dmi7

36.

C♯mi7    G♯mi7    D♯mi7    A♯mi7

## 5. *Correcting wrong voiceleading examples*

The following examples are a mixture of diatonic and circle-of-5ths/4ths progressions. One chord in each progression is incorrectly voiceled (i.e. the wrong inversion of the chord was used), resulting in an unnecessary top-note interval skip. You are to write asterisks over the incorrect voicing, and then write the correct inversion of the chord in the blank measure after each question, together with the appropriate chord symbol above the staff.

37.                                                     38.

39.                                                     40.

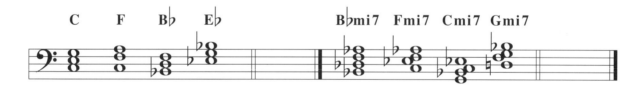

## Chapter Six Workbook Answers

### 1. *Diatonic triad voiceleading - answers*

**2.** *Diatonic four-part chord voiceleading - answers*

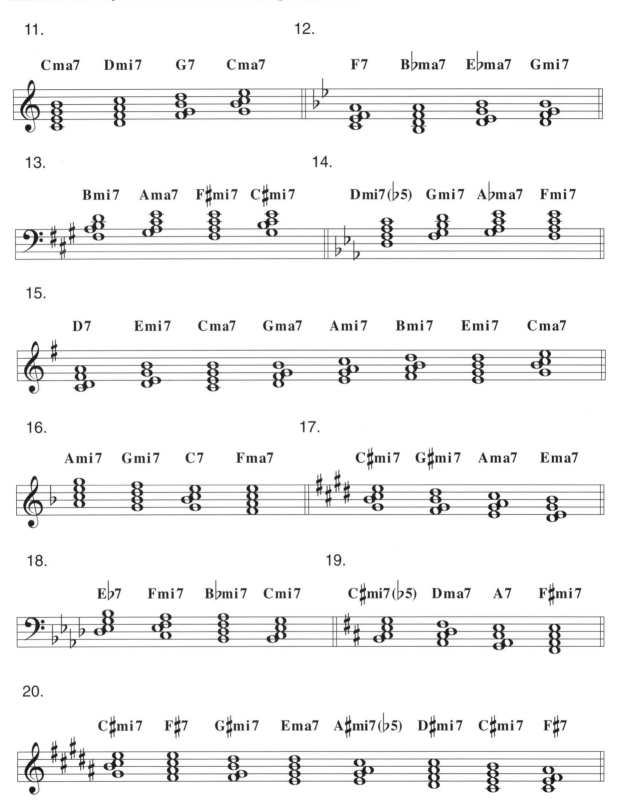

**3.** *Triad voiceleading around the circle-of-fifths/fourths - answers*

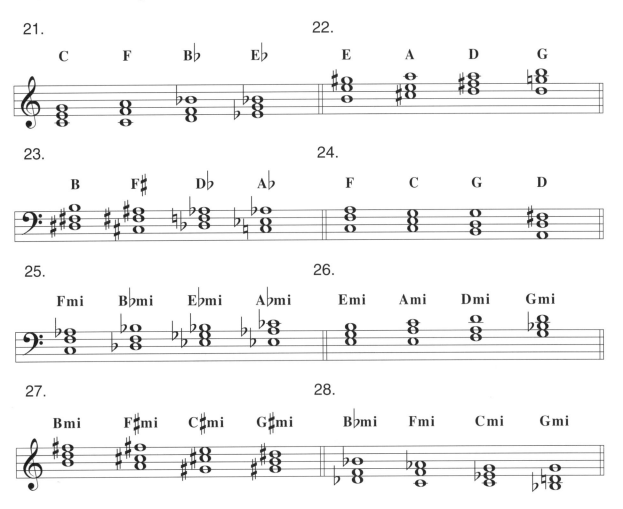

**4.** *Four-part chord voiceleading around the circle-of-fifths/fourths - answers*

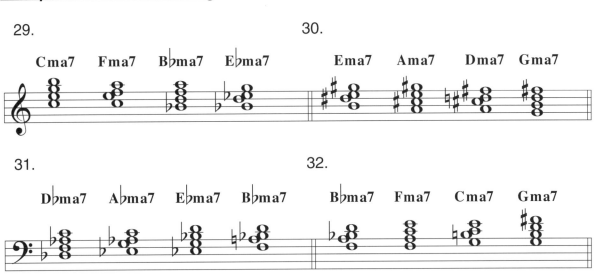

**4.** *Four-part chord voiceleading around the circle-of-fifths/fourths - answers (contd)*

33.                                              34.

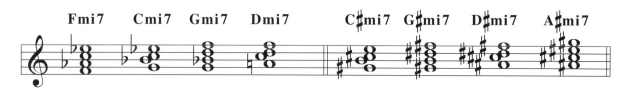

35.                                              36.

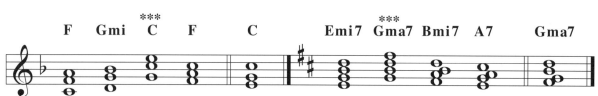

**5.** *Correcting wrong voiceleading examples - answers*

37.                                              38.

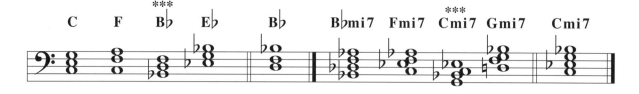

39.                                              40.

# *Chords using triad 'upper structures'*

## *Introduction*

Chords using triad 'upper structures' (also referred to as '**triad-over-root**' chords) are created by placing a major or minor triad over a root in the bass voice - for example the chord symbol **F/D** means an 'upper structure' of an **F major triad** is being placed over the note **D** in the bass voice. As this type of chord symbol contains a '/' (slash), these chords are also sometimes referred to as '**slash chords**'. This type of harmony is used in much of today's pop music.

We saw when working through *Chapters 2 - 5* that jazz and 'standard' styles are built around '**II - V - I**' chords (and substitutes) in major and minor keys. As these styles typically use key center changes in the harmony, we need the **definitive** quality of the '**II - V - I**' progression (and in particular the active tones in the dominant chord) to help our ear 'keep track of' the successive momentary keys being used.

By contrast, much of today's pop/rock/R'n'B music does not change keys nearly so much as jazz and 'standard' styles - therefore there is generally less need to keep defining the key center with '**II - V - I**'-type harmonies. These modern styles will instead typically use 'upper structure' chords, which have a transparent and 'open' quality and which are less definitive of a particular key (i.e. they can often belong to several keys). When analyzing progressions in these styles, we will therefore simply relate each chord to the **tonic of the overall key** - as opposed to our work on the jazz progressions in *Chapters 2 - 5* where we related each chord to a particular **momentary key** being used.

The application of 'triad-over-root' chords to a contemporary tune (i.e. working from a leadsheet or chord chart) will be in one or more of the following circumstances:-

*1)*    The required 'triad-over-root' chord may be **directly indicated** on the chart. For example, if we see the chord symbol **F/D** (as mentioned above) we can simply place the upper **F major triad** over **D** in the bass. *(Chord progression examples #1 - #6 in this chapter are presented in this manner i.e. with the 'slash' chords directly indicated).*

*2)*    We may need to **interpret** either a **composite** or a **basic triad** chord symbol by using a triad-over-root chord. (A '**composite**' chord symbol consists of a root note followed by a qualifier or 'suffix'). This interpretation will be in one of the following ways:-
-    We may be **literally translating** a chord symbol into a 'triad-over-root' chord. For example, if we see the composite chord symbol **Dmi7**, we may **literally translate** it to **F/D** (i.e. using a 'triad-over-root' chord which does not add or subtract any chord tones with respect to the original chord symbol).
-    We may be **upgrading** a chord symbol by using a 'triad-over-root' chord, if this is stylistically appropriate. For example, the basic triad symbol **Dmi** might be upgraded (effectively to a **Dmi7**) by using the **F/D** 'triad-over-root' chord as mentioned above.

## *Introduction (contd)*

In this chapter we will derive all commonly-used 'triad-over-root' relationships, and we will also see how these chords can be used (and analyzed) in major and minor keys. First we will summarize the four main types of chords which typically occur in contemporary pop styles, as follows:-

- **major** chords
- **minor** chords
- **dominant** chords (very frequently **suspended** in modern styles)
- **inverted** chords (i.e. placed over another chord tone such as the 3rd or 5th in the bass voice).

We will now derive 'triad-over-root' chords in each of the above categories.

## *Deriving 'triad-over-root' relationships for MAJOR chords*

In **Chapter 2** we have already created a five-part major chord (see derivation of the **Cma9** chord in **Fig. 2.17.**). Now in order to extract the required 'triad-over-root' relationships from the major chord 'stack', we need to extend this chord up to the **13th** as follows:-

### *Figure 7.1. C major 13th (with #11th) chord 'stack' and interval construction*

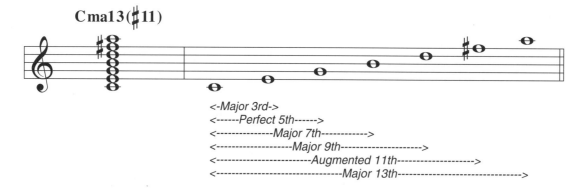

Note that this chord can be derived by taking the **Cma9** chord (as in **Fig. 2.17.**) and adding the notes which create **augmented 11th** and **major 13th** intervals from the root of the chord. The **11th** of this chord needs to be an **augmented 11th** (**F#** in this case) as the perfect 11th would clash with the **3rd** of the chord (**E** in this case).

Of course the above chord 'stack' (played all together) would sound very saturated and 'jazzy' - however we will now extract the required 'triad-over-root' relationships from this major chord 'stack', as shown on the following page:-

### Deriving 'triad-over-root' relationships for MAJOR chords (contd)

**Figure 7.2. 'Triad-over-root' relationships within the C major chord 'stack'**

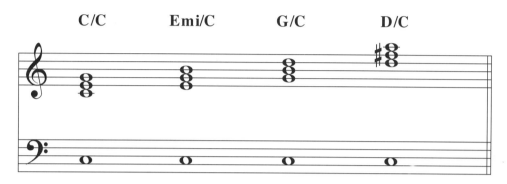

The following important general points should be made when discussing 'triad-over-root' relationships extracted from a chord 'stack', such as in the above example:-

- The upper triads shown above are only a 'subset' of those available within the overall chord 'stack' - however they are the combinations which are **most commonly used** in contemporary applications.
- Each of the above 'triad-over-root' relationships is a **potential voicing solution** for the type of chord in question (in this case a **major** chord).
- Each upper triad is '**built from**' a certain part of the overall chord. For example, the **Emi** triad shown above is built from the **3rd** of the overall **C major** chord, the **G** triad is built from the 5th of the overall **C major** chord, etc.
- Each upper triad could be used **in any inversion**, to accommodate melody or harmonic voiceleading considerations.
- The upper triads **do not by themselves define the chord** - they need to be placed **over** the root of the overall chord (in this case **C**) in the bass register, in order to create the required result.

Now we will look at the above 'triad-over-root' chords in greater detail, as follows:-

- ***C/C***      This is the most basic 'triad-over-root' voicing for a **C major** chord, and is suitable for simpler contemporary applications. (Although the symbol '**C/C**' has been used here for the purposes of illustration, generally the basic triad symbol '**C**' would be used in practice). This voicing consists of a **major triad built from the root of a major chord**, and we will therefore refer to it as a __1-3-5__ upper structure voicing.

*(This 'numeric' method of labelling upper structure triad voicings is also used in our contemporary keyboard method **The Pop Piano Book**, from **Chapter 5** onwards).*

## *Deriving 'triad-over-root' relationships for MAJOR chords (contd)*

### *(Explanation of triad-over-root chords in Fig. 7.2. contd)*

- **Emi/C**  This 'triad-over-root' voicing creates a fully-defined **major seventh** chord. (The term 'fully-defined' is used here because this voicing contains the **3rd** and **7th** of the chord, which as we have seen are the critical definitive tones). The chord symbol which is a **composite equivalent** of this **Emi/C** would be **Cma7**. This voicing consists of a **minor triad built from the 3rd of a major chord**, and we will therefore refer to it as a <u>3-5-7</u> upper structure voicing. Although useful in basic jazz and older pop music settings, this voicing may sound dated in modern contemporary styles.

- **G/C**  This 'triad-over-root' voicing creates a **major ninth** chord with the **third omitted**. The resulting transparent quality is highly useful in modern pop styles. The chord symbols which are **composite equivalents** of this **G/C** would be **Cma9(no3)** or **Cma9(omit3)**. This voicing consists of a **major triad built from the 5th of a major chord**, and we will therefore refer to it as a <u>5-7-9</u> upper structure voicing.

- **D/C**  This 'triad-over-root' voicing creates a **major thirteenth with sharped eleventh** chord, with the **third, fifth and seventh omitted**. This voicing has a sophisticated quality (mainly due to the sharped **11th**) which makes it useful in more evolved contemporary applications. (There is really no practical chord symbol which is a **composite equivalent** of this **D/C**). This voicing consists of a **major triad built from the 9th of a major chord**, and we will therefore refer to it as a <u>9-#11-13</u> upper structure voicing. *(Later in this chapter we will see that this voicing can also be used to imply an **inverted dominant** chord quality).*

## *Deriving 'triad-over-root' relationships for MINOR chords*

Now we will go through a similar process to derive the commonly-used 'triad-over-root' voicings for minor chords. Again the general observations noted on the previous page will also apply here. We recall that minor chords which are larger than triads (i.e. 4-part or above) may either have a **minor 7th** interval present (as in the **minor 7th** chord first seen in **Fig. 1.14.**) or a **major 6th** or **7th** interval present (as in the **minor 6th** and **minor major 7th** chords first seen in **Figs. 1.30.** and **1.29.**). Although the **minor 6th** and **minor major 7th** chords are very useful in jazz contexts, in modern contemporary applications we invariably use the **minor 7th** form (i.e. containing a **minor 7th** interval) when expanding the minor chord to 4-part or above.

This means that we will base our 'triad-over-root' relationships for minor chords, on the **minor 9th** chord 'stack' as derived in **Fig. 2.11.** However, we now need to extend this chord up to the **11th**, as shown in the example on the following page:-

### Deriving 'triad-over-root' relationships for MINOR chords (contd)

#### Figure 7.3. D minor 11th chord 'stack' and interval construction

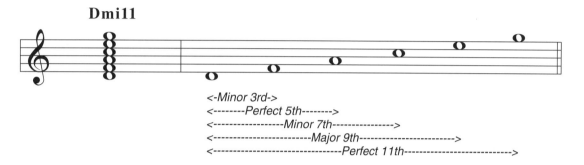

Note that this chord can be derived by taking the **Dmi9** chord (as in **Fig. 2.11.**) and adding the note which creates a **perfect 11th** interval from the root of the chord. Again as with the previous major chord 'stack', the above chord sounds rather dense if played all together - however we will now extract the required 'triad-over-root' relationships from this minor chord 'stack', as follows:-

#### Figure 7.4. 'Triad-over-root' relationships within the D minor chord 'stack'

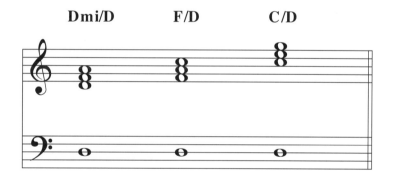

*(Again we have only extracted the 'triad-over-root' chords most commonly used in contemporary applications).*

Now we will analyze the above 'triad-over-root' chords as follows:-

- ***Dmi/D*** This is the most basic 'triad-over-root' voicing for a **D minor** chord, and is suitable for simpler contemporary applications. (Although the symbol '**Dmi/D**' has been used here for the purposes of illustration, generally the basic triad symbol '**Dmi**' would be used in practice). This voicing consists of a **minor triad built from the root of a minor chord**, and we will therefore refer to it as a <u>**1-b3-5**</u> upper structure voicing.

## *Deriving 'triad-over-root' relationships for MINOR chords (contd)*

**(Explanation of triad-over-root chords in Fig. 7.4. contd)**

- *F/D*     This 'triad-over-root' voicing creates a fully-defined **minor seventh** chord. (Again the term 'fully-defined' is used here because this voicing contains the **3rd** and **7th** of the chord). The chord symbol which is a **composite equivalent** of this **F/D** would be **Dmi7**. This voicing consists of a **major triad built from the 3rd of a minor chord**, and we will therefore refer to it as a <u>**b3-5-b7**</u> upper structure voicing. This 'triad-over-root' structure is widely used for minor and minor 7th-type chords in most pop music styles.

- *C/D*     This 'triad-over-root' voicing creates a **minor eleventh** chord with the **third** and **fifth omitted**. When used in a minor chord context, it has an 'open' and less defined quality. The chord symbol which would be an exact **composite equivalent** of this **C/D** would be **Dmi11(omit 3,5)** - although technically correct, this is a rather 'unwieldy' symbol which is less likely to be used in actual practice. This voicing consists of a **major triad built from the 7th of a minor chord**, and we will therefore refer to it as a <u>**b7-9-11**</u> upper structure voicing. *(We will shortly see that this voicing is also typically used for a **suspended dominant** chord).*

## *Deriving 'triad-over-root' relationships for DOMINANT chords*

Now we will look at the dominant chord to see if any useful 'triad-over-root' relationships can be derived. We recall that dominant chords can be **suspended** as in **Figs. 1.32.** and **2.15.**, and in the great majority of cases this suspended dominant quality is preferred in contemporary applications (see **Fig. 2.5.** and accompanying text). A 'triad-over-root' voicing which gave us this suspended dominant quality would therefore be very useful. As discussed in the text following **Fig. 2.15.**, the suspension on the dominant is equivalent to the **11th** of the chord - so we can extend the dominant chord 'stack' (derived in **Fig. 2.13.**) up to the **11th**, as follows:-

### *Figure 7.5. G dominant 11th chord 'stack' and interval construction*

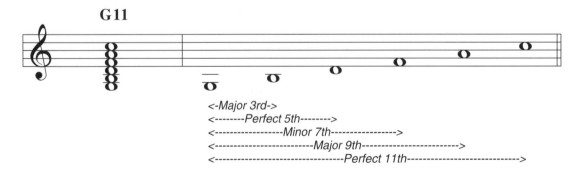

### Deriving 'triad-over-root' relationships for DOMINANT chords (contd)

Note that the dominant chord 'stack' shown at the bottom of the previous page, contains a conflict - the **3rd** of the chord (the note **B** in this case, required for the 'regular' or **unsuspended** dominant chord) clashes with the **11th** (the note **C** in this case, required for the **suspended** dominant chord). There are really no good-sounding 'triad-over-root' solutions for 'regular' or **unsuspended** dominant chords (although we will present a four-part 'upper structure' solution in *Chapter 8*). However, we can create a voicing for a **suspended** dominant chord, as shown within the following 'triad-over-root' relationships extracted from the dominant chord 'stack':-

### Figure 7.6. 'Triad-over-root' relationships within the G dominant chord 'stack'

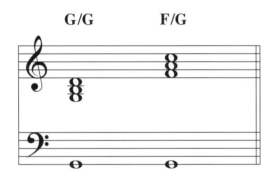

*(Again we have only extracted the 'triad-over-root' chords most commonly used in contemporary applications).*

Now we will analyze the above 'triad-over-root' chords as follows:-

- *G/G*    This voicing contained within the dominant chord 'stack' is the same as the basic <u>**1-3-5**</u> major chord voicing derived from the bottom of the major chord 'stack' - see **Fig. 7.2.** and accompanying text.

- *F/G*    This 'triad-over-root' voicing creates a **suspended dominant ninth** (also known as a **dominant eleventh**) chord. The presence of the **11th** of the chord (**C** in this case) implies that the **3rd** of the chord (**B** in this case) has been omitted. The other chord tone from the 'stack' which has been omitted is the **5th**, which is **not** an important definitive note on the chord. Therefore for all practical purposes, the chord symbols which are **composite equivalents** of this **F/G** would be **G9sus** or **G11** (review **Fig. 2.15.** and accompanying text as necessary). This voicing consists of a **major triad built from the 7th of a dominant chord**, and we will therefore refer to it as a <u>**b7-9-11**</u> upper structure voicing. Note that this 'triad-over-root' voicing was also available within the minor chord 'stack', as discussed on the previous page. In many cases however, this voicing will be heard and used in the **suspended dominant** capacity outlined above (particularly if the chord is resolving to the next chord on a **V - to - I** basis, as shown in the example on the following page).

## Deriving 'triad-over-root' relationships for DOMINANT chords (contd)

We will now look at an example of how the preceding **suspended dominant** chord (i.e. the **F/G**) might resolve to a **I** or **tonic** chord, as follows:-

### Figure 7.7. Suspended-dominant-to-tonic progression using 'triad-over-root' chords

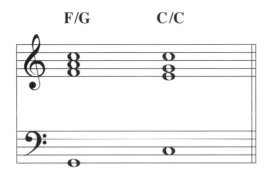

We can make the following observations concerning the above progression:-

- The first chord is a suspended dominant, using a **b7-9-11** 'triad-over-root' voicing as seen in **Fig. 7.6**.
- The second chord is a basic major chord, using a **1-3-5** 'triad-over-root' voicing as seen in **Fig. 7.2**.
- The upper triads (**F** to **C**) are actually moving in a **circle-of-4ths** sequence, even though the overall harmony is moving on a **V - to - I** basis (i.e. **circle-of-5ths**).
- The voiceleading of the upper triads follows the normal **circle-of-4ths** voiceleading rules (see **Chapter 6** and **Appendix 3**).

This type of progression and voicing solution is used in a great many pop tunes!

## Deriving 'triad-over-root' relationships for INVERTED chords

Now we will derive the 'triad-over-root' relationships used for inverted chords. Note here that we are **not** simply talking about the inversion of the upper triad (which as discussed may be in any inversion depending upon voiceleading requirements). Rather, this is referring to situations where chords are **placed over** tones other than the root in the bass voice (i.e. placed over the **3rd** or **5th** of the chord), thereby changing the **vertical quality** of the chord. For example, the 'triad-over-root' symbol **C/E** is an **inversion** as it indicates that a **C major** triad has been placed over its **3rd** in the bass voice.

### Deriving 'triad-over-root' relationships for INVERTED chords (contd)

This leads to an important distinction we need to make between the 'triad-over-root' voicing used so far (on **major**, **minor** and **dominant** chords) and these new 'triad-over-root' voicings used for **inversions**, as follows:-

- On **major**, **minor** and **dominant** chords, the **note to the right of the slash** (in the 'slash chord' symbol) was the **root of the 'real chord'**, and the **triad to the left of the slash** was the '**upper structure' on this chord**. For example, in the **F/D** chord shown in **Fig. 7.4.**, the note **D** is the the root of the chord (as discussed on **p212**, the composite equivalent is **Dmi7**), and the **F major** triad is an upper structure used on this chord.
- However on these **inverted** chords, the **triad to the left of the slash** indicates what the '**real chord'** is, and the **note to the right of the slash** indicates the **part of this chord** (i.e. 3rd, 5th etc.) which has been **placed in the bass voice**. For example, in the **C/E** chord mentioned on the previous page (and shown below), the **C** triad is <u>**not some upper structure of an E chord**</u> - this is still a **C** chord, but inverted over its **3rd** (**E**) in the bass.

So how do we tell the difference between these two overall categories of 'slash' chord symbols? A quick rule-of-thumb is to see if the note used in the bass voice (i.e. on the right of the slash) is within the upper triad (i.e. the triad to the left of the slash). If it is, then the chord symbol represents an inversion (or a basic **1-3-5** or **1-b3-5** voicing as shown in **Figs. 7.2.** and **7.4.**), otherwise it is some kind of 'upper structure' on a major, minor or dominant chord.

*(There is actually one potential exception to this rule that we need to be aware of! We already mentioned on **p210** that the **9-#11-13** upper structure on the major chord, can also function in an **inverted dominant** capacity - so this chord can actually belong to both of the above categories - more about this shortly).*

Now we will look at **major** and **minor** triads inverted over the **3rd** and **5th** in the bass voice. This is used very frequently in pop harmony (particularly on the major triad), and is often done to achieve a melodic bass line quality. First we will look at inversions below the major triad (using **C major** as an example), as follows:-

### Figure 7.8. 'Triad-over-root' relationships used for C major inversions

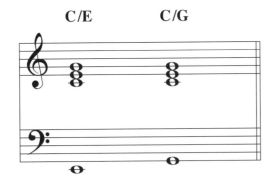

**215**

### Deriving 'triad-over-root' relationships for INVERTED chords (contd)

Again note that in the example at the bottom of the previous page, the upper triads can actually be in any inversion - the overall **inverted quality** is created here by the use of the **3rd** or **5th** of the triad in the **bass voice**. Now we will analyze these 'triad-over-root' inverted chords as follows:-

- **C/E**    This 'triad-over-root' voicing creates a **major triad inverted over its third**. It is arguably an 'unstable' inversion, as we feel that it wants to resolve or move to another chord (typically via a scalewise or circle-of-5ths root movement, as in a great number of David Foster tunes for example)! As this is still really a **C major** chord (see discussion on previous page), we will refer to it as a **1-3-5** upper structure voicing, but inverted over the **3rd** in the bass voice. Note however that this voicing is technically equivalent to a **minor triad with sharped 5th** i.e. **Emi(#5)** in this case - although you will sometimes encounter the **mi(#5)** symbol on charts and sheet music, this voicing will actually be heard and used as an **inverted major triad** (over the 3rd) in the great majority of cases.

- **C/G**    This 'triad-over-root' voicing creates a **major triad inverted over its fifth**. It has more 'stability' than the above inversion over the 3rd (and seems to be especially favoured in gospel styles). Again as this is still really a **C major** chord, we will refer to it as a **1-3-5** upper structure voicing, but inverted over the **5th** in the bass voice.

Now we will look at inversions below the minor triad (using **D minor** as an example):-

### Figure 7.9. 'Triad-over-root' relationships used for D minor inversions

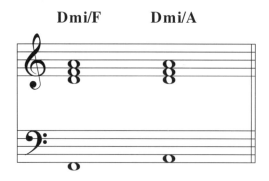

Now we will further analyze the above inversions as follows:-

- **Dmi/F**    This 'triad-over-root' voicing creates a **minor triad inverted over its third**. Again as this is still really a **D minor** chord, we will refer to it as a **1-b3-5** upper structure voicing, but inverted over the **3rd** in the bass voice.

- **Dmi/A**    This 'triad-over-root' voicing creates a **minor triad inverted over its fifth**. Again as this is still really a **D minor** chord, we will refer to it as a **1-b3-5** upper structure voicing, but inverted over the **5th** in the bass voice.

### Deriving 'triad-over-root' relationships for INVERTED chords (contd)

Now we will look at a final inversion example which is something of a 'special case' situation. We reviewed the construction and function of the basic **dominant 7th** chord in *Chapter 2* (i.e. in **Fig. 2.10.**) using a **G7** chord as an example. If we **remove the 7th** from the upper part of this chord and **place it in the bass voice**, a 'triad-over-root' relationship is created:-

**Figure 7.10. Creating a 'triad-over-root' relationship by placing the 7th of a G7 chord in the bass voice**

The above 'triad-over-root' chord is in fact a **dominant seventh chord inverted over its seventh**. In this context it is really a '**G**' chord rather than an '**F**' chord, and so we will refer to it as a **1-3-5** upper structure voicing, but inverted over the **b7th** in the bass voice. *NOTE HOWEVER* that this voicing is the same as the **9-#11-13** upper structure on the major chord seen in **Fig. 7.2.** (i.e. in different circumstances the **D/C** shown in **Fig. 7.2.** could function as an **inverted D7** chord). As noted on **p215**, this vertical structure therefore has two distinct and different functions:-

- as a **9-#11-13** upper structure on a major chord (as in **Fig. 7.2.**)
- as an **inverted dominant 7th** chord (**1-3-5** inverted over the **b7**) as described above.

We will now see an example of this chord functioning as an inverted dominant 7th chord:-

**Figure 7.11. Inverted-dominant to inverted-tonic progression using 'triad-over-root' chords**

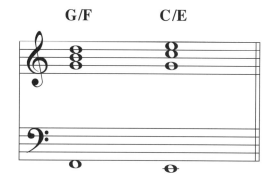

### *Deriving 'triad-over-root' relationships for INVERTED chords (contd)*

We can make the following observations concerning the progression shown at the bottom of the previous page:-

- The first chord is an **inverted dominant**, using a <u>1-3-5</u> 'triad-over-root' voicing inverted over the **7th**, as in **Fig. 7.10**.
- The second chord is an **inverted major** chord, using a <u>1-3-5</u> 'triad-over-root' voicing inverted over the **3rd**, as in **Fig. 7.8**.
- This progression is actually a <u>**V - to - I**</u> (dominant to tonic) progression in the key of **C**. However, instead of moving from **G** to **C** in the bass voice as might be expected, we instead move 'scalewise' from **F** to **E**. (From a '**solfeg**' standpoint, instead of a **SO to DO** circle-of-5ths movement in the bass, we have a **FA to MI** resolution).
- The upper triads (**G** to **C**) are moving in a **circle-of-5ths** sequence, and are following the normal **circle-of-5ths** voiceleading rules (see **Chapter 6** and **Appendix 3**).

This type of <u>**V - to - I**</u> progression using inversions is again frequently encountered.

### *Summary of upper structure 'triad-over-root' relationships derived so far*

We can summarize these commonly-used 'triad-over-root' voicings on **major**, **minor**, **dominant** and **inverted** chords as follows:-

| | | | |
|---|---|---|---|
| ***Major chords*** | <u>1-3-5</u> | as in **C/C**. | Basic major quality. |
| ***(Fig. 7.2.)*** | <u>3-5-7</u> | as in **Emi/C**. | Fully defined major 7th. |
| | <u>5-7-9</u> | as in **G/C**. | Transparent, 'modern' major. |
| | <u>9-#11-13</u> | as in **D/C** | Upper tension, sophisticated. |
| | | | |
| ***Minor chords*** | <u>1-b3-5</u> | as in **Dmi/D**. | Basic minor quality. |
| ***(Fig. 7.4.)*** | <u>b3-5-b7</u> | as in **F/D**. | Fully defined minor 7th. |
| | <u>b7-9-11</u> | as in **C/D**. | 'Open' and less defined minor. |
| | | | |
| ***Dominant chords*** | <u>b7-9-11</u> | as in **F/G**. | Suspended dominant quality. |
| ***(Fig. 7.6.)*** | | | |
| | | | |
| ***Inverted chords*** | <u>1-3-5, over the 3rd</u> | as in **C/E**. | Major triad inverted over the 3rd. |
| ***(Figs. 7.8. - 7.10.)*** | <u>1-3-5, over the 5th</u> | as in **C/G**. | Major triad inverted over the 5th. |
| | <u>1-b3-5, over the b3rd</u> | as in **Dmi/F**. | Minor triad inverted over the 3rd. |
| | <u>1-b3-5, over the 5th</u> | as in **Dmi/A**. | Minor triad inverted over the 5th. |
| | <u>1-3-5, over the b7th</u> | as in **G/F**. | Dominant chord inverted over the 7th. |

## Voiceleading 'triad-over-root' chords around the circle-of-5ths/4ths

As an exercise we could take any of the previous 'triad-over-root' voicings for major, minor, dominant or inverted chords and take them round the **circle-of-5ths** or **circle-of-4ths**. The upper (major or minor) triad shapes would then **voicelead** according to the principles established in *Chapter 6*. For example, if we built a **b7-9-11** upper structure voicing on a **D dominant** (or **D minor**) chord, this would use a **C major** upper triad (as seen in **Fig. 7.4.** in the context of a **D minor** chord). This structure could then be 'voiceled' around the circle-of-5ths:-

**Figure 7.12. Suspended dominant OR 'less defined' minor chord (using b7-9-11 upper structure as in Figs. 7.6. & 7.4.) moving around the circle-of-5ths**

(*Again note that the **b7-9-11** 'triad-over-root' voicing is available both on the **suspended dominant** chord as shown in **Fig. 7.6.**, and on the **minor** chord as shown in **Fig. 7.4.**).*

In the above example we can observe the following:-

- Each voicing above is a **b7-9-11** structure i.e. the upper major triad in each case is built from the **b7th** (minor 7th) of the chord defined by the root voice. A **suspended dominant** or (less defined) **minor** chord is therefore created in each case.
- The **b7-9-11** 'triad-over-root' voicings shown in **Fig. 7.4.** (i.e. the **C/D**) and in **Fig. 7.6.** (i.e. the **F/G**) are the first two chords in the above example, with the upper **C** and **F major** triads being in root position and 2nd inversion respectively.
- The voiceleading of the upper major triads follows the normal circle-of-5ths conventions as first seen in **Fig. 6.11.**

Next we will voicelead another 'triad-over-root' voicing around the entire circle-of-4ths. If we built a **3-5-7** upper structure voicing (as in **Fig. 7.2.**) on an **Ab major** chord, this would use a **C minor** upper triad. This structure could then be 'voiceled' around the circle-of-4ths as shown on the following page:-

## *Voiceleading 'triad-over-root' chords around the circle-of-5ths/4ths (contd)*

### *Figure 7.13. Major seventh chord (using 3-5-7 upper structure as in Fig. 7.2.) moving around the circle-of-4ths*

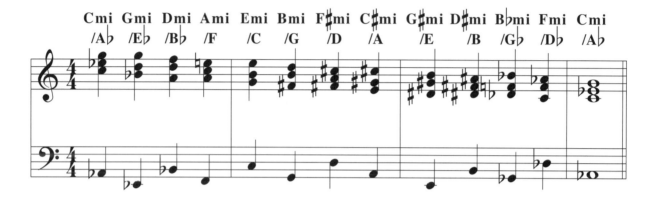

In the above example we can observe the following:-

- Each voicing above is a **3-5-7** structure i.e. the upper minor triad in each case is built from the **3rd** of the major chord defined by the root voice. A **major seventh** chord is therefore created in each case.
- The major 7th 'triad-over-root' voicing shown in **Fig. 7.2.** (i.e. the **Emi/C**) is the fifth chord in the above example, with the upper **E minor** triad being in 1st inversion.
- The voiceleading of the upper minor triads follows the normal circle-of-4ths conventions as first seen in **Fig. 6.14.**

  *(Please refer to **Chapter 5** of our contemporary keyboard method **The Pop Piano Book**, for playing exercises which take all of these 'triad-over-root' relationships around the circle-of-5ths and circle-of-4ths).*

## *Using 'triad-over-root' chord voicings within major keys*

In simpler pop music applications, it is common for all of the preceding 'triad-over-root' relationships to be used in a diatonic framework. It is therefore a useful exercise to determine which of the various upper structure voicings are contained within a particular major key. We can also analyze (using roman numerals) the scale degrees from which the upper structure triads and the roots are constructed. A chart of all the commonly-used 'triad-over-root' voicings within the key of **C major** (together with a 'roman numeral' analysis of the upper triads and roots) is now presented on the following page:-

## Using 'triad-over-root' chord voicings within major keys (contd)

### Figure 7.14. Chart and analysis of all 'triad-over-root' chords in the key of C major

## *Using 'triad-over-root' chord voicings within major keys (contd)*

It's important that we understand the chart shown in **Fig. 7.14.** on the previous page! The following notes should help you 'navigate' your way around this chart:-

- Each of the chords shown represents a **'triad-over-root'** relationship available within the key of **C major**.

- The **bottom** staff in the chart shows all of the available root voices in the key of **C major**.

- The chords are grouped in **columns**, corresponding to the **root voice** used in each chord (the note **to the right of the slash** in the chord symbol). For example, at the bottom of the first column we have the first available root voice of **C**, and above this (in the same column) we have all of the available 'triad-over-root' chords which use **C** as the root voice.

- The **type** of chord is indicated by the text on the left of the chart, as follows:-
    - the **top two** staffs contain **inverted** chords, as shown in **Figs. 7.8. - 7.11.**
    - the **third staff from the top** contains **suspended dominant** chords, as shown in **Figs. 7.6. - 7.7.** *(We also recall that these b7-9-11 structures occurred within the minor chord 'stack', as in Fig. 7.4.).*
    - the **fourth** and **fifth staffs from the top** contain **minor** chords, as shown in **Fig. 7.4.**
    - the **second**, **third** and **fourth staffs from the bottom** contain **major** chords, as shown in **Fig. 7.2.**
      *(Note that the G/F chord at the top of the middle column is marked with asterisks - this is to signify that, although on the chart it has been included within the inverted chords, it can also function as an 'upper structure' on a major chord - review Fig. 7.10. and accompanying text as necessary).*

- A **roman numeral** symbol is shown next to each chord in the table. This indicates the **relationship** of the **upper triad** and the **root voice** to the **key being used** (in this case **C major**). For example:-
    - on the top left of the chart we have an **F/C** chord, using the roman numeral symbol *IV/I*. This signifies that:-
        - the upper **F** major triad is a **IV** in the key of **C**.
        - the root voice of **C** is a **I** (or tonic) in the key of **C**.
    - the last (rightmost) chord on the second staff line is an **Emi/B** chord, using the roman numeral symbol *IIImi/VII*. This signifies that:-
        - the upper **E** minor triad is a **IIImi** in the key of **C**.
        - the root voice of **B** is a **VII** (i.e. is the 7th degree) in the key of **C**.

We will now use these **roman numeral** symbols to analyze how 'triad-over-root' chords are used in various contemporary applications.

## *Using 'triad-over-root' chord voicings within major keys (contd)*

The following contemporary progression examples are presented in the key of **C major**, for ease of reference to the 'triad-over-root' chart in **Fig. 7.14.** (However, these concepts will of course work in every major key). Each chord has been analyzed by applying a 'roman numeral' symbol, indicating the relationship of the chord to the key of **C major** (again as shown in **Fig. 7.14.**). As we said in the introduction to this chapter, this is a rather simpler analysis than was required for the more jazz-oriented progressions in *Chapters 2 - 5*, where we needed to establish the various **momentary keys** being used - here everything is being viewed as belonging to the (overall) major key. Here is our first progression analyzed using this method:-

*Figure 7.15. Harmonic analysis progression example #1 (this progression is typically used for the first eight measures of the Christopher Cross pop ballad "Sailing")*

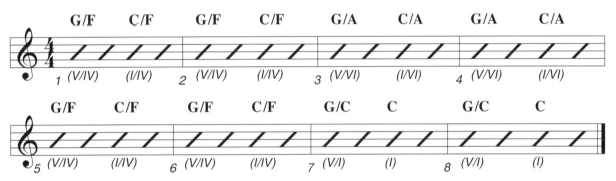

We can further describe the 'upper structure relationships' used on each chord (which are all contained within the summary at the bottom of **p218**) as follows:-

| | |
|---|---|
| ***Measures 1 & 2*** - | The **G/F** chord (which is a ***V/IV*** in the key of **C**) could be **either** a <u>9-#11-13</u> upper structure on an **F major** chord (see **Fig. 7.2.**) **or** an **inverted G7** dominant chord (i.e. a <u>1-3-5</u> inverted over the **b7**, as in **Fig. 7.10.**). In this context where the chord is 'alternating' with the **C/F** (another upper structure on an **F major** chord), it is more likely to be heard as a <u>9-#11-13</u> upper structure on this **F major** chord. |
| - | The **C/F** chord (which is a ***I/IV*** in the key of **C**) is a <u>5-7-9</u> upper structure on an **F major** chord (see **Fig. 7.2.**). |
| ***Measures 3 & 4*** - | The **G/A** chord (which is a ***V/VI*** in the key of **C**) is a <u>b7-9-11</u> upper structure with respect to the **A** in the bass. We know that this 'triad-over-root' chord functions in a **suspended dominant** capacity (as in **Fig. 7.6.**) as well as occurring within the **minor chord** 'stack' (as in **Fig. 7.4.**). In this context where the chord is 'alternating' with the **C/A** (an upper structure explicitly defining an **A minor 7th** chord, as in **Fig. 7.4.**), this chord is more likely to be heard as a <u>b7-9-11</u> upper structure within this (same) **A minor** chord. |
| - | The **C/A** chord (which is a ***I/VI*** in the key of **C**) is a <u>b3-5-b7</u> upper structure on an **A minor** chord (see **Fig. 7.4.**). |

## Using 'triad-over-root' chord voicings within major keys (contd)

*(Description of upper structure relationships within Fig. 7.15. contd)*

**(Measures 5 & 6**     *Same comments as for measures 1 & 2).*

**Measures**     -     The **G/C** chord (which is a *V/I* in the key of **C**) is a <u>**5-7-9**</u> upper structure
**7 & 8**                on a **C major** chord (see **Fig. 7.2.**).

              -     The **C** chord (which is simply a *I* in the key of **C**) is a <u>**1-3-5**</u> upper structure
                    on a **C major** chord (see **Fig. 7.2.**).

In the next progression example (again in the key of **C major**), the specific chord rhythm required is indicated using a **'rhythmic notation'** frequently found in contemporary charts:-

**Figure 7.16. Harmonic analysis progression example #2** *(this progression is typically used for the first four measures of the "Hill St. Blues" T.V. theme)*

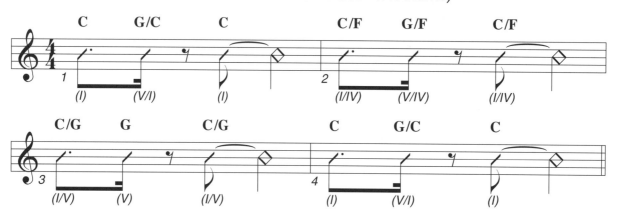

Again we can further describe the **'upper structure relationships'** used as follows:-

**Measure 1**     -     The **C** chord (which is simply a *I* in the key of **C**) is a <u>**1-3-5**</u> upper structure
                       on a **C major** chord (see **Fig. 7.2.**).

                 -     The **G/C** chord (which is a *V/I* in the key of **C**) is a <u>**5-7-9**</u> upper structure
                       on a **C major** chord (see **Fig. 7.2.**).

**Measure 2**     -     The **C/F** chord (which is a *I/IV* in the key of **C**) is a <u>**5-7-9**</u> upper structure
                       on an **F major** chord (see **Fig. 7.2.**).

                 -     The **G/F** chord (which is a *V/IV* in the key of **C**) is a <u>**9-#11-13**</u> upper
                       structure on an **F major** chord (see **Fig. 7.2.**).

**Measure 3**     -     The **C/G** chord (which is a *I/V* in the key of **C**) is a <u>**1-3-5**</u> upper structure
                       **inverted over its 5th** (see **Fig. 7.8.**).

                 -     The **G** chord (which is a *V* in the key of **C**) is a <u>**1-3-5**</u> upper structure
                       on a **G major** chord (see **Fig. 7.2.**).

**(Measure 4**     *Same comments as for measure 1).*

Now we will see which 'triad-over-root' voicings are available within the key of **C minor**, (again with a 'roman numeral' analysis relating to the tonic of **C**), as shown on the following page:-

## Using 'triad-over-root' chord voicings within minor keys

**Figure 7.17. Chart and analysis of all 'triad-over-root' chords in the key of C minor**

### Using 'triad-over-root' chord voicings within minor keys (contd)

Note that while the chart in **Fig. 7.14.** showed all of the commonly-used 'triad-over-root' voicings in the key of **C major** (i.e. within the **C major** scale), the chart in **Fig. 7.17.** on the previous page shows all of the commonly-used 'triad-over-root' voicings in the key of **C minor** (and within the **C natural minor** scale). Contemporary tunes in minor keys typically work within the restriction of the **natural minor** scale (as opposed to jazz applications which frequently 'combine' the different minor scales as needed). We recall from **Fig. 1.26.** that a **natural minor** scale results when we use a minor key signature with no additional accidentals - therefore all of the chords in **Fig. 7.17.** on the previous page, are available when the **C minor key signature** (i.e. three flats) is 'in force'.

The roman numeral analysis and chart 'layout' for **Fig. 7.17.** is essentially the same as for **Fig. 7.14.** (see comments on **p222**). Again note that:-

- the **Bb/Ab** chord at the top of the 2nd column from the right is marked with asterisks to signify that it could function as either an **inverted dominant** or an '**upper structure**' on a **major** chord - see comments on the **G/F** chord in the text following **Fig. 7.14.**
- the **suspended dominant** chords (shown on the third staff from the top) also occur within the respective **minor** chord 'stacks', again as noted on **p222**.

We will now use these 'triad-over-root' possibilities in minor keys, to analyze some further contemporary tune examples. Again for ease of reference these examples will be presented in the key of **C minor**, and a 'roman numeral' symbol will be applied indicating the relationship of the chord to the key of **C minor** (as shown in **Fig. 7.17.**). Here is our first minor key progression:-

**Figure 7.18. Harmonic analysis progression example #3** *(this progression is typically used for the first sixteen measures of the rock tune "Eye Of The Tiger")*

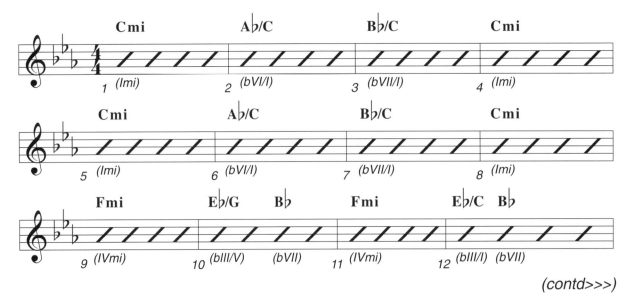

(contd>>>)

### Using 'triad-over-root' chord voicings within minor keys (contd)

**(Figure 7.18. contd)**

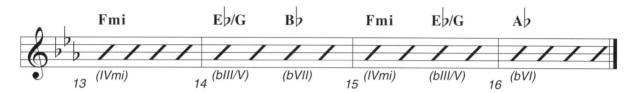

Again we can further describe the '**upper structure relationships**' used as follows:-

***Measure 1*** -  The **Cmi** chord (which is simply a *Imi* in the key of **C minor**) is a **1-b3-5** upper structure on a **C minor** chord (see **Fig. 7.4.**).

***Measure 2*** -  The **Ab/C** chord (which is a *bVI/I* in the key of **C minor**) is a **1-3-5** upper structure **inverted over its 3rd** (see **Fig. 7.8.**).

***Measure 3*** -  The **Bb/C** chord (which is a *bVII/I* in the key of **C minor**) is a **b7-9-11** upper structure, which is more likely to be heard as an upper part of a **C minor** chord (see **Fig. 7.4.**) than as a dominant suspension, due to the **Cmi** symbol immediately following.

*(**Measure 4*** *Same comments as for measure 1).*
*(**Measures 5 - 8*** *Same comments as for measures 1 - 4).*

***Measure 9*** -  The **Fmi** chord (which is a *IVmi* in the key of **C minor**) is a **1-b3-5** upper structure on an **F minor** chord (see **Fig. 7.4.**).

***Measure 10*** -  The **Eb/G** chord (which is a *bIII/V* in the key of **C minor**) is a **1-3-5** upper structure **inverted over its 3rd** (see **Fig. 7.8.**).

-  The **Bb** chord (which is a *bVII* in the key of **C minor**) is a **1-3-5** upper structure on a **Bb major** chord (see **Fig. 7.2.**).

*(**Measure 11*** *Same comments as for measure 9).*

***Measure 12*** -  The **Eb/C** chord (which is a *bIII/I* in the key of **C minor**) is a **b3-5-b7** upper structure on a **C minor** chord (see **Fig. 7.4.**). *(Note that this chord might also typically be represented by the composite symbol **Cmi7**).*

-  The **Bb** chord (which is a *bVII* in the key of **C minor**) is again a **1-3-5** upper structure on a **Bb major** chord (see **Fig. 7.2.**).

*(**Measures 13 - 14*** *Same comments as for measures 9 - 10).*

***Measure 15*** -  The **Fmi** chord (which is a *IVmi* in the key of **C minor**) is again a **1-b3-5** upper structure on an **F minor** chord (see **Fig. 7.4.**).

-  The **Eb/G** chord (which is a *bIII/V* in the key of **C minor**) is again a **1-3-5** upper structure **inverted over its 3rd** (see **Fig. 7.8.**).

***Measure 16*** -  The **Ab** chord (which is a *bVI* in the key of **C minor**) is a **1-3-5** upper structure on an **Ab major** chord (see **Fig. 7.2.**).

Now we will look at the next minor key progression, shown on the following page:-

## *Using 'triad-over-root' chord voicings within minor keys (contd)*

***Figure 7.19. Harmonic analysis progression example #4*** *(this progression is typically used for the first eight measures of the Christopher Cross rock tune "Ride Like The Wind")*

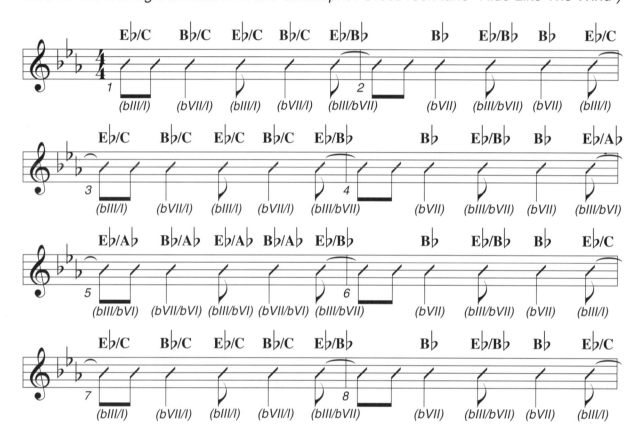

Again we can further describe the '**upper structure relationships**' used as follows:-

**Measure 1** -  The **Eb/C** chord (which is a *bIII/I* in the key of **C minor**) is a <u>b3-5-b7</u> upper structure on a **C minor** chord (see **Fig. 7.4.**). *(Note that this chord might also typically be represented by the composite symbol **Cmi7**).*

-  The **Bb/C** chord (which is a *bVII/I* in the key of **C minor**) is a <u>b7-9-11</u> upper structure, which is more likely to be heard as an upper part of a **C minor** chord (see **Fig. 7.4.**) than as a dominant suspension, due to the **Eb/C** symbols preceding and following.

-  The **Eb/Bb** chord (which is a *bIII/bVII* in the key of **C minor**) is a <u>1-3-5</u> upper structure **inverted over its 5th** (see **Fig. 7.8.**).

**Measure 2** -  The **Bb** chord (which is a *bVII* in the key of **C minor**) is a <u>1-3-5</u> upper structure on a **Bb major** chord (see **Fig. 7.2.**).

-  The **Eb/Bb** chord (which is a *bIII/bVII* in the key of **C minor**) is again a <u>1-3-5</u> upper structure **inverted over its 5th** (see **Fig. 7.8.**).

## Using 'triad-over-root' chord voicings within minor keys (contd)

**(Description of upper structure relationships within Fig. 7.19. contd)**

**Measure 2** - The **Eb/C** chord (which is a *bIII/I* in the key of **C minor**) is again a **b3-5-b7**
*(contd)* upper structure on a **C minor** chord (see **Fig. 7.4.**).
**(Measure 3** *Same comments as for measure 1).*
**(Measure 4** *Same comments as for measure 2), except for:-*
 - The **Eb/Ab** chord (which is a *bIII/bVI* in the key of **C minor**) is a **5-7-9**
upper structure on an **Ab major** chord (see **Fig. 7.2.**).
**Measure 5** - The **Bb/Ab** chord (which is a *bVII/bVI* in the key of **C minor**) is a **9-#11-13**
upper structure on an **Ab major** chord (see **Fig. 7.2.**).
 - The **Eb/Ab** chord (which is a *bIII/bVI* in the key of **C minor**) is again a
**5-7-9** upper structure on an **Ab major** chord (see **Fig. 7.2.**).
 - The **Eb/Bb** chord (which is a *bIII/bVII* in the key of **C minor**) is again a
**1-3-5** upper structure **inverted over its 5th** (see **Fig. 7.8.**).
**(Measure 6** *Same comments as for measure 2).*
**(Measures 7 - 8** *Same comments as for measures 1 - 2).*

So far then, we have dealt with 'triad-over-root' chords in the key of **C major** (as shown in **Fig. 7.14.**) and in the the key of **C minor** (as shown in **Fig. 7.17.**). Now we will look at what happens when we **combine** these possibilities from major and minor keys.

## Combining 'triad-over-root' chord voicings within major and minor keys

We recall from **Chapters 4** and **5** that major and minor keys are often 'combined' to form the **II - V - I** progressions commonly found in jazz and standard tunes. The 'pop' or contemporary equivalent to this situation, occurs when we **combine together the 'triad-over-root' chord options in major and minor**. For example, all of the chord options shown in **Figs. 7.14.** and **7.17.** can be combined together. These can all still be heard and used **with respect to the tonic of C as the 'home base'**. Technically we may be moving back and forth between the keys of **C major** and **C minor** during such a 'mixed' progression, although in a contemporary context where in general we are not changing the tonic of the key (as opposed to jazz styles), it is not really necessary to keep analyzing whether we are in major or minor - we can simply continue to relate each chord to the tonic (in this case **C**) using the 'roman numeral' symbols as shown on the examples so far in this chapter.

If we were then to combine together all of the 'triad-over-root' chord options within the key of **C major** (i.e. contained within the **C major** scale as shown in **Fig. 7.14.**) and within the key of **C minor** (i.e. contained within the **C natural minor** scale as shown in **Fig. 7.17.**), the results could be summarized as shown on the following page:-

## Combining 'triad-over-root' chord voicings within major and minor keys (contd)

### Figure 7.20. Chart of all 'triad-over-root' chords in the keys of C major and C minor

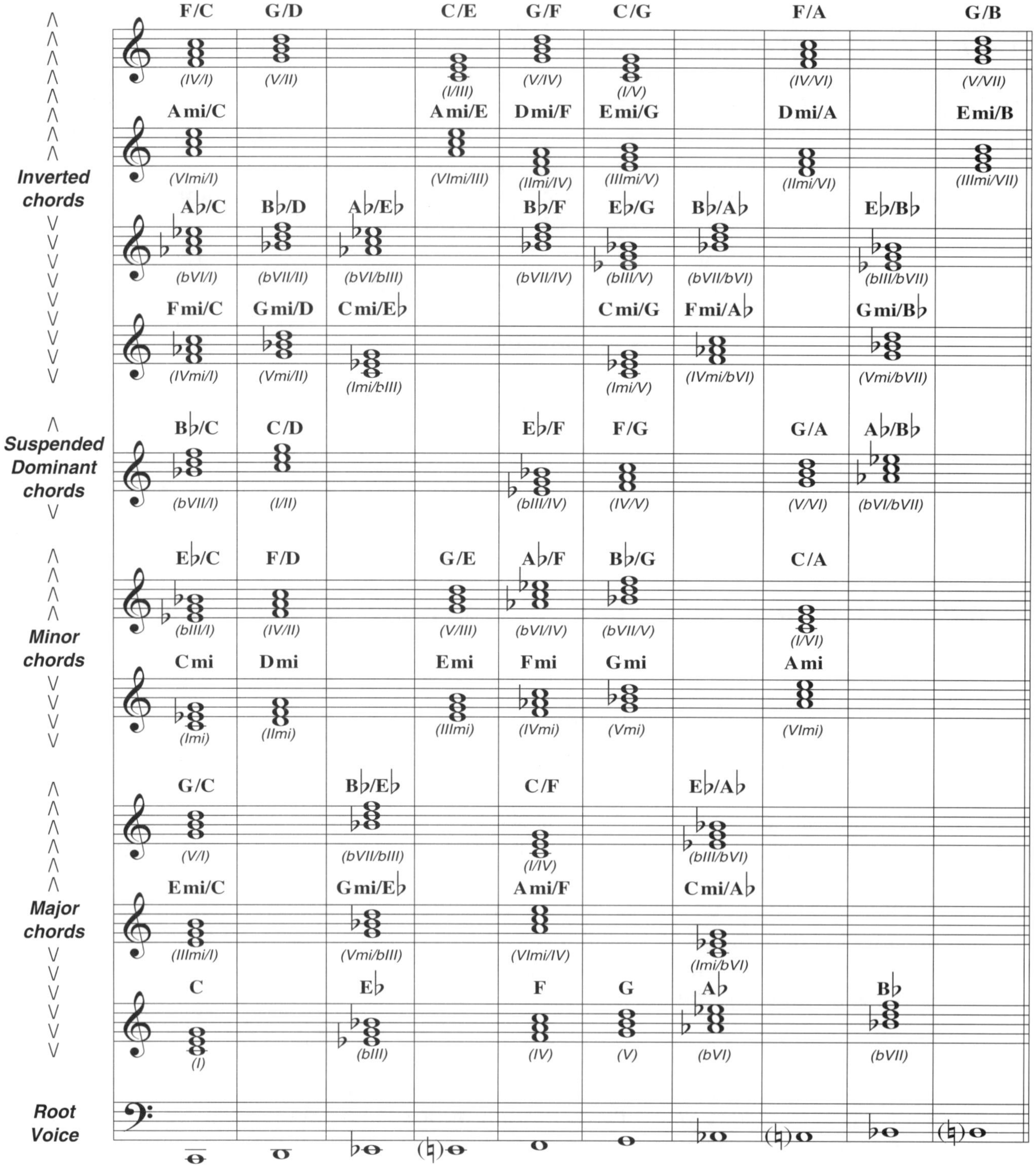

### *Combining 'triad-over-root' chord voicings within major and minor keys (contd)*

The harmony for a great many contemporary tunes is now contained within this combined **major & minor** 'triad-over-root' chart! We can make the following observations about **Fig. 7.20.**:-

- The chart layout, application of 'roman numeral' symbols etc. is essentially the same as for the previous charts in the keys of **C major** and **C minor** (although note that the top **four** staffs now contain **inverted** chords) - review comments on **p222** as necessary.
- If you wanted to find out whether a 'triad-over-root' chord on this chart came from either the **major** or **minor** key, a quick way to determine this would be to see if there was a '**b**' (flat sign) in the 'roman numeral' symbol for the chord - if so, this would indicate that the chord was derived from the **minor** key (in this case **C minor**).
- Each of these chords can actually be 'plural' to (i.e. contained within) a number of different keys - however, as discussed they will normally be heard in terms of their relationship to the **tonic** or **home-base** (in this case **C**) in contemporary applications.
- We should consider the role of the **key signature** in tunes using this type of combined major & minor 'upper structure' harmony. Generally (as on many actual charts) I think it is preferable to see the **major key signature corresponding to the tonic** being used. Any structures coming from the **minor key** built from the same tonic, would therefore require accidentals in the music. Therefore in the following progression examples using the combined major & minor possibilities in **Fig. 7.20.**, I have used the key signature of **C major** (i.e. no sharps and no flats). However you may see this situation handled in different ways (i.e. using the minor key signature for example) - so be prepared to make a contextual judgement in some cases!

We will now analyze some further progression examples using the combined possibilities within the keys of **C major** and **C minor**, again providing 'roman numeral' symbols as follows:-

*Figure 7.21. Harmonic analysis progression example #5* (this progression is typically used for the first eight measures of the Fleetwood Mac pop/rock tune "Don't Stop")

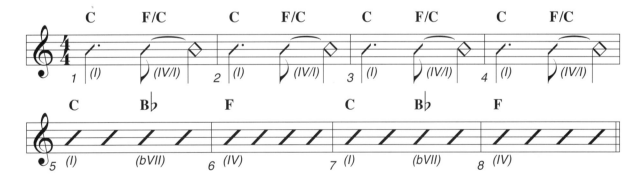

Again we can further describe the '**upper structure relationships**' used in the above example, on the following page:-

## Combining 'triad-over-root' chord voicings within major and minor keys (contd)

**(Description of upper structure relationships within Fig. 7.21.)**

*Measure 1*  -  The **C** chord (which is a *I* with respect to **C** as the tonic) is a **1-3-5** upper structure on a **C major** chord (see **Fig. 7.2.**).

-  The **F/C** chord (which is a *IV/I* with respect to **C** as the tonic) is a **1-3-5** upper structure **inverted over its 5th** (see **Fig. 7.8.**).

*(Measures 2 - 4*  *Same comments as for measure 1).*

*Measure 5*  -  The **C** chord (which is a *I* with respect to **C** as the tonic) is again a **1-3-5** upper structure on a **C major** chord (see **Fig. 7.2.**).

-  The **Bb** chord (which is a *bVII* with respect to **C** as the tonic) is a **1-3-5** upper structure on a **Bb major** chord (see **Fig. 7.2.**).

*Measure 6*  -  The **F** chord (which is a *IV* with respect to **C** as the tonic) is a **1-3-5** upper structure on an **F major** chord (see **Fig. 7.2.**).

*(Measures 7 - 8*  *Same comments as for measures 5 - 6).*

The above progression was fairly simple, in that most of the chords still came from the key of **C major**, and only the **Bb** chord in measures **5** & **7** came from the key of **C minor**. Now for the next 'mixed' major and minor progression example as follows:-

*Figure 7.22. Harmonic analysis progression example #6 (this progression is typically used for the first eighteen measures of the Elton John pop/rock tune "I'm Still Standing")*

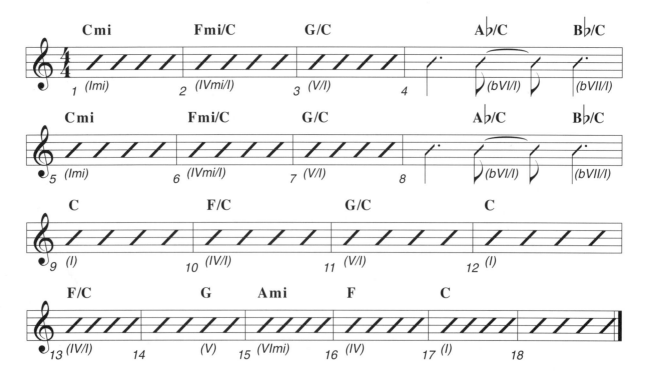

## Combining 'triad-over-root' chord voicings within major and minor keys (contd)

Again we can further describe the '**upper structure relationships**' used in the example at the bottom of the previous page, as follows:-

*Measure 1* - The **Cmi** chord (which is a *Imi* with respect to **C** as the tonic) is a **1-b3-5** upper structure on a **C minor** chord (see **Fig. 7.4.**).

*Measure 2* - The **Fmi/C** chord (which is a *IVmi/I* with respect to **C** as the tonic) is a **1-b3-5** upper structure **inverted over its 5th** (see **Fig. 7.9.**).

*Measure 3* - The **G/C** chord (which is a *V/I* with respect to **C** as the tonic) is a **5-7-9** upper structure on a **C major** chord (see **Fig. 7.2.**).

*Measure 4* - The **Ab/C** chord (which is a *bVI/I* with respect to **C** as the tonic) is a **1-3-5** upper structure **inverted over its 3rd** (see **Fig. 7.8.**).

- The **Bb/C** chord (which is a *bVII/I* with respect to **C** as the tonic) is a **b7-9-11** upper structure, which is more likely to be heard as an upper part of a **C minor** chord (see **Fig. 7.4.**) than as a dominant suspension, due to the **Cmi** symbol immediately following.

*(Measures 5 - 8* *Same comments as for measures 1 - 4).*

*Measure 9* - The **C** chord (which is a *I* with respect to **C** as the tonic) is a **1-3-5** upper structure on a **C major** chord (see **Fig. 7.2.**).

*Measure 10* - The **F/C** chord (which is a *IV/I* with respect to **C** as the tonic) is a **1-3-5** upper structure **inverted over its 5th** (see **Fig. 7.8.**).

*Measure 11* - The **G/C** chord (which is a *V/I* with respect to **C** as the tonic) is a **5-7-9** upper structure on a **C major** chord (see **Fig. 7.2.**).

*(Measures 12 - 13* *Same comments as for measures 9 - 10).*

*Measure 14* - The **G** chord (which is a *V* with respect to **C** as the tonic) is a **1-3-5** upper structure on a **G major** chord (see **Fig. 7.2.**).

*Measure 15* - The **Ami** chord (which is a *VImi* with respect to **C** as the tonic) is a **1-b3-5** upper structure on an **A minor** chord (see **Fig. 7.4.**).

*Measure 16* - The **F** chord (which is a *IV* with respect to **C** as the tonic) is a **1-3-5** upper structure on an **F major** chord (see **Fig. 7.2.**).

*(Measures 17 - 18* *Same comments as for measure 9).*

There will of course be some situations in which a contemporary tune uses chords outside the range of possibilities indicated on the 'combined' major and minor chart in **Fig. 7.20**. This is normally an indication of one of the following circumstances:-

- a 'momentary key change' (as discussed in our preceding work on jazz progressions) has after all occurred. In these cases, once you have determined the 'tonic' of the new key, it should then be possible to apply the chart with respect to that new 'tonic' for analysis purposes. You should in any case become familiar with this 'triad-over-root' chart using different 'tonics' (i.e. other than **C**) - please refer to ***Appendix 4*** as required.

*(contd>>>)*

### *Combining 'triad-over-root' chord voicings within major and minor keys (contd)*

*(Reasons why a contemporary tune may use chords outside the range of options in **Fig. 7.20.**, contd)*

- a 'modal harmonization' has occurred. A full presentation of modal harmony is beyond the scope of this **Level 2** book - however, we can briefly make the following points:-
  - The **C major** scale (used as the source for the chords in the key of **C major**, as in **Fig. 7.14.**) is also a **C Ionian** mode, and the **C natural minor** scale (used as the source for the chords in the key of **C minor**, as in **Fig. 7.17.**) is also a **C Aeolian** mode. So viewed from a modal standpoint, the **Ionian** and **Aeolian** are the most commonly used modes in contemporary applications.
  - However, the **Dorian**, **Lydian** and **Mixolydian** modes are also used (to a lesser degree) in modern styles. As you might imagine, these modes enable different 'triad-over-root' relationships to be created, not all of which are contained within the 'combined' table in **Fig. 7.20.** (although from a vertical quality standpoint, they would still typically be included in the summary at the bottom of **p218**).
  - In the context of using the note **C** as the overall tonic, the use of the following 'triad-over-root' chords (which are not present in **Fig. 7.20.**) are typical examples of this type of 'modal harmonization':-
    - **F/Eb**        -        from the **C Dorian** mode.
    - **F/Bb**        -        from the **C Dorian** or **C Mixolydian** modes.
    - **C/Bb**        -        from the **C Mixolydian** mode.
    - **D/C**        -        from the **C Lydian** mode, etc.

    *(For a review of basic modal concepts such as mode names, relative major scales etc. please refer to the **Level 1** book and/or **Chapter 1** of this book).*

### *Interpretation of contemporary charts using 'triad-over-root' chords*

For ease of analysis and illustration, the preceding progression examples **#1 - #6** were presented with the 'triad-over-root' or 'slash' chords already on the chart in each case. (This is also the manner in which many contemporary charts are actually written). However as mentioned in the introduction to this chapter, we may need to interpret either a **basic triad** chord symbol or a **composite** chord symbol with 'triad-over-root' structures. In all of these situations we will then typically need to **voicelead the resulting upper structure triads** according to the principles outlined in **Chapter 6**. As we will see in the following contemporary progression examples, we often need to voicelead the upper structure triads around the circle-of-5ths/4ths, even though the roots of the chords are not necessarily moving in a 'circular' manner.

When interpreting a chord symbol with a 'triad-over-root' structure, we will generally be doing one of the following (see next page):-

## *Interpretation of contemporary charts using 'triad-over-root' chords (contd)*

**1)**     **Literally translating** a triad or composite symbol to a 'triad-over-root' structure, i.e.:-
-     The chord symbol '**C**' can be translated to a **C/C** 'triad-over-root' structure (see **Fig. 7.2.**). No chord tones have been added or subtracted with respect to the original chord symbol.
-     The chord symbol '**Dmi7**' can be translated to a **F/D** 'triad-over-root' structure (see **Fig. 7.4.**). Again no chord tones have been added or subtracted with respect to the original chord symbol.

**2)**     **Upgrading** a triad or composite symbol by using a 'triad-over-root' structure, i.e.:-
-     The chord symbol '**C**' can be upgraded to a **G/C** 'triad-over-root structure' (see **Fig. 7.2.**). In comparison to the original chord symbol, the **3rd (E)** has been removed and the **7th (B)** & **9th (D)** have been added.
-     The chord symbol '**Dmi7**' can be upgraded to a **C/D** 'triad-over-root structure' (see **Fig. 7.4.**). In comparison to the original chord symbol, the **3rd (F)** & **5th (A)** have been removed and the **9th (E)** & **11th (G)** have been added.

So how do we know when to **literally translate** and when to **upgrade** these chords? Basically a stylistic judgement call needs to be made! In general, in older or simpler pop tunes it is often necessary to stick more closely to the basic chord symbols - however, in modern contemporary applications the type of 'upgrading' described above will frequently be desirable. This type of 'ear decision' is normally made on a case-by-case basis - however, here are some general points for you to consider:-

-     the type of upgrading described above, generally works best when the added tones are still **diatonic to the overall key** being used.
-     'triad-over-root' chords containing **upper extensions** (as mentioned in the '**upgrading**' paragraph above) often work well in conjunction with more **basic** 'triad-over-root' chords (as mentioned in the '**literally translating**' paragraph above), when used in an **alternating manner** i.e. back-and-forth over the same root. All of the progression examples so far in this chapter, use this approach in varying degrees. *(For a complete presentation of these 'alternating triad' concepts as used in pop-rock styles, please refer to **Chapter 12** of our contemporary keyboard method "**The Pop Piano Book**").*
-     here are **some hints** for commonly-used 'triad-over-root' chords in an upgrading context:-
  -     on major chords, the **<u>5-7-9</u>** (i.e. **G/C**, as in **Fig 7.2.**) is a very desirable modern sound - however, using it within older pop styles may be 'too hip for the room'!
  -     on minor chords, the **<u>b3-5-b7</u>** (i.e. **F/D**, as in **Fig 7.4.**) is almost always acceptable even in simpler pop styles.
  -     on dominant (suspended) chords, the **<u>b7-9-11</u>** (i.e. **F/G**, as in **Fig 7.6.**) as well as being a 'default' voicing of choice for the suspended dominant, might also be used **in place of** a 'regular' (i.e. unsuspended) dominant chord symbol on a chart, if the more modern (and less leading) sound of the suspension was preferred.

### *Interpretation of contemporary charts using 'triad-over-root' chords (contd)*

We will now look at some progression examples, containing symbols to be translated into 'triad-over-root' structures. First we will apply **literal translation** to the following progression:-

*Figure 7.23. Progression example #7 (to be translated using 'triad-over-root' chords)*

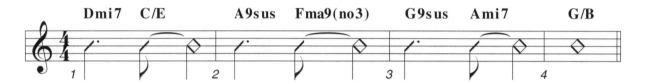

Note that some of the chord symbols in the above example are **already presented as 'slash' chords** - the major chords **C/E** and **G/B** are both <u>1-3-5</u> structures inverted over the **3rd** (as in **Fig. 7.8.**). The above example demonstrates a frequently-encountered mixture of '**slash**' and '**composite**' symbols, as follows:-

- the **inverted** chords (i.e. over the 3rd, 5th etc) are indicated using a 'slash' chord symbol, as there is often no other convenient way to notate these chords.
- **all other** chords (i.e. non-inverted) are indicated using a composite symbol, which we can then translate into a 'triad-over-root' structure.

Now we will present the 'triad-over-root' translation, which will include the following:-

- 'triad-over-root' or 'slash' **chord symbol equivalents** for the translated chords
- upper structure triad **voiceleading solution** for each chord
- '**roman numeral**' analysis for each chord (with respect to the tonic of **C**)

*Figure 7.24. Progression example #7 (translated using 'triad-over-root' chords)*

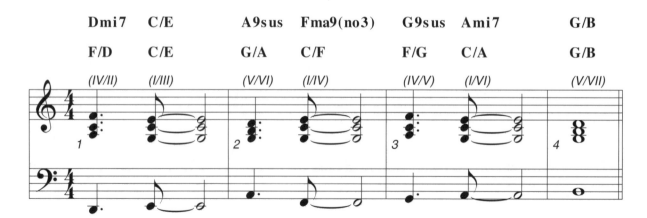

## *Interpretation of contemporary charts using 'triad-over-root' chords (contd)*

Note that in **Fig. 7.24.** at the bottom of the previous page, there are **two rows** of chord symbols - the **top** row are the original symbols from **Fig. 7.23.**, and the **bottom** row are the translated 'triad-over-root' symbols. We can further analyze this 'translated' solution as follows:-

*Measure 1* -    The **Dmi7** has been translated to an **F/D**, which is a <u>**b3-5-b7**</u> structure on a **D minor** chord (see **Fig. 7.4.**) and is also a *IV/II* with respect to **C** as the tonic. The upper **F major** triad has (arbitrarily) been placed in **1st inversion**.

-    The **C/E** has been derived directly from the original chord symbol, and is a *I/III* with respect to **C** as the tonic. The upper **C major** triad has been placed in **2nd inversion**, to **voicelead** from the preceding **F major** triad in a **circle-of-4ths** manner (see *Chapter 6* and *Appendix 3*).

*Measure 2* -    The **A9sus** has been translated to a **G/A**, which is a <u>**b7-9-11**</u> structure on an **A (suspended) dominant** chord (see **Fig. 7.6.**) and is also a *V/VI* with respect to **C** as the tonic. The upper **G major** triad has been placed in **root position**, to again **voicelead** from the preceding **C major** triad in a **circle-of-4ths** manner.

-    The **Fma9(no3)** has been translated to a **C/F**, which is a <u>**5-7-9**</u> structure on an **F major** chord (see **Fig. 7.2.**) and is also a *I/IV* with respect to **C** as the tonic. The upper **C major** triad has again been placed in **2nd inversion**, this time to **voicelead** from the preceding **G major** triad in a **circle-of-5ths** manner (see *Chapter 6* and *Appendix 3*).

*Measure 3* -    The **G9sus** has been translated to an **F/G**, which is a <u>**b7-9-11**</u> structure on a **G (suspended) dominant** chord (see **Fig. 7.6.**) and is also a *IV/V* with respect to **C** as the tonic. The upper **F major** triad has been placed in **1st inversion**, to again **voicelead** from the preceding **C major** triad in a **circle-of-5ths** manner.

-    The **Ami7** has been translated to a **C/A**, which is a <u>**b3-5-b7**</u> structure on an **A minor** chord (see **Fig. 7.4.**) and is also a *I/VI* with respect to **C** as the tonic. The upper **C major** triad has again been placed in **2nd inversion**, this time to **voicelead** from the preceding **F major** triad in a **circle-of-4ths** manner.

*Measure 4* -    The **G/B** has been derived directly from the original chord symbol, and is a *V/VII* with respect to **C** as the tonic. The upper **G major** triad has again been placed in **root position**, to **voicelead** from the preceding **C major** triad in a **circle-of-4ths** manner.

Note that in this example, all of the upper triad voiceleading was via **circle-of-5ths** or **circle-of-4ths**, even though the original progression (as first seen in **Fig. 7.23.**) does not look at all 'circular' in nature! Now we will look at a final progression example in which basic chord symbols will be **upgraded** using 'triad-over-root' structures, as shown on the following page:-

## *Interpretation of contemporary charts using 'triad-over-root' chords (contd)*

### *Figure 7.25. Progression example #8 (to be upgraded using 'triad-over-root' chords)*

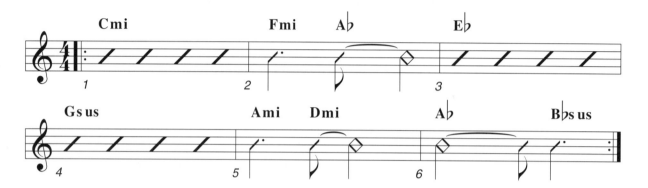

We will now **upgrade** these basic symbols using 'triad-over-root' structures, thereby achieving a more modern stylistic result as follows:-

### *Figure 7.26. Progression example #8 (upgraded using 'triad-over-root' chords)*

## *Interpretation of contemporary charts using 'triad-over-root' chords (contd)*

Again note that in **Fig. 7.26.** at the bottom of the previous page, there are **two rows** of chord symbols - the **top** row are the original symbols from **Fig. 7.25.**, and the **bottom** row are the upgraded 'triad-over-root' symbols. We can further analyze this 'upgraded' solution as follows:-

*Measure 1* -
The **Cmi** chord has been upgraded to an **Eb/C**, which is a <u>**b3-5-b7**</u> structure on a **C minor** chord (see **Fig. 7.4.**) and is also a *bIII/I* with respect to **C** as the tonic. This upgrading has **added the 7th** of the chord. The upper **Eb major** triad has (arbitrarily) been placed in **2nd inversion**.

*Measure 2* -
The **Fmi** chord has been upgraded to an **Ab/F**, which is a <u>**b3-5-b7**</u> structure on an **F minor** chord (see **Fig. 7.4.**) and is also a *bVI/IV* with respect to **C** as the tonic. This upgrading has again **added the 7th** of the chord. The upper **Ab major** triad has been placed in **1st inversion**, to **voicelead** from the preceding **Eb major** triad in a **circle-of-5ths** manner (see *Chapter 6* and *Appendix 3*).

-
The **Ab** chord has been upgraded to an **Eb/Ab**, which is a <u>**5-7-9**</u> structure on an **Ab major** chord (see **Fig. 7.2.**) and is also a *bIII/bVI* with respect to **C** as the tonic. This upgrading has **added the 7th & 9th,** and **removed the 3rd,** of the chord. The upper **Eb major** triad has again been placed in **2nd inversion**, this time to **voicelead** from the preceding **Ab major** triad in a **circle-of-4ths** manner (see *Chapter 6* and *Appendix 3*).

*Measure 3* -
The **Eb** chord has been upgraded to an **Bb/Eb**, which is a <u>**5-7-9**</u> structure on an **Eb major** chord (see **Fig. 7.2.**) and is also a *bVII/bIII* with respect to **C** as the tonic. This upgrading has again **added the 7th & 9th,** and **removed the 3rd,** of the chord. The upper **Bb major** triad has been placed in **root position**, to again **voicelead** from the preceding **Eb major** triad in a **circle-of-4ths** manner.

*Measure 4* -
The **Gsus** has been upgraded to an **F/G** (i.e. we have made the assumption that this basic suspension can be upgraded to a suspended dominant, which is often possible in more evolved contemporary styles). This is therefore a <u>**b7-9-11**</u> structure on a **G (suspended) dominant** chord (see **Fig. 7.6.**) and is also a *IV/V* with respect to **C** as the tonic. The upper **F major** triad has been placed in **1st inversion**, to again **voicelead** from the preceding **Bb major** triad in a **circle-of-4ths** manner.

*Measure 5* -
The **Ami** chord has been upgraded to a **C/A**, which is a <u>**b3-5-b7**</u> structure on an **A minor** chord (see **Fig. 7.4.**) and is also a *I/VI* with respect to **C** as the tonic. This upgrading has again **added the 7th** of the chord. The upper **C major** triad has been placed in **2nd inversion**, to again **voicelead** from the preceding **F major** triad in a **circle-of-4ths** manner.

*(contd>>>)*

## *Interpretation of contemporary charts using 'triad-over-root' chords (contd)*

*(Analysis of Fig. 7.26. contd)*

*Measure 5* - The **Dmi** chord has been upgraded to an **F/D**, which is a <u>**b3-5-b7**</u> structure
*(contd)* on a **D minor** chord (see **Fig. 7.4.**) and is also a *IV/II* with respect to **C** as
the tonic. This upgrading has again **added the 7th** of the chord. The upper
**F major** triad has again been placed in **1st inversion**, this time to **voicelead**
from the preceding **C major** triad in a **circle-of-5ths** manner.

*Measure 6* - The **Ab** chord has been upgraded to an **Eb/Ab**, which is a <u>**5-7-9**</u> structure
on an **Ab major** chord (see **Fig. 7.2.**) and is also a *bIII/bVI* with respect to
**C** as the tonic. This upgrading has again **added the 7th & 9th,** and **removed
the 3rd,** of the chord. The upper **Eb major** triad has again been placed in
**2nd inversion**, to continue the **upward voiceleading** direction from the
preceding **F major** triad (this voiceleading is not via circle-of-5ths or circle-
of-4ths this time).

- The **Bbsus** has been upgraded to an **Ab/Bb** (based on similar assumptions
as for the **Gsus** chord in measure **4**). This is therefore a <u>**b7-9-11**</u> structure
on a **Bb (suspended) dominant** chord (see **Fig. 7.6.**) and is also a *bVI/bVII*
with respect to **C** as the tonic. The upper **Ab major** triad has been placed
in **1st inversion**, to again **voicelead** from the preceding **Eb major** triad in
a **circle-of-5ths** manner.

Again note that all of the 'triad-over-root' chords used as a result of the various upgrading
decisions, are contained within the combined '**C major & C minor**' chord chart as shown in
**Fig. 7.20.**

# Chapter Seven Workbook Questions

## *1.* *Building 'triad-over-root' chord qualities*

For each question in Section **1** you are to write the upper triad (in root position) on the treble clef staff, and a triad-over-root chord symbol above the treble clef staff. In questions 1 - 8 you are to create a **dominant 11th** chord (with a <u>b7-9-11</u> upper structure major triad).

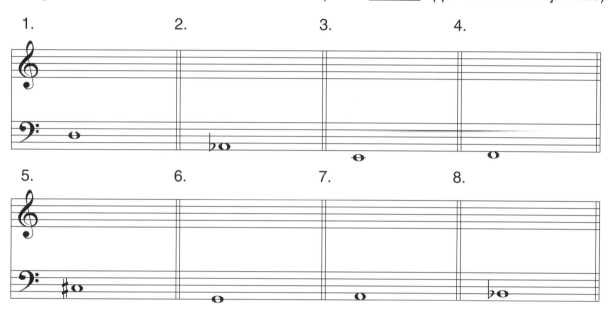

In questions 9 - 16 you are to create a **major chord inverted over the 3rd** (with a <u>1-3-5</u> upper structure major triad, inverted over the 3rd in the bass voice).

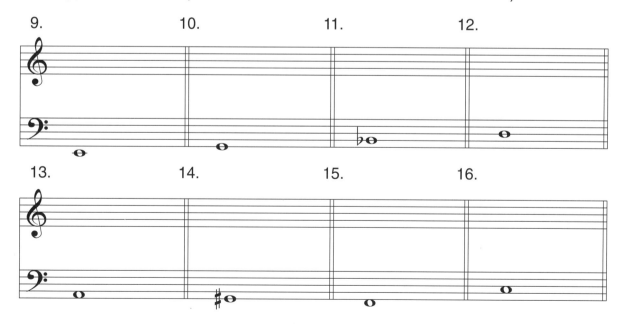

**1.** **_Building 'triad-over-root' chord qualities (contd)_**

In questions 17 - 24 you are to create a **major 9th (no 3rd)** chord (with a **5-7-9** upper structure major triad).

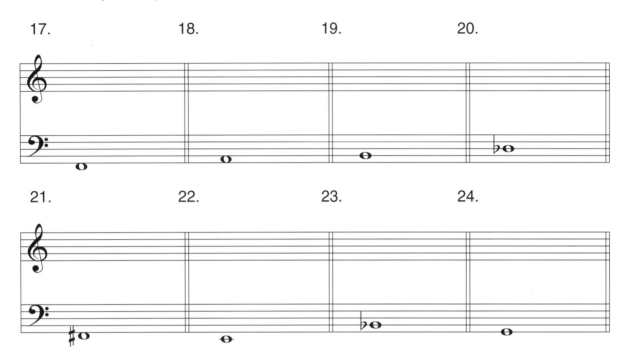

In questions 25 - 32 you are to create a **major 7th** chord (with a **3-5-7** upper structure minor triad).

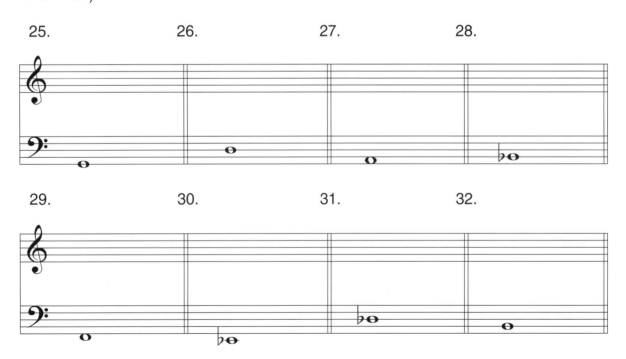

### 2. *Voiceleading 'triad-over-root' progressions*

You are to write the root on the bass clef staff, and the upper triad voicing on the treble clef staff, for the following progressions. You are to interpret the chord symbols as follows:-

- on the **minor 7th** chords, build a **b3-5-b7** voicing (i.e. major triad from the 3rd).
- on the **major 9th** chords, build a **5-7-9** voicing (i.e. major triad from the 5th).
- on the **suspended dominant 9th** chords, build a **b7-9-11** voicing (i.e. major triad from the 7th).
- on the **minor (#5)** chords, build a **1-3-5** voicing inverted over the 3rd (i.e. major triad with the 3rd in the bass voice - review **p216** comments as necessary).

You are to voicelead from the first triad-over-root chord voicing provided in each case.

Questions 33 - 36 each take a particular chord quality and move it around the circle-of-5ths or circle-of-4ths (potentially implying a new key center with each chord - see **Figs. 7.12.** and **7.13.** in the Textbook). The upper structure triads should be voiceled (in a circle-of-5ths/4ths manner) according to the rules established in *Chapter 6*.

33.                                                         34.

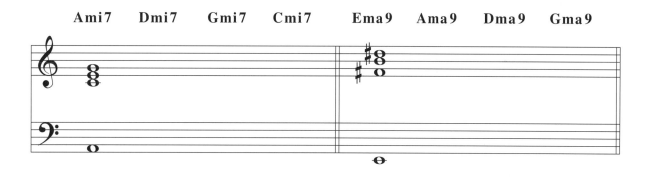

35.                                                         36.

### 2. *Voiceleading 'triad-over-root' progressions (contd)*

Questions 37 - 40 now contain a mixture of chord qualities, and the voiceleading between the upper triads may include movements other than circle-of-5ths/4ths. Each progression is now within a **combined major/minor key restriction** (for example, all the triad-over-root voicings required for questions 37 & 40 are contained within the combined **C major** and **C minor** chart shown in **Fig. 7.20.** in the Textbook). However, as no key signatures are provided, you still need to write all necessary accidentals.

For questions 37 - 38, where a commontone is not available as the top voice of consecutive chords, you are to voicelead the top voice in an *ascending* manner.

37. *(within the 'combined restriction' of the keys of **C major** & **C minor**)*

38. *(within the 'combined restriction' of the keys of **G major** & **G minor**)*

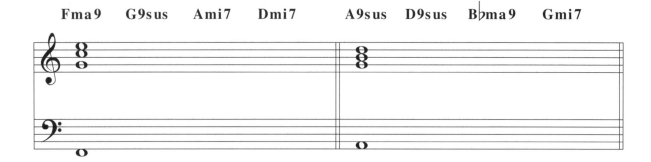

For questions 39 - 40, where a commontone is not available as the top voice of consecutive chords, you are to voicelead the top voice in a *descending* manner.

39. *(within the 'combined restriction' of the keys of **F major** & **F minor**)*

40. *(within the 'combined restriction' of the keys of **C major** & **C minor**)*

*(Review **Appendix 4** as necessary for the triad-over-root voicings available in all major/minor keys).*

## 3. Chord progression analysis

You are to determine the 'roman numeral' functions for each chord in the following progressions (as shown in various Textbook examples including **Fig. 7.22.**). Note that unlike the progressions analyzed in **Chapters 2 - 5**, these contemporary examples are to be analyzed **in relation to a single 'tonic' throughout** i.e. we are not looking for momentary key changes.

- Chord progression **#1** is to be analyzed with respect to the note **B** as the tonic, and is diatonic to the key of **B major** (i.e. the chords are wholly contained within a **B major** scale).
- Chord progression **#2** is to be analyzed with respect to the note **E** as the tonic, and is diatonic to the key of **E minor** (i.e. the chords are contained within an **E natural minor** scale).
- Chord progression **#3** is to be analyzed with respect to the note **D** as the tonic, and now combines together chords from the key of **D major** (using a **D major** scale) and the key of **D minor** (using a **D natural minor** scale).

### Chord progression #1
*(typically used for the first eight measures of the pop ballad "We've Got Tonight")*

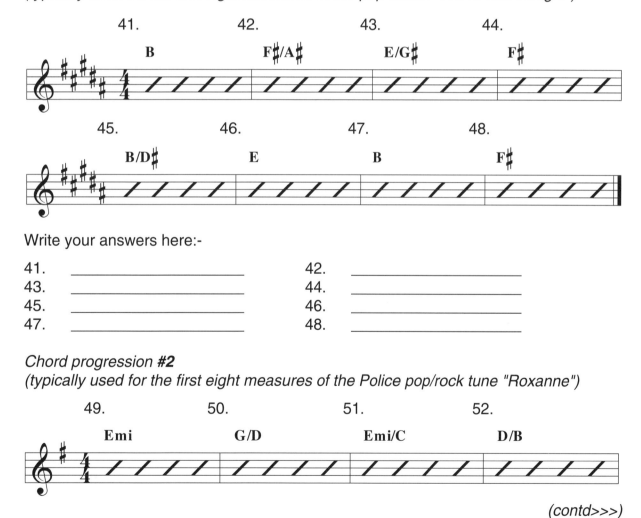

Write your answers here:-

| | | | |
|---|---|---|---|
| 41. | _____ | 42. | _____ |
| 43. | _____ | 44. | _____ |
| 45. | _____ | 46. | _____ |
| 47. | _____ | 48. | _____ |

### Chord progression #2
*(typically used for the first eight measures of the Police pop/rock tune "Roxanne")*

*(contd>>>)*

**3.** _**Chord progression analysis (contd)**_

_(Chord Progression **#2** contd)_

Write your answers here:-

49. _____
50. _____
51. _____
52. _____
53. _____
54. _____
55. _____

_Chord progression **#3**_
_(typically used for the first eight measures of the Elton John pop/rock tune_
_"Saturday Night's Alright For Fighting")_

Write your answers here:-

56. _____
57. _____
58. _____
59. _____
60. _____
61. _____
62. _____
63. _____

## Chapter Seven Workbook Answers

1. **Building 'triad-over-root' chord qualities - answers**

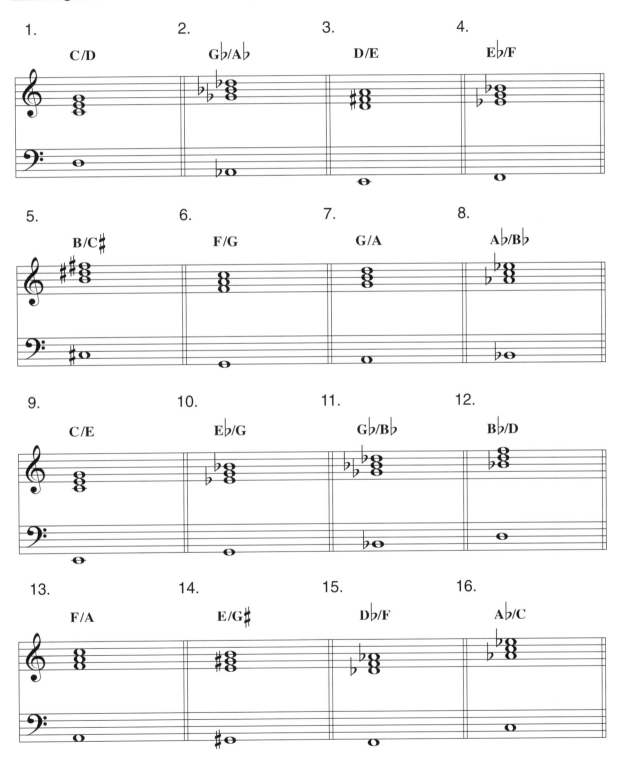

## 1. *Building 'triad-over-root' chord qualities - answers (contd)*

**2.** **_Voiceleading 'triad-over-root' progressions - answers_**

33.

34.

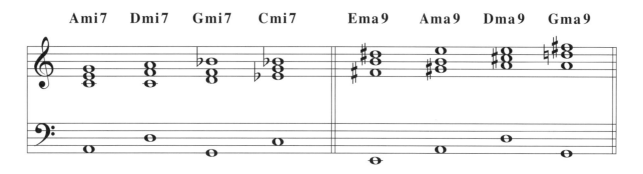

35.

36.

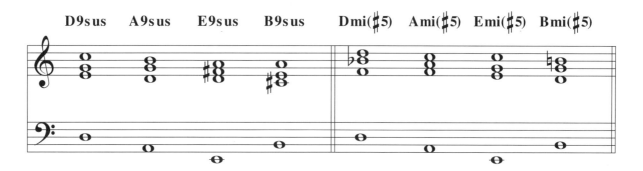

37.

38.

## 2. Voiceleading 'triad-over-root' progressions - answers (contd)

39.                                              40.

Abma9   C9sus   Dmi7   Dmi(♯5)        Cma9   G9sus   Ami7   Abma9

## 3. Chord progression analysis - answers

*(Chord Progression #1 - analyzed with respect to the note **B** as the tonic)*

| | | | | |
|---|---|---|---|---|
| 41. | *I* | 42. | *V/VII* |
| 43. | *IV/VI* | 44. | *V* |
| 45. | *I/III* | 46. | *IV* |
| 47. | *I* | 48. | *V* |

*(Chord Progression #2 - analyzed with respect to the note **E** as the tonic)*

| | | | | |
|---|---|---|---|---|
| 49. | *Imi* | 50. | *bIII/bVII* |
| 51. | *Imi/bVI* | 52. | *bVII/V* |
| 53. | *bVI/IV* | 54. | *bVI/bVII* |
| 55. | *Imi* | | |

*(Chord Progression #3 - analyzed with respect to the note **D** as the tonic)*

| | | | | |
|---|---|---|---|---|
| 56. | *IV/I* | 57. | *I* |
| 58. | *bIII/bVII* | 59. | *bVII* |
| 60. | *bVII/IV* | 61. | *IV* |
| 62. | *IV/I* | 63. | *I* |

# *Chords using four-part 'upper structures'*

## *Introduction*

In a similar manner as for the chords using triad 'upper structures' presented in *Chapter 7,* we will now focus on chords which use four-part 'upper structures'. These are formed by placing a four-part chord shape (typically a **major 7th** or **minor 7th**) over a root in the bass voice, and therefore can also be referred to as '**four-part-over-root**' chords. For example, the chord symbol **Fma7/D** means an 'upper structure' of an **F major 7th chord** is being placed over the note **D** in the bass voice. Again as this chord symbol contains a '/' (slash), it can also be referred to as a '**slash chord**'. These four-part 'upper structures' are widely used in more sophisticated pop and R'n'B styles to create (or imply) larger chord forms.

These voicings are more 'dense' and sophisticated than the preceding '**triad-over-root**' chords discussed in *Chapter 7*, and they can therefore be applied to some of the more '**II-V-I**'-oriented progressions discussed in *Chapters 2 - 5* (i.e. using **momentary key changes**), as well as more 'evolved' contemporary applications which may still **adhere to an overall major** and/or **minor key restriction**. This latter type of progression (used for the preceding *Chapter 7* examples) is also the basis of the contemporary examples presented in this chapter.

The application of 'four-part-over-root' chords to a contemporary tune (i.e. working from a leadsheet or chord chart) will be in one or more of the following circumstances:-

**1)**   The required 'four-part-over-root' chord may be **directly indicated** on the chart. For example, if we see the chord symbol **Fma7/D** (as mentioned above) we can simply place the upper **F major 7th** chord shape over **D** in the bass. *(Note however that, with the exception of certain suspended chords, this is less likely to occur in actual practice).*

**2)**   We more often need to **interpret a composite** (or a **basic triad**) chord symbol by using a 'four-part-over-root' chord, in one of the following ways:-

-   We may be **literally translating** a chord symbol into a 'four-part-over-root' chord. For example, if we see the chord symbol **Dmi9**, we may **literally translate** it to **Fma7/D** (i.e. using a 'four-part-over-root' chord which does not add or subtract any chord tones with respect to the original chord symbol).
-   We may be **upgrading** a chord symbol by using a 'four-part-over-root' chord (if stylistically appropriate). For example, the chord symbol **Dmi7** might be upgraded (effectively to a **Dmi9**) by using the 'four-part-over-root' chord **Fma7/D**.

In this chapter we will derive the commonly-used 'four-part-over-root' relationships in contemporary styles, and we will also see how these chords can be used (and analyzed) in major and minor keys. (Note that, while triads are often **inverted** over the 3rd or 5th in the bass voice as in *Chapter 7*, this occurs less often with four-part chord shapes). We will now derive 'four-part-over-root' chords within each of the following categories (as shown on the next page):-

## *Introduction (contd)*

- **major** chords
- **minor** chords
- **dominant** chords and **suspended dominant** chords.

We will now derive 'four-part-over-root' chords in each of the above categories.

## *Deriving 'four-part-over-root' relationships for MAJOR chords*

In **Chapter 2** we have already created a five-part major chord (see derivation of the **Cma9** chord in **Fig. 2.17.**). This chord 'stack' is shown again here for convenience:-

### *Figure 8.1. C major 9th chord 'stack' and interval construction*

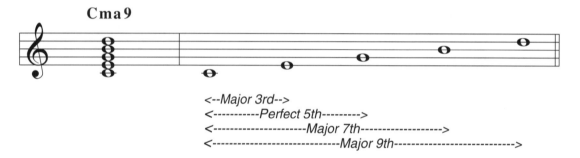

```
<--Major 3rd-->
<----------Perfect 5th--------->
<--------------------Major 7th-------------------->
<-----------------------------Major 9th--------------------------->
```

Now we will extract the required 'four-part-over-root' relationship from this major chord 'stack' as follows:-

### *Figure 8.2. 'Four-part-over-root' relationship within the C major chord 'stack'*

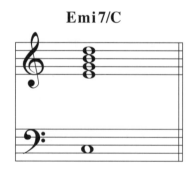

As with the 'triad-over-root' chords presented in **Chapter 7**, the following general points should be made when discussing 'four-part-over-root' relationships extracted from a chord 'stack' as in the above example (see following page):-

### *Deriving 'four-part-over-root' relationships for MAJOR chords (contd)*

- Each 'four-part-over-root' relationship shown is a **commonly used voicing solution** for the type of chord in question (in this case a single voicing is shown for a **major** chord).
- Each upper four-part shape is '**built from**' a certain part of the overall chord. For example, the **Emi7** (shown at the bottom of the previous page) is built from the **3rd** of the overall **C major** chord.
- Each upper four-part shape could be used **in any inversion**, to accommodate melody or harmonic voiceleading considerations. *(Note however that these four-part upper shapes are used less frequently in 1st inversion, due to the 'exposed' dissonance of the **2nd** interval on top).*
- Each upper four-part shape **does not by itself define the chord** - it needs to be placed **over** the root of the overall chord (in this case **C**) in the bass register, in order to create the required result.

Now we will look at the preceding 'four-part-over-root' chord in greater detail, as follows:-

- ***Emi7/C*** This 'four-part-over-root' voicing creates a fully-defined **major ninth** chord. (The term 'fully-defined' is used here because this voicing contains the **3rd** and **7th** of the chord, which as we have seen are the critical definitive tones). The chord symbol which is a **composite equivalent** of this **Emi7/C** would be **Cma9**. This voicing consists of a **minor 7th 'shape' built from the 3rd of a major chord**, and we will therefore refer to it as a **3-5-7-9** upper structure voicing. This voicing is widely used in R'n'B and more evolved pop styles.

*(This 'numeric' method of labelling four-part upper structure voicings is also used in our contemporary keyboard method **The Pop Piano Book**, from **Chapter 7** onwards).*

In comparing **Figs. 8.1. - 8.2.** on the previous page to **Figs. 7.1. - 7.2.** in *Chapter 7*, you may be wondering why we did not consider the four-part shape built from the root of the **C major** chord i.e. a **Cma7/C** (**1-3-5-7**) structure here, as we did include the triad built from the root of this chord i.e. a **C/C** (**1-3-5**) structure, in the last chapter. Well, as a general rule in contemporary styles I feel that it is redundant to duplicate the root of any four-part (or larger) chord form in the 'upper structure' voicing, if the root is already present in the bass voice. Therefore if an 'exact' voicing for a **Cma7** chord symbol was needed (i.e. without any 'upgrading' or interpretation), then the **Emi/C** 'triad-over-root' solution shown in **Fig. 7.2.** would generally be preferable to using a **Cma7/C** 'four-part-over-root' solution.

Next we will look at deriving 'four-part-over-root' upper structure relationships for minor chords, as discussed on the following page:-

### Deriving 'four-part-over-root' relationships for MINOR chords

Now we will go through a similar process to derive the commonly-used 'four-part-over-root' voicings for minor chords. Again the general observations noted on the previous page will also apply here. As noted in **Chapter 7**, in contemporary applications we invariably use the **minor 7th** form (i.e. containing a **minor 7th** interval) when expanding minor chords to 4-part or above.

In **Chapter 7** we already extended the minor chord 'stack' up to the 11th (in **Fig. 7.3.**) in order to derive the required 'triad-over-root' relationships. This minor chord 'stack' is shown again here for convenience:-

### Figure 8.3. D minor 11th chord 'stack' and interval construction

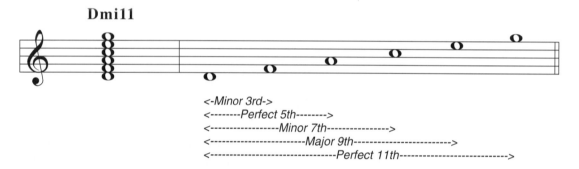

```
<-Minor 3rd->
<--------Perfect 5th-------->
<------------------Minor 7th---------------->
<-------------------------Major 9th------------------------->
<--------------------------------Perfect 11th--------------------------->
```

Now we will extract the required 'four-part-over-root' relationships from this minor chord 'stack' as follows:-

### Figure 8.4. 'Four-part-over-root' relationships within the D minor chord 'stack'

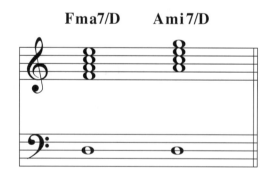

*(Again we have only extracted the 'four-part-over-root' chords most commonly used in contemporary applications).*

Now we will analyze the above 'four-part-over-root' relationships on the following page:-

### Deriving 'four-part-over-root' relationships for MINOR chords (contd)

- *Fma7/D* This 'four-part-over-root' voicing creates a fully-defined **minor ninth** chord. (Again the term 'fully-defined' is used here because this voicing contains the **3rd** and **7th** of the chord). The chord symbol which is a **composite equivalent** of this **Fma7/D** would be **Dmi9**. This voicing consists of a **major 7th 'shape' built from the 3rd of a minor chord**, and we will therefore refer to it as a <u>**b3-5-b7-9**</u> upper structure voicing. Again this voicing is widely used in R'n'B and more evolved pop styles.
- *Ami7/D* This 'four-part-over-root' voicing creates a **minor eleventh** chord with the **third omitted**. When used in a minor chord context, it has an 'open' and less defined quality. The chord symbol which would be an exact **composite equivalent** of this **Ami7/D** would be **Dmi11(omit 3)**. This voicing consists of a **minor 7th 'shape' built from the 5th of a minor chord**, and we will therefore refer to it as a <u>**5-b7-9-11**</u> upper structure voicing. *(We will shortly see that this voicing can also be used for a suspended dominant chord).*

### Deriving 'four-part-over-root' relationships for DOMINANT chords

Now will derive the commonly-used 'four-part-over-root' voicings for dominant chords. We recall from **Fig. 7.6.** that although the <u>**b7-9-11**</u> 'triad-over-root' voicing was very useful for a **suspended** dominant, we did not find a good-sounding 'triad-over-root' solution for a **regular** (i.e. <u>un</u>suspended) dominant chord in **Chapter 7**. Now however in examining the 'four-part over-root' options available, we find good solutions for both types of dominant chord. In order to derive these voicings, we now need to extend the dominant chord 'stack' up to the 13th, as follows:-

### Figure 8.5. G dominant 13th chord 'stack' and interval construction

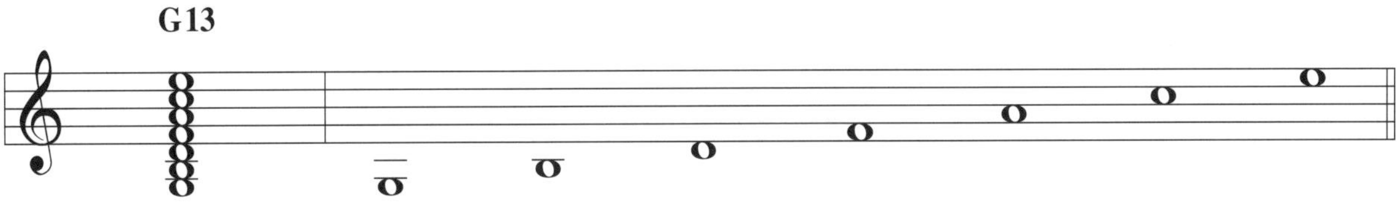

Again note that (as in **Chapter 7**) the dominant chord 'stack' above contains a conflict - the **3rd** of the chord (the note **B** in this case, required for the 'regular' or **unsuspended** dominant chord) clashes with the **11th** (the note **C** in this case, required for the **suspended** dominant chord). Depending on the type of dominant voicing required, one or other of these tones will be used.

### Deriving 'four-part-over-root' relationships for DOMINANT chords (contd)

Now we will extract the required 'four-part-over-root' relationships from the preceding dominant chord 'stack' as follows:-

**Figure 8.6. 'Four-part-over-root' relationships within the G dominant chord 'stack'**

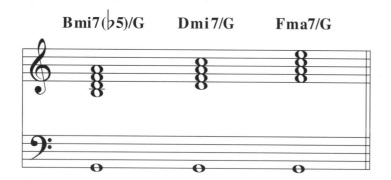

*(Again we have only extracted the 'four-part-over-root' chords most commonly used in contemporary applications).*

Now we will analyze the above 'four-part-over-root' chords as follows:-

- ***Bmi7(b5)/G***   This 'four-part-over-root' voicing creates a fully-defined (and <u>un</u>suspended) **dominant ninth** chord. (Again the term 'fully-defined' is used here because this voicing contains the **3rd** and **7th** of the chord). The chord symbol which is a **composite equivalent** of this **Bmi7(b5)/G** would be **G9**. This voicing consists of a **minor 7th with flatted 5th 'shape' built from the 3rd of a dominant chord**, and we will therefore refer to it as a <u>3-5-b7-9</u> upper structure voicing. This voicing is useful in contemporary situations where the more 'leading' and defined sound of the regular (i.e. <u>un</u>suspended) dominant is needed, but where the style does not permit the dominant chord to be **altered** - as in some R'n'B and gospel idioms.

- ***Dmi7/G***   This 'four-part-over-root' voicing creates a **suspended dominant ninth** (also known as a **dominant eleventh**) chord. The presence of the **11th** of the chord (**C** in this case) implies that the **3rd** of the chord (**B** in this case) has been omitted. The chord symbols which are **composite equivalents** of this **Dmi7/G** would be **G9sus** or **G11**. This voicing consists of a **minor 7th 'shape' built from the 5th of a dominant chord**, and we will therefore refer to it as a <u>5-b7-9-11</u> upper structure voicing. Note that this 'four-part-over-root' voicing was also available within the minor chord 'stack', as discussed on the previous page. In most cases however, this voicing will be heard and used in the **suspended dominant** capacity outlined above. This voicing can be considered a 'close relative' of the <u>b7-9-11</u> 'triad-over-root' voicing derived in **Fig. 7.6.**, with a 'denser' sound due to the addition of the **5th** of the overall suspended dominant chord. Unlike most of the 'four-part-over-root' voicings in this chapter which would be arrived at by **translating** or **upgrading** composite chord symbols, it is not uncommon to see this particular **'slash'** chord symbol (i.e. for the suspended dominant) on a leadsheet or chart.

## Deriving 'four-part-over-root' relationships for DOMINANT chords (contd)

**(Explanation of four-part-over-root chords in Fig. 8.6. contd)**

- **Fma7/G** This 'four-part-over-root' voicing creates a **suspended dominant thirteenth** chord. Again the presence of the **11th** of the chord implies that the **3rd** has been omitted. The other chord tone from the 'stack' which has been omitted is the **5th**, which is **not** an important definitive note on the chord. Therefore for all practical purposes, the chord symbol which is a **composite equivalent** of this **Fma7/G** would be **G13sus** (effectively a **G9sus** chord with the **13th** added).This voicing consists of a **major 7th 'shape' built from the 7th of a dominant chord**, and we will therefore refer to it as a **b7-9-11-13** upper structure voicing. Again in comparison to the **b7-9-11** 'triad-over-root' voicing derived in **Fig. 7.6.**, this voicing has a more sophisticated (and yet still **unaltered**) sound due to the addition of the **13th** of the overall suspended dominant chord. Again as for the preceding **5-b7-9-11** voicing, it is not uncommon to see this particular **'slash'** chord symbol shown on a chart.

## Summary of upper structure 'four-part-over-root' relationships derived so far

We can summarize these commonly-used 'four-part-over-root' voicings on **major**, **minor**, **dominant** and **suspended dominant** chords as follows:-

| | | | |
|---|---|---|---|
| **Major chords** (Fig. 8.2.) | 3-5-7-9 | as in **Emi7/C**. | Fully defined major 9th. |
| **Minor chords** (Fig. 8.4.) | b3-5-b7-9<br>5-b7-9-11 | as in **Fma7/D**.<br>as in **Ami7/D**. | Fully defined minor 9th.<br>Less defined minor 11th. |
| **Dominant chords** (Fig. 8.6.) | 3-5-b7-9 | as in **Bmi7(b5)/G**. | Fully defined (<u>unsuspended</u>) dominant 9th. |
| | 5-b7-9-11<br>b7-9-11-13 | as in **Dmi7/G**.<br>as in **Fma7/G**. | Suspended dominant 9th.<br>Suspended dominant 13th. |

## Voiceleading 'four-part-over-root' chords around the circle-of-5ths/4ths

As an exercise we could take any of the previous 'four-part-over-root' voicings for major, minor or dominant chords and take them round the **circle-of-5ths** or **circle-of-4ths**. The upper four-part shapes would then **voicelead** according to the principles established in **Chapter 6**. For example, if we built a **b7-9-11-13** upper structure voicing on a **D** (suspended) **dominant** chord, this would use a **C major 7th** upper 'shape'. This 'four-part-over-root' structure could then be 'voiceled' around the circle-of-5ths as shown on the following page:-

## Voiceleading 'four-part-over-root' chords around the circle-of-5ths/4ths (contd)

### Figure 8.7. Suspended dominant 13th chord (using b7-9-11-13 upper structure as in Fig. 8.6.) moving around the circle-of-5ths

In the above example we can observe the following:-

- Each voicing above is a **b7-9-11-13** structure i.e. the upper major 7th 'shape' in each case is built from the **b7th** (minor 7th) of the dominant chord defined by the root voice. A **suspended dominant 13th** chord is therefore created in each case.
- The suspended dominant 13th 'four-part-over-root' voicing shown in **Fig. 8.6.** (i.e. the **Fma7/G**) is the second chord in the above example, with the upper **F major 7th** 'shape' being in 2nd inversion.
- The voiceleading of the upper major 7th 'shapes' follows the normal circle-of-5ths conventions as first seen in **Fig. 6.25.**

Next we will voicelead another 'four-part-over-root' voicing around the entire circle-of-4ths. If we built a **3-5-7-9** upper structure voicing (as in **Fig. 8.2.**) on an **Ab major** chord, this would use a **C minor 7th** upper 'shape'. This structure could then be 'voiceled' around the circle-of-4ths as shown on the following page:-

## Voiceleading 'four-part-over-root' chords around the circle-of-5ths/4ths (contd)

### Figure 8.8. Major 9th chord (using 3-5-7-9 upper structure as in Fig. 8.2.) moving around the circle-of-4ths

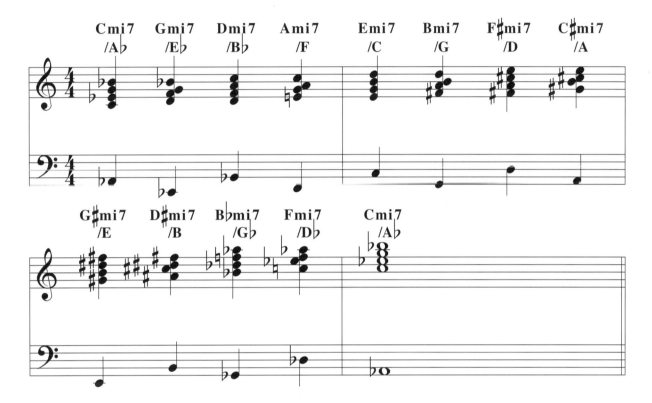

In the above example we can observe the following:-

- Each voicing above is a **3-5-7-9** structure i.e. the upper minor 7th 'shape' in each case is built from the **3rd** of the major chord defined by the root voice. A **major ninth** chord is therefore created in each case.
- The major 9th 'triad-over-root' voicing shown in **Fig. 8.2.** (i.e. the **Emi7/C**) is the fifth chord in the above example, with the upper **E minor 7th** 'shape' being in root position.
- The voiceleading of the upper minor 7th 'shapes' follows the normal circle-of-4ths conventions as first seen in **Fig. 6.28.**

*(Please refer to **Chapter 7** of our contemporary keyboard method **The Pop Piano Book**, for playing exercises which take these 'four-part-over-root' relationships around the circle-of-5ths and circle-of-4ths).*

### Using 'four-part-over-root' chords within major keys

Now we will present analysis 'tables' of the commonly-used 'four-part-over-root' chords in the keys of **C major** and **C minor**. For ease of illustration, these 'four-part-over-root' tables will again use the 'slash' chord symbol format. However, we will most often make use of these 'four-part-over-root' chords by **translating** (or **upgrading**) composite symbols on a chart. So within the next two progressions (**#1 - #2**) we will be **translating** composite chord symbols into 'four-part-over-root' chords where appropriate, and the last progression (**#3**) demonstrates some chord **upgrading**. In each case two sets of chord symbols are shown; the original (composite) symbols and the 'slash' symbol resulting from the chord translation or upgrading.

Note also that the 'triad-over-root' chords derived in **Chapter 7** can be freely mixed with 'these 'four-part-over-root' chords. We might use a 'triad-over-root' chord instead of a 'four-part-over-root' chord if a less 'dense' sound is required, or if using a 'triad-over-root' voicing enables us to stay within an overall key restriction (a consideration in less 'chromatic' styles). Now we will present a chart or 'table' of the commonly-used 'four-part-over-root' chords in the key of **C major**:-

### Figure 8.9. Chart and analysis of 'four-part-over-root' chords in the key of C major

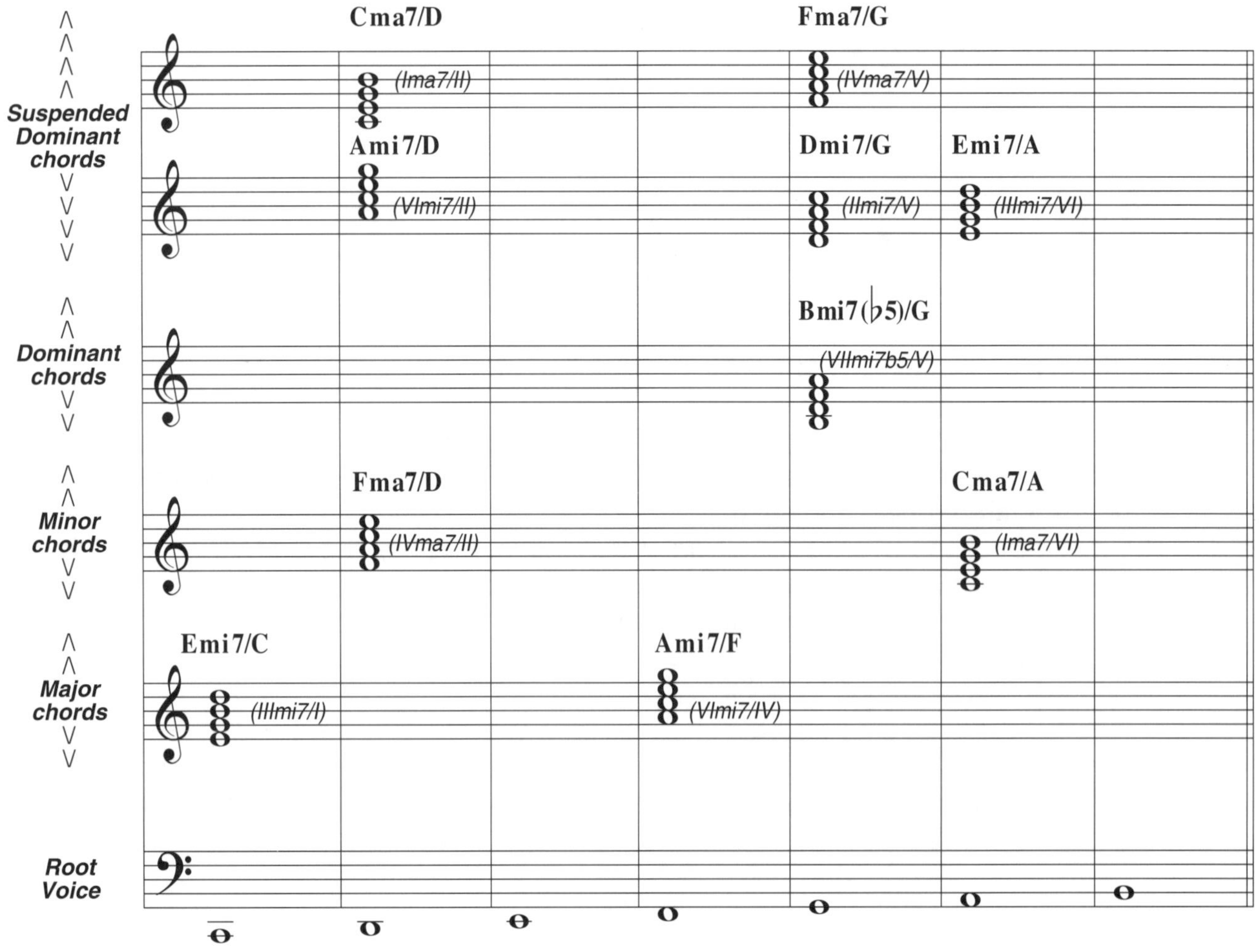

### *Using 'four-part-over-root' chords within major keys (contd)*

The information in the 'table' on the previous page, is presented in a similar manner as for the 'triad-over-root' charts shown in **Chapter 7**:-

- Each of the chords shown represents a **'four-part-over-root'** relationship available within the key of **C major**.

- The **bottom** staff in the chart shows all of the available root voices in the key of **C major**.

- The chords are grouped in **columns**, corresponding to the **root voice** used in each chord (the note **to the right of the slash** in the chord symbol). For example, at the bottom of the second column we have the root voice of **D**, and above this (in the same column) we have all of the available 'four-part-over-root' chords which use **D** as the root voice.

- The **type** of chord is indicated by the text on the left of the chart, as follows:-
    - the **top two** staffs contain **suspended dominant** chords, as shown in **Fig. 8.6**. (We also recall that the **5-b7-9-11** structure occurred within the minor chord 'stack', as in **Fig. 8.4.**).
    - the **third staff from the top** contains regular (i.e. <u>un</u>suspended) **dominant** chords, again as shown in **Fig. 8.6**.
    - the **third staff from the bottom** contains **minor** chords, as shown in **Fig. 8.4.**
    - the **second staff from the bottom** contains **major** chords, as shown in **Fig. 8.2.**

- A **roman numeral** symbol is shown next to each chord in the table. This indicates the **relationship** of the **upper four-part 'shape'** and the **root voice** to the **key being used** (in this case **C major**). For example:-
    - on the top of the fifth column (from the left) we have an **Fma7/G** chord, using the roman numeral symbol **IVma7/V**. This signifies that:-
        - the upper **F major 7th** 'shape' triad is a **IVma7** in the key of **C**.
        - the root voice of **G** is a **V** (i.e. is the 5th degree) in the key of **C**.
    - the only chord in the fourth column (from the left) is an **Ami7/F** chord, using the roman numeral symbol **VImi7/IV**. This signifies that:-
        - the upper **A minor 7th** 'shape' triad is a **VImi7** in the key of **C**.
        - the root voice of **F** is a **IV** (i.e. is the 4th degree) in the key of **C**.

The following progression examples are presented in the key of **C major**, for ease of reference to the 'four-part-over-root' chart on the previous page. Again as for the progressions shown in **Chapter 7**, each chord has been analyzed with a 'roman numeral' symbol indicating the relationship of the chord to the overall key of **C major**. We will now look at the first progression example, shown on the following page:-

## Using 'four-part-over-root' chords within major keys (contd)

***Figure 8.10. Harmonic analysis progression example #1*** *(this progression is typically used for the first eight measures of the David Gates pop ballad "Make It With You")*

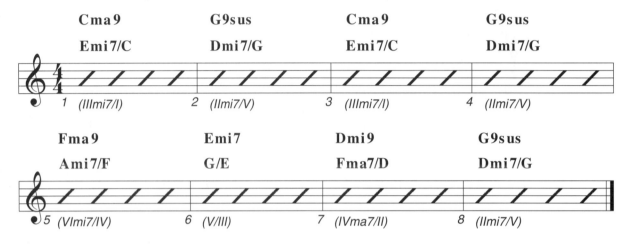

Again note that there are two sets of chord symbols in the above example:-

- the **top** row contains the **composite** chord symbols which we are more likely to see on leadsheets and charts.
- the bottom row contains the '**slash**' chord symbols which result from the **translation** of these composite symbols into 'four-part-over-root' (and in one case 'triad-over-root') chords.

We can further describe the '**upper structure relationships**' used on each chord (noting that the four-part upper structures are all contained within the summary on **p257**) as follows:-

*Measure 1* - The **Cma9** symbol has been translated into an **Emi7/C** 'four-part-over-root' chord. This <u>3-5-7-9</u> upper structure on a **C major** chord (see **Fig. 8.2.**) is also a *IIImi7/I* in the key of **C**.

*Measure 2* - The **G9sus** symbol has been translated into a **Dmi7/G** 'four-part-over-root' chord. This <u>5-b7-9-11</u> upper structure on a **G dominant** chord (see **Fig. 8.6.**) is also a *IImi7/V* in the key of **C**.

*(Measures 3 - 4* *Same comments as for measures 1 - 2).*

*Measure 5* - The **Fma9** symbol has been translated into an **Ami7/F** 'four-part-over-root' chord. This <u>3-5-7-9</u> upper structure on an **F major** chord (see **Fig. 8.2.**) is also a *VImi7/IV* in the key of **C**.

*Measure 6* - The **Emi7** symbol has been translated into a **G/E** 'triad-over-root' chord. This time we <u>**did not**</u> use a (four-part) <u>b3-5-b7-9</u> structure on the **E minor** chord, as the resulting ninth on this chord (**F#** in this case) would not have been in the key of **C major**. *(This type of judgement call will be needed in more diatonic styles).* This <u>b3-5-b7</u> upper structure on an **E minor** chord (see **Fig. 7.4.**) is also a *V/III* in the key of **C**.

## Using 'four-part-over-root' chords within major keys (contd)

**(Description of upper structure relationships within Fig. 8.10. contd)**

**Measure 7** - The **Dmi9** symbol has been translated into an **Fma7/D** 'four-part-over-root' chord. This **b3-5-b7-9** upper structure on a **D minor** chord (see **Fig. 8.4.**) is also a **IVma7/II** in the key of **C**.

**(Measure 8** *Same comments as for measure 2).*

## Combining 'four-part-over-root' voicings within major and minor keys

We recall from our work in **Chapter 7** (see **p229** comments) that 'triad-over-root' voicings can be combined together within the **major** and **minor key** built from the same tonic, and this is also the case for 'four-part-over-root' voicings, as shown in the following 'table':-

**Figure 8.11. Chart of all 'four-part-over-root' chords in the keys of C major and C minor**

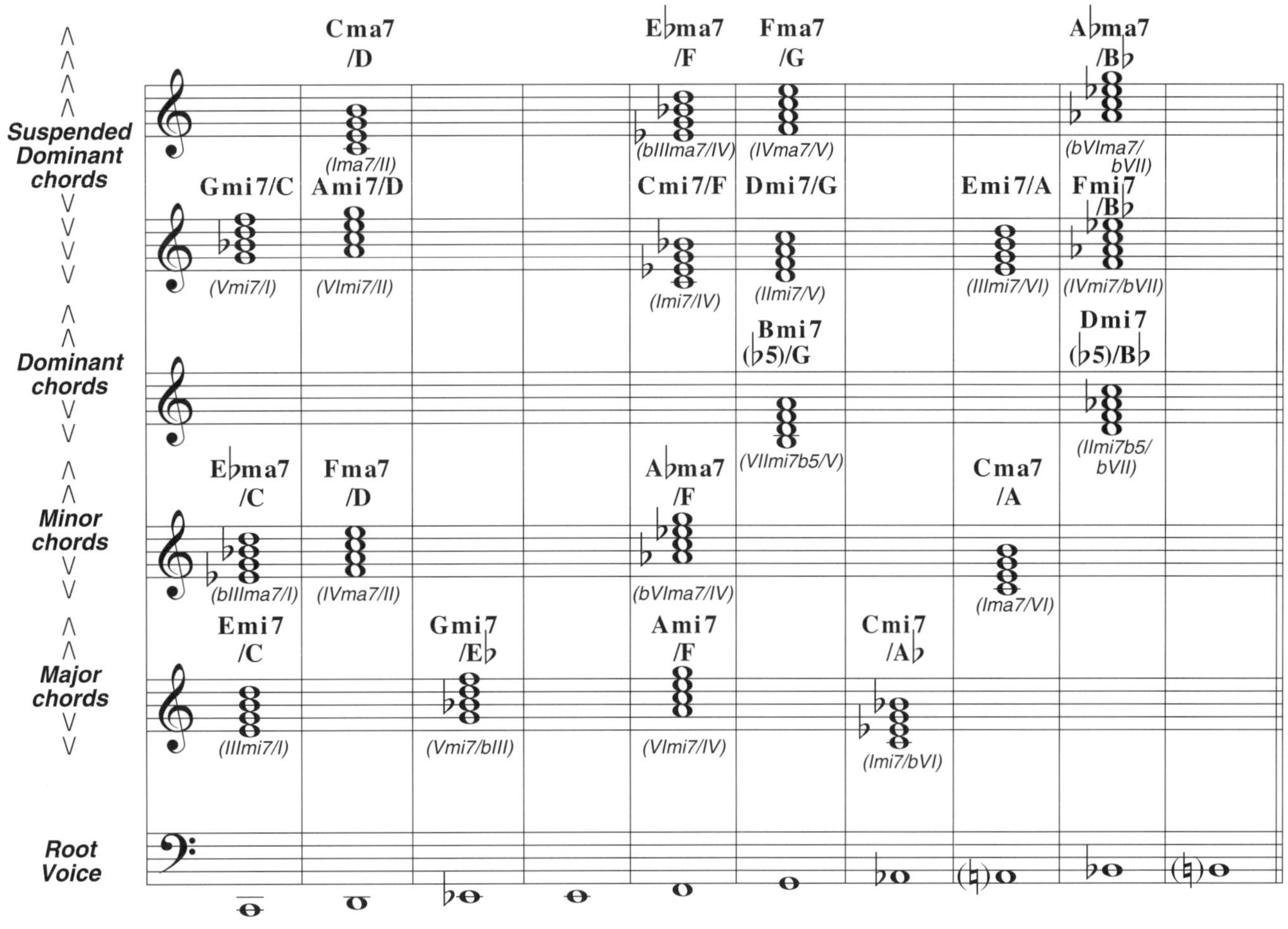

### Combining 'four-part-over-root' voicings within major and minor keys (contd)

The organization of the combined 'four-part-over-root' chart shown on the previous page, is essentially similar to the corresponding chart in **Chapter 7** for 'triad-over-root' chords - review **p231** comments as necessary. Again we have combined the possibilities for the key of **C major** (using the **C major** scale) and the key of **C minor** (using the **C natural minor** scale).

We will now look at another progression example, this time using the combined possibilities within the keys of **C major** and **C minor**. Again we are **translating** composite chord symbols into 'four-part-over-root' voicings, as shown in the following example:-

***Figure 8.12. Harmonic analysis progression example #2*** *(this progression is typically used for the first four measures of the Anita Baker R'n'B ballad "Sweet Love")*

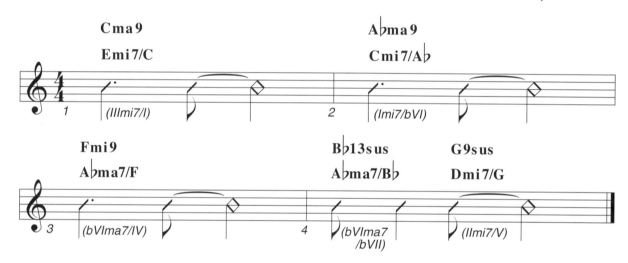

Again note that there are two sets of chord symbols in the above example - see **p262** comments. We can further describe the '**upper structure relationships**' used on each chord:-

***Measure 1*** - The **Cma9** symbol has been translated into an **Emi7/C** 'four-part-over-root' chord. This **3-5-7-9** upper structure on a **C major** chord (see **Fig. 8.2.**) is also a ***IIImi7/I*** with respect to **C** as the tonic.

***Measure 2*** - The **Abma9** symbol has been translated into a **Cmi7/Ab** 'four-part-over-root' chord. This **3-5-7-9** upper structure on an **Ab major** chord (see **Fig. 8.2.**) is also a ***Imi7/bVI*** with respect to **C** as the tonic.

***Measure 3*** - The **Fmi9** symbol has been translated into an **Abma7/F** 'four-part-over-root' chord. This **b3-5-b7-9** upper structure on an **F minor** chord (see **Fig. 8.4.**) is also a ***bVIma7/IV*** with respect to **C** as the tonic.

***Measure 4*** - The **Bb13sus** symbol has been translated into an **Abma7/Bb** 'four-part-over-root' chord. This **b7-9-11-13** upper structure on a **Bb dominant** chord (see **Fig. 8.6.**) is also a ***bVIma7/bVII*** with respect to **C** as the tonic.

## *Combining 'four-part-over-root' voicings within major and minor keys (contd)*

***(Description of upper structure relationships within Fig. 8.12. contd)***

**Measure 4** - 
*(contd)*          The **G9sus** symbol has been translated into a **Dmi7/G** 'four-part-over-root' chord. This <u>**5-b7-9-11**</u> upper structure on a **G dominant** chord (see **Fig. 8.6.**) is also a ***IImi7/V*** with respect to **C** as the tonic.

## *Upgrading of chord symbols using 'four-part-over-root' chords*

The preceding progression examples in **Figs. 8.10.** and **8.12.** have involved the translation of **composite** chord symbols into 'four-part-over-root' chords, which (as discussed) is typically required when reading contemporary charts. However, in the introduction to this chapter we also mentioned the possibility of **upgrading** triads or four-part symbols by using 'four-part-over-root' chords, which can be a very useful way of imparting a more sophisticated (and yet still unaltered) quality to a contemporary tune. Again as with upgrading using 'triad-over-root' chords (see **p235** comments), you may need to consider whether any added chord tones will work within the major and/or minor key being used. We will also need to voicelead the resulting upper (four-part) 'shapes' according to the principles outlined in *Chapter 6*, and again we may encounter circle-of 5ths/4ths voiceleading within these upper structures. We will now look at an example of a progression to be **upgraded** in this manner:-

*Figure 8.13. Progression example #3 (to be upgraded using 'four-part-over-root' chords)*

Note that the chords in the above example (which are all available within the 'combined' keys of **C major** and **C minor**) are presented as four-part symbols. In order to make this sound more sophisticated (which might be very appropriate for an R'n'B ballad treatment for example), we will now present an **upgraded** solution using 'four-part-over-root' chords, which will include the following:-

-     'four-part-over-root' or 'slash' chord symbols for the **upgraded** chords
-     upper structure four-part 'shape' **voiceleading solution** for each chord
-     '**roman numeral**' analysis for each chord (with respect to the tonic of **C**).

This solution is now shown on the following page:-

### *Upgrading of chord symbols using 'four-part-over-root' chords (contd)*

**Figure 8.14. Progression example #3 (upgraded using 'four-part-over-root' chords)**

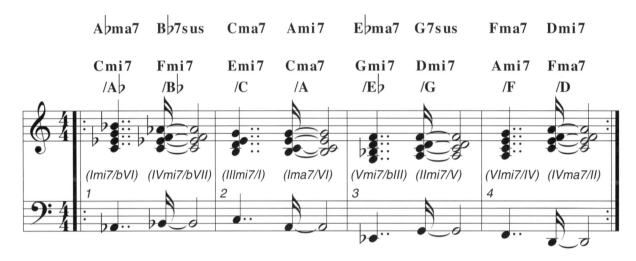

Note that we again have **two rows** of chord symbols - the **top** row are the original symbols from **Fig. 8.13.**, and the **bottom** row are the **upgraded** 'four-part-over-root' symbols. We will now further analyze this 'upgraded' solution (which has created '**9th**' or '**11th**' chords throughout):-

*Measure 1* - The **Abma7** has been upgraded to a **Cmi7/Ab**, which is a **3-5-7-9** structure on an **Ab major** chord (see **Fig. 8.2.**) and is also a *Imi7/bVI* with respect to **C**.

- The **Bb7sus** has been upgraded to an **Fmi7/Bb**, which is a **5-b7-9-11** structure on an **Bb dominant** chord (see **Fig. 8.6.**) and is also a *IVmi7/bVII* with respect to **C**.

*Measure 2* - The **Cma7** has been upgraded to an **Emi7/C**, which is a **3-5-7-9** structure on a **C major** chord (see **Fig. 8.2.**) and is also a *IIImi7/I* with respect to **C**.

- The **Ami7** has been upgraded to a **Cma7/A**, which is a **b3-5-b7-9** structure on an **A minor** chord (see **Fig. 8.4.**) and is also a *Ima7/VI* with respect to **C**.

*Measure 3* - The **Ebma7** has been upgraded to a **Gmi7/Eb**, which is a **3-5-7-9** structure on an **Eb major** chord (see **Fig. 8.2.**) and is also a *Vmi7/bIII* with respect to **C**.

- The **G7sus** has been upgraded to a **Dmi7/G**, which is a **5-b7-9-11** structure on a **G dominant** chord (see **Fig. 8.6.**) and is also a *IImi7/V* with respect to **C**.

*Measure 4* - The **Fma7** has been upgraded to an **Ami7/F**, which is a **3-5-7-9** structure on an **F major** chord (see **Fig. 8.2.**) and is also a *VImi7/IV* with respect to **C**.

- The **Dmi7** has been upgraded to an **Fma7/D**, which is a **b3-5-b7-9** structure on a **D minor** chord (see **Fig. 8.4.**) and is also a *IVma7/II* with respect to **C**.

Note that from the **1st** to the **2nd** chord, the upper minor 7th 'shapes' are voiceleading in a **circle-of-5ths** manner, and from the **5th** through to the **7th** chord the upper voiceleading is in a **circle-of-4ths** manner - review voiceleading concepts in *Chapter 6* as necessary.

## *Chapter Eight Workbook Questions*

**1.** *Building 'four-part-over-root' chord qualities*

For each question in Section **1** you are to write the upper four-part 'shape' (in root position) on the staff, and a four-part-over-root chord symbol above the staff. In questions 1 - 8 you are to create a **minor 9th** chord (with a <u>b3-5-b7-9</u> upper structure major 7th shape).

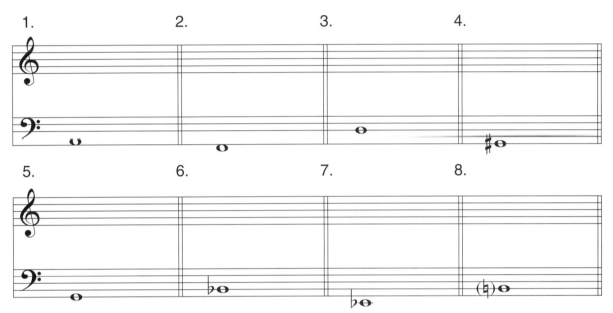

In questions 9 - 16 you are to create a **suspended dominant 13th** chord (with a <u>b7-9-11-13</u> upper structure major 7th shape).

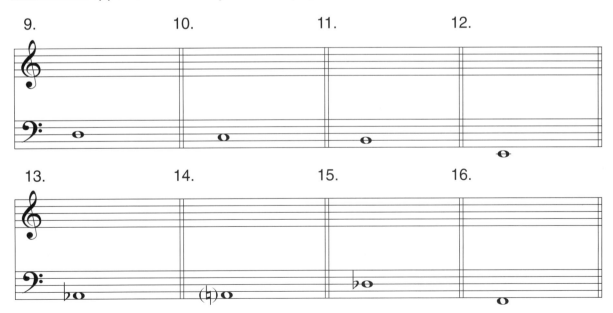

### 1. _Building 'four-part-over-root' chord qualities (contd)_

In questions 17 - 24 you are to create a **major 9th** chord (with a **3-5-7-9** upper structure minor 7th shape).

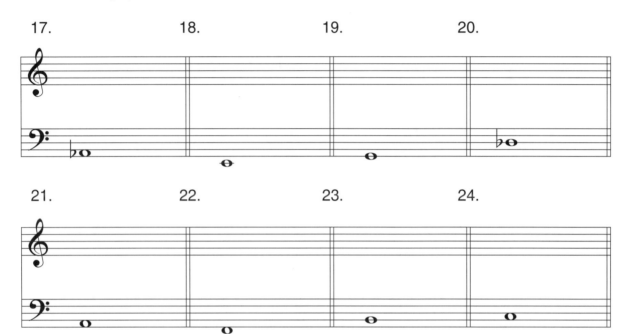

In questions 25 - 32 you are to create a **suspended dominant 9th** chord (with a **5-b7-9-11** upper structure minor 7th shape).

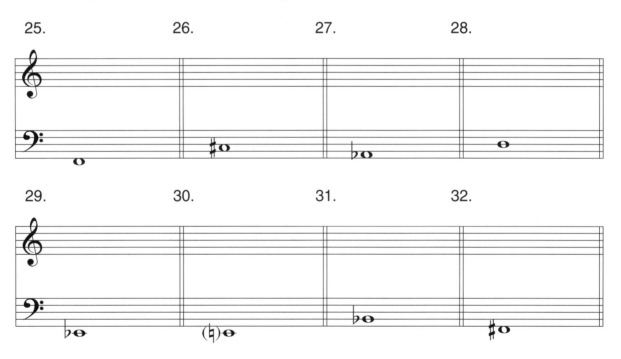

## 2. *Voiceleading 'four-part-over-root' progressions*

You are to write the root on the bass clef staff, and the upper four-part voicing on the treble clef staff, for the following progressions. You are to interpret the chord symbols as follows:-

- on the **minor 9th** chords, build a **b3-5-b7-9** voicing (i.e. *major seventh* from the 3rd).
- on the **major 9th** chords, build a **3-5-7-9** voicing (i.e. *minor seventh* from the 3rd).
- on the **suspended dominant 9th** chords, build a **5-b7-9-11** voicing (i.e. *minor seventh* from the 5th).
- on the **suspended dominant 13th** chords, build a **b7-9-11-13** voicing (i.e. *major seventh* from the 7th).

You are to voicelead from the first four-part-over-root chord voicing provided in each case.

Questions 33 - 36 each take a particular chord quality and move it around the circle-of-5ths or circle-of-4ths (potentially implying a new key center with each chord - see **Figs. 8.7.** and **8.8.** in the Textbook). The upper structure four-part shapes should be voiceled (in a circle-of-5ths/4ths manner) according to the rules established in *Chapter 6*.

2. *Voiceleading 'four-part-over-root' progressions (contd)*

Questions 37 - 40 now contain a mixture of chord qualities, and the voiceleading between the upper four-part shapes may include movements other than circle-of-5ths/4ths. Each progression is now within a **combined major/minor key restriction** (for example, all the four-part-over-root voicings required for question 37 are contained within the combined **C major** and **C minor** chart shown in **Fig. 8.11.** in the Textbook). However, as no key signatures are provided, you still need to write all necessary accidentals.

For questions 37 - 38, where a commontone is not available as the top voice of consecutive chords, you are to voicelead the top voice in an *ascending* manner.

37. *(within the 'combined restriction' of the keys of* **C major** *&* **C minor***)*     38. *(within the 'combined restriction' of the keys of* **G major** *&* **G minor***)*

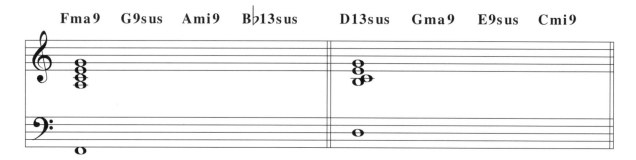

For questions 39 - 40, where a commontone is not available as the top voice of consecutive chords, you are to voicelead the top voice in a *descending* manner.

39. *(within the 'combined restriction' of the keys of* **Ab major** *&* **Ab minor***)*     40. *(within the 'combined restriction' of the keys of* **A major** *&* **A minor***)*

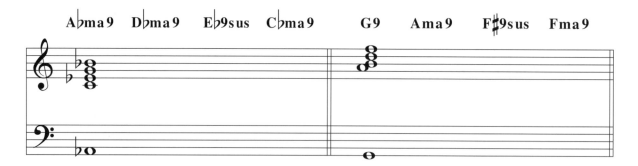

*(Review **Appendix 4** as necessary for the four-part-over-root voicings available in all major/minor keys).*

### 3. *Chord progression 'translation' and analysis*

You are to translate each 'composite' chord symbol in the following progressions, into a 'four-part-over-root' symbol according to the rules established in ***Chapter 8*** (and summarized on **p269** in the Workbook). You are then to determine the '**roman numeral**' functions for each resulting 'four-part-over-root' chord (as shown in various Textbook examples including **Fig. 8.12.**). Note that as with the progressions analyzed in ***Chapter 7***, these contemporary examples are to be analyzed **in relation to a single 'tonic' throughout** i.e. we are not looking for momentary key changes.

- Chord progression **#1** is to be analyzed with respect to the note **Eb** as the tonic, and is diatonic to the key of **Eb major** (i.e. the chords are wholly contained within an **Eb major** scale).
- Chord progression **#2** is to be analyzed with respect to the note **E** as the tonic, and now combines together chords from the key of **E major** (using an **E major** scale) and the key of **E minor** (using an **E natural minor** scale).

*Chord progression #1*
*(typically used for the first eight measures of the R'n'B ballad "Tonight I Celebrate My Love")*
*- note that question 51 will translate to a 'triad-over-root' symbol, as in* **Fig. 8.10.** *measure 6.*

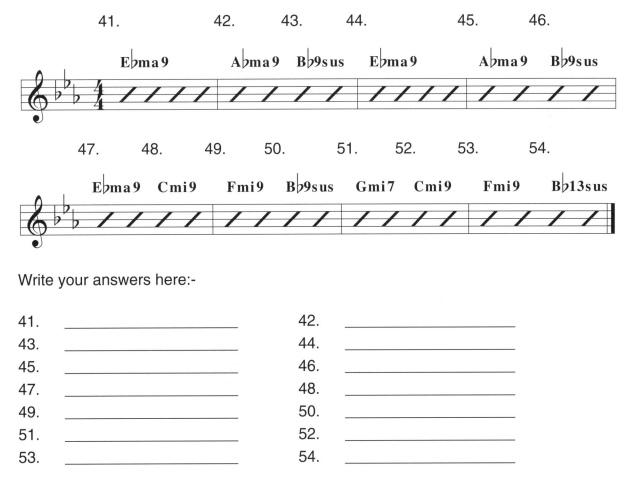

Write your answers here:-

| | | | |
|---|---|---|---|
| 41. | _____ | 42. | _____ |
| 43. | _____ | 44. | _____ |
| 45. | _____ | 46. | _____ |
| 47. | _____ | 48. | _____ |
| 49. | _____ | 50. | _____ |
| 51. | _____ | 52. | _____ |
| 53. | _____ | 54. | _____ |

### 3. _Chord progression 'translation' and analysis (contd)_

_Chord progression #2_
_(typically used for the chorus and bridge section of the R'n'B/pop tune "What's Goin' On")_

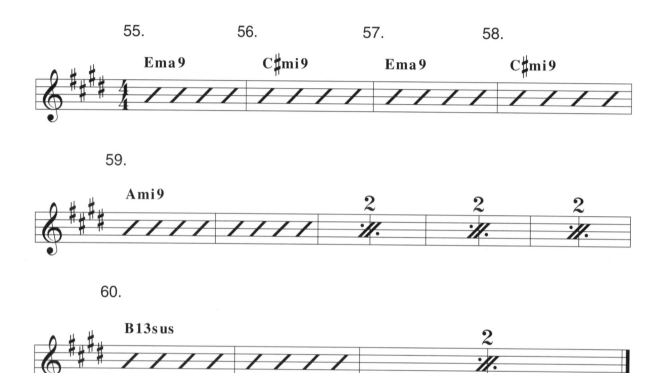

Write your answers here:-

55. _____    56. _____

57. _____    58. _____

59. _____    60. _____

## Chapter Eight Workbook Answers

**1.** *Building 'four-part-over-root' chord qualities - answers*

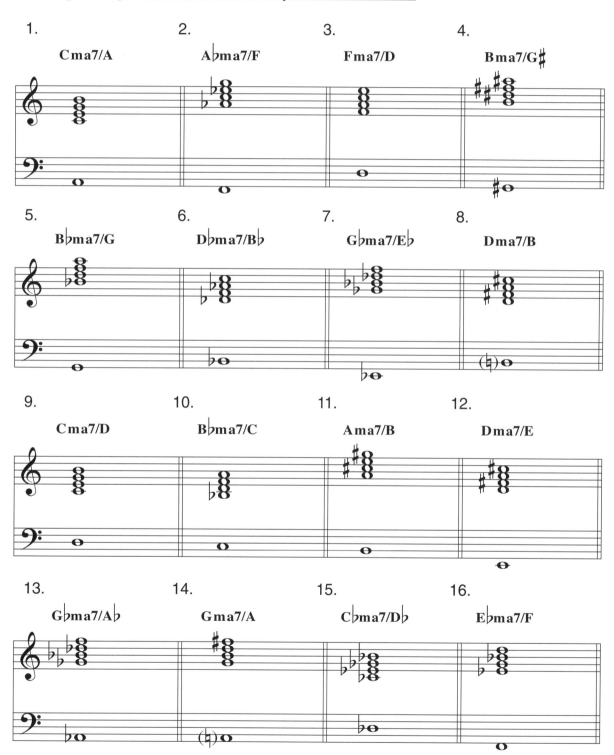

**1.** *Building 'four-part-over-root' chord qualities - answers (contd)*

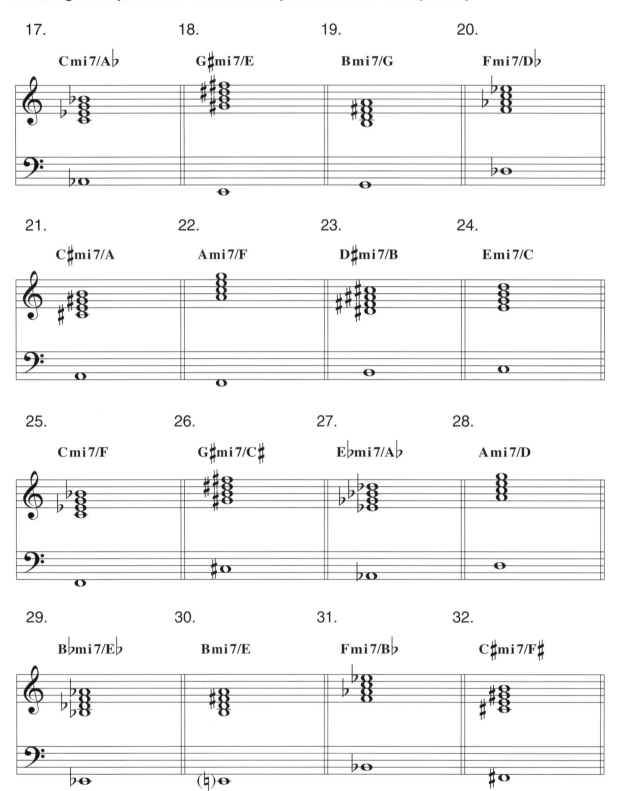

**2.** *Voiceleading 'four-part-over-root' progressions - answers*

33.

Ami9   Dmi9   Gmi9   Cmi9

34.

F#13sus   B13sus   E13sus   A13sus

35.

Cma9   Gma9   Dma9   Ama9

36.

B9sus   F#9sus   C#9sus   G#9sus

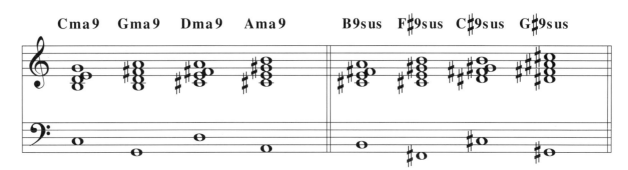

37.

Fma9   G9sus   Ami9   Bb13sus

38.

D13sus   Gma9   E9sus   Cmi9

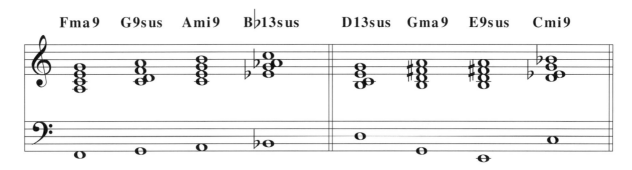

**275**

**2.** **_Voiceleading 'four-part-over-root' progressions - answers (contd)_**

39.                                            40.

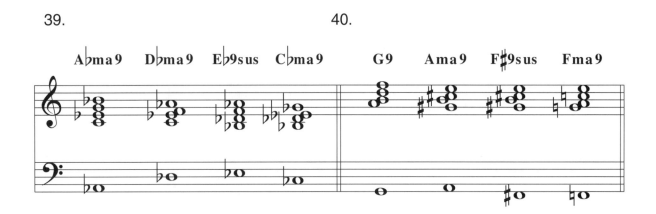

Abma9   Dbma9   Eb9sus   Cbma9        G9     Ama9    F#9sus   Fma9

**3.** **_Chord progression 'translation' and analysis - answers_**

*(Chord Progression #1 - analyzed with respect to the note **Eb** as the tonic)*

| | | | | | | |
|---|---|---|---|---|---|---|
| 41. | **_Gmi7/Eb_** | *(IIImi7/I)* | | 42. | **_Cmi7/Ab_** | *(VImi7/IV)* |
| 43. | **_Fmi7/Bb_** | *(IImi7/V)* | | 44. | **_Gmi7/Eb_** | *(IIImi7/I)* |
| 45. | **_Cmi7/Ab_** | *(VImi7/IV)* | | 46. | **_Fmi7/Bb_** | *(IImi7/V)* |
| 47. | **_Gmi7/Eb_** | *(IIImi7/I)* | | 48. | **_Ebma7/C_** | *(Ima7/VI)* |
| 49. | **_Abma7/F_** | *(IVma7/II)* | | 50. | **_Fmi7/Bb_** | *(IImi7/V)* |
| 51. | **_Bb/G_** | *(V/III)* | | 52. | **_Ebma7/C_** | *(Ima7/VI)* |
| 53. | **_Abma7/F_** | *(IVma7/II)* | | 54. | **_Abma7/Bb_** | *(IVma7/V)* |

*(Chord Progression #2 - analyzed with respect to the note **E** as the tonic)*

| | | | | | | |
|---|---|---|---|---|---|---|
| 55. | **_G#mi7/E_** | *(IIImi7/I)* | | 56. | **_Ema7/C#_** | *(Ima7/VI)* |
| 57. | **_G#mi7/E_** | *(IIImi7/I)* | | 58. | **_Ema7/C#_** | *(Ima7/VI)* |
| 59. | **_Cma7/A_** | *(bVIma7/IV)* | | 60. | **_Ama7/B_** | *(IVma7/V)* |

# *Pentatonic and blues scales, and their applications*

## *Introduction*

In this chapter we will derive and discuss the following scales:-

- **pentatonic** scale
- **minor pentatonic** scale (also sometimes referred to as a "blues pentatonic" scale)
- **blues** scale.

We will also analyze the relationship of these scales to each other and to the **major** scale (first reviewed in **Fig. 1.1.**), and we will see how we can use these scales as melodic and/or improvisational sources over different chords. Additionally we will introduce the concept of '**blues form**' as a vehicle for the use of blues scales over progressions.

## *Derivation of the PENTATONIC scale*

I believe that the simplest way to derive a pentatonic scale is to take a **major** scale and **remove the 4th and 7th degrees**. This method also enables a consistent approach to the 'scale degree numbering' of the pentatonic scale, as we will see in the following examples. First we will review the **C major** scale shown in **Fig. 1.1.**, now with the addition of 'scale degree numbers' as follows:-

### *Figure 9.1. C major scale showing intervals and scale degree numbers*

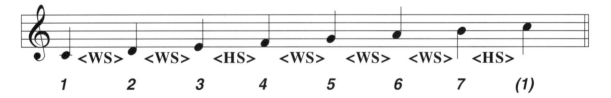

When we remove the **4th** and **7th** degrees from the major scale to create the pentatonic scale, the remaining notes will still retain the 'scale degree numbers' allocated above. This results in two important benefits:-

- it enables us to more easily relate the resulting scale to the original **major** scale above.
- it reminds us of the **intervals** between each of the scale degrees and the tonic of the scale.

Now we will derive the **C pentatonic** scale, as shown on the following page:-

## Derivation of the PENTATONIC scale (contd)

**Figure 9.2. C pentatonic scale showing intervals and scale degree numbers**

Note that the removal of the **4th** and **7th** degrees with respect to the **C major** scale in **Fig. 9.1.**, has created two **minor 3rd** intervals within the above **C pentatonic** scale (which consists entirely of minor 3rd and whole-step intervals). The lack of half-steps in the pentatonic scale gives it a less 'leading' quality and enables it to 'float' more easily over different harmonies (more about this shortly).

We can also consider the difference between the major and pentatonic scales, from a 'SOLFEG' (or active-and-resting) standpoint. We recall from **Chapter 2** (specifically the summary on **p20** and the text accompanying **Fig. 2.3.**) that the **4th** and **7th** degrees of a major scale/key ('SOLFEG' syllables **FA** and **TI** respectively) are the most 'active' in a major key, and typically require resolution to adjacent 'resting' tones. So what we did here was to take the major scale and remove the two 'hot notes' (i.e. **FA** and **TI**) of the scale - which is why I sometimes refer to the pentatonic scale as a "major scale with the teeth pulled" in my theory classes!

## Derivation of the MINOR PENTATONIC scale

If we now start the above **C pentatonic** scale from the scale degree corresponding to the **relative minor** of **C major** (this is the note **A** - review **p11** comments as necessary), we can now derive the **A minor pentatonic** scale as follows:-

**Figure 9.3. A minor pentatonic scale showing intervals and scale degree numbers**

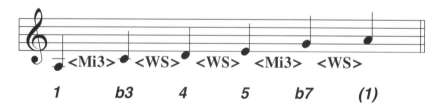

Note that the 'scale degree numbers' have now changed to reflect the intervals between each scale degree and the new tonic of **A**, which from left-to-right are **minor 3rd**, **perfect 4th**, **perfect 5th** and **minor 7th** intervals respectively.

## *Derivation of the MINOR PENTATONIC scale (contd)*

This scale is a favorite for guitar players and is widely used in rock styles! As mentioned in the introduction, this scale is sometimes referred to as a "**blues pentatonic**". I personally find this label potentially confusing - however it's important that you know what is meant by this term if you hear it used.

## *Derivation of the BLUES scale*

If we now take the **A minor pentatonic** scale as derived in **Fig. 9.3.**, and add an **extra half-step 'connector'** between scale degrees *4* and *5* (i.e. those which create **perfect 4th** and **perfect 5th** intervals from the tonic), we can derive the **A blues** scale as follows:-

*Figure 9.4. A blues scale showing intervals and scale degree numbers*

|   |    |   |       |   |    |     |
|---|----|---|-------|---|----|-----|
| 1 | b3 | 4 | #4/b5 | 5 | b7 | (1) |

Note that the 'scale degree numbers' again reflect the intervals between each scale degree and the tonic of **A**, and that the added scale degree (the note **D#** in the above example) could be described as either a *#4* or *b5* depending on the context. From left-to-right, between the tonic and the other scale degrees we now have **minor 3rd**, **perfect 4th**, **augmented 4th** or **diminished 5th**, **perfect 5th** and **minor 7th** intervals respectively.

The melodic strength and 'funky' character of the blues scale enable it to be used as a melodic and/or improvisational source in a great many different contexts (more about this later).

## *Application of pentatonic scales over different chords*

We will now discuss how pentatonic scales might be used as a source for melodic and/or improvisational ideas in contemporary applications. As a general rule, we can say that if a **major triad 'upper structure'** voicing is available for a particular chord (as detailed in *Chapter 7*), then the **pentatonic scale built from the root of the upper major triad** can be used over the chord. This is perhaps best seen by working through some examples, beginning on the following page:-

## Application of pentatonic scales over different chords (contd)

### Figure 9.5. Building a C pentatonic scale from the root of a C major chord

**C/C**         **C pentatonic/C**
Chord functions:-    1       9       3       5       6/13

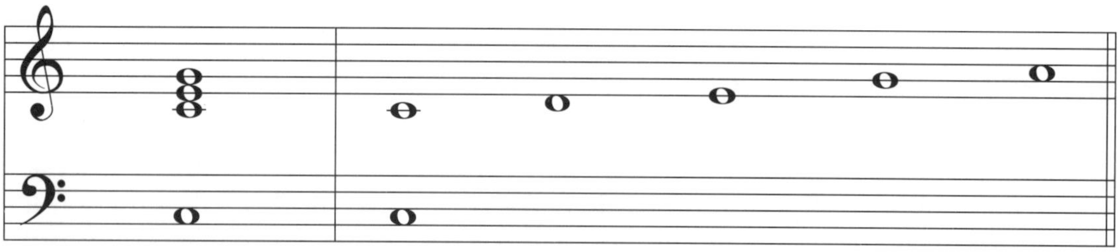

The information shown above can be described as follows:-

- In the left-hand measure a 'triad-over-root' chord is shown (in this case **C/C** - a basic voicing for a **C major** chord first seen in **Fig. 7.2.**).
- In the treble clef staff of the right-hand measure the **C pentatonic** scale is shown, together with the **chord functions** which result when this scale is 'used over' a **C major** chord. In comparing these **chord functions** with the **C pentatonic** 'scale degree numbers' shown in **Fig. 9.2.**, we note the following differences:-
    - while the note **D** is scale degree *'2'* in **Fig. 9.2.**, it is actually a **9th** on the above **C major** chord (review discussion on **p36** as necessary).
    - while the note **A** is scale degree *'6'* in **Fig. 9.2.**, it can actually be either a **6th** or a **13th** on the above **C major** chord (see **Figs. 1.13.** and **7.1.**).

Now we will look at some further 'triad-over-root' structures first derived in **Chapter 7**, and consider the corresponding pentatonic scale relationships available on these chords. For ease of illustration and comparison, we will continue to use the upper **C major** triad and **C pentatonic** scale over these different chords, beginning with the following example:-

### Figure 9.6. Building a C pentatonic scale from the third of an A minor (7th) chord

**C/A**         **C pentatonic/A(mi7)**
Chord functions:-    b3       11       5       b7       1

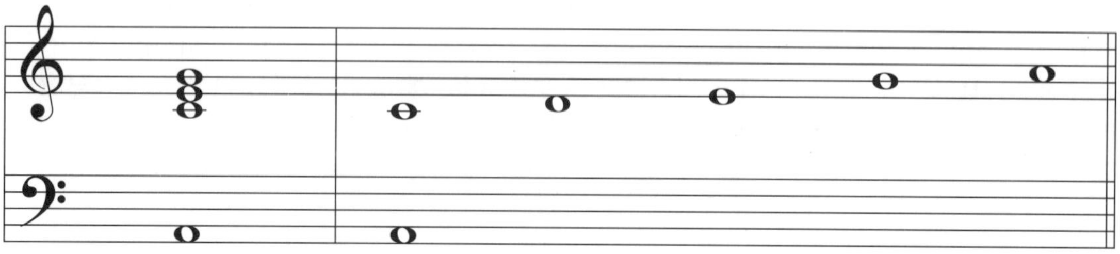

## *Application of pentatonic scales over different chords (contd)*

The information shown in the preceding **Fig. 9.6.** can be summarized as follows:-

- In the left-hand measure the 'triad-over-root' chord shown is **C/A**, which is a **b3-5-b7** 'triad-over-root' voicing (first seen in **Fig. 7.4.**) on an **A minor** chord. This creates an **Ami7** chord quality overall.
- In the right-hand measure we can see that the use of the **C pentatonic** scale over this **A minor** chord, creates the following **chord functions**:-
  - (minor) **3rd**, **11th** (sometimes referred to as the 4th), **5th**, (minor) **7th**, and **root**.

All of these tones are generally very 'safe' to use on the minor or minor 7th-type chord.

### *Figure 9.7. Building a C pentatonic scale from the fifth of an F major (9th) chord*

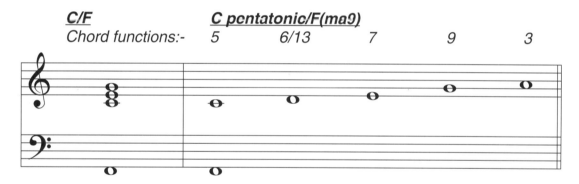

The information shown above can be summarized as follows:-

- In the left-hand measure the 'triad-over-root' chord shown is **C/F**, which is a **5-7-9** 'triad-over-root' voicing (first seen in **Fig. 7.2.**) on an **F major** chord. This creates an **Fma9(no3)** chord quality overall.
- In the right-hand measure we can see that the use of the **C pentatonic** scale over this **F major** chord, creates the following **chord functions**:-
  - **5th**, **6th/13th**, **7th**, **9th** and **3rd**.

In comparing the above functions to the chord tones created in **Fig. 9.5.** (where we built a pentatonic scale from the **root** of a major chord), we note the following differences:-
- the **7th** of the chord is now available
- the **root** of the chord is not available.
- other chord functions i.e. **3rd**, **5th**, **6th/13th** & **9th** are available in both cases.

Building a pentatonic scale from the **5th** of a major chord as in the above example, creates a fresh, contemporary sound which however is 'safe' to use in a large number of applications. This is a favorite device used by artists such as Bruce Hornsby for example!

## Application of pentatonic scales over different chords (contd)

***Figure 9.8. Building a C pentatonic scale from the seventh of a D minor (11th) or D suspended dominant chord***

| ***C/D*** | ***C pentatonic/D(mi11 or 9sus)*** | | | | |
|---|---|---|---|---|---|
| *Chord functions:-* | *b7* | *1* | *9* | *11* | *5* |

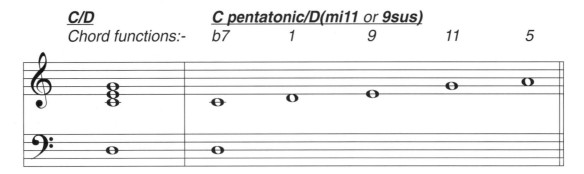

The information shown above can be summarized as follows:-

- In the left-hand measure the 'triad-over-root' chord shown is **C/D**, which is a **b7-9-11** 'triad-over-root' voicing available on both a **D minor** chord (creating an incomplete **Dmi11**, as in **Fig. 7.4.**) and on a **D suspended dominant** chord (creating a **D9sus** or **D11**, as in **Fig. 7.6.**)
- In the right-hand measure we can see that the use of the **C pentatonic** scale over this **D minor** or **D suspended dominant** chord, creates the following **chord functions**:-
  - (minor) **7th**, **root**, **9th**, **11th** (sometimes referred to as the 4th), and **5th**.

In comparing the above functions to the chord tones created in **Fig. 9.6.** (where we built a pentatonic scale from the **third** of a minor chord), we note the following differences:-

- the **9th** of the chord is now available
- the **3rd** of the chord is not available.
- other chord functions i.e. **11th**, **5th**, **7th** and **root** are available in both cases.

In a **minor chord** context, the use of the **9th** creates a more sophisticated sound here.

***Figure 9.9. Building a C pentatonic scale from the ninth of a Bb major (13th) chord***

| ***C/Bb*** | ***C pentatonic/Bb(ma13)*** | | | | |
|---|---|---|---|---|---|
| *Chord functions:-* | *9* | *3* | *#11* | *6/13* | *7* |

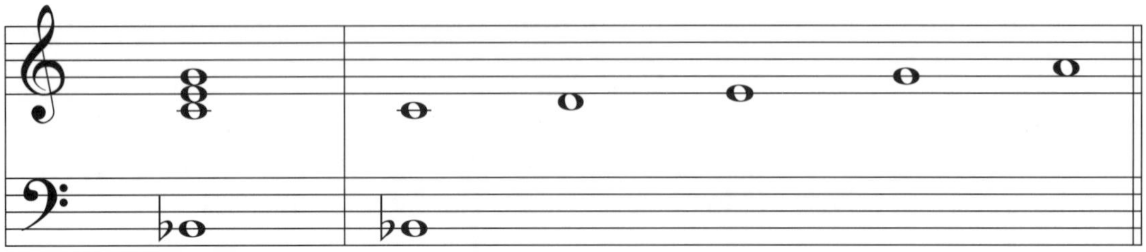

## *Application of pentatonic scales over different chords (contd)*

The information shown in the preceding **Fig. 9.9.** can be summarized as follows:-

- In the left-hand measure the 'triad-over-root' chord shown is **C/Bb**, which is a **9-#11-13** 'triad-over-root' voicing (first seen in **Fig. 7.2.**) on a **Bb major** chord. This creates an incomplete **Bbma13** chord quality overall.
- In the right-hand measure we can see that the use of the **C pentatonic** scale over this **Bb major** chord, creates the following **chord functions**:-
  - **9th**, **3rd**, **#11th** (sharped 11th), **6th/13th**, and **7th**.
  In comparing the above functions to the chord tones created in **Fig. 9.7.** (where we built a pentatonic scale from the **5th** of a major chord), we note the following differences:-
  - the **#11th** (sharped 11th) of the chord is now available
  - the **5th** of the chord is not available.
  - other chord functions i.e. **9th**, **3rd**, **6th/13th** & **7th** are available in both cases.
  Building a pentatonic scale from the **9th** of a major chord as in the preceding example, creates an 'altered' sound (due to the presence of the **#11th**) which is appropriate in more sophisticated settings.

## *Application of blues scales over different chords*

When building improvised lines or melodies over the chord changes in a tune, frequently one of two broad approaches will be used:-

- **Playing 'through' the changes.** This involves making decisions on a chord-by-chord basis as to the choice of notes available - for example by using pentatonic scales on different chords according to the rules outlined in **Figs. 9.5. - 9.9.**
- **Playing 'over' the changes.** This involves selecting a scale based on the overall key of the tune, and using it throughout. Blues scales are typically used for this purpose in both pop and jazz styles (which makes this technique a good starting point for the novice improviser).

When selecting a blues scale within which to create a melody or line in a tune (i.e. to play 'over' the changes), the two main ways to do this are as follows:-

- Play the blues scale built from the **tonic of the major key** (for example, using the **C blues** scale over a tune in the key of **C major**).
- Play the blues scale built from the **relative minor of the major key**, or from the **tonic of the minor key** (for example, using the **A blues** scale over a tune in the key of **C major** or **A minor**).

## *Application of blues scales over different chords (contd)*

We will now consider the application of these 'blues scale' techniques over a progression that is also an example of a 12-measure '**blues form**', typically encountered in pop/blues and simpler jazz/blues applications:-

### *Figure 9.10. 'C Blues' progression - basic 12-measure blues form*

We can make the following observations regarding the above 'blues form' example:-

- The chart is in the key of **C** (i.e. the key signature has no sharps and no flats). However, the '**home-base**' tonality is represented by a **C7** dominant chord, and not a **C major** chord as we might have expected. As mentioned in *Chapter 2* (see **p43** comments), blues applications typically build dominant chords from the **I**, **IV** and/or **V** of the overall (major) key, as is the case in the above example. In this style therefore (unlike the **II - V - I** styles covered in *Chapters 2 - 5*), we would **not** automatically analyze each dominant chord as being a **V** in a momentary key - here everything is heard with respect to the 'home-base' or tonic of **C**.
- The 'basic' 12-measure blues form is comprised of three 4-measure sections:-
  - Measures **1 - 4** are based around the **I7** chord (**C7** in this case), with the frequent variation of the **IV7** chord (**F7** in this case) being used on measure **2**.
  - Measures **5 - 8** normally begin with the **IV7** chord (**F7** in this case), working back to the **I7** chord (**C7** in this case) by measure **7**.
  - Measures **9 -12** normally begin with the **V7** chord (**G7** in this case), working back to the **I7** chord (**C7** in this case) by measure **11**, and frequently passing through the **IV7** chord (**F7** in this case) in measure **10**. The remainder of measures **11** and **12** is also commonly used as a 'turnaround', with many possibilities for chords leading back into measure **1** of the form.

### Application of blues scales over different chords (contd)

There are a great many variations on the preceding 'blues form' example, particularly when more jazz-influenced blues applications are considered. This basic progression example will however serve as a suitable vehicle to illustrate the use of blues scales '**over the changes**' as outlined in the comments on **p283**. We said then that the first way to do this was to build a blues scale from the tonic or 'home-base' of the overall (major) key, which in the case of the preceding 'blues form' example would be the note **C**. The **C blues** scale (built using the intervals and functions shown in **Fig. 9.4.**) is shown below:-

*Figure 9.11. C blues scale showing intervals and scale degree numbers*

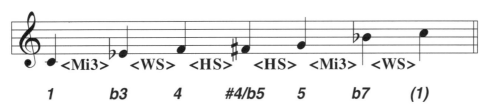

There are literally an infinite number of melodic and rhythmic phrases which could be constructed from this scale! We said on the previous page that the typical 'blues form' is often comprised of three 4-measure sections or phrases. Here is an example of a 4-measure melodic phrase using the notes within the **C blues** scale:-

*Figure 9.12. Four-measure melodic phrase using the C blues scale*

(Note this would typically be interpreted in a 'swing 8ths' or 'rolled 8ths' manner, in jazz/ blues or rock/shuffle contexts). In simpler blues applications, this 4-measure melodic phrase could simply be repeated across the entire 12-measure 'blues form' shown in **Fig 9.10.**, as follows:-

*Figure 9.13. 'C blues' 4-measure phrase used across entire 12-measure blues form*

(contd>>>)

## Application of blues scales over different chords (contd)

**(Figure 9.13. contd)**

You can see that some alterations and/or out-of-chord tones are created over these chords in some cases - however, these will typically be acceptable in a blues style due to the 'linear' and melodic strength of the blues scale being used. Again referring to our comments about playing '**over the changes**' on **p283**, we recall that the second way to do this was to use the blues scale built from the relative minor of the overall (major) key. If we were to do this on the preceding '**C Blues**' progression, we would then build a blues scale from the relative minor of **C** - this would therefore be the **A blues** scale (first shown in **Fig. 9.4.**). One possible 4-measure phrase built from an **A blues** scale is shown as follows:-

### Figure 9.14. Four-measure melodic phrase using the A blues scale

Again a simple solution would be to use this 4-measure phrase across the entire 12-measure 'blues form' shown in **Fig 9.10.**, as follows:-

### Figure 9.15. 'A blues' 4-measure phrase used across entire 12-measure blues form

## Application of blues scales over different chords (contd)

Again in the preceding example some alterations and/or out-of-chord tones are created, which however are frequently acceptable in this style as previously discussed. The blues scales built from the tonic of the major key, and from the relative minor (i.e. **C blues** and **A blues** in this case) can also be combined together and used 'over the changes' - this is a favorite blues/rock guitar technique for example.

Although the preceding examples have focused on blues scales being used '**over the changes**', it is also possible to approach the use of blues scales on a chord-by-chord basis, when considering their use in melodic and/or improvisational contexts. Again due to the great melodic 'strength' of the blues scale, it can be applied over numerous different chords (although care may be needed when out-of-chord tones and/or alterations are encountered). In the table below I have analyzed the implications of playing a **C blues** scale over various different chords:-

### Figure 9.16. C blues scale, and analysis of 'chord functions' over various chords

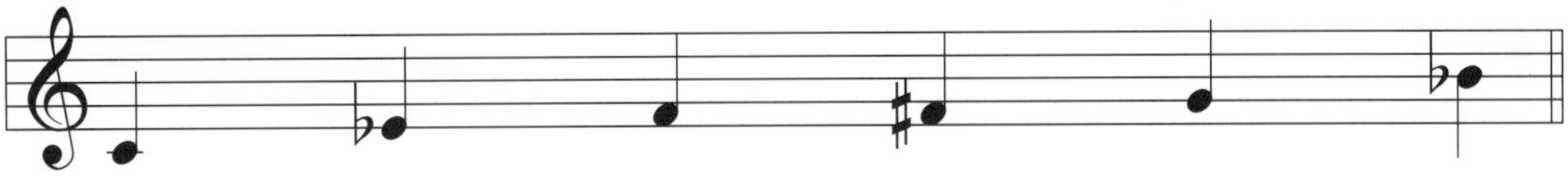

| | | | | | | |
|---|---|---|---|---|---|---|
| - **Cmi**, **Cmi7** etc. | 1 | b3 | 11 | **#11x** | 5 | b7 |
| - **C7** | 1 | (#9) | **11x** | (#11/b5) | 5 | b7 |
| - **Db**, **Dbma7** etc. | 7 | 9 | 3 | **11x** | (#11/b5) | 6/13 |
| - **D7** | b7 | (b9) | (#9) | 3 | **11x** | (b13/#5) |
| - **Eb**, **Ebma7** etc. | 6/13 | 1 | 9 | **b3x** | 3 | 5 |
| - **Eb7** | 13 | 1 | 9 | (#9) | 3 | 5 |
| - **Fmi**, **Fmi7** etc. | 5 | b7 | 1 | **b9x** | 9 | 11 |
| - **F7** | 5 | b7 | 1 | (b9) | 9 | **11x** |
| - **F7sus**, **F11** etc. | 5 | b7 | 1 | **b9x** | 9 | 11 |
| - **Gb**, **Gbma7** etc. | (#11) | 6/13 | 7 | 1 | **b9x** | 3 |
| - **Gb7** | (#11) | 13 | **7x** | 1 | (b9) | 3 |
| - **Gmi**, **Gmi7** etc. | 11 | **#5x** | b7 | **7x** | 1 | b3 |
| - **G7** | **11x** | (b13/#5) | b7 | **7x** | 1 | (#9) |
| - **G7sus**, **G11** etc. | 11 | **#5x** | b7 | **7x** | 1 | **#9x** |
| - **Ab**, **Abma7** etc. | 3 | 5 | 6/13 | **b7x** | 7 | 9 |
| - **Ab7** | 3 | 5 | 13 | b7 | **7x** | 9 |
| - **Adim**, **Adim7** | b3 | b5 | (b13/#5) | bb7 | **b7x** | **b9x** |
| - **Ami7(b5)** | b3 | b5 | (b13/#5) | **13x** | b7 | **b9x** |
| - **A7** | (#9) | (#11/b5) | (b13/#5) | 13 | b7 | (b9) |
| - **Bbmi**, **Bbmi7** etc. | 9 | 11 | 5 | **#5x** | (13) | 1 |
| - **Bb7** | 9 | **11x** | 5 | (b13/#5) | 13 | 1 |
| - **Bb7sus**, **Bb11** etc. | 9 | 11 | 5 | **#5x** | (13) | 1 |

## *Application of blues scales over different chords (contd)*

We can analyze the preceding table of blues scale usage over various chords as follows:-

- Each line indicates the **chord functions** created when the **C blues** scale is used over the chord(s) indicated in the left-hand column.
- Functions in **bold type**, underlined and followed by an '**x**' (for example the *#11x* on the first line) indicate an **out-of-chord tone** has been created. You are advised therefore to **not** place this note on a 'strong beat' (typically beats **1** and **3** in **4/4** time, or on a point of chord change) over the chord in question. These out-of-chord tones may however still be used as melodic embellishments or 'neighbor tones' of shorter duration, on the chord.
- Functions in **parentheses** indicate either an **upper 'tension'** tone on the chord, or an **available alteration** on the chord (typically either a **flatted 9th, sharped 9th, sharped 11th/flatted 5th**, or **flatted 13th/sharped 5th** on a **dominant** chord - see **p106** comments). A stylistic judgement call would be needed to determine the suitability of any 'tension' tones/alterations - although routinely used in jazz and jazz/blues styles, they would be less common in simpler contemporary applications.

## *Summary of pentatonic/blues scale options on major/minor/dominant chords*

In terms of looking at chord symbols and determining from which **chord functions** we can build pentatonic and blues scales for melodic and/or improvisation purposes, we can now summarize the conclusions reached in this chapter as follows:-

- On **major** chords we can:-
    - build a **pentatonic scale** from the **root**, **5th** and **9th** of the chord, as shown in **Figs. 9.5.**, **9.7.** and **9.9.** respectively.
    - build a **blues scale** from the **3rd**, **6th**, **7th** and **#11th** of the chord, as shown in **Fig. 9.16.** (and subject to the out-of-chord tones indicated and explained above).
- On **minor** & **minor 7th** chords we can:-
    - build a **pentatonic scale** from the **3rd** and **7th** of the chord, as shown in **Figs. 9.6.** and **9.8.** respectively.
    - build a **blues scale** from the **root**, **5th**, **9th** and **11th** of the chord, as shown in **Fig. 9.16.** (and subject to the out-of-chord tones indicated and explained above).
- On **dominant** chords we can:-
    - build a **blues scale** from the **root**, **3rd**, **5th**, **7th**, **9th**, **#9th**, **11th**, **#11th** and **13th** of the chord, as shown in **Fig. 9.16.** (and subject to the **altered** tones indicated and explained above).
- On **suspended dominant** chords we can:-
    - build a **pentatonic scale** from the **7th** of the chord, as shown in **Fig. 9.8.**
    - build a **blues scale** from the **5th**, **9th** and **11th** of the chord, as shown in **Fig. 9.16.** (and subject to the out-of-chord tones indicated and explained above).

## Chapter Nine Workbook Questions

### 1. Writing pentatonic scales

You are to write the following pentatonic scales on the staff provided. Be sure to include all necessary accidentals.

1. *C pentatonic*

2. *A pentatonic*

3. *Eb pentatonic*

4. *F pentatonic*

5. *D pentatonic*

6. *Ab pentatonic*

7. *Bb pentatonic*

8. *E pentatonic*

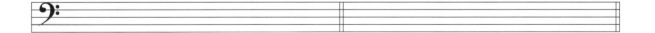

## 2. *Writing minor pentatonic scales*

You are to write the following minor pentatonic scales on the staff provided. Again be sure to include all necessary accidentals.

9. *A minor pentatonic*  10. *E minor pentatonic*

11. *G minor pentatonic*  12. *Bb minor pentatonic*

13. *F# minor pentatonic*  14. *G# minor pentatonic*

15. *F minor pentatonic*  16. *B minor pentatonic*

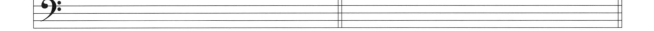

# Pentatonic and blues scales, and their applications

### 3. *Writing blues scales*

You are to write the following blues scales on the staff provided. Again be sure to include all necessary accidentals.

17. *C blues*                           18. *E blues*

19. *B blues*                           20. *D blues*

21. *F# blues*                          22. *Bb blues*

23. *G blues*                           24. *A blues*

### 4. *Identifying pentatonic, minor pentatonic and blues scales*

You are to identify the following pentatonic, minor pentatonic or blues scales. Don't forget that each scale name will have two parts - a starting note and a scale description (i.e. *pentatonic, minor pentatonic* or *blues* in this case).

25. _____ _____          26. _____ _____

27. _____ _____          28. _____ _____

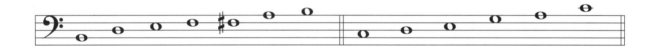

29. _____ _____          30. _____ _____

31. _____ _____          32. _____ _____

**4.** _Identifying pentatonic, minor pentatonic and blues scales (contd)_

33. ___ _____    34. ___ _____

35. ___ _____    36. ___ _____

37. ___ _____    38. ___ _____

39. ___ _____    40. ___ _____

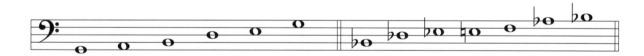

## 5. *Analysis of pentatonic scale usage over chords*

You are to determine which **pentatonic** scales can be used for embellishments/solos over the following chords (refer to **Figs. 9.5. - 9.9.** and the summary on **p288** in the Textbook as necessary):-

41. *Ami7* _____          42. *Fma7* _____
              _____                  _____
                                       _____

43. *D7sus* _____          44. *Emi7* _____
                                       _____

45. *Bmi7* _____          46. *Gma7* _____
              _____                  _____
                                       _____

47. *Eb7sus* _____          48. *Dma7* _____
                                       _____
                                       _____

You are to determine the chords over which the following **pentatonic** scales can be applied. For the purposes of this exercise, the available chord suffixes are **ma7**, **mi7** and **7sus** (again refer to **Figs. 9.5. - 9.9.** and the summary on **p288** as required).

49. *Ab pentatonic* _____ _____          50. *D pentatonic* _____ _____
                    _____ _____                             _____ _____
                    _____ _____                             _____ _____

51. *G pentatonic* _____ _____          52. *F pentatonic* _____ _____
                   _____ _____                             _____ _____
                   _____ _____                             _____ _____

53. *Eb pentatonic* _____ _____          54. *A pentatonic* _____ _____
                    _____ _____                             _____ _____
                    _____ _____                             _____ _____

55. *E pentatonic* _____ _____          56. *B pentatonic* _____ _____
                   _____ _____                             _____ _____
                   _____ _____                             _____ _____

**294**

## *Chapter Nine Workbook Answers*

**1.** *Writing pentatonic scales - answers*

1. *C pentatonic*           2. *A pentatonic*

3. *Eb pentatonic*        4. *F pentatonic*

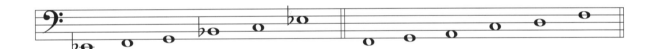

5. *D pentatonic*         6. *Ab pentatonic*

7. *Bb pentatonic*        8. *E pentatonic*

**2.** **_Writing minor pentatonic scales - answers_**

9.  *A minor pentatonic*

10.  *E minor pentatonic*

11.  *G minor pentatonic*

12.  *Bb minor pentatonic*

13.  *F# minor pentatonic*

14.  *G# minor pentatonic*

15.  *F minor pentatonic*

16.  *B minor pentatonic*

**3.** **_Writing blues scales - answers_**

17. *C blues*                    18. *E blues*

19. *B blues*                    20. *D blues*

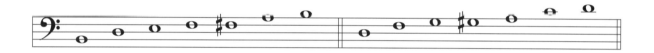

21. *F# blues*                   22. *Bb blues*

23. *G blues*                    24. *A blues*

**4.** *Identifying pentatonic, minor pentatonic and blues scales - answers*

| | | |
|---|---|---|
| 25. **G** *minor pentatonic* | 26. **Ab** *pentatonic* | 27. **B** *blues* |
| 28. **C** *pentatonic* | 29. **D** *minor pentatonic* | 30. **F** *blues* |
| 31. **Bb** *pentatonic* | 32. **D** *blues* | 33. **C** *minor pentatonic* |
| 34. **C** *blues* | 35. **F** *pentatonic* | 36. **A** *minor pentatonic* |
| 37. **E** *blues* | 38. **E** *minor pentatonic* | 39. **G** *pentatonic* |
| 40. **Bb** *blues* | | |

**5.** *Analysis of pentatonic scale usage over chords - answers*

(scales which work over the following chords:-)

| | | |
|---|---|---|
| 41. *Ami7* | **C** *pentatonic*<br>**G** *pentatonic* | 42. *Fma7*    **F** *pentatonic*<br>**C** *pentatonic*<br>**G** *pentatonic* |
| 43. *D7sus* | **C** *pentatonic* | 44. *Emi7*    **G** *pentatonic*<br>**D** *pentatonic* |
| 45. *Bmi7* | **D** *pentatonic*<br>**A** *pentatonic* | 46. *Gma7*    **G** *pentatonic*<br>**D** *pentatonic*<br>**A** *pentatonic* |
| 47. *Eb7sus* | **Db** *pentatonic* | 48. *Dma7*    **D** *pentatonic*<br>**A** *pentatonic*<br>**E** *pentatonic* |

(chords which work with the following scales:-)

| | | |
|---|---|---|
| 49. *Ab pentatonic* | **Abma7, Dbma7, Gbma7, Fmi7, Bbmi7, Bb7sus.** | 50. *D pentatonic*    **Dma7, Gma7, Cma7, Bmi7, Emi7, E7sus.** |
| 51. *G pentatonic* | **Gma7, Cma7, Fma7, Emi7, Ami7, A7sus.** | 52. *F pentatonic*    **Fma7, Bbma7, Ebma7, Dmi7, Gmi7, G7sus.** |
| 53. *Eb pentatonic* | **Ebma7, Abma7, Dbma7, Cmi7, Fmi7, F7sus.** | 54. *A pentatonic*    **Ama7, Dma7, Gma7, F#mi7, Bmi7, B7sus.** |
| 55. *E pentatonic* | **Ema7, Ama7, Dma7, C#mi7, F#mi7, F#7sus.** | 56. *B pentatonic*    **Bma7, Ema7, Ama7, G#mi7, C#mi7, C#7sus.** |

## *II-V-I definitive chords and substitutes in major keys*

**Key of
Eb Major**

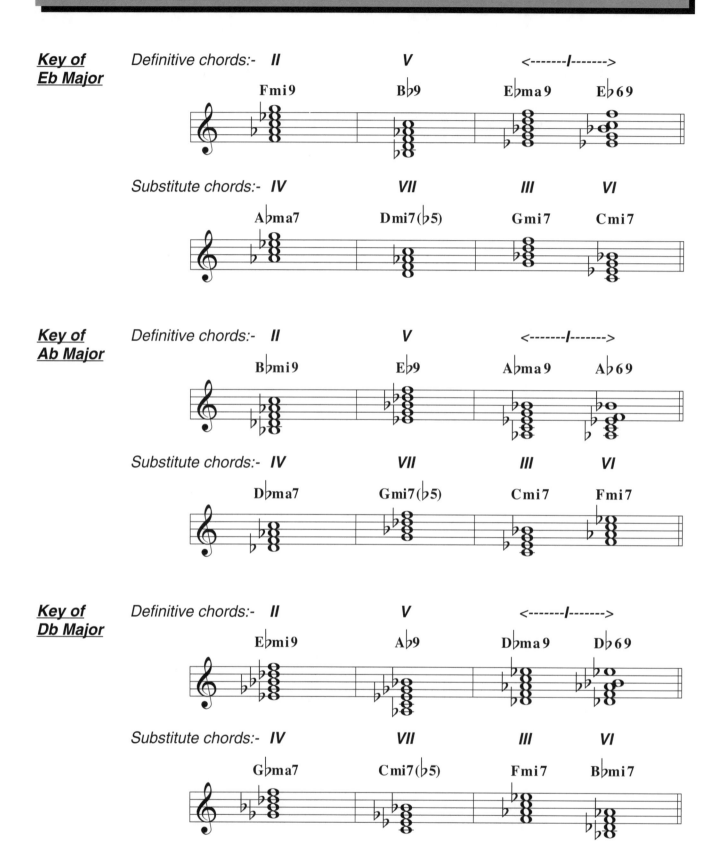

**Key of
Ab Major**

**Key of
Db Major**

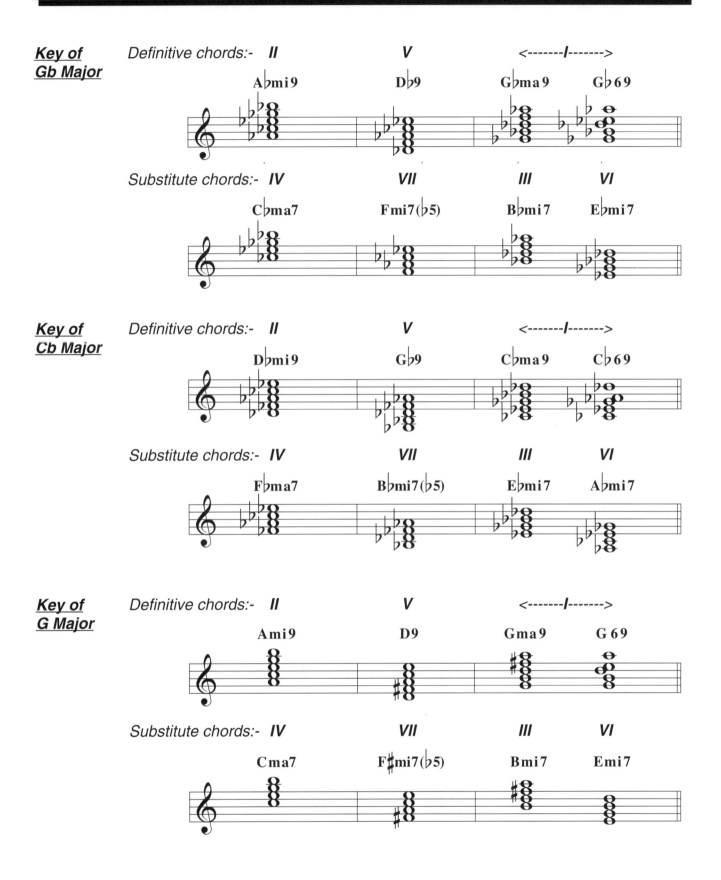

# II-V-I definitive chords and substitutes in major keys

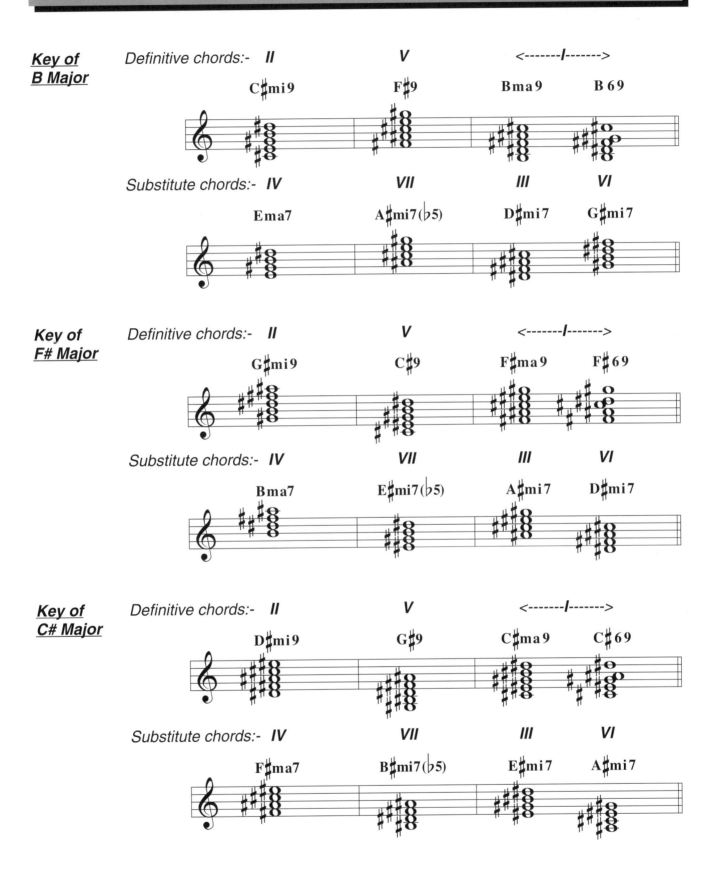

**303**

## *II-V-I definitive chords and substitutes in minor keys*

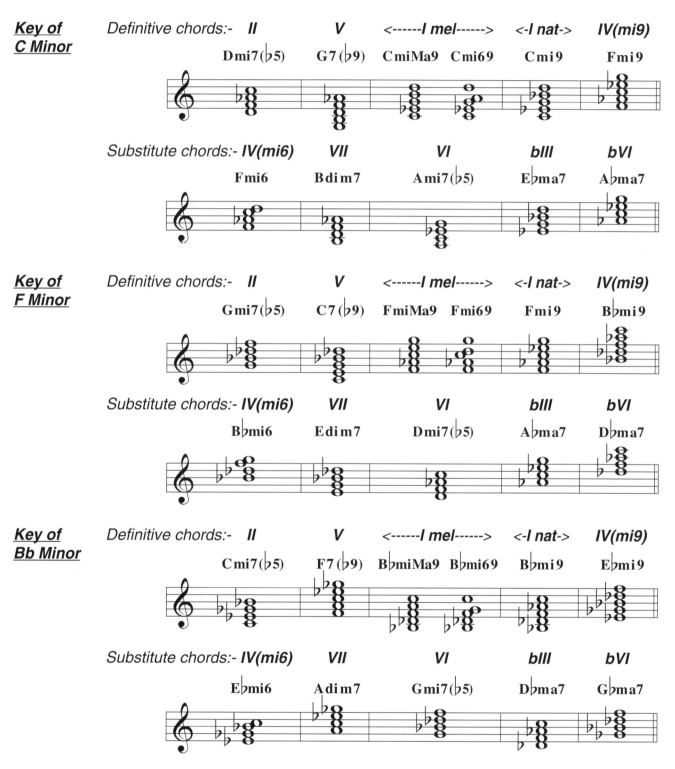

*('I mel' = I or tonic chords from **melodic minor**, and 'I nat' = I or tonic chord from **natural minor**).*

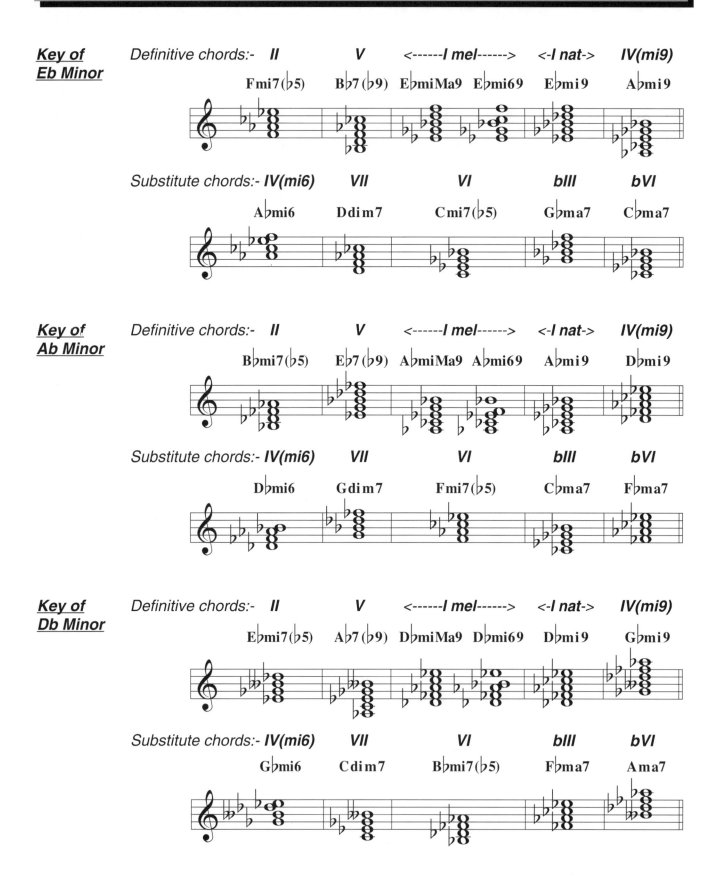

**Key of Eb Minor**

Definitive chords:- II     V     <------I mel------>     <-I nat->     IV(mi9)

Fmi7(b5)    Bb7(b9)    EbmiMa9   Ebmi69    Ebmi9    Abmi9

Substitute chords:- IV(mi6)     VII     VI     bIII     bVI

Abmi6    Ddim7    Cmi7(b5)    Gbma7    Cbma7

**Key of Ab Minor**

Definitive chords:- II     V     <------I mel------>     <-I nat->     IV(mi9)

Bbmi7(b5)   Eb7(b9)   AbmiMa9   Abmi69    Abmi9    Dbmi9

Substitute chords:- IV(mi6)     VII     VI     bIII     bVI

Dbmi6    Gdim7    Fmi7(b5)    Cbma7    Fbma7

**Key of Db Minor**

Definitive chords:- II     V     <------I mel------>     <-I nat->     IV(mi9)

Ebmi7(b5)   Ab7(b9)   DbmiMa9   Dbmi69    Dbmi9    Gbmi9

Substitute chords:- IV(mi6)     VII     VI     bIII     bVI

Gbmi6    Cdim7    Bbmi7(b5)    Fbma7    Ama7

*(While double accidentals are shown on the staff as required, some corresponding chord symbols have been enharmonically simplified).*

# II-V-I definitive chords and substitutes in minor keys

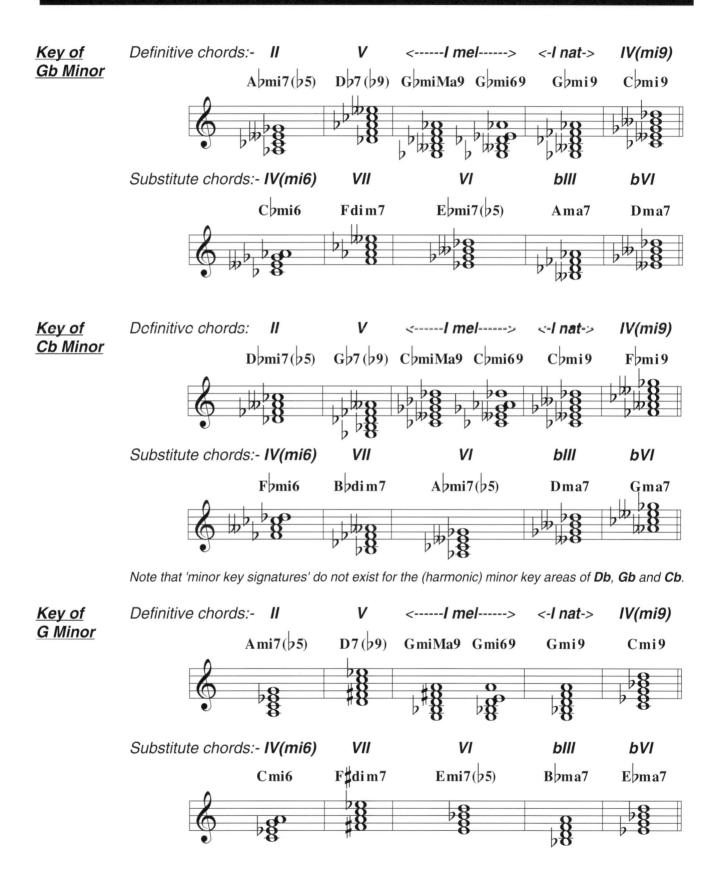

**Key of Gb Minor**

Definitive chords:- **II** — **V** — <------I mel------> — <-I nat-> — **IV(mi9)**

Abmi7(b5)  Db7(b9)  GbmiMa9  Gbmi69  Gbmi9  Cbmi9

Substitute chords:- **IV(mi6)** — **VII** — **VI** — **bIII** — **bVI**

Cbmi6  Fdim7  Ebmi7(b5)  Ama7  Dma7

**Key of Cb Minor**

Definitive chords: **II** — **V** — <------I mel------> — <-I nat-> — **IV(mi9)**

Dbmi7(b5)  Gb7(b9)  CbmiMa9  Cbmi69  Cbmi9  Fbmi9

Substitute chords:- **IV(mi6)** — **VII** — **VI** — **bIII** — **bVI**

Fbmi6  Bbdim7  Abmi7(b5)  Dma7  Gma7

*Note that 'minor key signatures' do not exist for the (harmonic) minor key areas of **Db**, **Gb** and **Cb**.*

**Key of G Minor**

Definitive chords:- **II** — **V** — <------I mel------> — <-I nat-> — **IV(mi9)**

Ami7(b5)  D7(b9)  GmiMa9  Gmi69  Gmi9  Cmi9

Substitute chords:- **IV(mi6)** — **VII** — **VI** — **bIII** — **bVI**

Cmi6  F#dim7  Emi7(b5)  Bbma7  Ebma7

*(While double accidentals are shown on the staff as required, some corresponding chord symbols have been enharmonically simplified).*

**307**

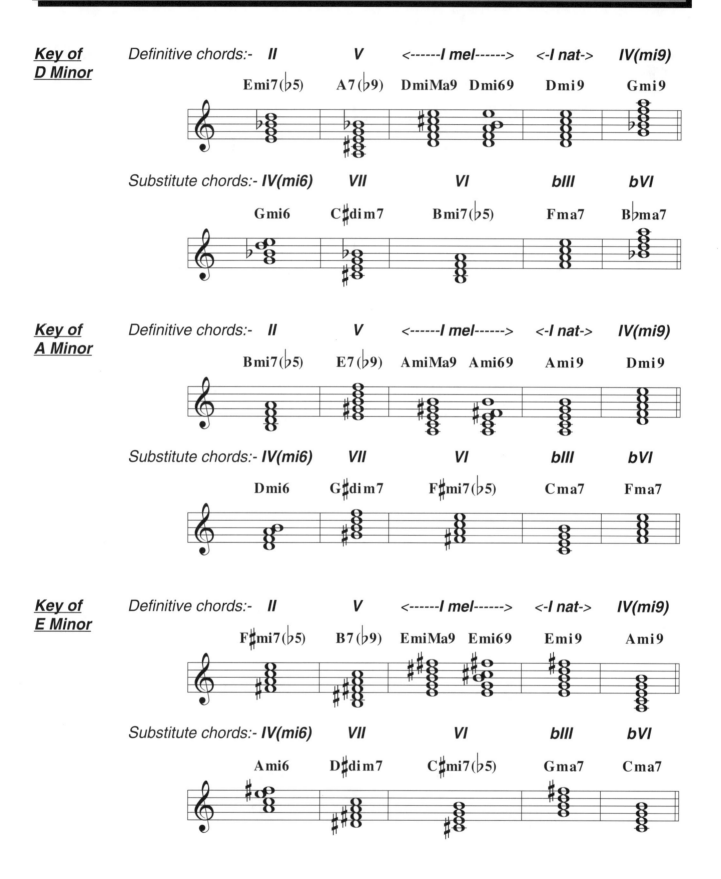

# II-V-I definitive chords and substitutes in minor keys

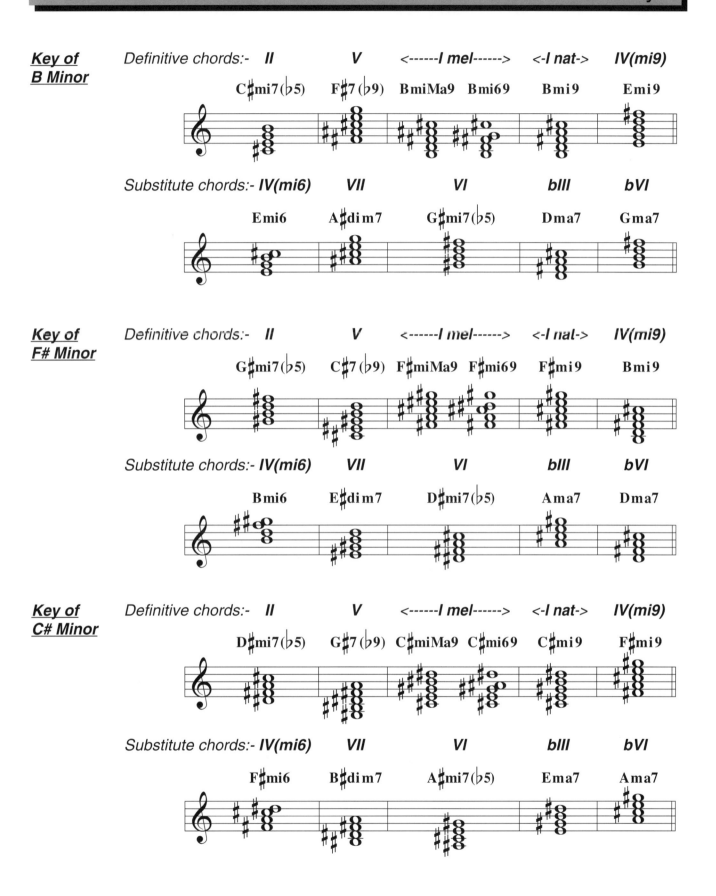

**Key of B Minor**

Definitive chords:- **II**      **V**      <------**I mel**------>    <-**I nat**->    **IV(mi9)**

C#mi7(b5)   F#7(b9)   BmiMa9   Bmi69   Bmi9   Emi9

Substitute chords:- **IV(mi6)**    **VII**    **VI**    **bIII**    **bVI**

Emi6   A#dim7   G#mi7(b5)   Dma7   Gma7

**Key of F# Minor**

Definitive chords:- **II**      **V**      <------**I mel**------>    <-**I nat**->    **IV(mi9)**

G#mi7(b5)   C#7(b9)   F#miMa9   F#mi69   F#mi9   Bmi9

Substitute chords:- **IV(mi6)**    **VII**    **VI**    **bIII**    **bVI**

Bmi6   E#dim7   D#mi7(b5)   Ama7   Dma7

**Key of C# Minor**

Definitive chords:- **II**      **V**      <------**I mel**------>    <-**I nat**->    **IV(mi9)**

D#mi7(b5)   G#7(b9)   C#miMa9   C#mi69   C#mi9   F#mi9

Substitute chords:- **IV(mi6)**    **VII**    **VI**    **bIII**    **bVI**

F#mi6   B#dim7   A#mi7(b5)   Ema7   Ama7

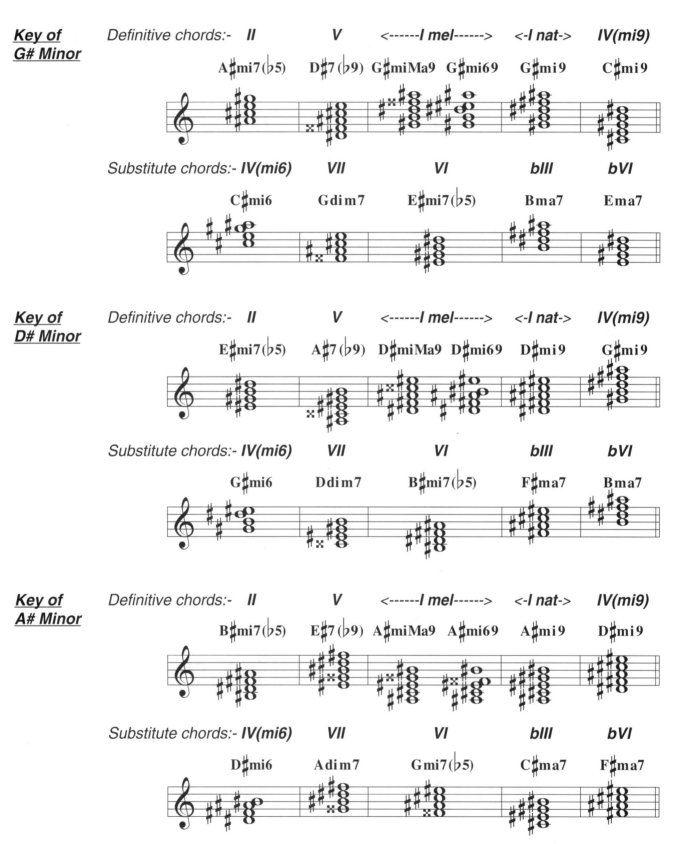

*(While double accidentals are shown on the staff as required, some corresponding chord symbols have been enharmonically simplified).*

# Voiceleading of triads & 4-part chords using the circle-of-5ths/4ths

*In all triad examples, the **inversions** (i.e. **Rt**, **1st** or **2nd**) are indicated below each chord, and the commontone (i.e. **\<b\>**, **\<m\>** or **\<t\>** signifying bottom, middle or top note) is indicated between each successive pair of chords.*

### Major triads voiced around the circle-of-fifths - starting with C major in root position

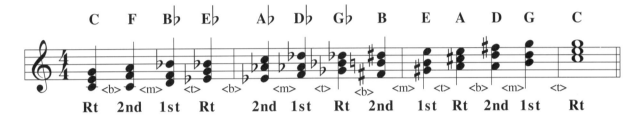

### Major triads voiced around the circle-of-fifths - starting with C major in 1st inversion

### Major triads voiced around the circle-of-fifths - starting with C major in 2nd inversion

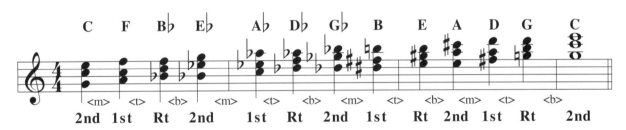

### Major triads voiced around the circle-of-fourths - starting with C major in root position

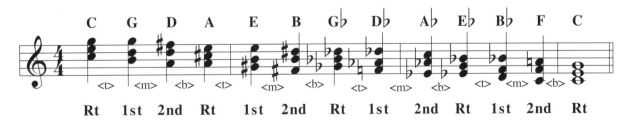

### *Major triads voiceled around the circle-of-fourths - starting with C major in 1st inversion*

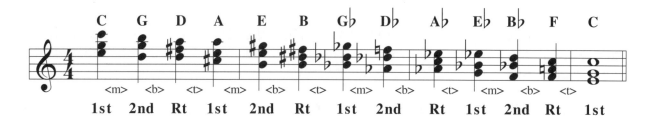

### *Major triads voiceled around the circle-of-fourths - starting with C major in 2nd inversion*

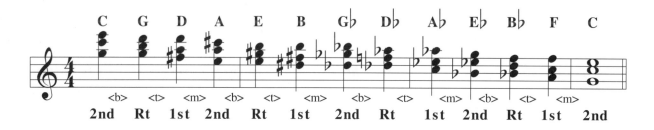

### *Minor triads voiceled around the circle-of-fifths - starting with C minor in root position*

### *Minor triads voiceled around the circle-of-fifths - starting with C minor in 1st inversion*

# Voiceleading of triads & 4-part chords using the circle-of-5ths/4ths

### *Minor triads voiceled around the circle-of-fifths - starting with C minor in 2nd inversion*

### *Minor triads voiceled around the circle-of-fourths - starting with C minor in root position*

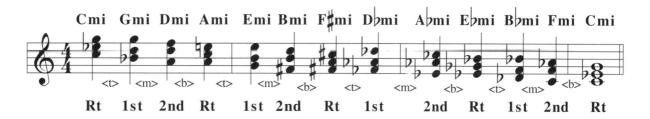

### *Minor triads voiceled around the circle-of-fourths - starting with C minor in 1st inversion*

### *Minor triads voiceled around the circle-of-fourths - starting with C minor in 2nd inversion*

313

### *Major 7ths voiceled around the circle-of-fifths - starting with C major 7th in root position*

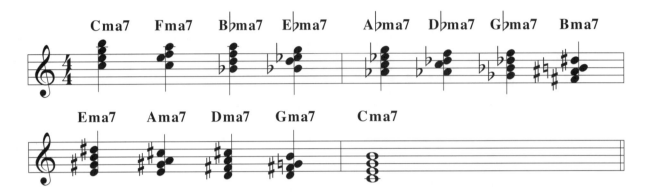

### *Major 7ths voiceled around the circle-of-fifths - starting with C major 7th in 2nd inversion*

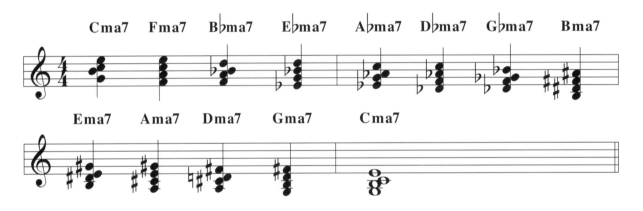

### *Major 7ths voiceled around the circle-of-fourths - starting with C major 7th in root position*

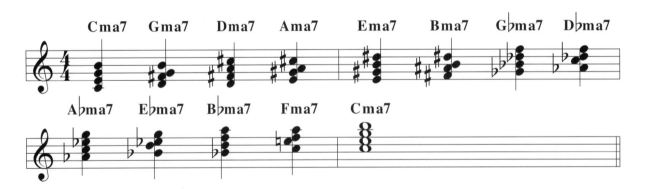

# Voiceleading of triads & 4-part chords using the circle-of-5ths/4ths

### *Major 7ths voiceled around the circle-of-fourths - starting with C major 7th in 2nd inversion*

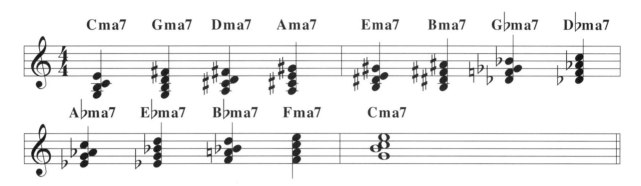

### *Minor 7ths voiceled around the circle-of-fifths - starting with C minor 7th in root position*

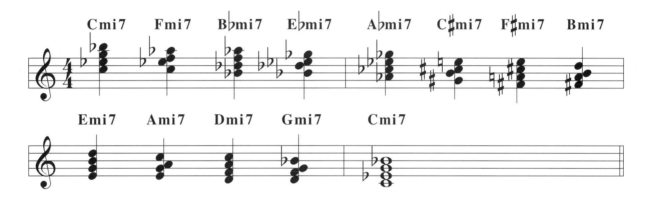

### *Minor 7ths voiceled around the circle-of-fifths - starting with C minor 7th in 2nd inversion*

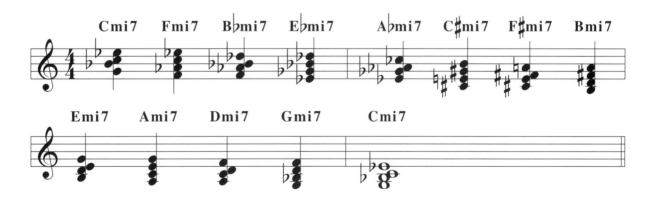

**_Minor 7ths voiceled around the circle-of-fourths - starting with C minor 7th in root position_**

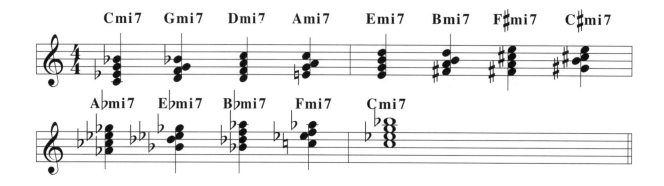

**_Minor 7ths voiceled around the circle-of-fourths - starting with C minor 7th in 2nd inversion_**

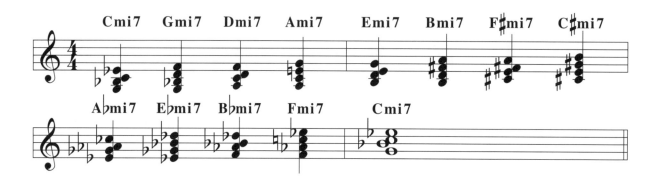

# 'Upper structure' chords in major and minor keys

## 'Triad-over-root' upper structure chords in major and minor keys

### Keys of C major & C minor *(using options within **C major** and **C natural minor** scales)*

*These 'triad-over-root' chord tables in all keys, are based upon **Fig. 7.20.** in the Textbook.*    **317**

## 'Triad-over-root' upper structure chords in major and minor keys (contd)

**Keys of F major & F minor** *(using options within **F major** and **F natural minor** scales)*

### 'Triad-over-root' upper structure chords in major and minor keys (contd)

#### Keys of Bb major & Bb minor *(using options within **Bb major** and **Bb natural minor** scales)*

## 'Triad-over-root' upper structure chords in major and minor keys (contd)

**Keys of Eb major & Eb minor** *(using options within* **Eb major** *and* **Eb natural minor** *scales)*

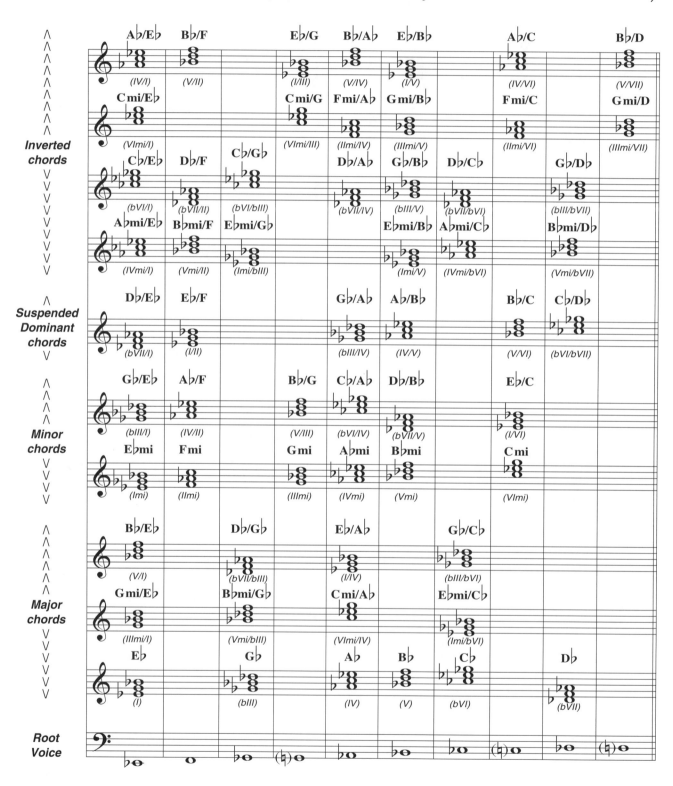

### 'Triad-over-root' upper structure chords in major and minor keys (contd)

**Keys of Ab major & Ab minor** (using options within **Ab major** and **Ab natural minor** scales)

## 'Triad-over-root' upper structure chords in major and minor keys (contd)

### Keys of Db major & Db minor (using options within Db major and Db natural minor scales)

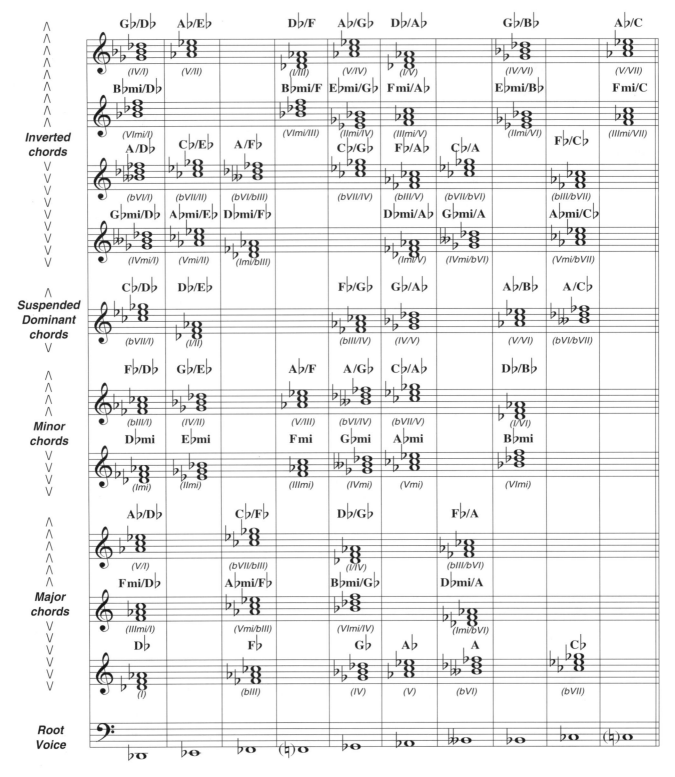

*(While double accidentals are shown on the staff as required, some corresponding chord symbols have been enharmonically simplified).*

## 'Triad-over-root' upper structure chords in major and minor keys (contd)

### Keys of Gb major & Gb minor (using options within Gb major and Gb natural minor scales)

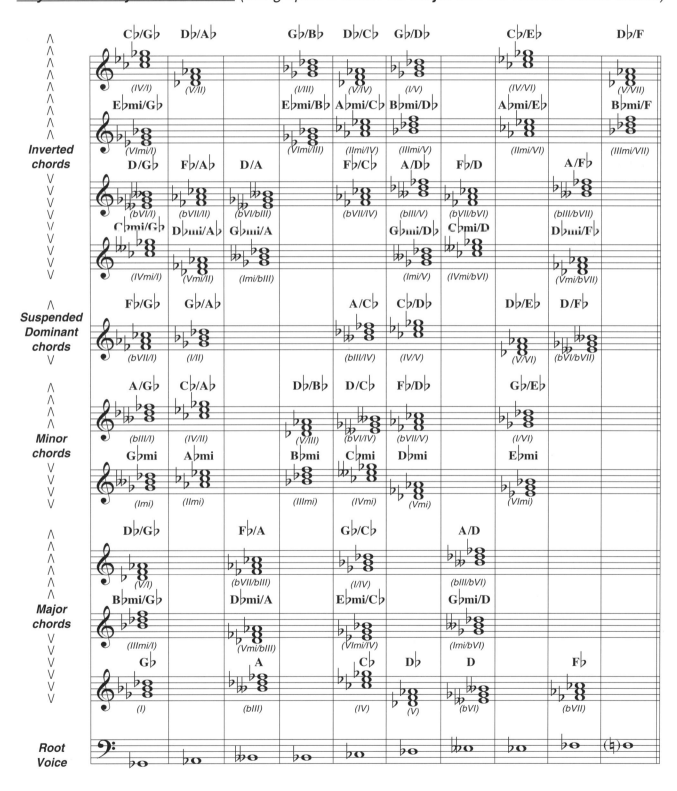

*(While double accidentals are shown on the staff as required, some corresponding chord symbols have been enharmonically simplified).*

## 'Triad-over-root' upper structure chords in major and minor keys (contd)

### Keys of Cb major & Cb minor (using options within Cb major and Cb natural minor scales)

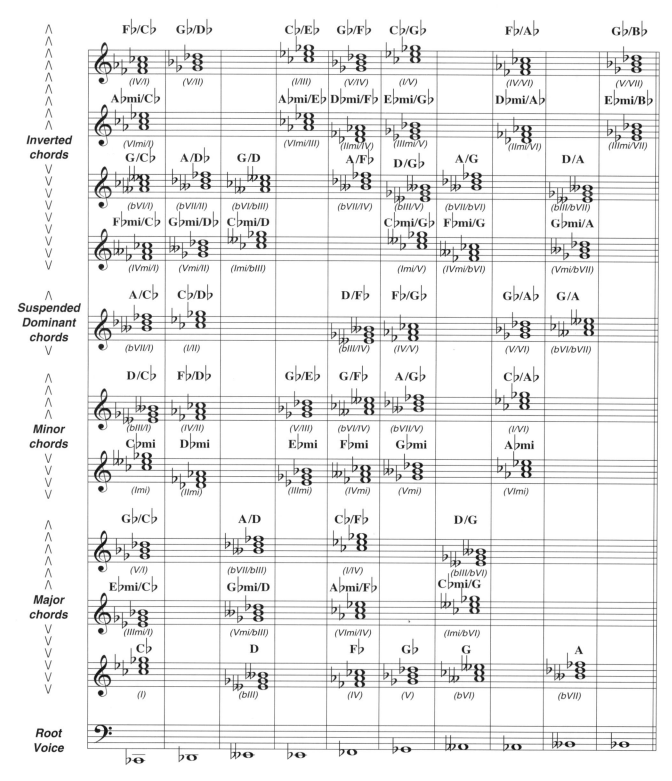

(While double accidentals are shown on the staff as required, some corresponding chord symbols have been enharmonically simplified).

### 'Triad-over-root' upper structure chords in major and minor keys (contd)

**Keys of G major & G minor** (using options within **G major** and **G natural minor** scales)

325

## 'Triad-over-root' upper structure chords in major and minor keys (contd)

### Keys of D major & D minor (using options within D major and D natural minor scales)

## *'Triad-over-root' upper structure chords in major and minor keys (contd)*

*<u>Keys of A major & A minor</u> (using options within **A major** and **A natural minor** scales)*

## 'Triad-over-root' upper structure chords in major and minor keys (contd)

### Keys of E major & E minor *(using options within **E major** and **E natural minor** scales)*

328

## 'Triad-over-root' upper structure chords in major and minor keys (contd)

### Keys of B major & B minor (using options within B major and B natural minor scales)

329

## 'Triad-over-root' upper structure chords in major and minor keys (contd)

### Keys of F# major & F# minor (using options within F# major and F# natural minor scales)

## 'Triad-over-root' upper structure chords in major and minor keys (contd)

### Keys of C# major & C# minor (using options within C# major and C# natural minor scales)

## 'Four-part-over-root' upper structure chords in major and minor keys

*Note that in comparison to **Fig. 8.11.** upon which these four-part-over-root chord 'tables' are based, the 'empty' columns over the 3rd and 7th degrees of the major scale (which for example are the root voices of **E** and **B** in the key of **C**) have been omitted for ease of illustration and to save space.*

**Keys of C major & C minor** *(using options within **C major** and **C natural minor** scales)*

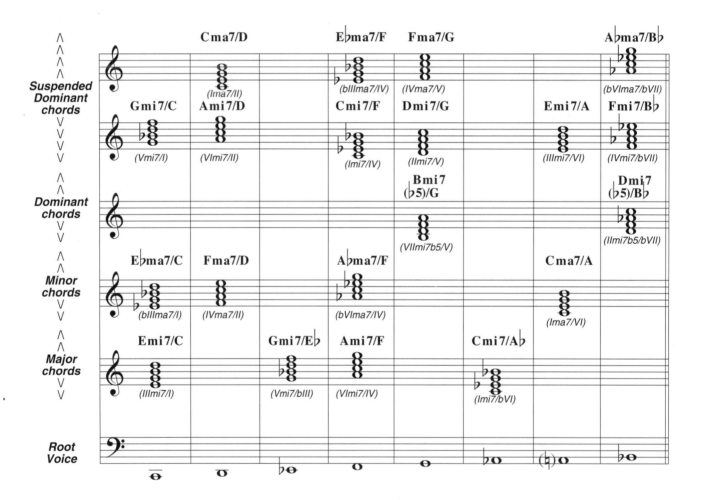

## 'Four-part-over-root' upper structure chords in major and minor keys (contd)

### Keys of F major & F minor (using options within F major and F natural minor scales)

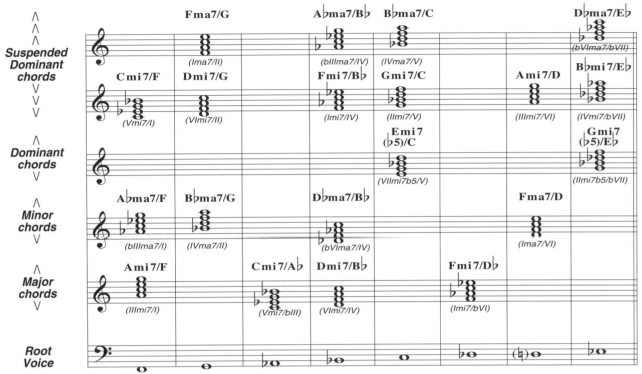

### Keys of Bb major & Bb minor (using options within Bb major and Bb natural minor scales)

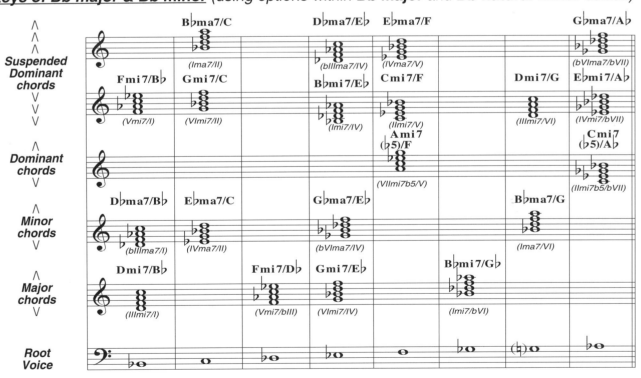

## 'Four-part-over-root' upper structure chords in major and minor keys (contd)

### Keys of Eb major & Eb minor *(using options within **Eb major** and **Eb natural minor** scales)*

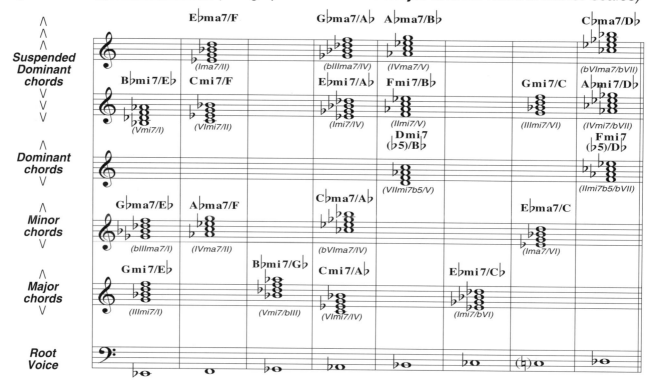

### Keys of Ab major & Ab minor *(using options within **Ab major** and **Ab natural minor** scales)*

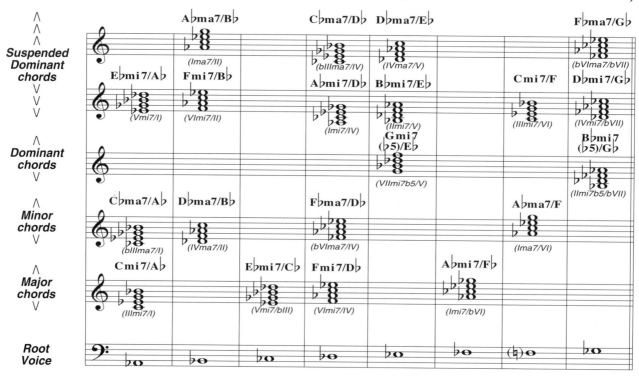

334

### 'Four-part-over-root' upper structure chords in major and minor keys (contd)

#### Keys of Db major & Db minor *(using options within **Db major** and **Db natural minor** scales)*

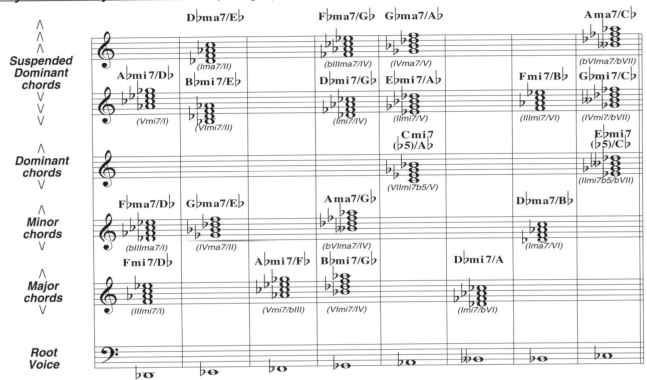

#### Keys of Gb major & Gb minor *(using options within **Gb major** and **Gb natural minor** scales)*

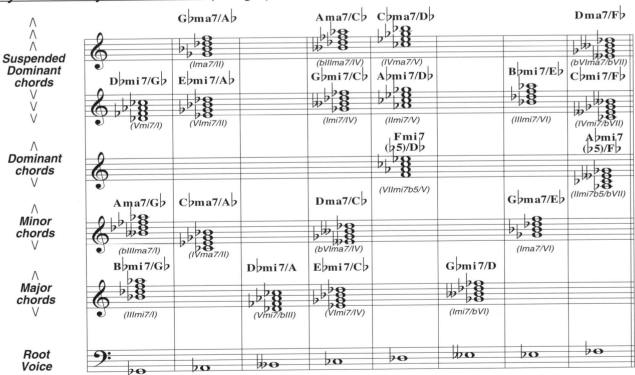

*(While double accidentals are shown on the staff as required, some corresponding chord symbols have been enharmonically simplified).*

**335**

## 'Four-part-over-root' upper structure chords in major and minor keys (contd)

### Keys of Cb major & Cb minor (using options within **Cb major** and **Cb natural minor** scales)

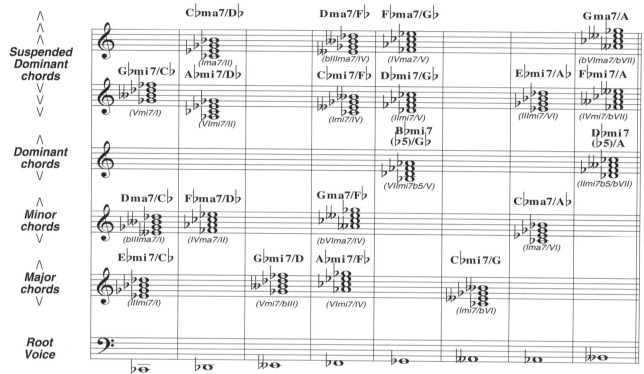

### Keys of G major & G minor (using options within **G major** and **G natural minor** scales)

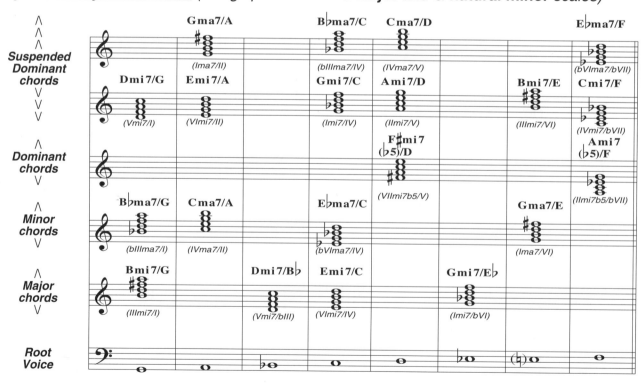

*(While double accidentals are shown on the staff as required, some corresponding chord symbols have been enharmonically simplified).*

## 'Four-part-over-root' upper structure chords in major and minor keys (contd)

### Keys of D major & D minor (using options within D major and D natural minor scales)

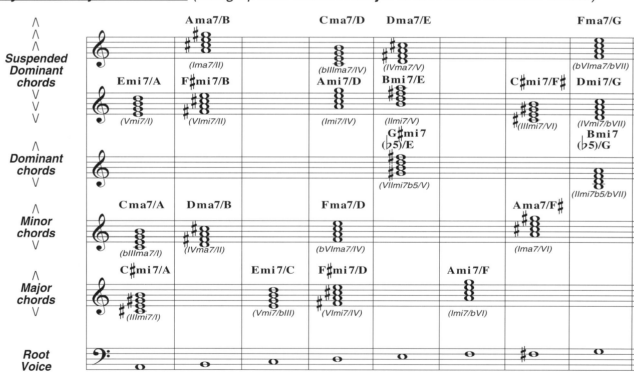

### Keys of A major & A minor (using options within A major and A natural minor scales)

## 'Four-part-over-root' upper structure chords in major and minor keys (contd)

### Keys of E major & E minor (using options within **E major** and **E natural minor** scales)

### Keys of B major & B minor (using options within **B major** and **B natural minor** scales)

### 'Four-part-over-root' upper structure chords in major and minor keys (contd)

**Keys of F# major & F# minor** (using options within **F# major** and **F# natural minor** scales)

**Keys of C# major & C# minor** (using options within **C# major** and **C# natural minor** scales)

# Pentatonic, minor pentatonic and blues scales

## Pentatonic scales

### C Pentatonic

### F Pentatonic

### Bb Pentatonic

### Eb Pentatonic

### Ab Pentatonic

### Db Pentatonic

### Gb Pentatonic

### Cb Pentatonic

## *Pentatonic scales (contd)*

### *G Pentatonic*

### *D Pentatonic*

### *A Pentatonic*

### *E Pentatonic*

### *B Pentatonic*

### *F# Pentatonic*

### *C# Pentatonic*

## Minor Pentatonic scales

### A Minor Pentatonic

### D Minor Pentatonic

### G Minor Pentatonic

### C Minor Pentatonic

### F Minor Pentatonic

### Bb Minor Pentatonic

### Eb Minor Pentatonic

### Ab Minor Pentatonic

### Minor Pentatonic scales (contd)

#### E Minor Pentatonic

#### B Minor Pentatonic

#### F# Minor Pentatonic

#### C# Minor Pentatonic

#### G# Minor Pentatonic

#### D# Minor Pentatonic

#### A# Minor Pentatonic

# Pentatonic, minor pentatonic and blues scales

### Blues scales

#### A Blues

#### D Blues

#### G Blues

#### C Blues

#### F Blues

#### Bb Blues

#### Eb Blues

#### Ab Blues

**345**

## *Blues scales (contd)*

### *E Blues*

### *B Blues*

### *F# Blues*

### *C# Blues*

### *G# Blues*

### *D# Blues*

### *A# Blues*

## *Glossary of terms used in this book*

*(The glossary in this **Contemporary Music Theory Level Two** book has been expanded to include terms which were first defined and used in our **Contemporary Music Theory Level One** book - see **page vi** for further info on our **Level One** book).*

| | |
|---|---|
| **Accidental** | Collective term for prefixes such as sharps, flats, and natural signs placed to the left of music noteheads. |
| **Active** | A scale degree has an 'active' quality if it has a tendency to resolve to an adjacent 'resting' or stable tone within the scale - see **p20** comments (and our **Contemporary Eartraining** courses). |
| **'Add nine' chord** | - See *'major add nine chord'*. |
| **'Add nine (omit 3)' chord** | - See *'major add nine (omit 3) chord'*. |
| **Aeolian (mode)** | The mode created when a major scale is displaced to start on its **6th** degree (see **p10** comments) - also equivalent to a natural minor scale. |
| **Alphabet** | - See *'music alphabet'*. |
| **Altered** | This is a general term applied to a chord, which signifies that the **5th** and/or the **9th** of the chord has been **flatted** or **sharped** by **half-step**:- |

- **altered 5ths** are available on major, minor and dominant chords - see **Figs. 1.36. - 1.38.**
- **altered 9ths** are only available on dominant chords (at least in conventional Western music styles!) - see **Fig. 4.15.** and accompanying text.

| | |
|---|---|
| **Altered chord** | See above comments regarding the term *'altered'*. |
| **Altered dominant chord** | A dominant chord in which the **5th** and/or **9th** has been altered - see above comments. |
| **Altered fifth *or* ninth** | See above comments regarding the term *'altered'*. |

| | |
|---|---|
| **Altered minor triad** | - See *'minor triad with sharped 5th'*. |
| **Altered minor 7th chord** | - See *'minor 7th with flatted 5th chord'* and *'minor 7th with sharped 5th chord'*. |
| **Altered major triad** | - See *'major triad with flatted 5th'*. |
| **Altered major 6th chord** | - See *'major 6th with flatted 5th chord'*. |
| **Altered major 7th chord** | - See *'major 7th with flatted 5th chord'* and *'major 7th with sharped 5th chord'*. |
| **Alternating triads** | The use of two 'upper structure' triads in an alternating manner over a constant bass note - see various **Chapter 7** examples. |
| **Augmented interval** | A **major** or **perfect interval** which has been **increased** by a **half-step** (see **p5** comments). |
| **Augmented triad** | A triad consisting of **major 3rd** and **augmented 5th** intervals (measured from the root of the chord - see **Fig. 1.8.**) - can also be derived by taking a major triad and raising the **5th** by a **half-step**. |
| **Bass clef** | The bass clef staff is typically used in contemporary music to notate pitches which are in the 'lower half' of the overall musical range i.e. from around the **Middle C** area downwards. |
| **Bass voice** | This term is typically used to describe the lowest pitch being played in a chord or voicing. (In contemporary styles, this is generally the root of the chord unless an inversion is being used). |
| **Beat** | A unit of rhythmic duration i.e. as in "a half note lasts for two beats". |
| **Blues form** | A 12-measure sequence based around dominant chords built from the **I**, **IV** and **V** of a key - see **Fig. 9.10.** and accompanying text. |
| **Blues scale** | A six-note scale consisting of **minor 3rd**, **perfect 4th**, **augmented 4th**, **perfect 5th** and **minor 7th** intervals respectively from the tonic. Can be derived by adding the **augmented 4th** interval (i.e. the half-step 'connector' between the **perfect 4th** and **perfect 5th** intervals) to a **minor pentatonic** scale - see **Fig. 9.4.** and accompanying text. |

| | |
|---|---|
| *Chart* | A written representation of a tune which typically contains the melody and chord symbols, which is then **interpreted** by the musicians according to their understanding of the style. (Specific instrument parts and rhythmic figures may also be indicated). See also *Fake Book*. |
| *Chord* | Term generally used to describe the harmony created when three or more pitches are used simultaneously, in a vertical 'stack'. Most contemporary styles are harmonically organized around 'chords'. |
| *Chord progression* | A series of chords used in sequence during a piece of music (as indicated on a chart for the particular tune). |
| *Chord quality* | The vertical sound created by the chord in question i.e. major, minor, suspended etc. |
| *Chord symbol* | The symbol used on the chart to indicate the chord required. |
| *Chromatic interval* | An interval in which the top note does not belong within the major scale built from the bottom note - see **p5** comments. |
| *Chromatic solfeg* | A collective term used to describe the 'solfeg syllables' for the tones which do **not** belong within the major scale or key in question - see **Figs. 4.2. - 4.3.** and accompanying text. |
| *Chromatic tones* | Tones which do **not** belong within the major scale or key in question. |
| *Circle-of-fifths* | A succession of major scales and keys based on a series of '**five-to-one**' relationships - see **Chapter 1 p2-3**. |
| *Circle-of-fourths* | A succession of major scales and keys based on a series of '**four-to-one**' relationships - see **Chapter 1 p2-3**. |
| *Common time* | Another way to describe **4/4** time. |
| *Commontone* | A term used to describe the same note being present in two (or more) consecutive chords or voicings. |
| *'Commontone top note'* | I have used this term to describe a **voiceleading** technique where a commontone is used as the top voice (i.e. the highest note) of consecutive chords - see *Chapter 6*. |

*349*

| | |
|---|---|
| *'Commontone voiceleading'* | I have used this term to describe a **voiceleading** technique around the circle-of-5ths/4ths, where the commontones retain their relative position between successive chords - see **Figs. 6.10. - 6.11.** and **6.13. - 6.14**. |
| *'Composite' chord symbol* | A chord symbol which consists of a root note followed by a qualifier or 'suffix', for example the symbol **Dmi7**. Often used in comparison or contrast to the term '**slash chord**' symbol. |
| *'Composite' (chord symbol) equivalent* | I have used this term to describe a **composite chord symbol** (see above definition) which is equivalent to, or a translation of, a '**slash chord**' symbol. |
| *Cut time* | Another way to describe **2/2** time. |
| *Definitive* | A term used to describe chord tones and/or scale degrees which explicitly convey the chord qualities and the key being used - for example, see **Fig. 2.8.** and accompanying text. |
| *DI (solfeg syllable)* | The (chromatic) solfeg syllable used to describe the 'raised' or sharped **DO** - see **Fig. 4.2**. |
| *Diatonic interval* | An interval in which the top note belongs within the major scale built from the bottom note - see **Fig. 1.5.** |
| *Diatonic solfeg* | A collective term used to describe the 'solfeg syllables' for the tones which belong within the major scale or key in question - see **Fig. 2.1.** and accompanying text. |
| *Diatonic triads* | Triads which belong to, or occur naturally within, the major scale or key in question. See **Fig. 1.11.** |
| *Diatonic four-part chords* | Four-part chords which belong to, or occur naturally within, the major scale or key in question. See **Fig. 1.17.** |
| *Diminished interval* | A diminished interval occurs when a **minor** or **perfect** interval is reduced by a **half-step** - see **p5** comments. |
| *Diminished triad* | A triad consisting of **minor 3rd** and **diminished 5th** intervals (see **Fig. 1.9.**) - can also be derived by taking a major triad and lowering the **3rd** and **5th** by a **half-step**. |

| | |
|---|---|
| ***Diminished 7th (seventh)*** | This term can be applied to a chord and an interval:- |

| | |
|---|---|
| ***Diminished 7th chord*** | A four-note chord consisting of **minor 3rd**, **diminished 5th**, and **diminished 7th** intervals (measured from the root of the chord - see **Fig. 5.7.**). |

***Diminished 7th interval***  - See *'seventh interval'*.

| | |
|---|---|
| ***Displaced scale*** | A scale beginning on a note other than the normal starting note or 'tonic'. For example, the modal scales reviewed on **p10-11** are all displaced major scales. |
| ***DO (solfeg syllable)*** | The (diatonic) solfeg syllable used to describe the **first** degree of a major key - see **Fig. 2.1.** |
| ***Dominant chord*** | A type of chord which is generally built from the **5th** degree of a major or minor key, and which has a tendency to resolve back to the **tonic** or 'I' chord of the key, due to the **active scale degrees** present (see discussion on **p21-24**). |
| ***Dominant 7th chord*** | A four-part chord consisting of **major 3rd**, **perfect 5th** and **minor 7th** intervals (measured from the root of the chord - see **Fig. 1.15.**). |
| ***Dominant 7th with flatted 5th chord*** | A dominant 7th chord in which the **5th** has been flatted - see **Fig. 1.38.** |
| ***Dominant 7th with sharped 5th chord*** | A dominant 7th chord in which the **5th** has been sharped - see **Fig. 1.38.** |
| ***Dominant 7th with flatted 9th chord*** | A dominant 7th chord to which the flatted **9th** has been added - see **Fig. 4.15.** and accompanying text. |
| ***Dominant 9th chord*** | A five-part chord consisting of **major 3rd**, **perfect 5th**, **minor 7th** and **major ninth** intervals (measured from the root of the chord - see **Fig. 2.13.**). |
| ***Dominant 9th suspended chord*** | - See *'suspended dominant 9th chord'*. |
| ***Dominant 11th chord*** | Equivalent to the *'suspended dominant 9th'* chord - see **p31** comments. |

*351*

**Dominant 13th chord**      The stack for this chord is shown in **Fig. 8.5.**, in which we saw that the **3rd** and the **11th** were mutually exclusive on this chord. Assuming that a regular (i.e. unsuspended) dominant is needed, this chord is typically obtained by adding the **major 13th** interval to the **dominant 9th** chord. An **11th** would not be present unless the chord was **suspended** (implying the **3rd** of the chord would not be used) or **altered** i.e. if the **11th** was 'raised' or sharped (an option mentioned on **p106**).

**Dorian (mode)**      The mode created when a major scale is displaced to start on its **2nd** degree (see **Figs. 1.18. - 1.19.**).

**Dotted eighth note**      A note with duration lasting for three-quarters of a beat.

**Dotted eighth note rest**      A rest with duration lasting for three-quarters of a beat.

**Dotted half note**      A note with duration lasting for three beats.

**Dotted half note rest**      A rest with duration lasting for three beats.

**Dotted quarter note**      A note with duration lasting for one-and-a-half beats.

**Dotted quarter note rest**      A rest with duration lasting for one-and-a-half beats.

**Eighth (8th) interval**      Another term for **octave** (see **Fig. 1.5.**).

**Eighth note**      A note with duration lasting for one-half of a beat.

**Eighth note rest**      A rest with duration lasting for one-half of a beat.

**Eleventh (11th) chord**      A general term which can be used to describe a chord containing tones up to and including the **11th** (potentially a **six-part** chord).

**Eleventh (11th) interval**      An interval derived by increasing a **fourth interval** by one **octave**. All possible versions of the **fourth** interval *(see glossary entry for fourth interval)* are also possible for the **eleventh** interval.

**Enharmonic**      A term used to describe alternative note (or solfeg) names for the same pitch. For example, **C#** and **Db** are considered enharmonic equivalent note names, and if **DO** were assigned to **C** then the corresponding solfeg syllables for these notes would be **DI** and **RA** (see **Figs. 4.2. - 4.3.**) - these are (solfeg) enharmonic equivalents.

*352*

**FA (solfeg syllable)**    The (diatonic) solfeg syllable used to describe the **fourth** degree of a major key - see **Fig. 2.1**.

**Fake book**    A book which contains **charts** of tunes (rather than written-out arrangements). The musician is left to create their own arrangement based on the melody and chord symbols provided, and on their understanding of the harmony and style.

**FI (solfeg syllable)**    The (chromatic) solfeg syllable used to describe the 'raised' or sharped **FA** - see **Fig. 4.2**.

**Fifth (5th) interval**    - A **perfect 5th** interval occurs between the tonic (**1st** degree) and the **5th** degree of a major scale i.e. **G** is the **5th** degree of **C major**, therefore **C** up to **G** is a **perfect 5th** interval (see **Fig. 1.5.**).
- A **diminished 5th** interval occurs when a **perfect 5th** interval is reduced by a half-step i.e. **C** up to **G** is a **perfect 5th** interval, therefore **C** up to **Gb** is a **diminished 5th** interval.
- An **augmented 5th** interval occurs when a **perfect 5th** interval is increased by a half-step i.e. **C** up to **G** is a **perfect 5th** interval, therefore **C** up to **G#** is an **augmented 5th** interval.

**First inversion**    A three- or four-part chord is in first inversion when the root has been moved up an octave and has become the highest note - see **Figs. 1.10.** and **1.16.**

**Five-part chord**    A five-note chord consisting of **3rd**, **5th** and **7th** (or **6th**) and **9th** intervals, measured from the root of the chord - also referred to as a '**ninth**' chord.

**Five-to-one**    A relationship created between successive stages around the **circle-of-5ths**, implying a movement from the **5th** degree to the **1st** degree of a major scale - see **Fig. 1.2**.

**Flashcards**    A set of flashcards contains one card for each note, with the note shown (on the treble or bass clef) on the front, and the note name (and keyboard location) on the back. A highly recommended tool for learning the notes on the staff!

**Flat**    A flat sign prefixed to a note requires that note to be lowered in pitch by one half-step. May also form part of a key signature.

**'Flat' keys**

A name sometimes given to those major keys which contain flats in the key signature - see **Fig. 1.3**.

**Four-four (4/4) time**

A time signature with four 'pulses' per measure, with the quarter note 'getting the beat' i.e. the pulse is felt on the quarter note.

**Four-part chord**

A four-note chord consisting of **3rd**, **5th** and **7th** (or **6th**) intervals, measured from the root of the chord - see **Figs. 1.12. - 1.17.**

**'Four-part-over-root' chord**

I have used this term to describe the chord created when a four-part chord 'shape' (for example a **major 7th** or **minor 7th**) is placed over another root in the bass voice - see **Chapter 8**.

**Four-part 'upper structure'**

Equivalent to 'four-part-over-root' chord described above.

**Fourteenth (14th) interval**

An interval derived by increasing a **seventh interval** by one **octave**. All possible versions of the **seventh** interval *(see glossary entry for seventh interval)* are also possible for the **fourteenth** interval.

**Fourth (4th) interval**

- A **perfect 4th** interval occurs between the tonic (**1st** degree) and the **4th** degree of a major scale i.e. **F** is the **4th** degree of **C major**, therefore **C** up to **F** is a **perfect 4th** interval (see **Fig. 1.5.**).
- An **augmented 4th** interval occurs when a **perfect 4th** interval is increased by a half-step i.e. **C** up to **F** is a **perfect 4th** interval, therefore **C** up to **F#** is an **augmented 4th** interval.

**Four-to-one**

A relationship created between successive stages around the **circle-of-4ths**, implying a movement from the **4th** degree to the **1st** degree of a major scale - see **Fig. 1.2**.

**'Fully defined'**

A term applied to a voicing which contains the 'definitive' **3rd** and **7th** of the chord, and which therefore conveys the **vertical quality** of the chord (for example, see **p210** comments on the **Emi/C** chord).

**Function**

This term is used as a way to connect a chord (in a progression) to a major or minor key area in which it is operating. For example, if in a progression we have analyzed that the "**G7** is functioning as a **V** in **C major**", this means that for the duration of this chord, we are in the (momentary) key of **C major**, and that the G7 chord is built from the **5th** degree of this key. See various examples in **Chapters 2 - 5**.

| | |
|---|---|
| *Grand staff* | A combination of **treble** and **bass** clef staffs, typically used to notate piano music. |
| *'Half-diminished' or 'Half-diminished 7th'* | These terms are sometimes used as alternative names for the **minor 7th with flatted 5th** chord (reviewed in **Fig. 1.37.**). |
| *Half note* | A note with duration lasting for two beats. |
| *Half note rest* | A rest with duration lasting for two beats. |
| *Half-step* | The smallest unit of interval measurement in conventional Western tonal music. There are twelve half-steps in one octave. |
| *Harmonic analysis* | The process of determining the function (and the key, in situations where momentary key changes are occurring) for each chord in a given progression. See examples in *Chapters 2 - 5* and *7 - 8*. |
| *Harmonic minor scale* | One of the three minor scales in common usage. A harmonic minor scale can be derived in the following ways:- |
| | - using the required tetrachords as in **Fig. 1.21.** |
| | - taking a major scale and flatting the **3rd** and **6th** degrees as in **Fig. 1.24.** |
| | - using the minor key signature and sharping the **7th** degree as in **Fig. 1.27.** |
| *Interval* | The distance in pitch between two notes. (See review on **p5**, and the individual glossary entries for the different types of intervals). |
| *Interval skip* | I have used this term to describe the results of 'poor voiceleading' between successive chords or voicings i.e. if the top note of a chord does not move by commontone or closest note to the top note of the next chord, an undesirable 'interval skip' may occur. For example, see **Fig. 6.1.** and accompanying text. |
| *Inversion, inverted chord* | This term is used in two ways:- |
| | - when applied to a specific 3- or 4-part chord 'shape' on the staff, it means the normal sequence of chord tones (from bottom to top) has been modified, as in **Figs. 1.10.** and **1.16.** |
| | - when used in a harmonic or 'chord quality' context, it means that some other chord tone apart from the root (i.e. the 3rd or 5th) is being used in the bass voice, as in **Figs. 7.8. - 7.9.** |

*355*

| | |
|---|---|
| *Ionian (mode)* | The mode name given to a major scale which is NOT displaced, i.e. still starting on the normal tonic (see review on **p10**). |
| *Key* | Term used to indicate tonality or the 'home base' for a piece of music. For example, in the keys of **C major** and **C minor**, the note **C** will be heard as the tonic or 'home base'. |
| *Key signature* | A group of sharps or flats placed at the beginning of a tune to indicate the key. (See **Figs. 1.3. - 1.4.** for major key signatures). Each key signature can also be used for a 'relative' minor key, built from the **6th** degree of the major key - see **p11**. |
| *LA (solfeg syllable)* | The (diatonic) solfeg syllable used to describe the **sixth** degree of a major key - see **Fig. 2.1.** |
| *LE (solfeg syllable)* | The (chromatic) solfeg syllable used to describe the flatted **LA** - see **Fig. 4.3.** |
| *'Leading' interval* | A strong interval which sounds natural and predictable. **Perfect fourth** and **fifth** intervals (as in the **circle-of-5ths** root movement in **Fig. 2.9.**) and **half-steps** (as in the upper '**7 - 3**' line movement in **Fig. 2.9.**) can be considered '**leading**' intervals. |
| *Leger line* | A short horizontal line used either above or below the staff, used to notate a pitch which would otherwise be beyond the normal range of the particular staff. |
| *Lettername* | A letter within the music alphabet (**A - G**) used for a note name. |
| *LI (solfeg syllable)* | The (chromatic) solfeg syllable used to describe the 'raised' or sharped **LA** - see **Fig. 4.2.** |
| *'Linking' chord* | I have used this term to describe a chord which 'belongs' to both the preceding and following momentary keys within a progression. See various examples in *Chapters 3 - 5*. |
| *Locrian mode* | The mode created when a major scale is displaced to start on its **7th** degree (see **p10**). |
| *Lower tetrachord* | The lower or left-hand portion of a scale created using tetrachords. The lower tetrachord contains the **1st** (tonic), **2nd**, **3rd** and **4th** scale degrees - see **Fig. 1.1.** (for a major scale) and **Figs. 1.20. - 1.22.** (for the minor scales). |

**Lydian mode**    The mode created when a major scale is displaced to start on its **4th** degree (see **p10**).

**Major interval**    The term **major** is applied to all **2nd**, **3rd**, **6th** and **7th** intervals (and octave displacements) which are diatonic i.e. in which the top note is within the major scale built from the bottom note - see **Fig. 1.5**.

**Major key**    - See *'key'*.

**Major key signature**    - See *'key signature'*.

**Major scale**    A set of interval relationships (*whole-step, whole-step, half-step, whole-step, whole-step, whole-step & half-step*) constituting the basic tonality or 'reference point' for most Western music (reviewed in **Fig. 1.1.**).

**Major tetrachord**    A 'scalewise grouping' of four notes containing the intervals *whole-step, whole-step* and *half-step* - used to construct the major scale as in **Fig. 1.1**.

**Major triad**    A triad consisting of **major 3rd** and **perfect 5th** intervals (measured from the root of the chord - see **Fig. 1.6.**) - can also be derived by taking the 1st, 3rd & 5th degrees of a major scale.

**Major triad with flatted 5th**    A major triad in which the **5th** has been flatted - see **Fig. 1.33**.

**Major 2nd (second) interval**    - See *'second interval'*.

**Major 3rd (third) interval**    - See *'third interval'*.

**Major 6th (sixth)**    This term can be applied to a chord and an interval:-

    **Major 6th chord**    A four-note chord consisting of **major 3rd**, **perfect 5th**, and **major 6th** intervals (measured from the root of the chord - see **Fig. 1.13.**).

    **Major 6th interval**    - See *'sixth interval'*.

**Major 6th with flatted 5th chord**   A major 6th chord in which the **5th** has been flatted - see **Fig. 1.35.**

**Major 7th (seventh)**   This term can be applied to a chord and an interval:-

**Major 7th chord**   A four-note chord consisting of **major 3rd**, **perfect 5th**, and **major 7th** intervals (measured from the root of the chord - see **Fig. 1.12.**).

**Major 7th interval**   - See *'seventh interval'*.

**Major 7th with flatted 5th chord**   A major 7th chord in which the **5th** has been flatted - see **Fig. 1.36.**

**Major 7th with sharped 5th chord**   A major 7th chord in which the **5th** has been sharped - see **Fig. 1.36.**

**Major 9th (ninth)**   This term can be applied to a chord and an interval:-

**Major 9th chord**   A five-note chord consisting of **major 3rd**, **perfect 5th**, **major 7th** and **major 9th** intervals (measured from the root of the chord - see **Fig. 2.17.**).

**Major 9th interval**   - See *'ninth interval'*.

**Major 'add 9' chord**   This chord is created when the note which is a **major ninth** interval from the root, is added to a **major triad**. Equivalent to a major ninth chord with the seventh omitted - see **Fig. 2.22.**

**Major 'add 9 omit 3' chord**   This chord is created when the 3rd is omitted from the **major 'add 9'** chord described above - see **Fig. 2.24.** and accompanying text.

**Major 69 (six nine) chord**   A five-note chord consisting of **major 3rd**, **perfect 5th**, **major 6th** and **major 9th** intervals (measured from the root of the chord - see **Fig. 2.19.**).

**Major 13th (#11) chord**   The stack for this chord is shown in **Fig. 7.1.**, as a source for various 'triad-over-root' voicings. In its 'complete' form however, this is a seven-note chord consisting of **major 3rd**, **perfect 5th**, **major 7th**, **major 9th**, **augmented 11th** and **major 13th** intervals from the root.

**Major 13th interval**   - See *'thirteenth interval'*.

**ME (solfeg syllable)**
The (chromatic) solfeg syllable used to describe the flatted **MI** - see **Fig. 4.3**.

**Melodic minor scale**
One of the three minor scales in common usage. A melodic minor scale can be derived in the following ways:-
- using the required tetrachords as in **Fig. 1.20.**
- taking a major scale and flatting the **3rd** degree as in **Fig. 1.23.**
- using the minor key signature and sharping the **6th** and **7th** degrees as in **Fig. 1.28.**

**'Melodic minor-based'**
I have used this term to describe **tonic** or **I** chords in a minor key, which are derived from a melodic minor scale - see **p108-112**.

**MI (solfeg syllable)**
The (diatonic) solfeg syllable used to describe the **third** degree of a major key - see **Fig. 2.1**.

**Middle C**
The note **C** which is in the middle of the piano keyboard, generally considered to be a central 'reference point' in Western music.

**Minor interval**
A **major interval** which has been **reduced** by a **half-step** (see **p5**).

**Minor key**
- See *'key'*.

**Minor key signature**
- See *'key signature'*.

**Minor pentatonic scale**
A scale created when the **pentatonic scale** is re-arranged to start on the **relative minor** (i.e. starting a **C pentatonic** scale on the note **A** as in **Fig. 9.3.**). Intervals created are **minor 3rd**, **perfect 4th**, **perfect 5th**, and **minor 7th** with respect to the tonic. This scale is also sometimes referred to as the "blues pentatonic" scale.

**Minor scale**
There are three minor scales in common usage - melodic, harmonic and natural. See **Figs. 1.20. - 1.28.** and individual glossary entries.

**Minor tetrachord**
A 'scalewise grouping' of four notes containing the intervals *whole-step*, *half-step* and *whole-step* - used to construct the minor scales as in **Figs. 1.20. - 1.22.**

**Minor triad**
A triad consisting of **minor 3rd** and **perfect 5th** intervals (measured from the root of the chord - see **Fig. 1.7.**) - can also be derived by taking the 2nd, 4th & 6th degrees of a major scale.

**Minor triad with sharped 5th**
A minor triad in which the **5th** has been sharped - see **Fig. 1.34.**

**359**

**Minor 2nd (second) interval**
- See *'second interval'*.

**Minor 3rd (third) interval**
- See *'third interval'*.

**Minor 6th (sixth)**
This term can be applied to a chord and an interval:-

**Minor 6th chord**
A four-note chord consisting of **minor 3rd**, **perfect 5th**, and **major 6th** intervals (measured from the root of the chord - see **Fig. 1.30.**).

**Minor 6th interval** - See *'sixth interval'*.

**Minor major 7th (seventh) chord**
A four-note chord consisting of **minor 3rd**, **perfect 5th** and **major 7th** intervals (measured from the root of the chord - see **Fig. 1.29.**).

**Minor 7th (seventh)**
This term can be applied to a chord and an interval:-

**Minor 7th chord**
A four-note chord consisting of **minor 3rd**, **perfect 5th**, and **minor 7th** intervals (measured from the root of the chord - see **Fig. 1.14.**).

**Minor 7th interval** - See *'seventh interval'*.

**Minor 7th with flatted 5th chord**
A minor 7th chord in which the **5th** has been flatted - see **Fig. 1.37.**

**Minor 7th with sharped 5th chord**
A minor 7th chord in which the **5th** has been sharped - see **Fig. 1.37.**

**Minor 9th (ninth)**
This term can be applied to a chord and an interval:-

**Minor 9th chord**
A five-note chord consisting of **minor 3rd**, **perfect 5th**, **minor 7th** and **major 9th** intervals (measured from the root of the chord - see **Fig. 2.11.**).

**Minor 9th interval** - See *'ninth interval'*.

**Minor 9th with flatted 5th chord**
A minor 9th chord in which the **5th** has been flatted - see comments on **p105**.

| | |
|---|---|
| *Minor 'add 9' chord* | This chord is created when the note which is a **major ninth** interval from the root, is added to a **minor triad**. Equivalent to a minor ninth chord with the seventh omitted - see **Fig. 2.23**. |
| *Minor 69 (six nine) chord* | A five-note chord consisting of **minor 3rd**, **perfect 5th**, **major 6th** and **major 9th** intervals (measured from the root of the chord - see **Fig. 4.19.**). |
| *Minor major ninth chord* | A five-note chord consisting of **minor 3rd**, **perfect 5th**, **major 7th** and **major 9th** intervals (measured from the root of the chord - see **Fig. 4.20.**). |
| *Minor 11th chord* | The stack for this chord is shown in **Figs. 7.3.** and **8.3.**, as a source for various 'upper structure' voicings. In its 'complete' form however, this is a six-note chord consisting of **minor 3rd**, **perfect 5th**, **minor 7th**, **major 9th**, and **perfect 11th** intervals from the root. |
| *'Mixed' II - V - I progression* | I have used this term to describe a **II - V - I** (two-five-one) progression in which the chords are being derived from both major and minor keys - see **Figs. 4.23. - 4.24.** and accompanying text. |
| *Mixolydian (mode)* | The mode created when a major scale is displaced to start on its **5th** degree (see **p10**). |
| *Mode, modal scale* | Terms used to describe a 'displaced' scale i.e. a scale starting from a note other than the normal tonic or first note of the scale. This concept is most frequently applied to major scales - see **p10**. |
| *Momentary key* | I have used this term to describe the various 'temporary' keys used throughout a tune (i.e. as evidenced by the chord symbols), which may differ from the 'overall' key of the tune (as indicated by the key signature). See discussion on **p43**, and examples in *Chapters 2 - 5*. |
| *Music alphabet* | The letters **A**, **B**, **C**, **D**, **E**, **F** and **G** which are used for note names. |
| *Music notation* | A convention of written symbols indicating musical pitch and rhythm. |
| *Natural* | A natural sign attached to a note cancels out a previously applied sharp or flat (from an earlier accidental, or from a key signature). |

*361*

**Natural minor scale**
One of the three minor scales in common usage. A natural minor scale can be derived in the following ways:-
- using the required tetrachords as in **Fig. 1.22.**
- taking a major scale and flatting the **3rd, 6th** and **7th** degrees as in **Fig. 1.25.**
- using the minor key signature **without** additional alterations as in **Fig. 1.26.**

**'Natural minor-based'**
I have used this term to describe **tonic** or **I** chords in a minor key, which are derived from a natural minor scale - see **Fig. 4.18**.

**Nine-eight (9/8) time**
A time signature with nine 'pulses' per measure, each of which consists of an eighth note.

**Ninth (9th) chord**
A general term which can be used to describe a chord containing tones up to and including the **9th** (potentially a **five-part** chord).

**Ninth (9th) interval**
An interval derived by increasing a **second interval** by one **octave**. All possible versions of the **second** interval *(see glossary entry for second interval)* are also possible for the **ninth** interval.

**Notation**
- See *'music notation'*.

**Octave**
The interval created between notes with the same name. For example, the interval between middle **C** and the next **C** in either direction is one octave - see **Fig. 1.5**.

**'Open' voicing**
I have used this term to describe a chord voicing in which the tones are separated by larger intervals, giving clarity and projection to the chord - for example the '**7 - 3**' (seven-three) voicing used in **Fig. 2.3**.

**Pentatonic scale**
A scale created when the **4th** and **7th** degrees are removed from the **major scale**, as in **Fig. 9.2**. Intervals created are **major 2nd, major 3rd, perfect 5th**, and **major 6th** with respect to the tonic.

**Perfect interval**
The term **perfect** is applied to all **4th** and **5th** intervals (and octave displacements thereof) which are diatonic i.e. in which the top note is within the major scale built from the bottom note - see **Fig. 1.5**.

**Phrygian (mode)**
The mode created when a major scale is displaced to start on its **3rd** degree (see **p10**).

| | |
|---|---|
| ***Playing 'over' the changes*** | Selecting a scale based on the key of the overall tune, and using it as a source of improvisational/solo ideas throughout - see **p283**. |
| ***Playing 'through' the changes*** | Making decisions on a chord-by-chord basis in a tune, when choosing notes for improvisational/solo purposes - see **p283**. |
| ***Plural, plurality*** | These terms can be used in the following contexts:- |

- A chord which occurs diatonically in different keys is said to be **plural** to those keys. For example, a **Dmi7** chord occurs within (and is plural to) the major keys of **C**, **Bb** and **F**.
- A chord which has a number of notes in common with another chord, is said to have **plurality** with that chord. For example, the **Dmi9** and **Fma7** chords in **Fig. 3.2.** have substantial plurality with one another.

| | |
|---|---|
| ***Plural substitute chord*** | A plural substitute chord is one which can be used in place of a **II**, **V** or **I** chord in a major or minor key. See ***Chapters 3*** and ***5***. |
| ***Progression*** | - See *'chord progression'*. |
| ***Quarter note*** | A note with duration lasting for one beat. |
| ***Quarter note rest*** | A rest with duration lasting for one beat. |
| ***RA (solfeg syllable)*** | The (chromatic) solfeg syllable used to describe the flatted **RE** - see **Fig. 4.3**. |
| ***RE (solfeg syllable)*** | The (diatonic) solfeg syllable used to describe the **second** degree of a major key - see **Fig. 2.1**. |
| ***Relative major*** | This term can be used in the following contexts:- |

- in a **modal** context, the relative major is the major scale which has been displaced to create the mode - see **p10-11**.
- in a **key signature** context, the relative major is the major key which shares the same key signature as the minor key in question - see review on **p11.**

| | |
|---|---|
| ***Relative minor*** | The minor key which shares the same key signature as the major key in question - see review on **p11.** |

**Resolution**

This term is used to describe the movement from an **active** to an adjacent **resting** tone within a key. See **p19-21**.

**Resting**

A scale degree has a 'resting' quality if it conveys a stable or resolved impression i.e. if it does **not** have a tendency to resolve to another degree of the scale - see **p20** comments (and our *Contemporary Eartraining* courses).

**Rhythm**

The organization of music in respect to time. (See individual glossary entries for the common rhythmic 'durations' used in music notation).

**Rhythmic value**

The number of beats (units of 'rhythmic duration') that a note or rest may last for. (See individual glossary entries for the common rhythmic 'durations' used in music notation).

**RI (solfeg syllable)**

The (chromatic) solfeg syllable used to describe the 'raised' or sharped **RE** - see **Fig. 4.2**.

**'Roman numeral' analysis**

I have used this term to describe the chord progression analysis technique used in *Chapters 7* and *8*, where the relationship of each chord to the overall key of the tune is expressed as a 'roman numeral'.

**Root**

A term normally used in the context of a chord - the root of a chord is the fundamental tone of the chord, as contained in the chord symbol i.e. the root of a **Bmi** triad is the note **B**.

**Root movement**

A term used to describe the intervals created between the roots of consecutive chords in a progression (as in the discussion on **p26** concerning the **II - V - I** progression).

**Root position**

A chord in which the notes appear in their normal vertical sequence i.e. root, 3rd, 5th etc. (as opposed to an inversion, in which case this sequence is modified). A **root position** chord will therefore have the **root** on the bottom of the chord. See **Figs. 1.10.** and **1.16.**

**'Root voice'**

- See *'bass voice'*.

**'Saturated' quality**

This term is used to describe the 'fuller' or 'denser' sound created by larger chord forms - for example, see the introduction to five-part chords on **p27**.

**Scale**

A sequence of notes governed by a specific interval relationship. (For example, the major scale is created via the intervals in **Fig. 1.1.**).

*364*

| | |
|---|---|
| **Scale degree** | A note which is part of (i.e. a 'scale degree' of) a particular scale. |
| **Scale source** | A scale from which a particular chord can be derived. |
| **Scalewise** | A movement occurring either up or down a scale by adjacent scale steps. |
| **SE (solfeg syllable)** | The (chromatic) solfeg syllable used to describe the flatted **SO** - see **Fig. 4.3**. |
| **Second (2nd) interval** | - A **major 2nd** interval occurs between the tonic (**1st** degree) and the **2nd** degree of a major scale i.e. **D** is the **2nd** degree of **C major**, therefore **C** up to **D** is a **major 2nd** interval (see **Fig. 1.5.**). <br> - A **minor 2nd** interval occurs when a **major 2nd** interval is reduced by a half-step i.e. **C** up to **D** is a **major 2nd** interval, therefore **C** up to **Db** is a **minor 2nd** interval. <br> - An **augmented 2nd** interval occurs when a **major 2nd** interval is increased by a half-step i.e. **C** up to **D** is a **major 2nd** interval, therefore **C** up to **D#** is an **augmented 2nd** interval. |
| **Second inversion** | A triad or four-part chord is in second inversion when the root and third have been moved up an octave, the third becoming the highest note - see **Figs. 1.10.** and **1.16**. |
| **Seventh (7th) chord** | A general term which can be used to describe a chord containing tones up to and including the **7th** (potentially a **four-part** chord). |
| **Seventh (7th) interval** | - A **major 7th** interval occurs between the tonic (**1st** degree) and the **7th** degree of a major scale i.e. **B** is the **7th** degree of **C major**, therefore **C** up to **B** is a **major 7th** interval (see **Fig. 1.5.**). <br> - A **minor 7th** interval occurs when a **major 7th** interval is reduced by a half-step i.e. **C** up to **B** is a **major 7th** interval, therefore **C** up to **Bb** is a **minor 7th** interval. <br> - A **diminished 7th** interval occurs when a **minor 7th** interval is reduced by a half-step i.e. **C** up to **Bb** is a **minor 7th** interval, therefore **C** up to **Bbb** (**B double-flat**, equivalent to the note **A**) is a **diminished 7th** interval. This interval has the same span as a **major 6th** interval. |
| **Seven-three (7-3) voicing** | This term is used to describe a voicing for a four-part (or larger) chord, which uses the definitive **7th** and **3rd** of the chord - see **Figs. 2.8. - 2.9**. |

*365*

| | |
|---|---|
| **Shape** | I have used this term to describe three- and four-note chord structures which can be placed over different roots to create 'upper structure' voicings - see **Chapters 7** and **8**. |
| **Sharp** | A sharp sign prefixed to a note requires that note to be raised in pitch by one half-step. May also form part of a key signature. |
| **'Sharp' keys** | A name sometimes given to those major keys which contain sharps in the key signature - see **Fig. 1.4**. |
| **SI (solfeg syllable)** | The (chromatic) solfeg syllable used to describe the 'raised' or sharped **SO** - see **Fig. 4.2**. |
| **Six-eight (6/8) time** | A time signature with six 'pulses' per measure, each of which consists of an eighth note. |
| **Sixteenth note** | A note with duration lasting for one-quarter of a beat. |
| **Sixteenth note rest** | A rest with duration lasting for one-quarter of a beat. |
| **Sixth (6th) interval** | - A **major 6th** interval occurs between the tonic (**1st** degree) and the **6th** degree of a major scale i.e. **A** is the **6th** degree of **C major**, therefore **C** up to **A** is a **major 6th** interval (see **Fig. 1.5.**). <br> - A **minor 6th** interval occurs when a **major 6th** interval is reduced by a half-step i.e. **C** up to **A** is a **major 6th** interval, therefore **C** up to **Ab** is a **minor 6th** interval. <br> - An **augmented 6th** interval occurs when a **major 6th** interval is increased by a half-step i.e. **C** up to **A** is a **major 6th** interval, therefore **C** up to **A#** is an **augmented 6th** interval. |
| **'Slash' chords** | The chord symbols for 'slash' chords contain a slash (/), implying that the chord **to the left** of the slash is to be placed over the bass voice **to the right** of the slash. See **p207** comments, and various examples throughout **Chapters 7** and **8**. |
| **SO (solfeg syllable)** | The (diatonic) solfeg syllable used to describe the **fifth** degree of a major key - see **Fig. 2.1**. |
| **Solfeg** | Short for 'solfeggio'. The solfeg system is a means of labelling all pitches with respect to the tonic of a key (to which the syllable '**DO**' is assigned). See **Figs. 2.1.**, **4.2.**, and **4.3.** (and our **Contemporary Eartraining** courses). |

| | |
|---|---|
| *Stack* | I have used this as a collective term to describe the pitches available within a particular chord. For example, the chord 'stack' in **Fig. 7.1.** shows all of the tones (and available extensions) within a **C major** chord. |
| *Staff* | A set of horizontal lines used in music notation. The lines (and spaces in between) are used to denote pitches, depending upon the **clef** (for example, bass clef or treble clef) being used. |
| *Standard* | A term used to describe a type of (vocal-based) jazz tune which has enduring popularity. 'Standards' are characterized by their strong melodies (and lyrics), and sophisticated jazz harmonizations. |
| *'Static' voiceleading* | I have used this term to describe a voiceleading technique in which the 'top note' of each successive chord voicing is moved as little as possible i.e. using commontones and small intervals. See *Chapter 6*. |
| *Substitutes* | - See *'plural substitutes'*. |
| *Suffix* | The part of the chord symbol following the root note name. For example, the chord symbol **Cma7** has a suffix of **'ma7'**. |
| *Sus, suspended* | A suspended chord is one in which the **3rd** is replaced by the **4th** (i.e. the note which is a **perfect 4th** interval above the root of the chord). See **p15**. |
| *Suspended triad* | See above comments, and **Fig. 1.31.** |
| *Suspended dominant 7th chord* | See above comments, and **Figs. 1.32. & 2.4.** |
| *Suspended dominant 9th chord* | See above comments, and **Figs. 2.15. - 2.16.** |
| *Suspended dominant 13th chord* | See above comments, and **Figs. 8.5. - 8.6.** |
| *TE (solfeg syllable)* | The (chromatic) solfeg syllable used to describe the flatted **TI** - see **Fig. 4.3**. |
| *'Tension tone'* | This term is used to describe an upper extension of a chord, which creates 'tension' against the basic tones of the chord - see **p288**. |

*367*

**Tenth (10th) interval**

An interval derived by increasing a **third interval** by one **octave**. All possible versions of the **third** interval *(see glossary entry for third interval)* are also possible for the **tenth** interval.

**Tetrachord**

A group of four notes arranged in a 'scalewise' sequence - used as a building block for major and minor scales.

**Third (3rd) interval**

- A **major 3rd** interval occurs between the tonic (**1st** degree) and the **3rd** degree of a major scale i.e. **E** is the **3rd** degree of **C major**, therefore **C** up to **E** is a **major 3rd** interval (see **Fig. 1.5.**).
- A **minor 3rd** interval occurs when a **major 3rd** interval is reduced by a half-step i.e. **C** up to **E** is a **major 3rd** interval, therefore **C** up to **Eb** is a **minor 3rd** interval.

**Third inversion**

A four-part chord is in third inversion when the root, third and fifth have all been moved up an octave (or when the 6th or 7th has been moved down an octave) - see **Fig. 1.16.**

**Thirteenth (13th) chord**

A general term which can be used to describe a chord containing tones up to and including the **13th** (potentially a **seven-part** chord).

**Thirteenth (13th) interval**

An interval derived by increasing a **sixth interval** by one **octave**. All possible versions of the **sixth** interval *(see glossary entry for sixth interval)* are also possible for the **thirteenth** interval.

**Three-four (3/4) time**

A time signature with three 'pulses' per measure, each of which consists of a quarter note.

**TI (solfeg syllable)**

The (diatonic) solfeg syllable used to describe the **seventh** degree of a major key - see **Fig. 2.1.**

**Time signature**

A pair of numbers (placed one above the other, at the beginning of the music staff) which indicates how many 'pulses' occur in each measure, and on which rhythmic unit (i.e. quarter note, eighth note etc.) this 'pulse' falls. See individual glossary entries for commonly-used time signatures.

**Tonic**

This term can be applied in the following contexts:-
- In a **scale degree** context, the tonic of a scale is the first degree of that scale.
- In a **key** context, the tonic of a key is the 'home base' (or **DO** when using the 'solfeg' system) of the key.
- In a **chordal** context, the tonic chord of a key is the chord 'built from' the first degree of that key.

| | |
|---|---|
| **_Top note_** | The 'top note' of a chord voicing is the highest pitch being used. Top note movement is critical when voiceleading - see **p178** comments, and examples throughout **_Chapter 6_**. |
| **_'Translating' chords (literally)_** | Composite chord symbols may be literally translated into 'upper structure' chord voicings where appropriate - see **Figs. 7.23. - 7.24.** and **Figs. 8.10. & 8.12.** (and **_Chapters 7_** & **_8_** text). |
| **_Treble clef_** | The treble clef staff is typically used in contemporary music to notate pitches which are in the 'upper half' of the overall musical range i.e. from around the **Middle C** area upwards. |
| **_Triad_** | A three-note chord consisting of **3rd** and **5th** intervals, measured from the root of the chord - see **Figs. 1.6. - 1.9.** |
| **_'Triad-over-root' chord_** | I have used this term to describe the chord created when a triad 'shape' (for example a **major** or **minor** triad) is placed over another root in the bass voice - see **_Chapter 7_**. |
| **_Triad 'upper structure'_** | Equivalent to 'triad-over-root' chord described above. |
| **_Twelve-eight (12/8) time_** | A time signature with twelve 'pulses' per measure, each of which consists of an eighth note. |
| **_Twelfth (12th) interval_** | An interval derived by increasing a **fifth interval** by one **octave**. All possible versions of the **fifth** interval _(see glossary entry for fifth interval)_ are also possible for the **twelfth** interval. |
| **_Two-five-one (II - V - I) progression_** | This term is used to describe the progression which uses chords built from the 2nd, 5th and 1st degrees of a major or minor key. Used extensively in jazz styles - see **Figs. 2.8. - 2.9.**, and examples throughout **_Chapters 2 - 5_**. |
| **_Two-two (2/2) time_** | A time signature with two 'pulses' per measure, each of which consists of a half note - also known as **cut time**. |
| **_'Unstable' inversion_** | I have used this term in the context of a triad inverted over the 3rd in the bass voice. This inverted chord has an 'unstable' quality as it has a tendency to resolve or move to another chord - see **Fig. 7.8.** and accompanying text. |

| | |
|---|---|
| **'Upgrading' chords** | Basic triad and composite chord symbols may be upgraded using 'upper structure' chord voicings where appropriate - see **Figs. 7.25. - 7.26.** and **Figs. 8.13. - 8.14.** (and *Chapters 7* & *8* text). |
| **Upper extensions** | Upper tones added to chords (beyond the basic root, 3rd and 5th of the chord). |
| **Upper structures** | Triad or four-part 'shapes' placed over another root in the bass voice, to create/imply larger chord forms - see *Chapters 7* and *8*. |
| **Upper structure voicings** | 'Triad-over-root' or 'four-part-over-root' chord voicings created as described above - see *Chapters 7* and *8*. |
| **Upper tetrachord** | The upper or right-hand portion of a scale created using tetrachords. The upper tetrachord contains the **5th**, **6th**, **7th** and **1st** (tonic) scale degrees - see **Fig. 1.1.** (for a major scale) and **Figs. 1.20. - 1.22.** (for the minor scales). |
| **Upper voices** | I have used this term in a 'seven-three' voicing context, to describe the chord tones used in the treble register, above the root of the chord - see **p26**. |
| **Vertical quality** | This term refers to the harmonic sound or impression created by a chord. For example, the **3rd** and **7th** (or 6th) of a four-part chord define the vertical quality of the chord - see **p14** and **p22**. |
| **Voiceleading** | A term used to describe the smooth horizontal movement between consecutive chord voicings - see *Chapter 6*. |
| **Voicing** | An **interpretation** of a given chord symbol. The 'seven-three' voicings in *Chapter 2*, and the upper structure voicings in *Chapters 7* and *8*, can all be considered as interpretations of chord symbols. |
| **Whole note** | A note with duration lasting for four beats. |
| **Whole note rest** | A rest with duration lasting for four beats. |
| **Whole-step** | An interval measurement equivalent to two **half-steps.** Together the whole-step and half-step intervals are the building blocks for most conventional scales (i.e. the major scale - see **Fig. 1.1.**). The whole-step is also equivalent to a **major 2nd** interval. |